Comparative Political Systems
An Inquiry Approach

Holt Social Studies Curriculum

GENERAL EDITOR   EDWIN FENTON

Comparative Political Systems

An Inquiry Approach

MINDELLA SCHULTZ

Pittsburgh Public Schools

Holt, Rinehart and Winston, Inc.

New York, Toronto, London

Contents

To the Student

This is a new kind of textbook. Most social studies texts you have read in the past contained information about a particular subject, like American history or geography. The texts were written by one or two authors who organized their material into chapters, each with an important theme. There were numerous illustrations in the form of pictures, graphs, tables, and charts. You read or examined this material to learn the facts and generalizations it contained.

Instead of twenty or thirty chapters written by one or two authors, this text has sixty readings. Each reading contains at least one piece of source material, taken from a newspaper, magazine, book, government document, or other publication. The piece of source material is preceded by an introduction, which links one reading with another, and by study questions, which will alert you to important points and issues in the source material. Within the source materials, bracketed definitions and explanations appear after unfamiliar terms and references.

You will not find many illustrations in this text, but filmstrips, a recording, and transparencies for the overhead projector have been provided for use with many of the readings.

Both the written and the audio-visual materials have been chosen with great care. These materials have been designed so that instead of merely memorizing facts and generalizations, you will identify problems, develop *hypotheses,* or tentative answers to questions, and draw your own conclusions from factual evidence. Throughout your course in Comparative Political Systems, you will be challenged to think for yourself and to make up your own mind.

Most students are able to study one reading in this text for each night's homework assignment. Because most classes meet from seventy-five to eighty-five times a semester and there are only sixty readings, there will be days when no readings from this book are assigned. Your teacher will find a variety of things he wishes to do on those days. He may wish to give tests, to assign supplementary readings, to analyze local or state government, to study current events, or to hold individual conferences with students to discuss their work in Comparative Political Systems.

During mankind's history a great variety of political systems has developed. This course concentrates on three types: The political system of a primitive tribe, a modern democracy, and a modern totalitarianism. There are many other kinds of political systems, and, of course, it is impossible to study every kind in just one semester. But in a semester you can learn how to approach the study of a political system. You can develop the tools that you need to analyze any political system at any time or any place.

We welcome you to an exciting adventure: the study of the ways in which different men solve similar political problems.

Edwin Fenton
General Editor
Holt Social Studies Curriculum

How To Use This Book

The text of *Comparative Political Systems* consists of sixty readings which have been edited from published works or written especially for this course. Each day's assignment follows a common pattern:

1. *The introduction.* Each introduction relates a reading to other readings in the course and supplies essential background information.
2. *Study questions.* A few study questions call your attention to the most important points of the reading so that you can think about them in preparation for class discussion.
3. *The source material.* Each piece of source material consists of a document, newspaper account, article from a magazine, or some other written material.

You are expected to read each day's lesson and to take notes on it before you come to class. Since your teacher will distribute dittoed material from time to time, you ought to get a three-ring looseleaf notebook which can hold both the material which will be distributed and your homework and classroom notes.

Note-taking is a vital skill. We suggest that you read and take notes on each reading in the following manner:

1. *Write the reading number and title at the top of a piece of paper.*
2. *Skim the entire reading.* Read the first sentence in each paragraph of the introduction. Next read the study questions and get them fixed in your mind. Finally, read the first sentence in each paragraph of the source material. When you have finished, try to state in your own words what the lesson for the day is all about. Skimming such as this should never take longer than a few minutes.

3. *Read the introduction and take running notes.* Do *not* read first and then read again for notes. Do *not* underline or mark the text in any way. Write down the major ideas from the introduction and any supporting evidence which seems particularly important. You need not use complete sentences, but remember that you may wish to study from the notes some months later, so take down enough information to make notes meaningful.

4. *Read the source material carefully and take running notes.* Do *not* read first and then read again for notes. Do *not* underline or mark the text in any way. Take the same sort of notes which you took for the introduction. Put any conclusions you draw in parentheses to show that they are your own ideas.

5. *Go over your notes, underlining key ideas or words.* This procedure is the best way to begin learning the information in the lesson.

6. *Try to answer the study questions.* When you have finished studying your notes, try to answer the study questions for yourself. Do *not* write out the answers to the study questions. You would only be repeating the information in your notes if you do this. Use this step to see whether or not you got the important points from the reading in preparation for class discussion.

Two other study techniques will be useful. First, keep a vocabulary list in which to enter all new words and their definitions. Second, keep your class notes and your reading notes on a lesson together in your notebook so that you can review for tests without flipping through a mass of paper to find material which goes together.

Your teacher will help you if you have trouble with this note-taking technique. Because some lessons are based upon material presented in charts or tables, the technique that is suggested here for taking notes cannot always be used. In such cases, your teacher will give you supplementary instructions. In addition, your teacher will occasionally spend time in class demonstrating good note-taking techniques and will criticize your notes in an individual conference if you request one. Do not hesitate to ask for help.

Supplementary Reading Material

At the end of this introduction you will find a bibliography of nine books containing articles about politics. Your teacher may have placed these books in your library or in the classroom. He may ask you to write reports from some of these volumes periodically throughout the course. Many teachers ask students to read one or more articles every week and to write reports about them.

At the end of each unit you will find a list of articles about subjects that are covered in that unit. These articles can all be found in the books listed in the bibliography. Beneath each article you will find a question. For a report about one of these articles, your teacher may ask you to answer the question in essay form. He will probably give you complete freedom to choose any of the articles which you find interesting from the list at the end of each unit. Keep your reports short, in no case longer than one hundred words.

The articles vary in length and in difficulty. Some are very easy to read; some are quite sophisticated. A number are only three or four pages long; some run ten or twelve pages. This variety has been provided so that you can find something which interests and challenges you.

Your teacher may wish to make special rules and regulations about the supplementary readings. Some teachers may choose not to use them at all. If you do use them, you will find varied and exciting articles about a wide variety of political issues.

ARMSTRONG, JOHN A., *Ideology, Politics, and Government in the Soviet Union.* New York: Frederick A. Praeger, 1962.

HAMILTON, HOWARD D., editor, *Political Institutions: Readings in Political Science.* Boston: Houghton Mifflin Company, 1962.

LEFEVER, ERNEST W. and WALTER V. HOHENSTEIN, editors, *Profile of American Politics.* Boston: Houghton Mifflin Company, 1960.

LISITZKY, GENE, *Four Ways of Being Human.* New York: The Viking Press, 1965

MEHLINGER, HOWARD, *Communism in Theory and Practice: A Book of Readings for High School Students.* San Francisco: Chandler Publishing Company, 1964.

MORLAN, ROBERT L., *Capitol, Courthouse and City Hall,* 3rd edition. Boston: Houghton Mifflin Company, 1966.

POWELL, THEODORE, editor, *Democracy in Action: The Voices of Men in American Government and Politics.* New York: The Macmillan Company, 1962.

RIEBER, ALFRED J. and ROBERT C. NELSON, editors, *The USSR and Communism: Source Readings and Interpretations.* Chicago: Scott, Foresman and Company, 1964.

SCOTT, ANDREW M. and EARLE WALLACE, editors, *Politics, U.S.A.: Cases on the American Democratic Process,* 2nd edition. New York: The Macmillan Company, 1965.

Unit One

Introduction to Comparative Political Systems

A POLITICAL SYSTEM is a society's way of regulating relations between individual people and groups of people. There are many kinds of political systems, but they all share certain characteristics. Every political system has leaders and those who are led. In every system, decisions must be made. Every system has goals toward which it strives.

You will learn to identify, analyze, and compare common characteristics of political systems as you proceed with this course. You will begin your study by analyzing the political systems of two relatively small societies—the first, a group of American prisoners of war who set up a government in a German prison camp; and the second, a tribe of American Indians. You will deal with these small societies first because it is easier to identify the political characteristics of small societies with fairly simple political systems. When you have learned how to analyze and compare these rather simple political systems, you will go on to analyze and compare the more complex systems of the United States and the Soviet Union.

Chapter 1

The Political System at Stoerpenberg Camp

STATING THE ISSUE Every society has a political system, for whenever people live in groups, they must have a way of regulating the relations between members of the groups. To regulate relations, a society must have rules, and it must develop positions and offices to be held by the people who will make, interpret, and enforce these rules. This set of positions and offices is a society's government.

Governments have a number of functions. They settle conflicts which arise among people in the same group. They provide services to the group, such as protection from fire, that individual members cannot provide for themselves. They also protect a group or a nation from its external enemies. All of us can think of a number of additional things which a government does.

Many forms of government have appeared in the past. Some have been dictatorships in which one man has ruled. Others have been organized as oligarchies in which a small group of men has held power. Still others have been organized to rule democratically. The institutions of government have been equally varied. Parliament, Congress, the King's Council, and the Supreme Soviet are all names of governmental institutions. Government is of endless variety.

Political scientists study governments and the political systems of which governments are a part. From their observations, they have discovered that, while all political systems are unique, within all of them there are political activities and forces which can be placed in several categories. These categories are called concepts of political science, and they help identify the themes that must be explored in studying any political system. Basic concepts of political science include the following:

1. Political Leadership: the group of people who make, interpret, and enforce the rules by which a political system operates
2. Political Decision-Making: the process by which these rules are made, interpreted, and enforced
3. Political Institutions: accepted organizations for or ways of handling political decision-making

4. Political Ideology: the body of beliefs, attitudes, values, and goals underlying political decisions
5. Citizenship: the role played by the individual in the system

Each concept is a guide to analytical questions that any student must ask as he seeks insight into the way a political system operates. In Chapter 1, you are going to analyze the political system of a World War II prisoner-of-war camp. The prisoners were told to select leaders and to make common decisions; that is, they had to create a government. So that you can guide your analysis and pick out meaningful details from the information you read, you must learn to ask analytical questions. There are many questions you might ask about the prisoner-of-war camp. How did the 160 American prisoners decide who their leaders would be? How did the prisoners make decisions? What governmental institutions did they set up? What ideology influenced them? What was the role of the individual citizen? These are the questions with which you begin your analysis.

1 Leadership and Institutions

Leadership plays a vital role in every political system. Whether the leader is a dictator who has seized and maintained power by force or a democratically elected official who is subject to the will of the electorate, the basic problem remains the same: all governments require political leaders. Each society must develop ways to recruit and train these leaders. Everywhere leaders must win and maintain support, for they cannot lead if no one will follow. Leaders must communicate with citizens and be responsive to their wishes; no leader, however strong, can afford to antagonize continuously those whom he leads.

What are the attributes, or personal characteristics, of political leaders? How are leaders different from those they lead? Are the characteristics of leaders in all societies the same, or do leaders differ from one society to another? Social scientists who study political systems frequently ask questions such as these.

Leaders work within an institutional framework. Our national government has three major branches: the executive, the legislative, and the judicial. The Presidency, the Senate and the House of Representatives, and the federal courts are institutions in which these branches of government operate. How do leaders work within institutions? How do institutions reflect the society of which they are a part? Political scientists ask a number of similar questions about the role of institutions in government.

Learning to ask questions will be one of the most important objectives of your education. Learning becomes sterile when it consists only of committing to memory a large amount of factual information. Many studies indicate that students rapidly forget most of the facts they have learned unless the facts are organized in such a way that one fact leads them on to another. Good questions often provide the framework on which one can build his factual knowledge. More important, questions provide a technique for studying new bodies of information. If a student knows what questions are vital to the study of one society's political system, he can ask them of another. Asking these questions often helps to make facts meaningful.

Before class, you are to read Part One of a short article which describes the political system in an American prisoner-of-war camp in Stoerpenberg, Germany, during World War II. As you read, think about the following questions:

1. How were the leaders at Stoerpenberg chosen?
2. What were the leaders like? What were their backgrounds and their most important character traits?
3. What governmental institutions were set up?

Stoerpenberg Camp (Part One)
GERALD HAINES

Adapted from "Stoerpenberg Camp," an unpublished case study of the Human Relations Department of the University of Kansas. Reprinted with permission of the department.

There were a hundred and sixty of them. They had been counted by the Germans, and the count had been checked. They moved about the building, peering out the windows at the drab winter landscape, or sat around the tables, now and then dropping down on a bunk, hands under head, to lie staring at the ceiling. One hundred and sixty American prisoners of war, who had been captured in the Battle of the Bulge two months ago, were now organized as a prisoner-of-war labor unit at Stoerpenberg, somewhere in western Germany.

During the first two days they had nothing to do but lie on their beds and wait to be fed. As men drifted from one bunk to another, they began to talk about their situation. They discovered that they were all privates who had been in combat units of one kind or another. They represented a fair cross section of the United States with men from every region of the nation included. Some of the men who had been able to talk to the guards had discovered that the camp was at the edge of a large town. The prisoners were to be used as laborers in nearby fields or for general utility work about the town.

The prisoners were housed in a gymnasium that had been part of a group of factory buildings. It evidently had been used as a workers' recreation center. At one end of the building, a few tumbling mats and gymnastic bars were all that remained of the building's former equipment. An aisle formed by two rows of tables ran down the center of the building. Behind the tables on each side were rows of double-decked bunks, while at the far end of the gymnasium, three rooms were partitioned off from the central part. The center room was fitted with washing troughs; to the north was a storage room, and to the south a lavatory. At the south end of the building on the outside lay a long narrow plot of ground used as an exercise yard for the prisoners. Within the building and the exercise yard the American prisoners formed a little society of their own.

By the second day the men had picked out bunks and taken regular places at the tables. There were ten tables, so sixteen men were grouped at each. Men who had known each other before they were captured tended to cluster together. None of the men could have known anyone else in the group for more than two months, but under the circumstances any familiar face was a welcome sight. A few men who had not yet made friends tended to drift to the table closest to their bunk.

On the third day the German officer in charge told the prisoners to choose a group leader. This leader would pass on to the group the regulations and orders of the German officers and would be responsible for carrying out rules for health and sanitation made by the prisoners.

After the interpreter told the prisoners this, they began to discuss the matter among themselves. They were seated around the tables where there was enough space for two or three of them to get together. They decided to hold an election. Very shortly men began to move from table to table campaigning for their favorite. Finally a few men were selected as candidates. Votes were taken by a show of hands. If a proposed candidate seemed to have a fairly large number of people behind him, he was considered in the running, and if not, his name was dropped. The choice soon narrowed down to a few men. Each man was presented to the group by his backers who made campaign speeches in his favor. After the speeches were finished, a final vote was taken by a show of hands. The choice was George Kent, a man of good physical appearance, who had demonstrated a commanding personality and superior social presence during the election of the leader. A college graduate, Kent had at one time been an acting sergeant and had distinguished himself in battle.

Kent immediately brought up the vital matter of how food was to be distributed. In a prisoner-of-war camp with limited rations, food was of vital importance to everyone and was without doubt the subject most constantly on every prisoner's mind. Kent suggested that the entire ration of food should be divided into ten parts, one for each table, and then distributed at the tables to the men. In order to supervise this final distribution of food, he suggested that each table elect a table leader to take charge. The men quickly responded to this suggestion. Gathered around the tables, they talked informally, and finally each table chose its representative. The men who were finally chosen as leaders had a few characteristics in common. Several were college graduates, and the remainder all had finished high school. A number of them had acted as noncommissioned officers at one time or another. Every one of them was a good talker who could communicate well with his fellows.

Shortly after the table leaders were chosen, several of them suggested to Kent that they set up a council to govern the unit. Kent agreed. In the following weeks the council met regularly. It consisted of Kent and the ten table leaders. At each meeting Kent passed on orders and information from the German administration of the camp so that the table leaders could inform the men in their group. The members of the council also discussed living arrangements, such as the choice of bunks, and made assignments to clean-up details.

2 Decision-Making

Government exists to make decisions about matters of vital concern to the people governed. If a society is small, the decisions are likely to be made informally. If a problem arises, it is brought to a leader or group of leaders, and a decision is arrived at.

Larger and more complicated societies organize elaborate institutions to make decisions. Our President, Congress, and court system are part of an enormously complicated decision-making process involving elections, political parties, and many other similar institutions.

In this reading you will study how the society at Stoerpenberg Camp made and enforced its decisions. To make and enforce these decisions, the prisoners set up simple political institutions, as the reading yesterday revealed. They had a leader, 10 table leaders organized as a council, and 160 voters. They did not try to set up an executive (president), legislature (congress), and judiciary (courts) because their society was so simple that one set of institutions and people could perform all three of these tasks. The leader and the table leaders passed laws subject to approval by the voters (the legislative function), carried out laws (the executive function), and interpreted laws by applying them to specific cases (the judicial function).

Studying the manner in which decisions were reached and enforced in the camp may reveal some interesting questions worth exploring when you investigate more complex political systems. The purpose of this assignment is to raise some of these questions. As you read, think about the following questions:

1. Who took initiative in bringing up suggestions for laws in the camp?
2. Who decided whether or not a question brought up for discussion was worth taking to a popular vote? Could these people control what was discussed?
3. How were laws made? How were they carried out?
4. What happened when a man broke the unwritten code? What role did Kent play in this incident? What did his role reveal about who really had power in the society? Do you think the President of the United States has similar influence?

Stoerpenberg Camp (Part Two)
GERALD HAINES

Adapted from "Stoerpenberg Camp," an unpublished case study of the Human Relations Department of the University of Kansas. Reprinted with permission of the department.

If a man felt that he had a legitimate "gripe," he complained to his table leader. If the table leader was unable to settle the matter on the spot, he would bring it before the council at the next meeting. Most matters brought up in this way were settled at the council, but when a new problem seemed to be particularly important, it was referred to the tables for discussion and a referendum [a popular vote]. Through this procedure the men were able to make rules by which they could govern themselves.

In a few weeks the camp was functioning very effectively. The men were organized into compact units. The routine of their lives had been worked out, with each man having certain duties to perform in a regular rotation for the benefit of all. Behind this formal organization was the code of the group. The code was not formal—no one had written it down or made speeches about it—yet everyone knew what it was and lived by it or knew what to expect if he did not.

The first and most important rule of this informal code was that no prisoner would steal from another, particularly that he would not steal food or tobacco. Stealing from the Germans was quite all right as long as a prisoner did not get caught. If he were caught, the prisoner's duty was clear—to identify himself as the sole participant and to bear the brunt of German displeasure. There were a few other important parts of the code. Everyone was expected to keep as clean as possible, although keeping clean required a great deal of effort. As to the work being done for the Germans, it was quite all right to do as little as possible as long as a prisoner did not get caught.

Within two weeks after the 160 prisoners had been thrown together in the gymnasium at Stoerpenberg, they had developed a

7

small but complete society. They had organized a government; they had made some laws; they had worked out an economic organization to distribute food; they had built up a social structure; and they had accepted an informal code which everyone obeyed.

In the third week of March 1945, as the result of an incident among the members of Table Five, the leaders of the work unit suddenly found themselves with a difficult problem. One of the men at the table was accused of stealing food, and the uproar over it threatened to break up the society. One of the members of Table Five was a man named Court. From the very first, Ainslee, the table leader of Number Five, had been aware that Court did not fit into any of the informal groups at the table, nor did he seem to have friends at any of the other tables. His manner was listless and apathetic. He seemed withdrawn from the life about him, and his reactions seemed rather slow and confused when any situation arose that required him to participate in some activity. His personal habits were very lax to the point that he was filthy, even though a room for washing was available. Ainslee thought that Court was mentally ill or had suffered some intense experience during his capture.

Whatever the reasons, Court was one of the few men who did not actively participate in the life of the group. His sole interest was food. Soon he began to save the bread from his daily rations. Each day he added another small portion to his store. He concealed the chunks of bread about his clothing and bunk. Court was very suspicious of his fellow prisoners and spent much of his free time carefully checking his hoard. By the middle of March, much of the bread he had managed to save was stale and unpalatable. He was not seen to eat any of it, but he seemed to get satisfaction from handling it and knowing that it was there when he wanted to look at it.

Bartrum, a tall, heavy man from Table Five, had been observing Court's behavior carefully. In casual conversations with others, he pointed out the futility of Court's actions. Many others agreed with him, and because food was so scarce, some felt that it was wrong for one man to waste what could be used so well by others.

Each evening the men of the work unit stood in the aisle to be counted by one of the German noncommissioned officers. Late in March Bartrum was late to formation. Immediately after the men were dismissed, he returned quietly to his bunk. A short time later the men around Table Five were startled by hoarse cries. Court was moving around and around his bunk, searching here and there, uttering moans, and weeping. Ainslee and several others moved quickly to Court to discover that much of his hoard of bread had been stolen. In a few minutes a large crowd had collected about Court's bunk. The news of his loss passed quickly among them. The low hum of many voices began to comment on the fact that Bartrum had been late to head count. The men began to suspect that he was the thief.

Ainslee had decided to go to Kent to organize a search among the members of the group when a few of the men walked over to Bartrum's bunk and began looking around. Bartrum protested when suddenly one of the men found a chunk of bread tucked away at one end of the bunk. He shouted and turned upon Bartrum. A thick knot of men rapidly swirled about him, cursing, shouting, and striking at him. Bartrum attempted to fight clear, stammering incoherently, as more and more men joined the melee. The room was filled with uproar which spread rapidly until every man there was involved.

Kent, the group leader, quickly caught the significance of the cries of the outraged men around Bartrum and realized that if he did not act quickly, Bartrum might be killed. Throwing himself into the crowd, he fought his way to Bartrum. Seizing him by the collar, Kent managed to get on top of a table where he could be seen above the mob, still holding Bartrum firmly. At first he could not make himself heard, but as more and more of the men saw who it was that held Bartrum, they became more quiet. Taking a deep breath, Kent tried again, "Okay," he said, "I hate the —— as much as you do, but this isn't the way to do it." Howls of protest greeted his statement, but he kept on talking, arguing that Bartrum must be handled by regular procedure and not by a mob. Meanwhile, several of the table leaders had fought their way to Kent and now began to ring about him. Slowly the protests began to lessen. Kent bore down on the fact that the group would have its chance to take action after the council had tried Bartrum. As the crowd became quieter, Kent felt that the immediate danger was over. Calling to the table leaders to come with him, he jumped down from the table and, holding tightly to Bartrum, pushed his way through the men. They let him pass. The leaders walked with Kent and Bartrum to the end of the room. Here on the old tumbling mats they sat down to consider what they should do.

Bartrum's trial was conducted with some formality. Kent presided and asked most of the questions. Bartrum began by denying the theft but soon admitted his guilt, justifying himself by saying that the bread was being wasted and should do someone some good. He surprised the council by saying that he was ready to accept any punishment that seemed fitting.

The council, after some deliberation, passed sentence on Bartrum. First, they placed him in isolation for a month; no one was to speak to him or have anything to do with him at all. Second, during this same month he was assigned to do two hours of additional work in the barracks each night after the work unit had returned from the fields. Finally, he was to replace from his own bread ration an amount equal to the bread he had stolen.

After passing the sentence, the table leaders returned to their tables and consulted their men. In general, most of the men seemed satisfied, and only a few felt that the sentence was too light. After each table had voted to accept the decision, the leaders returned to Kent and informed him of the results. Kent then sent Bartrum back to his bunk with a stern reminder that if he did not carry out his sentence properly, the next action would be very severe.

During the following two weeks, Bartrum was cut off from his fellow prisoners. No one spoke to him. Each evening he put in his two hours of extra labor. Each day he turned over part of his bread ration to Court, who either ate it or stored it away with the rest of his hoard. Ainslee supervised the return of the stolen rations and kept an accurate day-by-day record. He appointed a different man each day to make sure that Bartrum worked steadily during his extra hours in the evening. By refusing to have anything to do with Bartrum, every member of the group helped to enforce the rest of the sentence.

Note:

Two weeks after the sentence began, the gynmasium was hit by a bomb during an Allied air attack. The Germans then bundled the American prisoners into small groups to distribute them among a number of other work camps. The society which they had formed came to an end. Most of the prisoners never saw each other again.

3 Ideology and the Role of the Citizen

During the last two days you have investigated a political system set up by American prisoners in Stoerpenberg Camp. First you studied the leaders of the political system to find out about their backgrounds and their character traits. Then you examined the governmental institutions they developed. Finally you investigated the process of making and enforcing political decisions in the camp. Today's lesson concludes the study of the political system in Stoerpenberg.

What a person learns from a reading depends in part upon the questions he has in his mind as he reads. You have already read the Stoerpenberg article to learn about leadership, institutions, and decision-making in the camp. Today you are asked to reread the entire article, Parts One and Two—this time with new objectives—to investigate the ideology of the prisoners and the role of the citizen in the political system. Information about these topics can be found throughout "Stoerpenberg Camp." It is not necessary to read the two introductions again.

In American society, political activity occupies a comparatively small amount of the time of a typical citizen. He has a job, a family, a group of friends, and innumerable opportunities to go to movies, watch television, attend baseball games, or listen to a symphony orchestra. The attention of American citizens often focuses on these activities instead of on politics. Any American who considers entering politics must recognize that his time is a scarce resource which he must divide carefully among numerous activities. But time was not so scarce a resource in Stoerpenberg Camp. The prisoners there had little to do except work for part of the day in the fields and run their own society during their off-duty hours. This situation helped to make the nature of their political system quite different from the American political system. It particularly affected the role of the individual in politics.

Individuals play different roles in different political systems. Political scientists have identified a number of questions which help to reveal these differences and to analyze the citizen's role in politics. One such question is: How does a citizen gather information about politics? As you study this lesson, you may discover other questions which will help you to analyze political systems and to clarify the position of individuals within those systems.

The entire organization of governmental institutions, even those at Stoerpenberg, grows out of an *ideology* — the ideas, attitudes, values, and goals a group of people believe in. A particular type of political system reflects an ideology, and the ideology provides a set of explanations for and justifications of the governmental institutions. A political system's stated ideology is not always the same as the ideology reflected by the system's practices. Identifying ideology is frequently most difficult and requires the use of questions penetrating enough to help you look below the surface of what is said to find implications and hidden meanings. What can be implied from the way a decision is made? Who is involved in making the decision? Who is not included in the decision-making process? Is their exclusion significant?

As you reread Part One and Part Two of the Stoerpenberg article, think about the following specific questions:

1. The men at Stoerpenberg chose as their leaders men whose backgrounds and character traits they admired. What do examples of these backgrounds and traits tell you about what the men valued, or thought most of?
2. Review examples of the governmental institutions and ways of reaching decisions the men established. What do these examples tell you about what the men believed in and thought was a good form of government?
3. What was the source of the prisoners' ideology? What role did ideology play in helping to shape the election process and the procedure by which Bartrum was tried?

11

4 A Summary Exercise

In the previous three days you studied the political system of Stoerpenberg Camp. Obviously your major purpose was not to learn facts—names, events, dates—about Stoerpenberg. Neither Kent nor Court played an important part in world affairs. Their names will not appear on national examinations; only people who have read this account will ever hear of them. Hence, there is no reason to learn these facts for their own sake.

The major purpose in this chapter has been to introduce you to a method of analyzing political systems. Today's lesson provides a review and a way of checking what you have learned. Suppose you were told to analyze the political system of France during the period of Louis XIV (1643–1715). Assume that you know nothing about France during this period, that you can read French well, and that you have a large number of books, public papers, diaries, letters, newspapers, and so forth at your disposal. How would you proceed?

As homework for tomorrow's class, prepare a list of the major concepts which you think you ought to investigate in your analysis of the political system in France under Louis XIV. For example, the concept of political leadership would be important to your investigation. Under each concept, write one or more analytical questions which you can use to guide your note-taking. Use a new piece of paper for each concept and the questions which you want to use to analyze it. Then you can add additional questions to your list in the future. Use ink or a typewriter.

Chapter 2

The Political System of a Primitive Society

STATING THE ISSUE   In Chapter 1 you analyzed the political system of a prisoner-of-war camp and the government the prisoners developed to make and enforce the rules by which they lived. Chapter 2 turns your attention to another fairly simple political system, that of a primitive society, the Cheyenne Indians.

The Stoerpenberg readings made it possible for you to watch a political system develop from its start. Because the prisoners were part of a newly formed society, they had to plan a new government and put their plan into action. But a society which has existed for a long time inherits a political system from the past. Each new generation does not set up a new form of government. It does, however, adapt the government it inherits to fit the demands of the present. Some political systems are more flexible and adapt more easily than others. If a system fails to adapt sufficiently, it may be overthrown.

The extent to which the past influences those who govern depends upon a number of circumstances, but some political systems are more likely to be guided by the past than others. A traditional political system is most firmly rooted in the past. As its name suggests, this type of system is distinguished by its tendency to regulate political relationships in accordance with the dictates of custom. Decisions of the past are the models used for decisions of the present. A traditional system avoids change.

In analyzing a traditional political system, you can use as your guide the same basic concepts of political science identified in Chapter 1 — leadership, decision-making, institutions, ideology, and citizenship. Again you must pose analytical questions that will help you identify pertinent information concerning the Cheyenne political system. How did they choose their leaders? What types of leaders did they choose? How did their leaders make decisions? Your ability to pose penetrating questions determines your ability to find meaningful answers.

5 Leadership and Institutions: The Cheyenne

Trying to study the political systems of primitive societies creates a major problem. Where can one find information about these societies? In many cases there are no written records. In some cases, where there are written records, the language of the records is not fully understood. In still other cases there are written records that have been deciphered, but there are problems in interpreting what they mean.

Two anthropologists, E. Adamson Hoebel and K. N. Llewellyn, spent many years studying the development of law and government among the Cheyenne Indians. They studied written documents about the Cheyenne. They also lived among them for several years. At the time that they did their field work among the Cheyenne, there were tribesmen still living who remembered the days described in the accounts which you are going to read. These tribesmen told stories of events they remembered from their own experiences. Some tribesmen repeated stories told them by their parents, who may, in turn, have heard them from their parents.

Hoebel and Llewellyn wrote a book in which they related these stories just as the Cheyenne told them. They used the stories to construct a picture of the rules by which the Cheyenne tribes lived during the mid 1800's. Reading 5 tells the story of a Cheyenne named Pawnee who was punished by the Bowstring Soldiers. Use this story to see what information it can give you about the role of the Cheyenne leaders and the institutional framework within which they worked. As you read, keep in mind the following questions:

1. Who seem to be the leaders of the Cheyenne described here? What character traits did the leaders show?
2. What does the mention of Pawnee becoming a chief of the Fox Soldiers tell you about the way leaders gained power among the Cheyenne?
3. What clues do you find concerning how the Cheyenne governed themselves? What governmental institutions did they have?

Pawnee Punished by the Bowstring Soldiers and Rehabilitated by High Backed Wolf

K. N. LLEWELLYN AND E. ADAMSON HOEBEL

Black Wolf, a member of the Northern Cheyenne, told this story to Hoebel and Llewellyn. The events he describes took place sometime between the 1840's and the 1860's. The Bowstring Soldiers were one of several soldier troops, or military societies, within the Cheyenne tribe. From The Cheyenne Way *(pp. 6-9) by Karl N. Llewellyn and E. Adamson Hoebel, Copyright 1941 by the University of Oklahoma Press.*

Pawnee was a Southern Cheyenne when he was a very young man, but in his later years he lived up here with us. He was all the time looking out after the people's morals and counseling the boys on good behavior. I have heard him tell his story many times when I was a youth, because he was always telling it to us as a lesson. He had been an awful rascal down there in Oklahoma when he was young, stealing meat from people's racks, taking their horses for joyrides without asking them for them, and then when he got to where he was going, he would just turn the horse loose and let it wander back to its owner—if it did. He was disrespectful to people and sassed them back. Everyone thought he was a mean boy, and whatever happened in the camp, he got blamed for it. This story I am going to tell happened just after that trouble Wolf Lies Down had over the borrowed horse when the soldiers made the rule that no one in the camp could take another person's horse without permission. This is what Pawnee used to tell us:

Down there [in Oklahoma] were two spotted horses well liked in their family. One day I took them and headed west. Three days passed, and I found myself still safe. Now I was out of trouble's way, so I began to feel pretty good. On the fourth day, as I looked back I saw some people coming up. "It is nothing," I thought, "just some people traveling." When they overtook me, I saw they were Bow-string Soldiers out after me.

"You have stolen those horses," they cried as they pulled me from my horse. "Now we have trailed you down." They threw me on the ground and beat me until I could not stand; they broke up my weapons and ruined my saddle; they cut my blankets, moccasins, and kit to shreds. When they had finished, they took all my food and went off with the horses, leaving me alone on the prairie, sore and destitute, too weak and hurt to move.

The next day I started back, traveling as best I could all day long. I knew there was a small camp of buffalo hunters out, and for them I was looking. I traveled all day. The next day I thought I would die. I had no food, only water. Late in the afternoon I camped on a creek. My feet were bleeding, and I could not walk farther. I crawled slowly on my hands and knees to the brow of a high hill to find a place to die. I waited in mourning. Far to the south of me, I could see the rolling country; to the west my view was blocked. My pipe and tobacco were gone. Without smoke I sat there thinking of a great many things as I watched the blood drip from my swollen feet.

As I gazed steadfastly into the south, a hunter came up the hill from behind me. When he saw me, he stopped and watched me for a long time. After three days and two nights in my condition, I must have been nearly deaf, for I did not hear him until he spoke from his horse right behind me. I was naked. I fell over in a fright when I heard his voice start out in the silence.

This man dismounted and hugged me. He wept, he felt so bad at seeing my plight. It was High Backed Wolf, a young man, but a chief. He put his blanket about me and took me home. The camp was on the creek below, hidden just around a bend where I had not seen it. His wife gave me food and nourished me.

Then High Backed Wolf sent for the chiefs who were in the camp. Four or five came, one of whom was a soldier chief.

High Backed Wolf spoke to the soldier chief first. "This is the first time since I have become a big [tribal] chief that I have happened upon such a poor man; now I am going to outfit him. Until he is fixed up, I shall ask no questions. Then we shall learn how he came to be naked. I am not going to ask you to give anything unless you wish to do so. I know this man," he said. "He is a great smoker. But I shall give him no smoke until he has first eaten." (In my own mind I said, "I'd rather smoke first.")

First they gave me a little soup; then some meat.

High Backed Wolf then filled the pipe. As he held it to the five directions, he prayed, "This is my first good act as chief. Help this man to tell the truth." Then he held the pipe for me to smoke; then he gave it to the next man and to the others. Now he faced me again. "Now you tell the truth. Have you been caught by enemies and stripped? Or was it something else? You saw me smoke this pipe; you have touched it with your own lips. That is to help you tell the truth. If you tell us straightly, Maiyun [the Supernatural] will help you."

I told them the whole story. I told them whose horses they were, and I told them it was the Bowstrings who had punished me.

High Backed Wolf knew I was a rascal, so he lectured to me. "You are old enough now to know what is right," he preached. "You have been to war. Now leave off this foolishness. If it had been that I had not ridden out into the hills today, you would have died. No one would have known the end of you. You know how we Cheyenne try to live. You know how we hunt, how we go to war. When we take horses, we take them from enemies, not from Cheyenne. You had better join a military society. You can learn good behavior from the soldiers. Yet I ask only one thing of you. Be decent from now on! Stop stealing! Stop making fun of people! Use no more bad language in the camp! Lead a good life!

"Now I am going to help you out. That is what I am here for, because I am a chief of the people. Here are your clothes. Outside are three horses. You may take your choice!" He gave me a six-

16

shooter. "Here is a mountain-lion skin. I used to wear this in the parades. Now I give it to you." He offered me all these things, and I took them.

The others gave me beaver skins to braid in my hair, beads, and extra moccasins, and two more horses.

Then High Backed Wolf ended it. "Now I am not going to tell you to leave this camp. You may stay here as long as you wish. I shall not tell you which direction to go, west or south."

I had a sweetheart in the south, but when these people did this for me, I felt ashamed. I had all those things with which to look beautiful, but I did not dare to go back, for I knew she would have heard what the Bowstrings had done to me. I thought it wisest to go north until the thing was dead.

When the Arrows were next renewed [the Renewal of Arrows was a Cheyenne religious ceremony], the Foxes [one of the military, or soldier, societies] put up their lodge to get more men. I went in [joined]. Still, I never got it out of my heart that it had been those Bowstrings. Whenever my Fox troop was on duty, I was out looking for those men or their families to do something wrong. I always looked for a Bowstring to slip, so I could beat him well. I stayed with the Northern Cheyenne a long, long time, until the Horse Creek Treaty [a treaty which several Indian tribes signed in 1851, agreeing to peace among themselves and with the white people]. Though I came to be a chief of the Fox Soldiers among the northern people, I never amounted to much with the southern bands. Those people always remembered me as a no-good.

You boys remember that. You may run away, but your people always remember. You just obey the rules of the camp, and you'll do all right.

6 Decision-Making: The Cheyenne

By the early 1800's the Cheyenne were settled in permanent villages constructed of earth lodges, where they grew corn, beans, and squash and relied on hunting only to supplement their food supplies. The rules by which they lived were fairly well established. But then the Cheyenne were introduced to horses. By 1830, the Cheyenne had enough horses to abandon their villages for the more profitable life of the hunter. Bison covered the plains, and these animals were a rich source of food and leather.

The Cheyenne whom Llewellyn and Hoebel studied were the Cheyenne of the mid 1800's who were thoroughly adapted to the use of horses. The rules they had lived by as villagers did not cover all the situations in which they found themselves as hunters. During the summer the Cheyenne hunted as a single group, but during the fall, winter, and spring they broke up into smaller groups because it was impossible to feed the larger group during the severe weather. The Cheyenne had to adopt rules for governing the small groups as well as the large group.

The cases "The Tribal Ostracism and Reinstatement of Sticks Everything Under His Belt" and "Cries Yia Eya Banished for the Murder of Chief Eagle" are evidence of the kinds of political decisions the Cheyenne had to make and how they made them. Keep the following questions in mind as you read these cases because they will help you to analyze political decision-making among the Cheyenne Indians:

1. Who made the political decisions in the Cheyenne tribe?
2. How were the decisions made? Was there any formal machinery set up for decision-making?
3. What generalization can you make about the way the Cheyenne made decisions?

1. The Tribal Ostracism and Reinstatement of Sticks Everything Under His Belt

K. N. LLEWELLYN AND E. ADAMSON HOEBEL

Black Wolf also told Hoebel and Llewellyn this story. The "Sun Dance" to which he refers was a Cheyenne ceremony which lasted several days. Each Sun Dance was inaugurated by a "pledger," or sponsor, who organized it. The ceremony combined different elements: the building of a new lodge, rituals performed by priests, public dancing, and various forms of self-torture for the purpose of making sacrifice. One form of self-torture consisted of "hanging from the pole"—a young man would drive skewers through his breasts, attach the skewers by rope to a wooden pole, and then dance around the pole until he could pull himself free of the skewers. From The Cheyenne Way *(pp. 9–13) by Karl N. Llewellyn and E. Adamson Hoebel. Copyright 1941 by the University of Oklahoma Press.*

Once, at a time when all the Cheyenne tribe was gathered together, Sticks Everything Under His Belt went out hunting buffalo alone. "I am hunting for myself," he told the people. He was implying that the rules against individual hunting did not apply to him because he was declaring himself out of the tribe—a man on his own.

All the soldier chiefs and all the tribal chiefs met in a big lodge to decide what to do in this case, since such a thing had never happened before. This was the ruling they made: no one could help Sticks Everything Under His Belt in any way; no one could give him smoke; no one could talk to him. They were cutting him off from the tribe. The chiefs declared that if anyone helped him in any way, that person would have to give a Sun Dance.

When the camp moved, Sticks Everything Under His Belt moved with it, but the people would not recognize him. He was left alone, and it went to his heart, so he took one of his horses (he had many) and rode out to the hilltops to mourn.

His sister's husband was a chief in the camp. This brother-in-law felt sorry for him out there mourning, with no more friends. At last he took pity on his poor brother-in-law; at last he spoke to his wife, "I feel sorry for your poor brother out there, and now I am going to do something for him. Cook up all those tongues we have! Prepare a good feast!"

Then he invited the chiefs to his lodge and sent for his brother-in-law to come in. This was after several years had passed, not months.

When the chiefs had assembled, the brother-in-law spoke. "Several years ago you passed a ruling that no one could help this man. Whoever should do so, you said, would have to give a Sun Dance. Now is the time to take pity on him. I am going to give a Sun Dance to bring him back in. I beg you to let him come back to the tribe, for he has suffered long enough. This Sun Dance will be a great one. I declare that every chief and all the soldiers must join in. Now I put it up to you. Shall we let my brother-in-law smoke before we eat, or after?"

The chiefs all answered in accord, "Ha-ho, ha-ho [thank you, thank you]. We are very glad you are going to bring back this man. However, let him remember that he will be bound by whatever rules the soldiers lay down for the tribe. He may not say he is outside of them. He has been out of the tribe for a long time. If he remembers these things, he may come back." . . .

The lodge was not big enough to hold all the chiefs who had come to decide this thing, so they threw open the door, and those who could not get in sat in a circle outside. Then they filled a big pipe, and when it was lighted, they gave it to Sticks Everything Under His Belt. It was so long since he had had tobacco that he gulped in the smoke and fell over in a faint. . . . The chiefs waited silently for him to come to again, and then the pipe was passed around the circle.

When all had smoked, Sticks Everything Under His Belt talked. "From now on I am going to run with the tribe. Everything the people say, I shall stay right by it. My brother-in-law has done a great thing. He is going to punish himself in the Sun Dance to bring me back. He won't do it alone, for I am going in, too."

After a while the people were getting ready for the Sun Dance. One of the soldiers began to get worried because he had an ugly growth on his body which he did not want to reveal to the people. He was a good-looking young man named Black Horse. Black Horse went to the head chiefs asking them to let him sacrifice himself alone on the hilltops as long as the Sun Dance was in progress.

"We have nothing to say to that," they told him. "Go to the pledger. This is his Sun Dance."

Black Horse went to the brother-in-law of Sticks Everything Under His Belt, who was a brother-in-law to him as well. "Brother-in-law," he begged, "I want to be excused from going into the lodge. Can't you let me go into the hills to sacrifice myself as long as you are in there. . . ?"

"No," he was rebuffed, "you know my rule is that all must be there."

"Well, brother-in-law, won't it be all right if I set up a pole on the hill and hang myself to it through my breasts? I shall hang there for the duration of the dance."

This brother-in-law of his answered him in these words, "Why didn't you take that up when all the chiefs were in the lodge? I have agreed with them that everyone must be in the lodge. I don't want to change the rule. I won't give you permission to go outside."

Then Black Horse replied, "You will not make the rules my way. Now *I* am going to put in a rule for everybody. Everyone in there has to swing from the pole as I do."

"No," countered the brother-in-law. "That was not mentioned in the meeting. If you want to swing from the pole, that is all right, but no one else has to unless he wishes to."

When they had the Sun Dance, everyone had a good time. Black Horse was the only one on the pole, and there were so many in the lodge that there was not room enough for all to dance. Some just had to sit around inside the lodge. Though they did not dance, they starved themselves for four days. This dance took place near Sheridan, Wyoming, seven years before Custer. . .

2. Cries Yia Eya Banished for the Murder of Chief Eagle

K. N. LLEWELLYN AND E. ADAMSON HOEBEL

Calf Woman related this story to the two anthropologists. From The Cheyenne Way *(pp. 12–13) by Karl N. Llewellyn and E. Adamson Hoebel. Copyright 1941 by the University of Oklahoma Press.*

Cries Yia Eya had been gone from the camp for three years because he had killed Chief Eagle in a whiskey brawl. The chiefs had ordered him away for his murder, so we did not see anything of him for that time. Then one day he came back, leading a horse packed with bundles of old-time tobacco. He stopped outside the camp and sent a messenger in with the horse and tobacco who was to say to the chiefs for him, "I am begging to come home."

The chiefs all got together for a meeting, and the soldier societies were told to convene, for there was an important matter to be considered. The tobacco was divided up, and chiefs' messengers were sent out to invite the soldier chiefs to come to the lodge of the tribal council, for the big chiefs wanted to talk to them. "Here is the tobacco that that man sent in," they told the soldier chiefs. "Now we want you soldiers to decide if you think we should accept his request. If you decide that we should let him return, then it is up to you to convince his family that it is all right." . . . The soldier chiefs took the tobacco and went out to gather their troops. Each [soldier] society met in its own separate lodge to talk among themselves, but the society servants kept passing back and forth between their different lodges to report on the trend of the discussion in the different companies.

At last one man said, "I think it is all right. I believe the stink has blown from him. Let him return!" This view was passed around, and this is the view that won out among the soldiers. Then the father of Chief Eagle was sent for and asked whether he would accept the decision. "Soldiers," he replied, "I shall listen to you. Let him return! But if that man comes back, I want never to hear his voice raised against another person. . . ."

Cries Yia Eya had always been a mean man, disliked by everyone, but he had been a fierce fighter against the enemies. After he came back to the camp, however, he was always good to the people.

7 Ideology and the Role of the Citizen: The Cheyenne

Analyzing the ideological base of a political system is particularly difficult for the beginning student. The ideology underlying political decisions is rarely stated explicitly. The prisoners at Stoerpenberg did not discuss their ideas about an individual's right to participate in his government. However, when they were called upon to choose leaders or to make political decisions, they all participated. Their actions reflected the belief that all citizens should have a voice in government. Insight into ideology depends not only upon knowing what was said or done but also upon recognizing the implications of what was said or done.

The development of insight requires both skill and knowledge. As a student being exposed to your first course in political science, you are obviously not going to gain the same insight by reading about the Cheyenne that Hoebel or Llewellyn did in studying them. But each of you is capable of gaining some insight, depending upon the questions you ask and the store of information and skills you bring with you to the task.

The first step you must take to sharpen your ability to infer and to see implications is to approach material with a question mark in mind. Reading 7 tells the story of Two Twists who led the Cheyenne against the Crows. What questions must you ask to help you identify the parts of the story that give clues about what the Cheyenne believed? What Cheyenne practices seem strange viewed from an American point of view? Do these practices imply different values? What Cheyenne practices seem similar to American practices? Does the similarity imply a shared value?

Developing a knowledge about the role played by the individual among the Cheyenne is easier. The questions you must ask are more direct. Are individuals, other than those designated by the system as government officials or accepted leaders, involved in the process of making, interpreting, or enforcing the rules by which relations are regulated? Who are these individuals? What is the source of their political power?

As you read the case of "When Two Twists Led the Cheyenne Against the Crow," keep the following questions in mind:

1. What did the Cheyenne believe in? What traits and acts did they value? What kinds of behavior did they believe were good? What kinds were bad?
2. What part did their beliefs play in the kind of political system they had—its leaders and its way of making and enforcing decisions?
3. What role did the individual play in the Cheyenne political system?

When Two Twists Led the Cheyenne Against the Crow

K. N. LLEWELLYN AND E. ADAMSON HOEBEL

Stump Horn told this story to Hoebel and Llewellyn. From The Cheyenne Way *(pp. 3–6) by Karl N. Llewellyn and E. Adamson Hoebel. Copyright 1941 by the University of Oklahoma Press.*

Red Robe's two sons were killed by the Crows quite a while back; their father in his grief stood before his lodge in mourning and called out, "All of my horses are for those who take them." He threw the whole herd away, not keeping even one for himself to ride upon.

The Dog Soldiers went out to herd his horses together, because they simply were not going to see the old man afoot. "No one is going to take these horses," they said. Then they sent an old man to see Red Robe.

"Your sons died like men," this messenger reminded him. "They died the glorious death, not in bed sick. Why don't you take back some ponies?"

"No," Red Robe replied, "Maiyun [the Supernatural] wanted my sons to die in battle, and it wants that I should be afoot awhile." Whatever they said, they could not budge him.

Finally, four soldier troops [the Elk, Bowstring, Dog, and Fox] decided to go talk to him. He had been a good man in the tribe, and here he was destitute. When the camp moved, he was the last to come along. He had nothing to camp with, but just stayed in the open. This had gone on three or four months when the soldiers got together. They all came to Red Robe, but one or two did the talking for them all. "We are begging you to do what we ask you — we are not alone — see them all — every company among us is here. We still have your horses. Come in among the people."

Still he was unmoved by all their pleading. At last Two Twists, a chief of the Bowstring Soldiers, came forward. "Say yes," he implored the old man. "Say yes, and we will promise you to go to war against the Crows wherever they may be. Say yes, and I'll get revenge for you whatever the risks. If they be in breastworks [fortifications], I'll drive them out."

"I accept," the bereaved old man finally answered. "I did not want to take those horses back after giving them away. It's like taking back a thing given to a friend."

"No, it is not like that to us," the soldiers all assured him.

So Red Robe came into camp. In the days which followed after, Two Twists prepared his pipe, taking it to all the soldier societies. Everyone smoked, whole troops pledging themselves to vengeance on the Crows. When all was ready, the societies moved to the raid in a body. Women and children went too, for the whole tribe was on the march. Two Twists was the leader of them all.

When they had come close to the enemy, Two Twists rode about the camp accompanied by his crier, who called for the people to listen. Two Twists spoke in this vein. "Look at me now. Soon I am about to follow the two sons of Red Robe. My friends, behold me; I shall never return from this raid."

The women all came out of their lodges to gaze at him. They sang him many heartening songs of which one was this — "Only the rocks lie here and never move. The human being vapors away." That night Two Twists sang the war songs of the Bowstring Soldiers.

The people were anxious to face the enemy, but the chiefs held them in. In the meantime the Crow scouts had spotted the Cheyenne and warned their camp. That night they built a breastwork of all their tepees arranged in a semicircle.

The next morning Two Twists was out in the camp again. "I sing for the last time," he cried. "People, behold me! This is my last time to walk on earth."

From all around folks brought him feathers to help him in the thing he was to do. They tied them to his war bonnet, to his horse's mane, and to its tail.

At last the fighters went toward the Crow camp. Two Twists led them, armed only with a saber. When they were before the enemy, he ordered his followers to hold back; he had his promise to fulfill. And so they all watched as he rode out alone toward the waiting enemy.

Straight at the tepees and into the breastwork he charged, slashing off the head of a Crow warrior as he broke through. He wheeled about, charging into the thick of them again, working havoc where his sword fell. The Crows shot, but missed and missed. Then our people saw Two Twists disappear among them in hand-to-hand struggle.

Then the Cheyenne charged into the Crows, killing them on all sides. Red Robe's wife charged with an ax. Wherever she found a Crow dead or wounded, she split his skull to smear the blood of the enemy upon her face and arms [pantomimed by the informant with proper gusto] . . . .

Two Twists was not killed, and from his deeds he derived the greatest honor. People said he had done his work; they would never let him do so again; he need not fulfill his vow to die. Back in camp, Two Twists sent for Red Robe and his two wives and children. He himself stripped them of their mourning rags and dressed them well. Many things were given to the women, and now Red Robe took back his horses. They, too, participated in the victory joy of the camp.

Red Robe went back to his lodge and in his turn sent for a crier to get Two Twists. Red Robe was accepting felicitations [congratulations] from everybody. To each person who came to greet him, he gave a horse. He painted the faces of all adult comers with black charcoal—the symbol of joy in the death of the enemy. Of all his horses he kept only a few for himself, and this time he was not stopped by the soldiers.

At the end, he adopted Two Twists for his son. Two Twists was not a tribal chief then, only the leader of a soldier society; later he was made a big chief, but on that one occasion he had charge of the whole tribe. He had wanted to wear the Medicine Hat [a Cheyenne religious relic] in the battle; and he had told the keeper he wished to wear it, but the keeper gave no answer. It was the keeper's wife who refused him. "You are going to war never to return. I do not think it right for us to give you the hat. You will get it bloody; you would bring us great trouble; blood on the hat would mean blood for all the tribe."

8 A Summary Exercise

When you finished reading Chapter 1, you prepared a list of concepts for use in analyzing the political system under which Louis XIV reigned. Under each concept, you identified questions to help you in your analysis. Turn to those questions now.

Concepts such as political leadership and decision-making help dissect political systems into categories that can be identified and studied. For purposes of comparison, these categories are too broad to be helpful. It is significant to know that in all political systems there are leaders, decisions to be made, and institutions established which reflect ideology. But to make a meaningful comparison between systems, you must also note what it is about their leadership that makes the systems different. What are the features of the decision-making process that reflect the system's ideology? Is it the way they choose those who are to make the decisions? Is it the freedom decision-makers are given to carry out their decisions? What is it about the decision-making process that distinguishes one system from another?

You have now studied two political systems. How would you go about comparing them?

Listing the five concepts you have studied would be a good starting point. Now, what analytical questions can you ask about each of these concepts that would give you the answers you need to describe the political systems of the Cheyenne Indians and the Stoerpenberg prisoners? Use the set-up below as a model to help you organize your ideas. Do not write in your book; but on a sheet of paper, write the concepts, and under each one, write the analytical questions you think would be useful.

A. Political Leadership
1. How many individuals are involved in the process of choosing the political leaders?
2. Who are they?
3.
What other questions can you ask about political leadership?

B. Political Decision-Making
1. Who is involved in making major political decisions?
2.
3.
What other questions can you ask about decision-making?

C. Political Institutions
1. How are political decisions carried out?
2.
3.
What other questions can you ask about institutions?

D. Political Ideology
   1. What goals are implied by the decisions that are made?
   2.
   3.
   What other questions can you ask about ideology?

E. Citizenship
   1. How much influence does the individual citizen have on political decisions?
   2.
   3.
   What other questions can you ask about the role of the citizen in his political system?

After you have made a written list of all of the questions you can think of that would help you understand the political systems of the Stoerpenberg prisoners and the Cheyenne Indians, glance through Readings 1 to 7. Do you find any clues that will help you answer the questions you have posed? Come to class tomorrow prepared to discuss the questions you have asked and their answers.

SUGGESTED READINGS

LISITZKY, GENE, *Four Ways of Being Human.*
   "The Kinship Band," pp. 33–40.
   Question: How do the Semang govern? What are the functions of the "leaders"? How does one become a leader?
   "The Odyssey of Kridlarssuark," pp. 100–09.
   Question: Why was Kridlarssuark accepted as a leader by the Eskimos?
   "Mana and Tapu," pp. 140–51.
   Question: How did the concepts of *mana* and *tapu* influence the way in which the Maori were governed?
   "The Warriors," pp. 151–66.
   Question: What were the "rules" that governed warfare among the Maori?
   "The Artists," pp. 167–81.
   Question: What was the role of the artist in the Maori political system?
   "Making a Living," pp. 181–92.
   Question: What was the relationship between the individual and the Maori chief?
   "Making a Maori," pp. 192–203.
   Question: How were Maori children taught Maori ways of doing things?
   "Hopis: People of the Desert," pp. 211–94.
   Question: What is the basic ideology of the Hopi people? How has their ideology influenced their political system?

Unit Two

Political Institutions and Ideologies: The U.S. and the U.S.S.R.

AT STOERPENBERG and among the Cheyenne, the groups governed were relatively small, and individuals could easily gain access to their leaders. Those who disagreed with political decisions could say so, and they would be heard directly by those who made the decisions. Procedures for compromising differences of political opinion were informal and responsive to the demands of a particular situation.

As societies get larger and more complex, those governed are farther removed from those who govern. Decision-making becomes more formalized. Rules are agreed upon and recorded. Procedures for making, interpreting, and enforcing the rules are adopted. In short, a society establishes many political institutions through which those who govern must operate.

Often a society sets down this formal plan of government in a constitution, a statement of a political system's philosophy of government. A constitution establishes the framework within which the government must work.

In Unit Two you will examine the constitutions of the United States and the Soviet Union, as well as other materials which you can use to analyze and compare the ideologies and institutions of these two complex political systems.

Chapter 3

The United States: A Democratic Political System

STATING THE ISSUE   Political systems can be compared in a number of different ways. You can compare them in terms of the number of people living within the systems. You can compare them in terms of their stability: that is, the extent to which people living within the systems accept them. You can compare them in terms of the amount of influence the general public has over political decision-making or in terms of the extent to which power is concentrated in the hands of a few. However you compare political systems, you should avoid certain pitfalls.

A common pitfall is the tendency to try to fit every political system into a rigid category. No political system fits neatly into any category, for no system exists in pure form. There are shades of difference. For example, some systems are more democratic than others; none is a perfect democracy. It is the extent to which a system leans one way rather than another that identifies the kind of system it is.

A second pitfall is the tendency to judge political systems in terms of your own values. While you cannot divorce yourself from the particular way you view an event, you can be aware of the fact that what you consider "good" or "bad" is very much affected by who you are, what you believe, how you were raised and educated, and what is happening to you right now. You cannot erase your values from your mind, but you can be alert to the way in which they color what you see. You can examine the yardstick you choose to measure a system. Is it a fair measure? Are the generalizations you draw related to that yardstick? Are your generalizations backed up by the information at hand?

In Chapter 3 you will be called upon to analyze the political system of the United States in terms of the ideology upon which its government is based. You will also analyze the institutions developed to express this ideology. After you have gained some insight into the background of American political ideology, you will turn to the Constitution for evidence concerning American political institutions and the values they reflect. The Constitution contains a wealth of material that can be used to answer such questions as these: What are the values expressed by the American political system? What are the roots of these values?

9 American Ideology

When the American prisoners at Stoerpenberg Camp were told to make rules to govern themselves, they agreed to hold an election in which everyone would vote. Candidates were nominated, and prisoners then campaigned for their favorites. Why did these men choose this particular way to organize their political activities? Obviously, their backgrounds guided them in this direction. The ideology and institutions upon which they built their system were borrowed from the political system which they knew best, that of the United States.

In 1787, each of the newly united American states sent delegates to Philadelphia to write a constitution setting forth new rules by which to govern the nation. Like the Stoerpenberg prisoners, these men brought political and social backgrounds to their task. Their backgrounds were not identical. Some framers of the Constitution were aristocratic southern planters. Others were New England tradesmen. All of them, however, shared a political background which helped to form a common ideology.

This background was rooted in a political heritage developed over centuries and extending beyond the borders of the American continent. It included such acts as the signing of the Magna Carta, an agreement limiting the power of the English kings over their feudal lords in the thirteenth century. It included as well the more recent writings of such political philosophers as the seventeenth-century Englishman John Locke. Locke was widely read in both England and the colonies. He believed that men were born free and were entitled by nature to life, liberty, and property. In 1690, he published two books in which he explained his concept of government. According to Locke, free men voluntarily united in a "social contract" that gave government the powers it needed to protect each man's life, liberty, and property from invasion by others. Government properly existed only where men willed it for the preservation of order in their society.

In addition to sharing a knowledge about the writings of men like Locke, most members of the Constitutional Convention shared common experiences in colonial, county, or town governments. These experiences were also a part of the background they brought with them to Philadelphia. There they faced the task of writing a document which would express the goals of the American people, compromise the differences of opinion among Americans, win acceptance among the leaders of each colony, and create a national government powerful enough to control the newly united states. Reading 9 describes the colonial governments which the members of the convention knew so well. As you read, keep the following questions in mind:

1. What were the major features of colonial governments? What influence did colonial government probably have on the ideas of the members of the Constitutional Convention?
2. What sort of constitution would men with backgrounds like these be likely to write?
3. Is it reasonable to expect men who have lived in a primitive society such as an African tribe to write the same sort of constitution, once they win their freedom? If they did write such a constitution, would it be likely to work well? Give reasons for your answers.

Government in the American Colonies

EDWIN FENTON

Each of the thirteen American colonies grew up more or less independently of the others. They were founded by different men during a period lasting more than a century. The first colony, Virginia, was established in 1607 and the last, Georgia, in 1732. Each began under its own charter which the king granted to a trading company, such as the Massachusetts Bay Company, or to a lord proprietor, such as William Penn, the founder of Pennsylvania. The charters and the subsequent agreements with settlers established individual and different governments in each colony. Moreover, the backgrounds and ideas of settlers differed from one colony to another. A Virginia aristocrat would have felt quite uncomfortable living in Boston or Salem, Massachusetts. Yet beneath all the differences, the governments and the people of the thirteen colonies had much in common.

Almost everyone, for example, assumed that a government ought to have a written charter or constitution. Each colony did. The famous Mayflower Compact served as a primitive constitution for the Pilgrim settlers of Plymouth, Massachusetts. Other colonists, as you have seen, procured written charters from the trading companies or the proprietors who owned the land where they had settled. Everywhere in the colonies, men became accustomed to referring to their charters to find out what political rights they had. They were not likely to start a government in which rights and duties of government and citizen were not clearly defined on paper.

The colonists had an inbred fear of a powerful central government. The king or his representatives in England had often *vetoed,* or refused to approve, bills passed by colonial governments. Governors appointed by the king had also exercised the veto too frequently to please independent colonists. Moreover, the royal government had taxed the colonists and regulated their trade. Because central gov-

30

ernments had acted in this manner, the colonists had learned to rely on local institutions and to give central authorities as little power as possible.

One tested way to limit the power of government was to separate its three branches, the executive, legislative, and judicial. During the eighteenth century, executive power in most colonies was in the hands of the colonial governors, who were usually appointed by the king. Colonial legislatures had two houses, one elected by the voters and the other appointed. Judges were usually appointed by the governor or by the king himself. Although the upper house of the legislature often heard court cases, the three branches of government performed different functions and were usually responsible to different authorities. In many cases, one branch could *check*, or control, the power of another. A government in which all power was centralized in one man or in one institution would have been unthinkable to our colonial ancestors.

The colonial governments were not entirely democratic. Most of the governors and the members of the upper house of the legislature were appointed. Even the elected branches of the legislature did not spring entirely from the people. Neither women nor slaves could vote. In addition, all of the colonies had either property or religious qualifications for voting. On the whole, since most people owned property, the right to vote was widespread among free white males, more so in New England than in the South. A member of a colonial legislature usually had to own more property than a mere voter, and by custom, he had to live in the district which elected him. No responsible official would have hoped to include in a constitution a provision granting every adult the right to vote. Nor could the founding fathers have agreed on who should have had the right to vote when each of the thirteen colonies had somewhat different provisions from all the others.

Nor would a provision for political parties have made sense. In our meaning of the term, the colonies had no real political parties. Each colony did have groups of people who disagreed with each other. In some cases, supporters of the colonial governor contended with his opponents. In others, men from the coast regions opposed inlanders who faced somewhat different problems, such as defense against the Indians. But these alliances based on common interests never became firm enough to form into distinct political parties which drew up platforms and carried on campaigns from one election to another.

Local government also varied widely from one colony to another. Southern colonies such as Virginia often reproduced the English pattern, transplanting the county as the basic unit with a sheriff appointed by the colonial governor and a court made up of appointed justices of the peace. In New England, the basic unit of local government was the town, run by elected officials and focusing on an annual town meeting in which all the voters decided issues by direct vote. In the middle colonies such as New York and Pennsylvania, both the county and the town forms of government appeared together. It would have been quite difficult to get colonial people to agree on one system of local government for all sections of the country. They could agree, however, that criticism of a government, if true, was not libelous. This principle was established in the trial of a New York publisher named Peter Zenger in 1734, a case which helped to establish the principle of liberty of the press for all the colonies.

With all these differences, what held the colonies together? Not direct political ties. Each colonial government had more direct ties to England than to each other. The flow of petitions and orders all centered in His Majesty's government. The governor of Massachusetts and the governor of Virginia had no official relationships to each other. Both had well-established relationships to London. Attempts were made to form alliances among the colonies, but none succeeded before the American Revolution.

Even before the Revolutionary War, a few nonpolitical factors did tie the colonies together, however. The steady growth of population produced an almost continuous line of settlements down the Atlantic seacoast. Coastal trade, the gradual construction of roads, and the improvement of the colonial postal service all formed links between colonies. The presence of two enemies, the Indians and the French, on the western frontier brought common problems which colonies were forced to face together and which helped to unify them. The common English language and the common set of customs that the colonists imported from abroad also helped link one colony to another.

Then came the quarrel with England. After 1763, the British government began to pass additional laws to regulate life in the colonies. A few Americans in every colony protested, and they began to correspond with each other and to support each other's protests. Here was the real beginning of the ties which bound the leaders of the colonies to each other.

The Revolutionary War strengthened these ties. Soldiers from every colony, northern as well as southern, served in the army under the command of a Virginian, General George Washington. The wartime government, which was made up of delegates from all the rebelling colonies, was very weak, but it encouraged leaders to think along national instead of local lines. The military victory which the revolutionists finally secured signified that all thirteen colonies had won in a common cause.

10 American Institutions: Federalism

In May 1787, the Constitutional Convention met in Philadelphia. All of the delegates to it agreed upon this fundamental premise: government exists because men have agreed that it should, and governments have power to the extent that men give them power. But disagreements arose over how this power should be divided.

More than ten years prior to the Constitutional Convention, during the Revolutionary War, the states had attempted to solve their joint problems by forming a *confederation,* or loose union. They had adopted the Articles of Confederation, a written constitution which gave the national government virtually no power. Though on paper these Articles gave the national government the right to levy taxes, the states had not given the Confederation the power to enforce taxation. On paper the Confederation had the right to coin money, but the states had not given the national government the power to secure the gold and silver for coining it. Because the states retained so much power, they prevented the development of a strong and tyrannical national government. But they also prevented the establishment of a national government that could meet their joint needs.

The Constitutional Convention met to create a national government which would have sufficient power to cope with the problems of the United States but which could not destroy the individual states. To meet these conditions, the delegates adopted a system called *federalism.* Federalism divides power between the national government and the state governments. The national government has only those powers given, or delegated, to it by the Constitution. The state governments retain all powers not delegated to the national government, except those specifically denied by the Constitution. Federalism represented a compromise between those favoring confederation, or the retention of most political power by the governments of the individual states, and those who favored a form of government in which more power would be delegated to the national government.

Broadly, the Constitution divides political power into these six categories:

1. Powers delegated to the national government (*enumerated* and *implied powers*)
2. Powers retained by state governments (*residual powers*)
3. Powers that can be exercised by both national and state governments (*concurrent powers*)
4. Powers denied state governments
5. Powers denied the national government
6. Powers denied both governments, national and state

Reading 10 is a collection of Articles from the Constitution of the United States of America. (The complete Constitution appears in the appendix, pages 275–88.) These Articles were selected because they deal with the division of political power between the national and state governments. The wording has been simplified. Read these Articles carefully. Write answers to the following questions in your notebook and bring them to class. In organizing your answers, you might find it convenient to keep the six categories listed above in mind.

1. What powers are delegated to the national government? What powers are retained by the state governments? What powers are shared by national and state governments?
2. What powers are denied state governments? What powers are denied the national government? What powers are denied both governments?
3. What are the main areas of concern to the national government? What are the main areas of concern to the state governments?

Excerpts from the Constitution of the United States

Article I

Section 1. A Congress of the United States, which shall consist of a Senate and House of Representatives, shall have the power to make all national laws.

Section 4. The times, places, and manner of holding elections to choose senators and representatives shall be decided in each state by its legislature. . . .

Section 8. Clause 1. Congress has the right to collect taxes of various kinds to pay the debts of the national government, to defend the nation against enemies, and to provide for the welfare of the people. Taxes must be uniform; they must not discriminate against any section of the nation.

Section 8. Clause 2. Congress may borrow money.

Section 8. Clause 3. Congress may control trade with foreign nations, among the states, and with Indian tribes.

Section 8. Clause 4. Congress may make rules concerning how people may become citizens of the United States and what must be done when a person cannot pay his debts.

Section 8. Clause 5. Congress may coin money and regulate its value. It may also regulate the value of foreign money used in the United States. Congress may set standards to be used for weighing and measuring.

Section 8. Clause 6. Congress may pass laws specifying how those who counterfeit money should be punished.

Section 8. Clause 7. Congress can establish post offices and roads over which mail is to be carried.

Section 8. Clause 8. Congress may encourage the progress of science and useful arts by securing for authors and inventors exclusive rights to their writings and discoveries for a limited period of time.

Section 8. Clause 10. Congress may decide on the punishment for crimes committed on the high seas and crimes in which foreign countries are involved.

Section 8. Clause 11. Congress may declare war.

Section 8. Clause 12. Congress may create an army and raise money to pay for its expenses. Only enough money to pay for two years' expenses can be given the army at any one time.

Section 8. Clause 13. Congress may create a navy and provide money to support it.

Section 8. Clause 14. Congress may make rules governing its armed forces.

Section 8. Clause 15. Congress may call out the National Guard to enforce the laws of the Union, to suppress internal rebellion, and to repel foreign invasions.

Section 8. Clause 16. Congress may organize, arm, and discipline a citizens' army (the National Guard). The states may appoint the officers of this army, but the states must train them in the way Congress directs.

Section 8. Clause 17. Congress may make all rules governing the national capital and all other areas in which such national operations as forts or arsenals are located.

Section 8. Clause 18. Congress may make all laws necessary to carry out the powers delegated to the national government by this Constitution. [Clause 18 is referred to as the *elastic clause*.]

Section 9. Clause 2. Individuals cannot be held prisoner unless there is sufficient evidence to hold them. [This is the privilege of the writ of *habeas corpus,* a court order which demands that a prisoner be brought before a judge who determines whether or not there is enough evidence to hold the prisoner.] Congress may suspend this privilege only if public safety is threatened by it.

Section 9. Clause 3. Congress may pass no law whose intent is to punish a particular person without a jury trial. [Such a law is called a *bill of attainder*.] Neither can Congress pass a law that would punish someone for doing something that was not against the law at the time he did it. [Such a law is an *ex post facto* law.]

Section 9. Clause 5. Congress must not tax goods sent out of any state.

Section 9. Clause 6. Congress shall make no laws that would give the ports of one state an advantage over the ports of others.

Section 9. Clause 8. No title of nobility shall be granted by the United States . . . .

Section 10. Clause 1. State governments must not do the following: enter into agreements with foreign nations; issue coins or paper money; pass any bill of attainder [see Article I, Section 9, Clause 3] or ex post facto law [see Article I, Section 9, Clause 3]; pass laws that destroy contracts agreed to by individuals; grant any title of nobility.

Section 10. Clause 2. No state shall, without the consent of Congress, tax goods entering or leaving their territory, except to cover the cost of inspection . . . .

Section 10. Clause 3. No state shall, without consent of Congress, tax ships entering its ports; maintain an army or navy in times of peace; make treaties with other states or with foreign powers; engage in war, unless actually invaded or in such immediate danger that delay is impossible.

Article IV

Section 1. Each state shall respect the laws of all other states.

Section 2. Clause 1. The citizens of one state shall be entitled to the privileges and immunities of citizens in all states.

Section 2. Clause 2. If a person charged with a crime in one state flees from that state, he shall, on request of the governor, be returned to the state from which he fled.

Section 4. The United States shall guarantee to every state in this Union a republican form of government [that is, a government where the power rests in the hands of the voters]. It shall protect each state against invasion and, at the request of the state, shall protect each state against domestic violence.

Article VI

Clause 2. The Constitution and the laws of the United States shall be the supreme law of the land. Judges in every state shall be bound by them, even when state laws and state constitutions conflict with the national laws.

11 American Institutions: Checks and Balances

The national government, often referred to as the federal government, is divided into three branches: the executive, the legislative, and the judicial. The executive branch of the government includes not only the President but all the executive departments, bureaus, and agencies required to carry out the decisions made by the President. Each member of the President's Cabinet heads an executive department. The legislative branch of the government includes the two houses of Congress plus such divisions as the Library of Congress and the Government Printing Office, which help Congress with its work. The judicial branch of government includes the entire system of federal courts, headed by the Supreme Court of the United States.

The men who wrote the American Constitution were torn by differences concerning how much power should be given to the federal government. They were also in conflict concerning how the power given to the federal government should be divided among the three branches of government. Some wanted a strong executive, independent of the legislature, who could provide the country with direct and vigorous leadership. Others, who feared tyranny, wanted an executive controlled completely by the legislature.

Again, the framers of the Constitution reached a compromise. They divided power among all three branches of the government, and they built a system of balances into the Constitution. Power granted one branch of government was checked by power granted another. No branch was to dominate the others.

Reading 11 is a collection of Articles from the Constitution that deal with the division of power at the federal level of government. Again, the wording has been simplified, and, in some cases, the Article shortened. Answer the following questions in your notebook:

1. What powers are given by the Constitution to Congress? to the President? to the federal court system?
2. In general, what kinds of powers are given to the legislative branch? to the executive branch? to the judicial branch?

3. How many instances can you find in which the power given one branch of government is checked by a power given another branch?

Excerpts from the Constitution of the United States

Article I

Section 1.   A Congress of the United States, which shall consist of a Senate and House of Representatives, shall have the power to make all national laws.

Section 2. Clause 5.   The House of Representatives shall have the right to *impeach,* or bring charges against, officials of the United States suspected of serious wrongdoing.

Section 3. Clause 4.   The Vice-President of the United States shall be the President of the Senate. He shall preside over the Senate when it is in session, but will vote only in case of a tie.

Section 3. Clause 5.   The Senate shall choose their other officers, and also a temporary president [President *pro tempore*], who shall preside over the Senate when the Vice-President is absent.

Section 3. Clause 6.   The Senate shall have the right to try impeached officials. Ordinarily the President of the Senate shall preside at impeachment trials, but if the President of the United States has been impeached, the Chief Justice of the Supreme Court shall preside at his trial. No official shall be convicted of the charges brought against him unless two thirds of the senators present at his trial find him guilty.

Section 3. Clause 7.   Congress can punish impeached officials found guilty only by removing them from office and forbidding them ever to hold another federal office. After impeachment, however, officials can be tried by a regular court and, if found guilty, punished in accordance with the law.

Section 4. Clause 1.   The times, places, and manner of holding elections to choose senators and representatives shall be decided in each state by its legislature, but the United States Congress may at any time change any of these regulations except regulations concerning where elections shall be held.

Section 5. Clause 1.   Each house of Congress may judge whether its members were chosen by a fair election and whether they are properly qualified to be members of Congress. A representative or a senator may be kept from taking office if a majority of the members of the body to which he was elected vote him ineligible. . . .

Section 5. Clause 2. Each house of Congress may make rules governing its work. They may also punish members for behaving improperly and may expel them from the group if two thirds of the members of that house vote to do so.

Section 7. Clause 1. All bills having to do with the raising of money, or *revenue*, must be introduced in the House of Representatives. However, the Senate can offer changes, or amendments, to revenue bills.

Section 7. Clause 2. Every bill that is passed by the House of Representatives and the Senate shall be presented to the President. If he approves the bill, he shall sign it, thus making it law. If he does not approve, he may veto the bill. If he vetoes the bill, he shall return it, with his objections, to the house where the bill originated. That house shall then reconsider the bill. If, after reconsideration, two thirds of the members of that house still vote to pass the bill, it shall be sent, with the President's objections, to the other house. It shall be reconsidered there, and if approved by two thirds of that house also, the bill shall become law without the President's signature.

If a bill is not signed by the President within ten days of being presented to him (not counting Sundays), it shall automatically become law anyway, unless Congress has adjourned during those ten days, thus preventing the President's returning the bill to them within that time. If Congress adjourns during this ten-day period and the President does not sign the bill, the bill shall not become law. [This procedure of holding the bill until Congress adjourns is called a *pocket veto*.]

Section 8. Clause 1. Congress has the right to collect taxes of various kinds to pay the debts of the national government, to defend the nation against enemies, and to provide for the welfare of the people. Taxes must not discriminate against any section of the nation.

Section 8. Clause 2. Congress may borrow money.

Section 8. Clause 3. Congress may control trade with foreign nations, among the states, and with Indian tribes.

Section 8. Clause 4. Congress may make the rules governing how individuals become citizens of the United States. . .

Section 8. Clause 5. Congress may coin money and regulate its value. . . .

Section 8. Clause 11. Congress may declare war.

Section 8. Clause 12. Congress may create an army and raise money to pay for its expenses. . . .

Section 8. Clause 13. Congress may create a navy and provide money to support it.

Section 8. Clause 14. Congress may make rules governing its armed forces.

Section 8. Clause 18. Congress may make all laws necessary to carry out the powers delegated to the national government by this Constitution.

Article II

Section 2. Clause 1. The President shall be Commander in Chief of the Army and Navy of the United States and of the militias of the several states when they are called into the service of the United States. He may call for written reports from the heads of each of the executive departments [the members of his cabinet] upon any subject relating to the work of their departments. He may grant pardons to persons convicted of crimes against the federal government or order their punishment to be delayed, except in the case of impeached government officials.

Section 2. Clause 2. The President shall have the power to make treaties. These treaties must be approved by two thirds of the senators present when the treaties are voted on. The President shall nominate and, with the approval of the Senate, appoint ambassadors, other public ministers and consuls, judges of the Supreme Court, and any other officers of the United States whose appointments have, by law, been provided for. . . .

Section 3. The President shall from time to time give Congress information concerning the state of the Union. He may suggest for congressional consideration conditions which he feels require legislation. He may call special sessions of Congress and may adjourn Congress if the two houses cannot agree on an adjournment time.

Section 4. The President, Vice-President, and all civil officials of the federal government may be removed from office if Congress impeaches and convicts them of treason, bribery, or other crimes.

Article III

Section 2. Clause 1. Federal courts shall rule on conflicts concerning interpretations of the Constitution and of federal laws. . . They have the power to rule on disagreements between the federal government and other governments or individuals. They may settle arguments between the states or between citizens of different states or between states and their citizens and foreign countries.

12 The Rights of the American Individual

After more than three months of debating, delegates to the Constitutional Convention agreed upon a document which they would present to their states to *ratify*, or accept, as the Constitution of the United States. The arguments between those who favored a strong national government and those who favored a confederation had been compromised. The delegates had reached agreement concerning the distribution of powers among the three branches of government. But still, considerable doubt remained as to whether the Constitution would be generally acceptable to the American people and to their state governments.

Delegates to the convention had been instructed to suggest amendments to the Articles of the Confederation. They had gone much further. They had set aside the Articles of Confederation completely and had written a new Constitution. They recognized that there was little chance of getting the Constitution adopted by all the states. Therefore, the delegates ruled that the Constitution would go into effect as soon as it was ratified by nine of the thirteen states. But even ratification by only nine states was not to prove easy.

One of the stumbling blocks was the delegates' failure to include in the Constitution a clear definition of rights retained by the individual over which no government had any power. The Constitution did mention a few individual rights, but many, about which the people had strong feelings, were ignored. There were no provisions guaranteeing freedom of speech or religion, or the right to assemble or petition.

Several states refused to ratify the Constitution until they were promised that amendments which guaranteed individual rights would be added. When the first session of Congress met, the members went to work to keep this promise.

They wrote ten amendments to the Constitution dealing with the rights of the individual. By the end of 1791, the states ratified this "Bill of Rights" and it became a part of the Constitution.

The Bill of Rights was written to protect the rights of the individual. But sometimes the rights of the individual come into conflict with the public interest. At such times a dilemma occurs. Is the cost of upholding the rights of an individual worth the possibility of doing harm to the general welfare?

An issue that currently poses this dilemma is the question of permitting evidence secured by wiretapping to be used in courts to convict known criminals. Most citizens are not against the conviction of racketeers and gangsters, yet there is sufficient feeling against the use of wiretap evidence to prevent its use.

Reading 12 is in two parts. The first part consists of the Bill of Rights, the first ten amendments to the Constitution. Their wording has been simplified. The second part contains a newspaper account concerning the dropping of charges against seven men who, in the words of the district attorney in the case, were guilty "beyond all doubt" of selling narcotics. Charges were dropped because the evidence needed to convict these men was obtained by wiretapping. As you read, consider the following questions:

1. Which of the first ten amendments have bearing on the use of evidence obtained by wiretapping?
2. What is the cost of not permitting the use of wiretap evidence in a trial?
3. What would the cost to all citizens be of permitting the use of wiretap evidence in the case of known criminals?
4. Do you think wiretap evidence should be allowed in court?

1. First Ten Amendments to the Constitution of the United States

Amendment I

Congress shall make no law that restricts people from worshiping as they please, from speaking freely, from assembling peaceably, or from complaining to the government if they think they have been treated unfairly. In addition, Congress shall not pass any law that restricts the freedom of the press.

Amendment II

Since a citizens' army is necessary to the security of a free state, people shall be allowed to keep and bear arms.

Amendment III

People shall not be forced to give room and board in their homes to soldiers in times of peace. Nor shall they be forced to quarter soldiers in time of war unless a law is first passed requiring it.

Amendment IV

Government officials cannot search individuals or their homes or belongings unless a judge has first issued an official order authorizing the search. No warrant shall be issued unless there is reasonable evidence that a crime has been committed and will be exposed as a result of the search.

42

Amendment V

No person shall be
(1) tried for a serious crime unless a grand jury has first examined the evidence and decided that a trial is warranted, except in cases arising in the armed forces in times of public danger;
(2) tried for the same crime twice;
(3) forced, in a criminal case, to be a witness against himself; *wire taping*
(4) executed, imprisoned, or fined without a fair trial;
(5) deprived of his property for public use unless he has first been given a fair price for it.

Amendment VI

Any person being tried for a criminal offense is entitled to
(1) a speedy and public trial;
(2) an impartial jury chosen from citizens of the state and district in which the crime was committed;
(3) knowledge of why he is being tried;
(4) see and hear the witnesses who testify against him;
(5) force witnesses who can give evidence in his favor to come to court to testify;
(6) defense by a lawyer appointed by the court if he cannot afford to pay for one himself.

Amendment VII

In law suits involving things valued at more than $20, individuals have the right to a jury trial. [Today, people usually do not bring law suits unless they involve a great deal more than $20.]

Amendment VIII

Individuals accused of a crime cannot be required to pay excessive bail. Individuals found guilty of crimes cannot be required to pay excessive fines, nor can cruel or unusual punishments be inflicted.

Amendment IX

The fact that certain individual rights are guaranteed by the Constitution should not be interpreted to mean that rights not specifically mentioned in the Constitution are denied the individual.

Amendment X

The Constitution delegates certain powers to the national government of the United States. All other powers are retained by the states or by the people, except those powers specifically denied to the states by the Constitution.

2. Wiretap Evidence Barred by Hogan Until U.S. Backs It

JACK ROTH

The article from which these excerpts are taken appeared in The New York Times *on November 15, 1961. The events described took place in New York. © 1961 by The New York Times Company. Reprinted by permission.*

. . . Assistant District Attorney Irving Lang moved for the discharge of seven narcotics defendants — men he said were "guilty beyond any doubt."

Mr. Lang, who is in charge of narcotics cases for the prosecutor's office, said he was abandoning the prosecution because the law prevented him from using wiretap evidence, and the "key" pieces of evidence in the case, "cementing the conspiracy and convicting the defendants by their own words, are the wiretaps."

The defendants were indicted [charged with a crime] in January 1960. At the time Mr. Hogan [the district attorney] said they had operated a multi-million-dollar narcotics ring in the metropolitan area for five to ten years. He described them as among the top narcotics distributors in the nation.

After reviewing before Judge Mitchell D. Schweitzer how the defendants had been apprehended through the use of court-authorized wiretaps [wiretapping for criminal investigation is legal under New York State law] and detailing their backgrounds, Mr. Lang said: "Ordinarily the district attorney moves for the discharge of defendants either because he cannot prove guilt beyond a reasonable doubt or in the interests of justice. Neither reason motivates the application in the instant case.

"The people feel the guilt of these defendants can be established, not only beyond a reasonable doubt but beyond all doubt. And, indeed, the interests of justice would require the prompt isolation of these men from society.

"However, the people cannot proceed further with this case.

"The United States Court of Appeals for the Second Circuit has held that the introduction of wiretap evidence in a trial constitutes a violation of the Federal Communications Act and that those who testify to or introduce wiretaps commit a federal crime."

Chapter 4

The Soviet Union: A Totalitarian State

STATING THE ISSUE As you worked with Chapter 3 and dealt with American ideology and American institutions, you were on fairly familiar ground. For many years you have been hearing and learning about the American Constitution, about man's right to life, liberty, and the pursuit of happiness, about the President and Congress and the Supreme Court.

Now you approach ground which in all likelihood is not so familiar. In dealing with political systems that evolved from backgrounds different from your own, you run the risk of equating the unfamiliar with the unreasonable or the bad. While the ways of other people may seem unreasonable or undesirable viewed through your eyes, these strange ways may well seem more reasonable when you see them placed in their own setting.

Chapter 4 gives you the opportunity to see examples of beliefs different from yours. You will take a look at some of the events and beliefs that shaped the Soviet ideology. You will see some of the institutions the Soviets have developed to carry out the objectives of their ideology. Above all, you will see that to evaluate Soviet institutions, you must determine how effective they are in reaching the objectives of the ideology from which they spring.

Use the readings in Chapter 4 to help you discover answers to these questions: What forces have shaped the beliefs of the Soviet Union? What are these beliefs? What political institutions have been established as a result of the Soviet ideology?

13 Soviet Ideology

A society's ideology and institutions are by no means immune to change. As history unfolds and pressures develop, societies are sometimes forced to reexamine their beliefs. The institutions that evolve from such reexaminations tend to reflect some of the values of the past as well as the beliefs of the present.

In 1917, the existing Russian political system was overthrown by a revolution. The leaders who came to power brought with them a belief in the ideology expressed in the writings of Karl Marx. While the new leaders and their followers believed in this ideology, there were many Russian citizens who had never even heard of Karl Marx and his philosophy of communism.

The new leaders had to meet the problem of developing a political system that would be capable of regulating relationships among all those living within the Soviet Union. In their attempt to form a stable government, they developed a number of political institutions. Some proved successful and are still part of the Soviet government. Others had to be abandoned as ineffective. To be effective, these institutions had to be responsive to attitudes and values that were remnants of the past as well as expressive of the communist ideology.

So that Reading 13 can deal with the old and the new, it is divided into two parts. The first part is a brief account of prerevolutionary Russian history. The second is a short excerpt from Marx's *Communist Manifesto*. As you read the first part, consider these questions:

1. How would you describe social and economic conditions in Russia prior to 1860, compared with the United States or Western Europe?
2. What adjectives could you use to describe the type of government the Russian serf was accustomed to prior to 1860? What adjectives could you use to describe the type of government that ruled the Russian serf during the period between 1860 and 1917?

The Russian Background
HARRY SCHWARTZ

From The Soviet Union—Communist Economic Power *by Harry Schwartz. Copyright © 1963 by Curriculum Resources, Inc. Published in cooperation with Scott, Foresman and Company, Glenview, Illinois.*

. . . For centuries before the czar was toppled from his throne in 1917, Russia was backward compared with Western Europe or the United States. This was the result of several special factors, notably the long period 1240–1480 during which the Russian people lived under Mongol rule. The Renaissance—the era of re-awakening scholarship and science—had little impact upon Russia. In the years Western Europe's intellectual horizons were being broadened by the discovery of America and by a host of new scientific and intellectual ideas, Russia was almost unaffected. It had very little contact with the West and was preoccupied with recovering from the impact of the long, stifling Mongol rule. In short, Russia was a comparative latecomer to the modern world of science and industry. It had to compress into decades the progress and change which the West had made over centuries.

For several centuries before 1860, large numbers of Russians were serfs on large estates owned by the czar, members of the nobility, and other large landowners. Illiterate, poverty-stricken, almost a slave, the typical serf worked the land belonging to the estate owner and received little in return. Serfs could be, and often were, bought and sold with the land they lived on. Many of them were treated brutally by their masters, and often their anger at their hard life flared into rebellions which were crushed mercilessly.

William Richardson, an Englishman, visited Russia just before the American Revolution and summed up his impressions of the serfs in these words: "Those poor unhappy men who are bought and sold, who are beaten, loaded with fetters, and valued no higher than a dog, treated with unabating rigor, become inhuman; insulted with un-remitting contempt, become base; and, forever afraid of rapacious injustice, they grow deceitful."

By the accident of history, the Russian serfs were liberated at about the same time that the Negro slaves were freed in the United States. Unlike Negroes here, the freed Russian serfs were given part of the land they had tilled for their own use. The land given to these serfs was taken from the nobility, who were paid by the government for this loss. In turn, the government expected the former serfs to pay for the land they had received at some time. This debt was considered the collective debt of each village. In order to permit the village to pay this debt and to prevent peasants from running away and escaping their shares of this obligation, the czarist government gave the village a great deal of control over its members.

As a result, for decades after the end of serfdom, the free individual farmer of the sort that dominated American agriculture was almost unknown in many parts of Russia. The burden of debt on the freed serfs and the fact that large areas of the land remained the property of the nobility embittered the peasants. That bitterness increased as the population rose rapidly after the 1860's and the pressure of additional mouths to feed worsened the economic situation of many living in the countryside. The peasants were convinced that all the land should belong to them and that they had been swindled when they were freed. The peasants' resentment and desire for land played an important role in creating the dissatisfaction that erupted in the unsuccessful revolution of 1905 and again in the stormy events of 1917. "All land to the peasants!" was the slogan Lenin used to try to win peasant support for the Bolshevik regime in the difficult days after the successful revolution of November 1917.

In March 1917, the government of the czar simply collapsed as a result of pressures created by World War I. For a few months moderates, attracted to Western political systems, controlled the government. In November the moderates were overthrown by the Bolsheviks, led by Vladimir Lenin.

Lenin was a Russian intellectual who had been exiled from his homeland for many years prior to the revolution because of his attempts to arouse the people. He wrote pamphlets and made speeches encouraging them to revolt against the commands of an oppressive government. Lenin believed the prerevolutionary Russian government was based on a false ideology. He preached a new ideology, an ideology that represented a revolt from the unfairnesses of the past and an acceptance of values defined by a German economist-philosopher, Karl Marx.

Marx, who became the spokesman of a working-class movement called the League of Communists, wrote in the mid 1800's. He formulated his theories on the basis of his observations of industrialized Western Europe. His observations led him to theorize that the history of all existing societies is a history of class struggles. At times the struggle has taken place between freeman and slave, between aristocrat and peasant, between lord and serf, between guildmaster and journeyman. Regardless of how the classes were labeled, Marx believed that, throughout history, all people could be divided into two classes, the oppressors and the oppressed. Marx went on to note that the industrialization of modern Europe failed do away with this natural antagonism. It merely established new classes and new conditions under which the struggle took place.

The new class of oppressors was called the *bourgeoisie.* Among the bourgeoisie Marx included all those who controlled the new commercial and industrial interests that now dominated Western Europe. Small shopkeepers, landlords, bankers, and industrialists were all described as oppressors. The oppressed were called the *proletariat,* which included those who provided the labor needed to promote the commerical and industrial interests of the bourgeoisie.

Seeing society in perpetual conflict and seeing this conflict polarized around two naturally antagonistic forces, Marx wrote *The Manifesto of the Communist Party.* When you have read the excerpts from this document, answer the following questions:

1. What is Marx's view of private property? What does he say should be done about it?
2. What does Marx envision that the role of the workingman should be?

The Manifesto of the Communist Party
KARL MARX and FRIEDRICH ENGELS

Karl Marx and Friedrich Engels are co-authors of The Manifesto. *Its basic ideas, however, are considered to be "Marxist." Several of these ideas appear in these excerpts from* The Manifesto.

. . . The theory of the Communists may be summed up in a single sentence: Abolition of private property. . .

You are horrified at our intending to do away with private property. But in your existing society, private property is already done away with for nine tenths of the population; its existence for the few is solely due to its nonexistence in the hands of those nine tenths. . . .

Communism deprives no man of the power to appropriate the products of society; all that it does is to deprive him of the power to subjugate the labor of others by means of such appropriation. . . .

The Communists are further reproached with desiring to abolish countries and nationality.

The workingmen have no country. We cannot take from them what they have not got. Since the proletariat must first of all acquire political supremacy, must rise to be the leading class of the nation, must constitute itself *the* nation, it is, so far, itself national, though not in the bourgeois sense of the word. . . .

The proletariat will use its political supremacy to wrest, by degrees, all capital from the bourgeoisie, to centralize all instruments of production in the hands of the state; that is, of the proletariat organized as a ruling class; and to increase the total of productive forces as rapidly as possible. . . .

When, in the course of development, class distinctions have disappeared and all production has been concentrated in the hands of a vast association of the whole nation, the public power will lose its political character. Political power. . . is merely the organized power of one class for oppressing another. If the proletariat during its contest with the bourgeoisie is compelled, by the force of circumstances, to organize itself as a class, if, by means of a revolution, it makes itself the ruling class, and, as such, sweeps away by force the old conditions of production, then it will, along with these conditions, have swept away the conditions for the existence of class antagonisms, and of classes generally, and will thereby have abolished its own supremacy as a class.

In place of the old bourgeois society with its classes and class antagonisms, we shall have an association in which the free development of each is the condition for the free development of all. . . .

The Communists disdain to conceal their views and aims. They openly declare that their ends can be attained only by the forcible overthrow of all existing social conditions. Let the ruling classes tremble at a communistic revolution. The proletarians have nothing to lose but their chains. They have a world to win.

14 Soviet Institutions: The Soviet Government

Lenin was a man dedicated to Marxist ideology when he assumed leadership of the Russian government in November 1917. He faced the need to rebuild a nation devastated by war and revolution, a nation accustomed to having its political decisions made by czars. The czar had absolute power over the people; he ruled, and the people obeyed.

During the year following the start of the Communist regime, several attempts were made to overthrow the new leaders. Civil war raged, but finally the Communists gained firm control of the government.

By 1920, the Russian economy, shattered by the war, was virtually paralyzed. The years 1921 to 1928 were devoted to rebuilding the economy. To rebuild the economy, the Communist leaders frequently had to adjust their Marxist ideology and, in some instances, abandon it to meet the immediate demands of survival.

In 1924 Lenin died. He was replaced, after a period of political maneuvering, by Joseph Stalin. Under Stalin the economy gained strength, and several of the Communist institutions which had been abandoned during the 1920's were reinstated. Under Stalin the present constitution of the Soviet Union was adopted in 1936. An English version of several chapters of the 1936 constitution amended to January 1, 1964, appears in the appendix, pages 289–99.

The chart at the right shows the structure of government that the constitution established. Study the levels of the structure and note that at each level there is a *soviet*, or council. As you read more and more about the Soviet political system, you will find frequent mention of soviets and the other governmental bodies shown here.

Chapter II, Article 13 of the Soviet constitution (page 290) defines the federal nature of the Union of Soviet Socialist Republics.

Chapters III and V of the Soviet constitution (pages 292–95 and 295–97) deal with the top level in the governmental structure—the Supreme Soviet, its two chambers (the Council of Union and the Council of Nationalities), its Presidium, and its Council of Ministers.

The chairman of the Council of Ministers is the Premier of the U.S.S.R., the highest office in the Soviet government.

Chapters IV and VI (pages 295 and 297–98) deal with the structure of government at the union republic level—the Union Republic Supreme Soviet, its presidium, and its council of ministers.

Chapter VIII (pages 298–99) deals with what the chart shows as provincial, district, and village soviets and their executive committees.

Look through the chapters of the constitution in the appendix, and, in your notes, write brief answers to the following questions:

1. Why does the U.S.S.R. call itself a "federal state"?
2. According to the constitution, what is the job of the Supreme Soviet? How are its members selected? What is its Presidium? What is its Council of Ministers?
3. What is the job of the Union Republic Supreme Soviet? How are members selected? What is its presidium? its council of ministers?
4. What is the job of the provincial, district, and village soviets? How are members selected? What are the executive committees?

STRUCTURE OF THE SOVIET GOVERNMENT

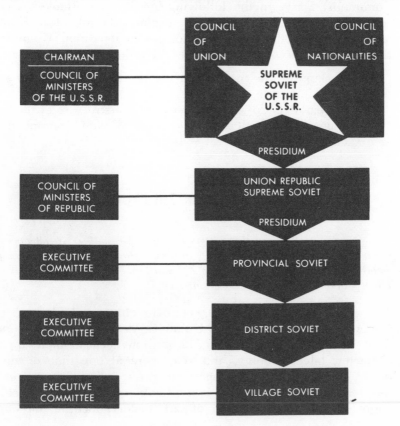

Soviet – member of Communist party

15 Soviet Institutions: The Communist Party

It is not possible to understand the way in which the Soviet Union is governed without first examining the role that the Communist Party plays. Article 126 of the constitution of the Soviet Union describes the role of the Communist Party: "In conformity with the interests of the working people, and in order to develop the organizational initiative and political activity of the masses of the people, citizens of the U.S.S.R. are guaranteed the right to unite in public organizations: trade unions, cooperative societies, youth organizations, sport and defense organizations, cultural, technical, and scientific societies; and the most active and politically conscious citizens in the ranks of the working class, working peasants, and working intelligentsia voluntarily unite in the Communist Party of the Soviet Union, which is the vanguard of the working people in their struggle to build a Communist society and is the leading core of all organizations of the working people, both public and state."

In the Soviet Union, there is but one political party—the Communist Party. Membership within the party is exclusive; a person must be invited to join. The chart at the right shows the structure of the Communist Party. In the following article, Max Frankel, a correspondent for *The New York Times*, explains the role of the Communist Party within the government of the Soviet Union. Examine the chart, read this account, and answer the following questions:

1. How large is the membership of the Communist Party of the Soviet Union?
2. What parallels do you find between the structure of the Soviet Union's government and the structure of the Communist Party?
3. What is the Secretariat?

The 8,708,000 "Elite" of Russia
MAX FRANKEL

Because this article was written in 1960, it reflects census figures of that time. More recent statistics show about 12 million party members in a population of over 235 million. © *1960 by The New York Times Company. Reprinted by permission.*

. . . The 8,708,000 Soviet citizens who belong to the Communist Party of the Soviet Union [C.P.S.U.] today were recruited from among a population of 212 million because their apparent character, talent, energy, and zeal were at one time or another deemed appropriate to management of the nation. The owner of a red leatherette Communist Party book is expected to excel his countrymen in the knowledge of party history, doctrine, and dogma;

STRUCTURE OF THE COMMUNIST PARTY

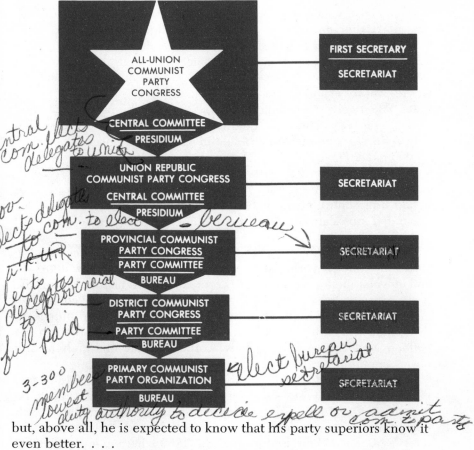

but, above all, he is expected to know that his party superiors know it even better. . . .

The essential difference between the Communist and republican systems of government is the Communist Party of the Soviet Union's recognized and supreme authority over the Soviet government itself and its long reach into the management of every factory and farm, dance troupe, fire brigade, and infantry batallion. Through a giant network of inspectors-general, the Communists audit all books and supervise all activity. They control the press and radio. Party members responsible to the party hierarchy have offices beside those of factory directors, university rectors, infantry colonels.

Though the party is . . . superior to the government, how it exerts control at every level is not so easily defined. It has legal standing, forceful backing, and ideological justification for supremacy, but it must earn its authority with organizational skills and the direct influence of its members. . . .

. . . The theoretical rationale for party superiority is disarmingly simple: Marx said that workers were the only producers of wealth and thus should run society; therefore, added Lenin, the ideal form of government is a dictatorship of the proletariat—namely the Communist Party, which considers itself the "vanguard of the proletariat." *Marxism-Leninism* this "science" is called.

To know everything best, the C.P.S.U. needs the best men in everything. To control everything, it needs to control the leaders of everything. The country's problems are its problems. And, of course, as the country changes, the C.P.S.U. changes.

In 1905, twelve years before it seized power, the party was a band of 8,500 outlaws. The chief qualification of membership was skill at subversion. At the start of the fateful year of 1917, it still had only 23,000 members.

Responsibility brought expansion. Men were needed to seize all property, to keep the factories going, and to fight the civil war. Until it had firm control of the nation, however, the party of conspirators expanded most carefully. It did not admit its millionth member until 1926.

Its rapid growth began with Stalin's five-year plans [a continuing series of Soviet governmental plans for economic and social growth and development]. To manage the breakneck industrialization, the party now needed not only politicians but planners and economists, engineers and city builders, gifted diplomats and shrewd propagandists, men to control the growing army and to restore order on the collectivized farms, and zealous workers to set the high factory norms of output.

In the next decade the party had a net gain of only another 1,000,000 members, but many times that number passed through its ranks to be tested and discarded or purged. Energetic, educated, and, above all, disciplined organization men were wanted, not romantic Socialist reformers. . . . When Stalin died in 1953, there were 6,880,000 names on the rolls.

The doors were flung open . . . as soon as Nikita Khrushchev felt himself in command. . . . He. . . admitted 2,000,000 new members in an intensive search for young blood capable of controlling a complex industrial society, now a world power. . . .

The pressure for results runs through the party from top to bottom. More, higher, greater, better, cheaper—more, comrades, there must be more. The party member is the bearer of these exhortations, and he is judged by his success at keeping others happily and productively at work. The ordinary party member also has the difficult assignment of listening to and promising to act on gripes, complaints, and criticism from below.

At the base of the party pyramid are machinists and bricklayers, tractor drivers and teachers, musicians and nuclear physicists. They spend long evenings at meetings to be attuned to the party line at every moment and to become fluent in the special rhetoric of the faith. . . .

The party man must exhort, explain, and defend. When volunteers are called, he must rush to volunteer—to work on Sunday or to move to Siberia. He must not get drunk. He must not be seen in church. And no matter how exemplary his behavior, when things go wrong and hundreds are at fault, he gets the blame.

Because they appreciate the difficulties of life in the party, non-party Russians judge members as they would anyone else, without special envy or resentment. They know that Communists live well for their station in life, but they know too that the Communist is always at work. He is known to sacrifice much of his individuality for the vague satisfactions of organizational triumph. There are strident bossy comrades in the party, too, of course. But they are disliked for their human qualities, not because they own a party book. Enlistment in the party is an act of individual faith, a complex act inspired by a desire to serve, to know, to succeed, to lead. The zealous lathe operator, always surpassing his assigned quota, the influential professor, the outstanding milkmaid, and the high-ranking army officer need not seek membership. It seeks them, and they rarely refuse.

The road to membership for the ambitious Soviet youngster is through excellence on the job or in school, clean living, enthusiasm for party doctrine, helpfulness at election time or harvest time. A good record in the Young Communist League is especially valuable.

The big step is into candidate membership—a year's probation to test the character, loyalty, and knowledge of the newcomer. Any three party members may propose anyone over eighteen; approval by a local party cell completes the admission process. To expel a member, formal charges must be filed by the local unit and extensive hearings and a review by the next highest party organ be held.

Party members are divided into about 500,000 cells, with a membership of from three to several hundred each. They operate in plants, stores, ministries, institutes, villages, and even submarines.

The born glad hander and the obvious leader can normally expect to reach at least one higher rung on the party ladder. As a secretary of a large cell or city or county committee, he becomes one of the several hundreds of thousands of full-time party workers responsible for whole districts or industries, for the operation of government, the administration of justice, and the morals of the population. . . .

As in an army, the routine is strict, and party officials are expected to fit in anywhere from the Baltic to the Pacific. . .Naturally, the leadership of key industrial or population centers tends to catapult a party man to national influence. . . .

At the top of the party hierarchy are a Central Committee (a forum of prominent regional military and special functionaries), the Committee's Presidium (a senior brain trust or policy panel—the Presidium presently consists of twelve full members and six alternate members), and the Committee's Secretariat. The Secretariat is the party's nerve center; it devises workaday policies and translates them into directions for subordinate secretariats throughout the organization.

[The Secretariat is headed by the First Secretary and five other secretaries. The First Secretary, or General Secretary, is the highest office in the Communist Party.] . . . The Secretariat is divided into sections—foreign affairs, agitation and propaganda, political administration of the military, education, and culture. How many sections there are, how they are staffed, and how they do their work is not known. But history is a witness to the power and stamina of the Secretariat and the party it heads. For both Stalin and Khrushchev it was a small step from leadership of the Secretariat to undisputed leadership of the entire nation. . . .

From Secretariat to tiniest cell, discipline plus agility have enabled the party to survive the enormous stresses of wars, famines, purges, changes of leadership, the collectivization of agriculture, and the social upheaval of industrialization.

Grate as it may on his Democratic-Republican conscience, the American must appreciate the viability of this so strange, so different "party." And he must understand that this is no lifeless machine but a living body politic evolving with the people from which it sprang. . . .

16 A Summary Exercise

You have now begun to examine two very complex political systems. Go back to the analytical questions about ideology and institutions that you assembled in your notebooks as you worked with the summary exercises for Chapters 1 and 2. Add any additional questions that you have learned to ask about these two concepts. Keeping these questions in mind, read Chapter I of the Soviet constitution (pages 289–90). Then review Readings 9 to 15. Note the ideological beliefs implied by the constitutions of both the United States and the Soviet Union. Note the political institutions that each constitution describes. Arrange your information in the form of a chart like this one:

	United States	Soviet Union
Ideological Beliefs		
Political Institutions		

SUGGESTED READINGS

ANDERSON, WILLIAM, "Rivals or Partners," *Capitol, Courthouse and City Hall,* pp. 24–29.

Question: What arguments are used by those who oppose increasing the powers of the national government? How are these arguments refuted?

ANTHONY, KATHERINE, "Catherine the Great—A Successful Tyrant," *The USSR and Communism,* pp. 73–75.

Question: What made Catherine a successful tyrant?

ARMSTRONG, JOHN A., "The Background," *Ideology, Politics, and Government in the Soviet Union,* pp. 5–23.

Question: What Russian experiences help explain the rise of the Soviet political system?

"The Ideology," *Ideology, Politics, and Government in the Soviet Union,* pp. 26–44.

Question: Which principles of Marxism-Leninism were emphasized by the Soviet Union? Why might these principles appeal to under-developed nations?

"The Soviets and the Nationalities," *Ideology, Politics, and Government in the Soviet Union,* pp. 101–30.

Question: Why are the national republics maintained as separate states within the Soviet Union?

BARON, SAMUEL H., "Plekhanov, Father of Russian Marxism," *The USSR and Communism,* pp. 116–20.

Question: How did Plekhanov adapt Marxism to fit the Russian political situation?

BECKER, CARL, "The Nature of Constitutions," *Political Institutions,* pp. 11–14.

Question: Why do nations write constitutions?

DEVTSCHER, ISAAC, "Joseph Stalin: Socialism in One Country," *The USSR and Communism,* pp. 124–28.

Question: What was the ideological struggle between Trotsky and Stalin? How did Stalin's victory affect the political development of the Soviet Union?

KIRK, RUSSELL and ERIC F. GOLDMAN, "Is Washington Too Powerful?", *Politics, U.S.A.,* pp. 84–91.

Question: What are the arguments for a strong federal government? What are the arguments against it?

LENIN, V. I., "On Communist Party Organization," *Communism in Theory and Practice,* pp. 22–24.

Question: What did Lenin mean by "dictatorship of the proletariat"?

LOCKE, JOHN, "The Social Contract," *Political Institutions,* pp. 3–5.

Question: According to Locke, why do men form political systems?

LOCKHART, SIR ROBERT BRUCE, "The Revolutions of 1917," *The USSR and Communism,* pp. 106–11.

Question: What circumstances were influential in the overthrow of the government of Nicholas II? Why was Kerensky unsuccessful in his attempt to establish a democracy in its place?

MARX, KARL and FRIEDRICH ENGELS, "Manifesto of the Communist Party," *Communism in Theory and Practice,* pp. 6–11.

Question: Why did Marx and Engels consider the rise of communism inevitable?

MENKEN, JULES, "Autocracy and the First Tsar," *The USSR and Communism,* pp. 56–61.

Question: What political institutions were developed under the reign of Ivan the Terrible?

MUSKIE, EDMUND S., "$ and ¢ of Federalism," *Capitol, Courthouse and City Hall,* pp. 331–33.

Question: Why is the concept of federalism so frequently challenged?

PROWDIN, MICHAEL, "Mongol Rule and the Rise of Muscovy," *The USSR and Communism,* pp. 53–56.

Question: How would you describe the political system imposed upon the Russians by Batu?

RIEBER, ALFRED J. and ROBERT NELSON, "Communist Theory and Doctrine," *The USSR and Communism,* pp. 112–14.

Question: How did the individual leaders of the Soviet people adjust Marxist ideology to fit the needs of their regime?

"The Russian Past," *The USSR and Communism,* pp. 50–53.

Question: How do events of the past help explain the present?

RIVERS, WILLIAM L., "The Politics of Pollution," *Politics, U.S.A.,* pp. 99–106.

Question: What are the arguments for giving the federal government the authority to enforce anti-pollution regulations? What are the arguments against giving this authority to the federal government?

ROSTOW, EUGENE, "The Supreme Court and the People's Will," *Political Institutions,* pp. 259–62.

Question: What is the value of viewing the Constitution as a living document?

SCHAPIRO, LEONARD, "How Communism Came to Russia," *The USSR and Communism,* pp. 146–53.

Question: Why did Lenin adopt a dictatorial approach to political decision-making?

STALIN, JOSEPH, "The Superiority of the Soviet State," *Political Institutions,* pp. 62–64.

Question: Why does Stalin consider the Soviet constitution superior to all others? Do you agree with his point of view?

STURM, ALBERT L., "Making a Constitution," *Capitol, Courthouse and City Hall,* pp. 69–74.

Question: What steps had to be taken before Michigan could adopt a new constitution?

TOLSTOY, LEO, "Study in Misery," *The USSR and Communism,* pp. 90–94.

Question: How does this story help explain why Soviet leaders had difficulties persuading the Russian peasant to adopt Communist ideology?

TROYAT, HENRY, "A Worker's Life under the Last Tsar," *The USSR and Communism,* pp. 95–97.

Question: What were the conditions of factory workers in the 1800's in Russia? How might this affect their willingness to accept Communist ideology?

Unit Three

Political Leadership: The U.S. and the U.S.S.R.

IN THE FIRST UNIT of the course, you studied two simple political systems, one in a prisoner-of-war camp and the other among Indians on the Great Plains. These societies faced relatively simple problems. The political institutions they developed to deal with their problems were uncomplicated compared to those of the United States and the Soviet Union which you studied in Unit Two. Because their institutions were uncomplicated, they needed few leaders. Frequently one man performed many political functions. He may have proposed legislation, carried it out, and helped to interpret it.

The successful operation of complex political systems like those of the United States and the Soviet Union demands a variety of leaders with different talents for different functions. Some of these men are elected, but many of them are appointed to their posts.

As you study Unit Three, you will analyze political leadership in the United States and in the Soviet Union. Some of the leaders you will study hold or have held positions of great political power; others hold or have held minor leadership positions. All leaders, no matter what their position in the political system, have greater impact upon government than do men whose political function is limited to voting. Gaining an understanding of their roles in their political systems will help you both as a student learning to analyze political systems and as a citizen who will one day be a voter in a democracy.

Chapter 5

Personal Characteristics of American Leaders

STATING THE ISSUE   Every individual plays many roles in the society in which he lives. His age, sex, job, and family all help to determine what these roles will be. A high school student may be a paper boy, a football player, a grandchild, a scout leader, and a choir boy all at the same time. As he performs each of these roles, he exhibits different characteristics and different behavior. As a football player, he must be in top physical condition. He must be able to tackle and block and perhaps to pass or kick a ball. When he is a choir boy, quite different characteristics and behavior become important.

The role a political leader plays is defined by the political system in which he plays it. One useful way to study political systems is to examine their leaders and to ask questions about the roles they play. In a complex political system, there are many kinds of political leaders and, therefore, many political leadership roles to be played. In the American system there are four kinds of political leaders who are particularly important.

Because the United States has a representative government, elected officials make many of the political decisions. Among these officials are the President, governors, mayors, state and national senators and representatives, city councilmen, and various other state and local elected officials.

Appointed officeholders may also hold positions of political leadership. Many of these officeholders win their appointments through competitive examinations administered by the Civil Service Commission. This commission has as its primary objective seeing to it that appointments to government offices are given on the basis of merit. Another, much smaller group of appointed officeholders win their appointments without competitive examination. In this group are Supreme Court justices, cabinet members, and foreign ministers.

Political leadership is not restricted only to elected and appointed government officeholders. Theorists who analyze political systems and try to interpret government actions may also be thought of as political leaders, for they often influence both government officials and ordinary voting citizens. Then, too, there are individuals who influence political activity from behind the scenes. Big city political "bosses" and chairmen of political parties at both the state and national levels are examples of still another kind of political leader.

Chapter 5 examines leadership in the American political system. It emphasizes analysis of the nature of political leadership and the forces that determine the role a political leader must play to function effectively. It raises a number of questions: What are the characteristics required to be a leader in the American political system? How does one get to be a leader? Will a leader in one situation be a leader in another? These are some of the questions you will work with in Chapter 5.

17 Leadership and Situation

As you saw in "Stating the Issue" of this chapter the American political system demands many different kinds of political leaders. This demand results from the existence of so many different political situations in which leaders must play roles.

For example, look at two political situations: The first one is a city where many thousands of people live. There are a number of different groups of people, and they are likely to expect conflicting courses of action from their city government. The city treasury is on the verge of bankruptcy. The second political situation is a suburban town which has only a few thousand people. The people are more or less similar in the amount of money and education they have. They can pay fairly substantial taxes to run their town government.

Obviously, these are two quite dissimilar situations. Would the same political leader be as effective in one as in the other?

Reading 17 presents you with another situation and the leader who worked within it. Again, it is an account of a prisoner-of-war camp, this time in Japan. The account begins as a young American, known to his buddies as Moochie, and his fellow prisoners are being released and returned to the United States. As you read, think about the following questions:

1. What characteristics made Moochie a leader in the prisoner-of-war camp? How useful are some of these characteristics in civilian life?
2. Would these characteristics make Moochie a good President?

member of the House of Representatives? judge? Secretary of Defense? Give reasons for your answer in each case.
3. List three personal characteristics which you think are important in fulfilling the jobs of the officeholders listed in Question 2.

Moochie, the Magnificent
WALDEMAR A. NIELSON

Reprinted from "Moochie, the Magnificent," The New Yorker, *February 1, 1947. Copyright © 1947 by* The New Yorker. *Reprinted by permission of the author.*

. . . One morning . . . as I was walking to work, I saw in a store window a poster announcing a wrestling show. The semifinal bout was between Moochie the Magnificent and someone whose name meant nothing to me. Under Moochie's name, in small letters, were the words "Marine Hero of Jap Prison Camp." His picture was on the poster, and I recognized him. In September of 1945, soon after the surrender of Japan, I had heard a lot about him in Osaka, and I had ridden with him on a train from Osaka to Yokohama. Moochie had a lower directly across the aisle from me. The train was filled with American, British, and the Australian former prisoners of war, the last of some 4,300 men who had been rounded up in the vicinity of Osaka. . . .

Moochie had come from a small town in upstate New York. He had quit high school to work in a garage and had spent his spare time in poolrooms or playing baseball for the town team. In 1940, he had joined the Marines, had been sent to Guam, and three days after Pearl Harbor was captured there, together with all the others in his outfit.

They were moved by the Japanese from one island to another, and finally to Japan. Some of the camps were all right, but most of them were bad. The prisoners did all kinds of labor—unloading ships, digging drydocks, and building barracks. In May of 1943, ninety prisoners were taken to a camp near Osaka, and from then until the end of the war, they worked as coolies on the railroad docks. The work was hard, and the food was bad. The men lost weight steadily, and a number of them fell sick. They often had long discussions about food—descriptions of meals they had once eaten, the kinds of food they liked best, the smells of food, the tastes, the colors, army food, navy food, marine food. They had food dreams at night, and some of them talked in their sleep about food. Constant hunger blotted out thoughts of home, of women, and of everything except food for long periods of time.

But even worse than the trouble about food was their continuous sense of insecurity. In the narrow world of the prison camp, which consisted of a circle of bare earth and a few wooden barracks surrounded by barbed wire and armed guards, death was a constant possibility. The prisoners were under the protection of neither civil nor military law. The comfort of physical strength was gone. They were ninety foreigners in a hostile country, and they were helpless. Except for a daily trip to the railroad docks, they were confined to their little compound. As the months dragged on, rumor, suspicion, and anxiety wore away at the men's spirits. Then, gradually, and without design, Moochie became the leader of the prison camp. He was reckless and fearless, and he had always been big—on Guam, before he was taken, he had weighed 235 pounds. He was friendly and cheerful by nature, and he laughed easily. In the prison camp, these commonplace civilian virtues, which in ordinary life had brought him very little reward, became respected and admired. He made jokes at the expense of the guards and took his punishment without flinching. He devised a system by which the prisoners regularly looted the cargoes they unloaded of quantities of sugar and fish. When the men fell sick, his laughter was their only medicine.

Moochie's final elevation to a minor form of greatness came almost accidentally, as such things usually do. In February and March of 1945, American air raids and strafing attacks were added to the prisoners' complement of sorrows. Twice they were burned out of their camp, and once they were machine-gunned. In retaliation for the raids, the Japanese in charge of the camp became even more ruthless in their treatment of the prisoners. For the slightest infraction of the rules, men were beaten until they couldn't move, and a rumor spread through the camp that if more raids came, they were all to be killed.

One evening, when the prisoners were leaving the railroad docks, a guard discovered several pouches of stolen sugar strapped to the body and legs of one of them. Moochie met the danger of that much-feared moment head on. He felled the guard with a single blow, and then knocked another down. A free-for-all began, in which some of the Japanese coolies on the dock took part on the side of the prisoners. When the fight was over, eighteen of the guards were laid out unconscious on the tracks.

For his leadership in this uprising, Moochie was thrown into solitary confinement, and the other prisoners were locked in the compound. All of them expected to be killed. Moochie was compelled to stand at attention sixteen hours a day for nineteen days; then he was released and sent back to work. He had lost thirty pounds during his ordeal. His release was a genuine victory. It was taken to mean that in the eyes of the Japanese, the prisoners had a little value and could therefore count on some small measure of clemency. The men knew that, whereas Japanese coolies drew wages, P.W.s were free labor for the shipping companies, and they considered it likely that to save ninety pay envelopes a week, someone had picked up a telephone and made a practical plea for lenience.

Whatever the source of their protection or the identity of their protector, the memory of Moochie's victory provided for the last few months of the war the thread by which hung their common faith that they might, after all, come out of it alive.

I watched Moochie with interest that night on the train. He was wearing only an undershirt above his trousers, and I could see the well-separated muscles of his great shoulders and arms. He had a mane of black hair, a long jaw, and a big pleasant face.

For several hours after we pulled out of Osaka, the men who had lived through so much with him kept lurching down the aisle to his berth and paying awkward tribute to his leadership. Some of them sat on the edge of his berth beside him, others stood up in the aisle. There was a great quantity of Japanese beer aboard and almost unlimited amounts of American Army food. With their belt knives, the men opened bottles of beer and punched open cans of K-ration cheese and biscuits. They passed around opened cans of tomatoes. Someone brought out a gasoline stove and set it in the middle of the aisle, and they made a large tin can of hot coffee.

As the men ate, they talked about the camp and about happenings on the docks, and told jokes on one another. Moochie ruled over the group with easy, kingly grace. He was the magnetic center toward which the others pointed their conversation, and in little ways they deferred to him and showed their regard. When, now and then, a man left to go to his berth, he generally gave Moochie a friendly punch on the arm or tousled his hair.

And then, along about one o'clock in the morning, Moochie's crown was lifted from him. Quietly and rather suddenly, it just disappeared. The conversation had slowed down from time to time before that, and the silent gaps between stories had begun to grow longer and longer. Finally, everyone stopped talking. There was a long pause. A sailor who had been taken in the Philippines and who had spent a couple of years with Moochie in camp said, "Listen . . . let's stop talking about it. It's over now, and I'm ready to forget it. From now on, I'm concentrating on getting home."

"Right!" someone added quickly. "I'm ready to knock it off. Let's change the subject to something pleasant, something natural."

Just that suddenly, the conversation turned a corner. The talk from then on concerned home, wives, and Stateside things, and camp world passed into memory, and Moochie moved from the center to the periphery of the group. At first, neither he nor the others seemed to be aware of the change that had taken place. The next time I glanced across at him, Moochie was looking out of the train window at the dark, and the bull session was gradually breaking up. When I went to sleep, Moochie was still staring out of the window. . . .

18 Characteristics Helpful in Winning Elections

Men often appear on the political scene who seem to have many of the characteristics required to function effectively in a particular political office. Yet they may never be given the opportunity. Adlai Stevenson was nominated for the Presidency twice by the Democratic Party, but he never won election. Robert A. Taft, a Republican senator from Ohio, never succeeded in winning his party's nomination, although he was frequently referred to as "Mr. Republican." Both men appeared to have the personal, social, and intellectual qualities required of a President, yet neither was ever elected to the office.

Political scientists have studied the attributes of political leaders. They have written hundreds of books and articles on the subject. Some have done surveys of men who held offices as senators or representatives, trying to identify the characteristics they have in common. Others have followed politicians through an entire campaign or through a typical workday to see what they actually do. These studies have given new insights into the democratic process.

Reading 18 describes a typical day in the life of a congressman campaigning for reelection. As you read about the activities of a candidate for national political office, keep these questions in mind:

1. What characteristics did Voorhis show as a campaigner?
2. Would these characteristics be important to a man running for any elective political office? Why?
3. Are these same characteristics of any importance in determining a congressman's effectiveness in doing his job once elected?

A Day in a Campaign
JERRY VOORHIS

Democrat Jerry Voorhis was first elected to the U.S. House of Representatives in 1936. During much of his ten years as congressman from the Twelfth District in California, he fought for legislation that would help solve such problems as postwar housing for veterans, farm surpluses, inflation, labor-management relations, and unemployment. In the reading that follows, the year is 1946 and Congressman Voorhis is campaigning for his sixth straight term in office. From Confessions of a Congressman *by Jerry Voorhis. Copyright 1947 by Jerry Voorhis. Reprinted by permission of Doubleday & Company, Inc.*

The warm sunshine of a late California summer fills the room. We are home for the campaign. We have to be. Congressmen either campaign every two years, or they don't remain congressmen. Sometimes they don't anyway.

"Daddy, which is stronger, a buffalo or a mountain lion?" I try to pry my eyes open. I shake my head. I manage to push my feet out of bed, and somehow my legs follow them. I get myself tipped up to a sitting position. It seems only a moment ago that I crawled into bed.

Fumbling for the watch—twenty minutes after seven. Should have waked up sooner.

"But, Daddy, which is stronger, a buffalo or a mountain lion?" Our eight-year-old really wants to get some information.

I try, as I stagger into the bathroom, to defend the buffalo, but to no avail, because the picture in the book shows the mountain lion getting the best of it.

I should be downstairs already. But first comes the seemingly interminable job of shaving. Hope we get through with breakfast before something happens.

But we don't. The phone rings. A good friend is on the line to say: "They have a whispering campaign going on. They say you haven't done anything to help the district. No big government installations like they have in the Nineteenth District. They're comparing you with the congressman from over in that district. I understand they're fixing up an ad which will list all the government projects in the Nineteenth District and contrast it with a much shorter list of the ones here. How can we answer this?"

"We can't," I tell him, "because it's at least partly true. I never claimed to be much good at delivering projects unless there were good solid reasons why they should be located here. About all we can do is point out that the very same fellows complain because I don't induce the government to spend more money in the district and also because the budget isn't balanced."

My friend isn't very well satisfied.

We talk more about other subjects. Then we say good-by.

I go in and eat some breakfast. But the family is all through, and it's no fun eating alone.

By now it is going on nine o'clock. In another hour and a half I should be clear at the other end of the district to attend a community meeting. But there is the mail to be answered before that and a great number of matters I have promised people I would attend to—soldier's dependents' allowances, housing priorities, rent adjustment problems, et cetera.

My secretary, Harold Herin, is in the office already. So we start. We get through part of the letters. While I'm dictating, I make notes of other things that must be done. Who is going to speak for the state ticket at the South Pasadena meeting? I must phone about that. Does the A. F. of L. primary endorsement carry over into the finals, or does it have to be renewed? Can we publish it in our campaign leaflet? Better find out for certain. Will Mrs. Voorhis or our daughter, Alice, please type the news release we wrote last night? It ought to be in the mail today.

All of this interrupts the dictation. But it can't be helped. Phone calls keep coming in, and we try to do both jobs at once. I look at my watch—almost ten. I ought to be on my way. I can barely make it to Monterey Park by ten-thirty. Just one more letter, then I'll go.

The phone rings again. This time it's about an allocation of scarce material for one of the district's small companies. Unless they get it, they're out of business. It takes several minutes to work out the facts, decide what steps to take with the Department of Agriculture. I look at the watch again—ten-fourteen!

I grab my brief case, climb in the car, and dash off. All the way to Monterey Park I wonder if I'll be in time. Traffic is bad, and I seem to hit every single red light. As I drive along, I have a pad on the seat beside me to jot down more things to remember.

At last, here's Monterey Park. I go to the place appointed for the morning ceremonies. I am too late. They began exactly on time and were very short. A friend tells me my not getting there wasn't "too serious."

There are forty minutes left before I have to speak to the Lions Club. So I call at the newspaper office and pay my respects to the editor and his staff. . . . The editor and I talk briefly about current problems, and then I say good-by.

I call at a couple of other places.

By this time it is noon, and I am due at the Women's Clubhouse for the Lions Club meeting. I start to walk. As I pass the drugstore, a young veteran who works there comes out and stops me. He is president of a new organization of veterans who are trying to find homes to live in. A certain very new construction and real estate company has taken deposits from them of a hundred dollars and more each. But no homes have been completed, and there seems to be great doubt whether more than a handful will ever be built. Most of the boys, therefore, stand to lose their deposits unless something can be done to force the company to pay. Everybody is fearful the company won't have funds to do so, and now something new has come up. I was at their meeting the night before and made a few suggestions to them. One of the metropolitan Los Angeles papers has been carrying feature articles about their problems, so they submitted a story about the meeting to one of its reporters. Just an hour ago the reporter called up to say the paper wouldn't run the story because Congressman Voorhis's name was mentioned in it. What do I think of that? . . . I will call the paper just as soon as I can get to a phone.

I am worried over this as I enter the little building where the Lions are meeting. A lot of them are my good friends, and it is good to see them. I try to put other things out of my mind. Pretty soon I'll have to start speaking. It is hard to eat. At last the program chairman takes over and introduces me. For thirty minutes I give a talk on the need for dynamic American leadership in the world and what will be required of each of us if our country is to give that leadership.

The talk is well received apparently. The meeting adjourns, and though I wish I could stay around for a few minutes and talk informally with some of the men, I have to break away almost at once because I am due at an old-age pension meeting in Whittier at two-thirty and want to see a veterans' housing project on the way. So off I dash to see the housing project. . . .

I arrive in Whittier and go to the park where about a hundred people, mostly old folk, are sitting on the benches listening to the speeches. I find the president of the local club, and he takes me up on the platform and, as he has promised, lets me speak almost at once. I only talk a few minutes about how I believe a national old-age pension system would help keep the nation's buying power in balance with production and about some of the principles to which I believe such a system should conform. It takes a half-hour, however, to leave the park because a number of people want to talk about various problems, and I'm no good at cutting short such conversations. At last, however, I do go.

I glance at the lists I've been making of things to do that afternoon. Most urgent are some phone calls. At least I must find out about that veteran story not being printed. So I go to our congressional field office in the federal building in Alhambra and start putting in calls. I get through to the secretary of the Central Labor Council of the A. F. of L. to ask whether their primary endorsement is still valid for the finals. . . . He tells me it is still valid and that I can state publicly that I have their endorsement. . . . I try the newspaper . . . and . . . reach the vice-president. Did the paper kill the veteran's housing story because my name was mentioned? He says he's sure that can't be the case. Will he make certain their story is run? I ask. If it makes any difference please omit my name—but run the story. . . .

It's after five, and I have a dinner meeting and later a mass meeting coming along in only an hour's time. A man with a problem drops into the office, but he has all the facts written out and is most kind when I explain that I have to make my notes for the evening speeches. I start to outline the talk for the dinner.

I work quietly for a while. Then I look at my watch. Barely time to get to the poultrymen's dinner, twenty minutes away—but I make it in fifteen. Mrs. Voorhis is there ahead of me, and it is good to see her. . . . We find our places and sit down. . . .

During the meal I make some notes of what I want to speak about—the problems poultrymen have faced and how we tried to meet them . . . As people call one another by name, I jot them down — so I won't forget next time.

They let me speak first so we can leave for our other meeting. I have trouble in cutting my speech as short as it ought to be, but finally I sit down. We shake hands with those at the head table, slip out, and get into the car.

Now comes the crucial meeting of the whole day — a joint meeting with my opponent. . . .

Here we are. . . . The meeting is about to start, so I rush down to the platform. Almost before I know it, I have been introduced and am facing the crowd. Each of the main speeches is only fifteen minutes long. I know to start with that I cannot begin to do justice to the program I want to present. I talk first about foreign policy, outline what I believe our nation's duty is, say I believe our policy generally is now a correct one. I see there are only five minutes left. I attempt to pack into those five minutes as much as possible of the domestic "full production-full consumption" program in which I so earnestly believe. . . .

My opponent is introduced. He speaks easily, and I wonder whether the audience may not prefer his lighter touch to my rather ponderous manner of presenting one big problem after another. . . .

Then comes the question period.

Was I once a registered Socialist?

Yes, I was during the late twenties and the worst part of the depression when it seemed neither major party had any effective answer to the people's problems.

Why did I permit the bill to pass the Congress which reduced on-the-job training payments to veterans?

It was only on the floor for a very few minutes; no real explanation was made of it; it was passed under suspension of the rules without any record vote.

Should not I have been present at the time and stopped it?

Of course I should have been, but so should I have been doing a dozen other tasks, to one of which I was attending. . . .

And so on until at last about eleven o'clock the meeting is brought to an end. There is handshaking and talking afterward in the hall — and then some more outside. It is part of the job — meeting people, the American people, who were interested enough in their government to come.

We drive home.

As always at the end of a day in a campaign, I am so exhausted I wonder if I can make it until Election Day. But it has been done before. It can be done again. . . .

[*Mr. Voorhis, who had been a successful campaigner so many times, lost the election that year to a young assistant attorney — Richard M. Nixon.*]

19 Characteristics Helpful
in Maintaining Authority

Getting elected is only half the battle. Once in office, an official has a job to do. In order to get elected, officials often have to promise voters, or at least imply to them, that they will support particular points of view. If possible, they try to fulfill their promises because they want to be reelected. A member of the House of Representatives of the United States has to stand for reelection every two years. A United States senator goes before the electorate every six years. Every time a political leader asks the members of his electorate for their votes, he is being judged. When he first stands for election, he is judged on the basis of his characteristics and background, as well as his ability to convince the voters of his intentions. When he goes back to his constituency for reelection, the outcome of the election can depend largely on the decisions he made in office.

The characteristics an elected official needs vary with his job and the nature of the electorate to which he is responsible. A member of the House of Representatives from a congressional district in a major city can vote against legislation favoring farmers with little worry that his constituents will be offended. A senator represents an entire state. Therefore, if he represents a state where 15 per cent of the voters are farmers, he cannot ignore their wishes. A man who has been in the national legislature for many years, has been reelected a number of times, and is well known and respected by his electorate can devote a larger proportion of his time and energies to national problems than can a man whose reelection and reputation are uncertain. No politician can ever completely ignore his constituency.

In Reading 19, David S. Broder, a political reporter for a Washington, D.C., newspaper, analyzes the characteristics of great senators. As you read his analysis, think about the following questions:

1. What characteristics help a person to succeed as a United States senator? Do the great senators selected by the author share all of these characteristics?
2. Would these same characteristics be important in fulfilling the tasks required of any elected executive, such as a President or a governor? of a big city boss? of an appointed official, such as a cabinet member?

What Makes a Great Senator?
DAVID S. BRODER

This article appeared in The New York Times Magazine *on June 14, 1964.* © *1964 by The New York Times Company. Reprinted by permission.*

. . . Just what qualities mark a man as fit for membership in the world's most self-exalted legislative body are undefined. But the imprecision of the standards in no way lessens the intensity of the belief that there are standards to be maintained.

The difficulty of judging the quality of a senator was discussed in this magazine seven years ago by John F. Kennedy. "There are no standard tests to apply to a senator," he wrote, "no Dun and Bradstreet rating, no scouting reports. His talents may vary with his time; his contributions may be limited by his politics. To judge his true greatness . . . is nearly an impossible task."

Mr. Kennedy, at the time, was engaged in the task of selecting the five greatest senators, whose portraits were to adorn the senate reception room. But the difficulty of picking the outstanding men in the history of the institution is essentially the same as the problem of defining the qualities that make for distinction in the Senate today.

Must the "good senator" be a man of eloquence, who can supply the oratorical gloss to finished legislation during floor debate? Or is it more important that he have the legal skills that make him a superb craftsman behind committee doors?

Is it sufficient that the good senator excel at protecting his state's interests and representing its point of view on the issues of the day? Or must he also don the toga and advise the Secretary of State and the President on how to handle their jobs?

Is the good senator the man who adheres always to the dictates of his own conscience—a relentless investigator, a shunner of compromise? Or is he the cheerful pragmatist whose willingness to split the difference makes it possible to pass a bill now and then?

Is he a John Kennedy or a Barry Goldwater, using the Senate as the base for a national campaign? Or is he a Carl Hayden or a George Aiken, whose labors are scarcely noticed by the public?

Simply to raise these questions is to suggest that there is room in a hundred-man Senate for men of differing tastes and talents. Any arbitrary standard that ignores these individual variations is certain to be wrong.

In one basic sense, Washington's belief in the distinctiveness of the Senate is well justified. The most striking single fact about the senators we have is that they are *uncommon* Americans. Professor Donald R. Matthews described the typical senator of the post-World War II decade as "a late middle-aged or elderly, white, Protestant, native-born man with rural or small-town and upper-middle-class origins, a college-educated lawyer and a 'joiner.'" As Mr. Matthews noted in his classic study, *U.S. Senators and Their World,* this combination of characteristics is so far from the norm of American society that "probably less than 5 per cent of the American people have any significant chance of ever serving in the Senate so long as the present informal 'requirements' for the office hold."

The major abnormality about senators, in career terms, is that they are professional officeholders. Mr. Matthews found that almost half the postwar senators achieved their first public office before they turned thirty and that three quarters of them were on the public payroll before they were forty. The average member had spent approximately half his adult life in officeholding—even before he became a senator.

Of the hundred current senators, sixty-six came to that body directly from other public offices; twenty-one more relied chiefly on the fame won in prior public service—service which, in most cases, had terminated only briefly before their Senate campaigns began. That leaves only thirteen of today's senators who launched their campaigns from reputations earned outside public office. Most of these men are "political accidents" of one sort or another.

With so much similarity in their backgrounds, what determines which senators rise to distinction and which stay submerged in the pack? Again, one must be wary of generalizations.

A favorite myth, for example, is that governors—or other executive types—fare badly in the Senate. They are, according to legend, extremely unhappy at sharing their sovereignty and command authority with ninety-nine others. But then comes a man like the late Robert Kerr, from the governorship of Oklahoma, who finds the paths to power in the Senate ridiculously easy to explore. No one was ever more at home or more skillful in committee machinations or in floor debates than ex-Governor Kerr.

In a body dominated by lawyers, there is a strong tendency to think that lawyers have a special calling for the Senate. Even Joe Clark of Pennsylvania, normally a man to deride the prejudices of "The Senate Establishment," is convinced that "lawyers make the best senators; to make laws you have to know law." But Lyndon Johnson, the ablest leader the Senate has had in years, was no lawyer, nor is Mike Mansfield, nor is Hubert Humphrey.

Energy, eloquence, wit, good humor, intelligence, frankness, honor —all these are worthy qualities, esteemed by senators, as by most men, in their fellows. But to catalog these virtues is not to describe the *special* qualities that make a man a good senator. For, in candor, there have been good senators, even great ones, who were a mite bad-tempered or a mite dull or less than irreproachable in their personal codes.

Thus, all the popular generalizations prove false, in some degree. One comes closer to the truth by noting that the best senators, generally, are those who have acquired seniority and who use their powers, not simply for the advantage of their states, but also to serve their conception of the national interest.

It takes time to develop influence in the Senate, and a senator's greatness is measured by the reach of his influence. It is a place, as

Lee Metcalf of Montana has remarked, "where you have to do a lot of favors for others before they start doing them for you." It is a unique political structure—an assemblage of delegates from sovereign states, each man, in theory, the equal of any other. The seniority system is its only acknowledged ranking order, and its influence is pervasive.

The five men selected by Mr. Kennedy's committee to be enshrined in the Senate's Hall of Fame—Henry Clay, Daniel Webster, John C. Calhoun, Robert LaFollette, and Robert A. Taft—served a total of eighty-six years. Their first responsibility, no less than that of the lowliest of today's freshman senators, was to gain reelection. Only with the confidence of his own constituency, renewed at the polls, can a senator play his role on the national stage.

But if seniority is an essential for effective and distinctive senatorial service, it is obviously not a guarantee of such a career. A special combination of personal qualities and political circumstances marks the history of the best members.

What are those qualities? First is the instinct or the drive in some men that takes them to the heart of the issues of their time. The late Robert Taft and the late Styles Bridges were contemporaries in the Senate, and both achieved great power. But Bridges confined himself by choice to the private, back-room trades of projects, patronage, and appropriations, while Taft engaged himself publicly in all the major debates of his era—touching the responsibilities of American government in foreign affairs, domestic welfare, and labor relations. It is Taft, not Bridges, who has a memorial on Capitol Hill today.

A second quality is diligence, again well typified by Taft or by his successor in the Republican leadership today, Everett Dirksen of Illinois. Senator Dirksen owes much of his influence to the simple fact that he studies more intensively and knows more intimately the provisions of the bills he is debating than the vast majority of his colleagues.

A third quality is breadth of interest, a refusal to be bound by the parochial [limited] concerns of one's own state. Senators have achieved great reputations in the past as spokesmen for their states and regions, but as our politics have become national and international, so have the perspectives of the best senators. It is the man who can see beyond the borders of his own state whose contribution is remembered—George Norris of Nebraska sponsoring the Tennessee Valley Authority, Lyndon Johnson of Texas guiding the first civil rights bill in a century into law, Arthur Vandenberg of Michigan leading the Senate into an acceptance of its world responsibilities.

The Senate, for all the criticism it receives, is a tolerant place. It finds uses for all sorts of talents. Most members take the established route up the seniority ladder to a committee chairmanship and increasing influence with The Establishment. But the Senate, to its credit, also provides outlets for the "angry men" who cannot conform to these comfortable career lines.

An Estes Kefauver investigating drugs, a John McClellan exposing labor racketeering, or a John Williams documenting financial chicanery are not the most congenial companions for "The Club" members. But persistence and publicity are forces the Senate recognizes. The iconoclasts, too, can make their mark in the history books.

There are circumstances which can disqualify senators from playing the roles of which they are capable, as with the Southerners today. The southern senators are men of ability, and some — like J. W. Fulbright and Richard Russell — have achieved distinction in special fields like foreign policy and defense. But their isolation from the mainstream of American politics on the central question of race relations bars them from leadership roles, to their own loss and the loss of the country.

By and large, though, seniority, talent, diligence, breadth of vision, and a grasp of major issues will enable a senator to contribute his full share to the making of national policy. The Senate has its shortcomings, but it is not arbitrary nor capricious in the way it weighs its members and judges them for what they are. . . .

20 Ethics and Leadership

Each day many of the decisions you make are made, consciously or unconsciously, on the basis of your own code of ethics. What do you think is right? What do you consider wrong? Political leaders, too, must wrestle with ethical questions. Some of these questions involve clear-cut choices: Should I or should I not accept a bribe? Other questions involve choices that are not so clear-cut: Should I, as an elected official, accept a color television set as a Christmas gift from a friend who may later want a political favor? Should I accept a necktie from him? In other words, when does a gift become a bribe?

Other questions involving a man's code of ethics are even more difficult to resolve. For example, what should a politician do when his conscience tells him to vote one way and his chances of being reelected demand that he vote the other? Suppose that you were a senator and that you, personally, favor a bill which would make the crime of lynching a federal offense. Most of your constituents might oppose this bill, arguing that such crimes have traditionally been punished at the state or local level and are not properly the concern of the federal government. If you vote for the bill, your constituents very likely will elect your opponent in the coming election. He is a man who tends to support almost every major measure you oppose. Should you vote for the anti-lynching bill, help your opponent win the next election, and then watch him vote against measures that you would have supported during the next six years? Or, should you vote against the bill in spite of your convictions that such a stand is morally wrong?

Reading 20 tells of a senator who confronted such a problem — the choice between conscience and political obscurity. It is taken from a book written by former President John F. Kennedy. As you read about Senator Edmund G. Ross's role in the trial of President Andrew Johnson, think about the following questions:

1. Who impeached the President? On what charges? Who was to try him? What vote was required to convict him?
2. Why did Ross vote as he did?
3. What happened to Ross's career as a result of this episode?

Edmund G. Ross
JOHN F. KENNEDY

At the time of Andrew Johnson's impeachment trial in 1868, Edmund G. Ross, a former journalist, had been in the U.S. Senate about two years. Abridgement of "Edmund G. Ross" from Profiles in Courage *by John F. Kennedy. Copyright © 1955 by John F. Kennedy. Reprinted by permission of Harper & Row, Publishers.*

In a lonely grave, forgotten and unknown, lies "the man who saved a President," and who as a result may well have preserved for ourselves and posterity constitutional government in the United States — the man who performed in 1868 what one historian has called "the most herioc act in American history, incomparably more difficult than any deed of valor upon the field of battle" — a United States Senator whose name no one recalls: Edmund G. Ross of Kansas.

The impeachment of President Andrew Johnson, the event in which the obscure Ross was to play such a dramatic role, was the sensational climax to the bitter struggle between the President, determined to carry out Abraham Lincoln's policies of reconciliation with the defeated South, and the more radical Republican leaders in Congress, who sought to administer the downtrodden southern states as conquered provinces which had forfeited their rights under the Constitution. It was, moreover, a struggle between executive and legislative authority. Andrew Johnson, the courageous if untactful Tennessean who had been the only southern member of Congress to refuse to secede with his state, had committed himself to the policies of the Great Emancipator to whose high station he had succeeded only by the course of an assassin's bullet. He knew that Lincoln, prior to his death, had already clashed with the extremists in Congress who had opposed his approach to reconstruction in a constitutional and charitable manner and sought to make the legislative branch of the government supreme. And his own belligerent temperament soon destroyed any hope that Congress might now join hands in carrying out Lincoln's policies of permitting the South to resume its place in the Union with as little delay and controversy as possible.

. . . Early in 1867, Congress enacted over the President's veto the tenure-of-office bill which prevented the President from removing without the consent of the Senate all new officeholders whose appointment required confirmation by that body. At the time nothing more than the cry for more patronage was involved, cabinet members having originally been specifically exempt.

On August 5, 1867, President Johnson—convinced that the Secretary of War, whom he had inherited from Lincoln, Edwin M. Stanton, was the surreptitious tool of the Radical Republicans and was seeking to become the almighty dictator of the conquered South—asked for his immediate resignation; and Stanton arrogantly fired back the reply that he declined to resign before the next meeting of Congress. Not one to cower before this kind of effrontery, the President one week later suspended Stanton and appointed in his place the one man whom Stanton did not dare resist, General [Ulysses S.] Grant. On January 13, 1868, an angry Senate notified the President and Grant that it did not concur in the suspension of Stanon, and Grant vacated the office upon Stanton's return. But the situation was intolerable. The Secretary of War was unable to attend cabinet meetings or associate with his colleagues in the administration; and on February 21, President Johnson, anxious to obtain a court test of the act he believed obviously unconstitutional, again notified Stanton that he had been summarily removed from the office of Secretary of War.

While Stanton, refusing to yield possession, barricaded himself in his office, public opinion in the nation ran heavily against the President. He had intentionally broken the law and dictatorially thwarted the will of Congress! Although previous resolutions of impeachment had been defeated in the House, both in committee and on the floor, a new resolution was swiftly reported and adopted on February 24 by a tremendous vote. Every single Republican voted in the affirmative, and Thaddeus Stevens of Pennsylvania—the crippled, fanatical personification of the extremes of the Radical Republican movement, master of the House of Representatives, with a mouth like the thin edge of an ax—warned both houses of the Congress coldly: "Let me see the recreant [coward] who would vote to let such a criminal escape. Point me to one who will dare do it, and I will show you one who will dare the infamy of posterity." . . .

. . . As the trial progressed, it became increasingly apparent that the impatient Republicans did not intend to give the President a fair trial on the formal issues upon which the impeachment was drawn, but intended instead to depose him from the White House on any grounds, real or imagined, for refusing to accept their policies. Telling evidence in the President's favor was arbitrarily excluded. Prejudgment on the part of most senators was brazenly announced. Attempted bribery and other forms of pressure were rampant. The chief interest was not in the trial or the evidence, but in the tallying of votes necessary for conviction.

Twenty-seven states (excluding the unrecognized southern states) in the Union meant fifty-four members of the Senate, and thirty-six votes were required to constitute the two-thirds majority necessary for conviction. All twelve Democratic votes were obviously lost, and the forty-two Republicans knew that they could afford to lose only six of their own members if Johnson were to be ousted. To their dismay, at a preliminary Republican caucus, six courageous Republicans indicated that the evidence so far introduced was not in their opinion sufficient to convict Johnson under the Articles of Impeachment. "Infamy!" cried the *Philadelphia Press*. The republic has "been betrayed in the house of its friends!"

But if the remaining thirty-six Republicans would hold, there would be no doubt as to the outcome. All must stand together! But one Republican senator would not announce his verdict in the preliminary poll—Edmund G. Ross of Kansas. The Radicals were outraged that a senator from such an anti-Johnson stronghold as Kansas could be doubtful. "It was a very clear case," Senator Sumner of Massachusetts fumed, "especially for a Kansas man. I did not think that a Kansas man could quibble against his country."

When the impeachment resolution had passed the House, Senator Ross had casually remarked to Senator Sprague of Rhode Island, "Well, Sprague, the thing is here; and, so far as I am concerned, though a Republican and opposed to Mr. Johnson and his policy, he shall have as fair a trial as an accused man ever had on this earth." Immediately the word spread that "Ross was shaky." "From that hour," he later wrote, "not a day passed that did not bring me, by mail and telegraph and in personal intercourse, appeals to stand fast for impeachment. . . ."

Ross and his fellow doubtful Republicans were daily pestered, spied upon, and subjected to every form of pressure. Their residences were carefully watched, their social circles suspiciously scrutinized, and their every move and companions secretly marked in special notebooks. They were warned in the party press, harangued by their constituents, and sent dire warnings threatening political ostracism and even assassination. Stanton himself, from his barricaded headquarters in the War Department, worked day and night to bring to bear upon the doubtful senators all the weight of his impressive military associations. The *Philadelphia Press* reported "a fearful avalanche of telegrams from every section of the country,"a great surge of public opinion from the "common people" who had given their money and lives to the country and would not "willingly or unavenged see their great sacrifice made naught." . . .

But with no experience in political turmoil, no reputation in the Senate, no independent income, and the most radical state in the Union to deal with, Ross was judged to be the most sensitive to criticism and the most certain to be swayed by expert tactics. A committee of congressmen and senators sent to Kansas and to the states of the other doubtful Republicans this telegram: "Great danger to the peace of the country and the Republican cause if impeachment fails. Send to your senators public opinion by resolutions, letters, and delegations." A member of the Kansas legislature called upon Ross at the Capitol. A general urged on by Stanton remained at his lodge until four o'clock in the morning determined to see him. His brother received a letter offering $20,000 for revelation of the senator's intentions. Gruff Ben Butler [Massachusetts congressman and Radical Republican] exclaimed of Ross, "There is a bushel of money! How much does the —— scoundrel want?" The night before the Senate was to take its first vote for the conviction or acquittal of Johnson, Ross received this telegram from home:

> Kansas has heard the evidence and demands the conviction of the President. (signed) D.R. Anthony and 1,000 Others.

And on that fateful morning of May 16, Ross replied:

> To D. R. Anthony and 1,000 Others: I do not recognize your right to demand that I vote either for or against conviction. I have taken an oath to do impartial justice according to the Constitution and laws, and trust that I shall have the courage to vote according to the dictates of my judgment and for the highest good of the country. (signed) E. G. Ross

That morning spies traced Ross to his breakfast; and ten minutes before the vote was taken, his Kansas colleague warned him in the presence of Thaddeus Stevens [leader of the Radical Republicans] that a vote for acquittal would mean trumped up charges and his political death.

But now the fateful hour was at hand. Neither escape, delay, nor indecision was possible. As Ross himself later described it: "The galleries were packed. Tickets of admission were at an enormous premium. The House had adjourned, and all of its members were in the Senate chamber. Every chair on the Senate floor was filled with a senator, a cabinet officer, a member of the President's counsel, or a member of the House." Every senator was in his seat, the desperately ill Grimes of Iowa being literally carried in. . . .

The voting tensely commenced. By the time the Chief Justice reached the name of Edmund Ross, twenty-four "guilties" had been pronounced. Ten more were certain, and one other practically certain. Only Ross's vote was needed to obtain the thirty-six votes necessary to convict the President. But not a single person in the room knew how this young Kansan would vote. Unable to conceal the suspense and emotion in his voice, the Chief Justice put the question to him: "Mr. Senator Ross, how say you? Is the respondent Andrew Johnson guilty or not guilty of a high misdemeanor as charged in this article?" Every voice was still; every eye was upon the freshman senator from Kansas. The hopes and fears, the hatred and bitterness of past decades were centered upon this one man.

As Ross himself later described it, his "powers of hearing and seeing seemed developed in an abnormal degree."

Every individual in that great audience seemed distinctly visible, some with lips apart and bending forward in anxious expectancy, others with hand uplifted as if to ward off an apprehended blow, . . . and each peering with an intensity that was almost tragic upon the face of him who was about to cast the fateful vote. . . . Every fan was folded, not a foot moved, not the rustle of a garment, not a whisper was heard. . . . Hope and fear seemed blended in every face, instantaneously alternating, some with revengeful hate . . . others lighted with hope. . . . The senators in their seats leaned over their desks, many with hand to ear. . . . It was a tremendous responsibility, and it was not strange that he upon whom it had been imposed by a fateful combination of conditions should have sought to avoid it, to put it away from him as one shuns, or tries to fight off, a nightmare. . . .

I almost literally looked down into my open grave. Friendships, position, fortune, everything that makes life desirable to an ambitious man were about to be swept away by the breath of my mouth, perhaps forever. It is not strange that my answer was carried waveringly over the air and failed to reach the limits of the audience, or that repetition was called for by distant senators on the opposite side of the chamber.

Then came the answer again in a voice that could not be misunderstood—full, final, definite, unhesitating and unmistakable: "Not guilty." The deed was done, the President saved, the trial as good as over, and the conviction lost. The remainder of the roll call was unimportant; conviction had failed by the margin of a single vote, and a general rumbling filled the chamber until the Chief Justice proclaimed that "on this article thirty-five senators having voted guilty and nineteen not guilty, a two-thirds majority not having voted for conviction, the President is, therefore, acquitted under this article."

The "open grave" which Edmund Ross had foreseen was hardly an exaggeration. A justice of the Kansas Supreme Court telegraphed him that "the rope with which Judas Iscariot hanged himself is lost, but Jim Lane's pistol is at your service." An editorial in a Kansas newspaper screamed:

On Saturday last Edmund G. Ross, United States senator from Kansas, sold himself and betrayed his constituents; stultified his own record; basely lied to his friends; shamefully violated his solemn pledge; . . . and to the utmost of his poor ability, signed the death warrant of his country's liberty. This act was done deliberately, because the traitor, like Benedict Arnold, loved money better than he did principle, friends, honor, and his country, all combined. Poor, pitiful, shriveled wretch, with a soul so small that a little pelf [money] would outweigh all things else that dignify or ennoble manhood.

Ross's political career was ended. To the *New York Tribune,* he was nothing but "a miserable poltroon and traitor." The *Philadelphia Press* said that in Ross "littleness" had "simply borne its legitimate fruit," and that he and his fellow recalcitrant Republicans had "plunged from a precipice of fame into the groveling depths of infamy and death." The *Philadelphia Inquirer* said that "they had tried, convicted, and sentenced themselves." For them there could be "no allowance, no clemency." . . .

Neither Ross nor any other Republican who had voted for the acquittal of Johnson was ever reelected to the Senate, not a one of them retaining the support of their party's organization. When he returned to Kansas in 1871, he and his family suffered social ostracism, physical attack, and near poverty.

Who was Edmund G. Ross? Practically nobody. Not a single public law bears his name, not a single history book includes his picture, not a single list of Senate "greats" mentions his service. His one heroic deed has been all but forgotten. But who might Edmund G. Ross have been? That is the question—for Ross, a man with an excellent command of words, an excellent background for politics, and an excellent future in the Senate might well have outstripped his colleagues in prestige and power throughout a long Senate career. Instead, he chose to throw all of this away for one act of conscience. . . .

Chapter 6

The Process of Becoming an American Leader

STATING THE ISSUE Chapter 5 examined characteristics of American political leaders. You looked at political leadership in terms of the leader himself—what kind of man he appears to be and what he has to be able to do. Chapter 6 concentrates on the process of becoming a leader in the American political system.

The way a person becomes a political leader varies from one political system to another, depending on the system's ideology and institutions. At Stoerpenberg Camp, Kent became a political leader because he was elected to the position by his fellow prisoners, all of whom either knew him or had seen him around. In their simple political system the men needed no elaborate preelection procedures. They merely followed the informal election process they knew in civilian life—suggesting candidates, campaigning for favorites, and voting on a one man-one vote basis.

The American political system is too large and complex to make such personal contact and simple procedure possible in all elections. Most often, it is impossible for a political candidate to meet all the potential voters. Therefore candidates resort to television and radio to contact a large number of their constituents. The majority of American voters never even see in person many of the candidates for whom they vote. As to procedure, it is surely impossible for the enormous number of voters in the United States to get together informally to choose their candidates. More formal procedures are required.

Article I, Section 4 of the United States Constitution delegates to each state the right to prescribe the manner in which elections to the national legislature will be held. Consequently, election laws do vary from state to state. Some states require *primary elections,* in which each political party takes a vote among its members to determine which candidates the party will support in a general election. In other states, political party leaders select candidates after conferring with individuals and groups whose thinking influences large segments of the voting population. Despite these differences, political leaders do follow similar procedures to reach positions of power.

In Chapter 6 you will analyze these routes to power. What is the role of elections in choosing American political leaders? What part do political parties play in the process? What is the impact of interest groups? How is leadership transferred from one person to another?

21 The Role of American Elections

It is difficult to generalize about American election procedures. Not only does the process vary from state to state, but the rules governing elections have changed over the years. In 1789, only about one adult in thirty was eligible to vote. No women or slaves could vote, and in many states a man had to belong to a certain church or had to own property or pay taxes to be eligible to vote. These religious and property qualifications barred many adult white males from the polls.

Gradually, more people were *enfranchised*, or given the right to vote. Property and religious restrictions were dropped in most states by the 1830's. In theory, the Fifteenth Amendment, added to the Constitution shortly after the Civil War, extended the right to vote to all men regardless of "race, color, or previous condition of servitude." This right, agreed upon by Congress and ratified by the states, is still in the process of being won in practice in some states. In 1920, the Nineteenth Amendment gave women the right to vote. With this change, the constitutional privilege of voting was extended to almost all adult Americans.

As stated earlier, rules governing election procedures vary from state to state. For example, both Kentucky and Georgia permit eighteen-year-olds to vote, while in other states, people under twenty-one do not have this privilege. Residence requirements, too, differ among states. In some states a United States citizen is permitted to vote six months after he takes up residence. In other states he must wait two years. Even within a state, residence requirements may vary from county to county.

In Reading 21 you will meet a young man going through the election procedure in his state, the state of Washington. As you read about his drive for election to the state legislature, consider the following questions:

1. What did Wes Uhlman do to get elected? Make a list of the activities he and his supporters undertook.
2. What contribution did each of these activities make to his campaign?
3. Would these activities differ if he had been running for governor? for President?

The Election of Wes Uhlman
WILLARD LEAVEL

Willard Leavel, "The Election of Wes Uhlman" in Cases in State and Local Government, *edited by Richard T. Frost,* © *1961. By permission of Prentice-Hall, Inc., Englewood Cliffs, New Jersey.*

Early in the spring of 1958, two University of Washington law students found themselves discussing, with greater and greater frequency, the chances of a young, unknown candidate for the state legislature.

Wes Uhlman was only twenty-three, but he was hardly a political novice. He had served a term as president of the University of Washington Young Democrats and was vice-president of the 32nd District Democratic Club in Seattle. Jim Wanamaker, then president of the campus Y.D.'s, had been raised among politicians, and for many years his mother had held public office. The two were not only fascinated by the picture of a young law student holding public office, but they were interested in the Young Democrats and hoped to find some way to rouse it from its lethargy.

They quickly determined that nothing could do more for the Young Democrats than to run their own candidate for public office. When the plan was discussed with the active members of the Y.D.'s, they responded enthusiastically.

A seat in the Washington State House of Representatives from the 32nd Legislative District . . . was the goal. . . .

[*If Wes Uhlman was to reach this goal, he had to win not one but two elections. First, he had to* file, *or submit his name, as a candidate in the primary, an election held in order to select a candidate to run against the other party's candidate. If he won the primary, he would be eligible to enter the general election later on.*]

The active campaign began in April with a series of strategy meetings to determine what types of campaign materials to use, what particular groups in the district to appeal to, what geographic areas to work the hardest, and, above all, how to build an organization for the campaign. . . .

In the primary, four Democratic candidates were vying for nomination to the two seats.

Wes Uhlman was the first Democrat to file.

A second candidate was Donna McArthur, an attractive young lawyer. . . . Miss McArthur was a graduate of the University of Washington and was in her late twenty's.

The third candidate was Frank Gustin. Gustin had graduated from the University of Washington Law School in June 1958. Also in his late twenty's, he was an accomplished speaker, and had been president of the student body while at the University. . . . The fourth candidate, John Carroll . . . was an elderly, retired man. . . .

In May, the Uhlman forces began to feed stories to the newspapers. Hardly a week passed that a story did not appear in most of the district weeklies, and some success was achieved in the daily papers. A highly effective publicity story was Uhlman's selection by the University of Washington Young Democrats for their first annual Man of the Year award—a most fortunate, if not entirely accidental, event.

Literature was designed carefully. One folder had to do for all the district. It was to be used when "doorbelling," and included in all mailings. . . .

Uhlman's strategists . . . felt that name familiarity, more than issues, would probably be the dominant factor in determining the winner. Hence, a sign campaign began that took a sizeable percentage of available time and money. A young artist contributed silk screens for the primary and general election campaigns. Five hundred signs were then printed by the candidate and his workers at a saving of hundreds of dollars. They were posted nightly to compete with the hundreds that sprang anew each night during Washington's election season.

The second part of the campaign was a number of carefully organized mailings to a list of some 1,300 known Democrats in the district. The core of this list had been compiled by the district organization over the years from the names of voters who had bought tickets for Democratic dinners, raffles, and the like. As Uhlman's workers campaigned, they wrote down the name of anyone who identified himself to them as a Democrat. This method rapidly expanded the list. In spite of the proportionately high cost of mailing, the Uhlman forces assumed that reaching a voter who publicly identified himself with a party and who, therefore, was most likely to be at the polls on primary day was worth the cost. . . .

Uhlman felt that to have any chance at a seat in the state house, he had to place first among the Democratic candidates in the primary. One of the Republican incumbents, Richard Ruoff, was considered invulnerable, making it possible for only one Democratic candidate to win in November. Moreover the state party and the lobbies would be likely to invest funds only in the Democratic candidate who was number one in the primary. . . .

The third campaign technique, and the one initially considered the most important, was old-fashioned doorbell-ringing. This was the operation that involved the most workers and gave the candidate his only direct contact with casual voters. Uhlman found that the political speech and political rally had almost vanished. He did appear, of course, at a number of meetings of the 32nd District Democratic Club, but he made no formal speeches, and few attended who were not already committed among the candidates. The only other meeting attended was an all-candidate affair sponsored by the League of Women Voters and the P.T.A. . . .

The real burden of the "doorbelling," as with everything else, fell upon Uhlman and his wife, Laila. . . .

Uhlman and his wife worked almost every night, going from door to door with a smile, an introduction, and a folder. . . . Three large work parties were held. Groups of from twelve to sixteen met at the home of an Uhlman supporter in a district, and from this point they were assigned to surrounding precincts to work. After nine, they reassembled for talk, drink, and rest. [Precincts are small subdivisions of an election district.]

The fourth and final part of the master campaign plan was a throwaway to be distributed the night before and on election day. This was a simple, inexpensive flyer that said little more than "Be Sure—Vote Uhlman." . . .

In twenty precincts this throwaway was placed on front porches the night before the primary election. In another fifteen precincts workers stood near the polls handing the flyer to passers-by for part or all of election day.

Newspaper ads were used to a limited extent in the neighborhood papers. A limited budget held the number and size down, and their effectiveness was questioned.

The primary campaign was climaxed the Saturday before the election with a parade through the entire district. . . .

Wes Uhlman placed first among the Democratic candidates, winning 2,591 votes. . . .

Winning a primary is not an unadulterated blessing. With victory comes the knowledge that all the work that won the primary, and all the thought, deals, and tensions, must be doubled and spent again. And a good deal more money must be found. Uhlman had largely financed his own primary. . . .

Pressure groups beat no path to the door of the candidate. . . . The Uhlman campaign had little trouble staying pure in the general election—it wasn't tempted.

In the general election the party, and especially the district party organization, did make substantial financial contributions. It was up to the candidate again, however, to dig deeply into his own pocket.

The election campaign strategy was much the same as that of the primary. The literature was almost identical. The major change was the emphasis on Uhlman's endorsements. The fact that he had Railroad Brotherhood endorsement, . . . endorsement by the public school teachers' association, and was then the only candidate rated above average by the Municipal League of King County was used extensively. . . .

Doorbell-ringing was not started until early October . . . because the primary election results indicated that "doorbelling" more than a month before the election was largely wasted effort.

The sign campaign never stopped. . . . Between the beginning of the primary campaign and general election day, some 1,250 signs were posted.

Mass mailings were sent out. Known Democrats were mailed items several different times to insure their votes and to attempt to get money, workers, and offers to put Uhlman bumper strips on cars or Uhlman signs in yards. All University employees in the district were sent a letter by the candidate stressing his interest in the University. Public school teachers received a second mailing, as did the retired teachers in the district and all P.T.A. officers. . . .

Between mailings, the sign campaign, and door-to-door canvassing, little time was left for the candidate or his workers to do anything else. . . .

Between forty-five and fifty precincts were worked by Uhlman, or his crew, in the general election campaign. A worker rang the doorbell, introduced himself, and asked if he could leave a folder for his friend, Wes Uhlman, who was running for the state legislature. No more time was usually spent with each voter for two reasons. There were too few workers and too many precincts; and very few voters were willing to spend many minutes with a political worker. The candidate himself attempted to meet the voters in those precincts in which he had done badly in the primary. . . .

By election eve no one would have bet on anything. There were no hopes of beating Richard Ruoff, but it was felt that a good campaign could mean Uhlman would run second in the district and win the other seat in the legislature. . . . The last weeks of the campaign were spent working in the heaviest Republican territory where warm welcomes came seldom.

Final returns showed: Uhlman, 7,542; Ruoff, 6,871; Carroll, 6,557; Oakes, 6,195. Of the eighty-four precincts in the district, Uhlman ran first in forty and second in another twenty. He ran third in twenty-three and fourth in only one. Comparing Uhlman's votes to those of other Democratic candidates for this office in recent elections, gains came in every part of the district. He ran ahead of the party ticket as a whole. In the Republican University district he cut heavily into the Republican vote, running first or second in well over half of these precincts.

22 The Role of Political Parties

Political parties play a major role in the process of selecting American political leaders. The way in which the parties play this role is significant. A political system is democratic only as long as those who govern are responsive to those who are being governed.

To test whether American political parties are a hindrance to democracy or an agency of it, you must ask a few questions. What is the major function of political parties in the United States? How do they perform this function?

Political parties are most active during primaries, when candidates for political office are being selected to represent the parties, and during general elections, when the candidates chosen by the parties compete for positions of political leadership. In local elections, the part played by political parties varies considerably. In the election of Wes Uhlman, the party seemed to play a minor part. In some areas, parties exercise tight control. In others, candidates who are independent of parties run with little party resistance. The political party plays its most dramatic role once every four years when it attempts to have one of its members elected President.

The American party system is basically a two-party system. At the national level, the two major parties have within them factions supporting many different causes. Selecting a candidate considered a suitable leader for all factions is a difficult task.

Every four years, each major party holds a national convention to choose its candidate for President and its candidate for Vice-President. The party organization in each state in the Union sends a delegation to select these two national candidates. Probably you have seen either a Republican National Convention or a Democratic National Convention on television and have watched the state delegations being called upon to cast their votes. You may have seen the final step in the selection of the party's candidates. But what do you know about the earlier stages in the process of selecting the candidates? What goes on within the party before the final selection is made?

Reading 22 gives you an opportunity to see a party at work. It describes how the Democratic Party in California selected its delegation to the national convention in 1960 and how the members of that delegation participated in the selection of a candidate for the Presidency of the United States.

1. Who were the California delegates to the Democratic National Convention in 1960?
2. What choices were available to the delegates?
3. Did the Democratic Party leaders dictate the final choice? Was this choice in any way responsive to the will of the people?

Choosing a Presidential Candidate
MINDELLA SCHULTZ

Every four years, delegates from every state in the Union meet in national convention to select the candidates who are going to become the leading contenders in the election for the Presidency of the United States. To the television viewer, the convention resembles a riotous outing of the national leaders of the two major political parties, highlighted by the noisy and fervent demonstrations that follow the nomination of each of the potential candidates. Yet, in the hands of the demonstrators lies the choice of the candidate who is going to be given the opportunity to run for the Presidency and who is going to have the political and financial backing of the party that chose to nominate him.

The delegates who attend a convention can greatly influence the outcome of that convention. Yet there are no national rules designating how these delegates will be selected. In some states, delegates are chosen by voters in a primary election. More often, delegates are chosen at state or congressional district conventions of the political parties. Delegates include governors, mayors, senators, prominent businessmen, labor leaders, and housewives. They represent a cross-section of the American public.

In the 1960 Democratic National Convention, delegates representing the state of California controlled 81 of the 761 votes that a contender would need to be nominated as the Democratic Party's candidate for the Presidency. Thus, winning the support of the California delegation represented a big prize for any candidate, but the delegation arrived in Los Angeles badly split over who would get California's votes. The votes were actually in the hands of 162 delegates, each delegate having only half a vote. The delegates had been chosen in accordance with California's Election Code. An executive committee of party leaders was authorized to select delegates and alternates from each of the congressional districts in the state. The executive committee included California's Democratic Party state chairman, the northern California chairman, the state women's vice-chairman, the Democratic national committeeman and committee-woman, president of the California Democratic Council, temporary president of the state senate, the speaker of the state assembly, the chairman of the Democratic congressional delegation, a congressman, and a United States senator—leaders of the many different official groups within the Democratic Party.*

Party leaders may differ when it comes to evaluating the candidates who wish to stand for election, but they all agree on one major point. They all want to pick the candidate who represents the party's best chance of winning the election. Since, in the election, the party must attract votes from a coalition of interests representing many different groups, these groups must be considered in choosing the delegates who have the authority to choose a candidate. The 162 delegates chosen by California's executive committee included representatives

*John Bunzel and Eugene C. Lee, "California Democratic Delegation of 1960," *Case Studies in American Government* (Englewood Cliffs: Prentice-Hall 1962) p. 140.

of the many groups who would be needed for a Democratic victory in the fall. Some delegates were chosen from those who had been large contributors to Democratic elections in the past. Some were chosen to represent the local party workers who would be needed to line up volunteers, get out mailings, make local campaign arrangements, and, in general, manage the thousand and one details connected with getting a candidate elected. Some delegates represented California's labor unions. Some represented religious groups. Some represented ethnic groups. There were delegates who were farmers as well as delegates prominent in city politics. There were delegates from both the northern and southern parts of the state. There were delegates who were known to favor each of the candidates who was a serious contender for nomination as the Democratic candidate for the Presidency of the United States.

A number of candidates were vying for the nomination. There was Adlai Stevenson who twice had failed in his bid for the Presidency. An eloquent, thoughtful man, Stevenson still had a magnetic appeal for America's "eggheads," or intellectuals. There was Lyndon Johnson, the dynamic senator from Texas with an impressive record as Senate majority leader. There was Hubert Humphrey, senator from Minnesota, whose faith in the common man was convincing. There was Chester Bowles, who had been Ambassador to India and in that post had convinced many Americans that he not only had compassion but a real understanding of the needs of the Asiatic world—a world whose development or lack of it was threatening America's peace. There was Stuart Symington, senator from Missouri, a handsome man from an industrialized border state, a man with a record of success in business and government. And there was John Kennedy, senator from Massachusetts with a vigorous team of bright young men masterminding his campaign.

The delegation from California was going to the convention formally committed to vote for California's "favorite son," its governor, Edmund G. (Pat) Brown. Brown had, at one time, been thought of as a serious contender for the candidacy; but long before the convention, a series of political mishaps had removed him from the list of those who could conceivably win not only the nomination but also the election. For many reasons, however, the decision was made to hold the delegates to their commitment to vote for Brown, at least through the convention's first ballot.

The strategy of the Stevenson supporters was to work for a deadlock that would throw convention support to Stevenson as a compromise candidate.* As they saw it, if Kennedy could be kept from getting the

*Theodore White, *The Making of the President 1960* (New York: Atheneum, 1961) p. 123.

necessary 761 votes on the first ballot, none of the other candidates could win either. In the search for a compromise, the man most likely to be acceptable to a majority of candidates might well be the man who was their choice in 1952 and in 1956, Adlai Stevenson. Stevenson supporters favored California's commitment to Pat Brown. A vote for Governor Brown was not a vote for Kennedy. Supporters of senators Symington and Johnson favored Brown on the first ballot for the same reason.

While the California delegation was committed to Brown on the first ballot, the delegation was not in agreement about whom it would vote for on subsequent ballots. Governor Brown was pledged to support Kennedy, but not all members of the California delegation agreed with his choice. A sizable faction in the delegation favored Kennedy, but there were factions supporting the other candidates as well, and they wanted to "stop Kennedy." They wanted a poll of the delegation to be taken in order to show that the delegates were not united behind Kennedy and that they favored other candidates. Pressure was put on Brown to poll his delegates to disclose their preferences.

On July 10, Governor Brown declared himself for Kennedy and tried to release his delegation from their commitment to cast a "favorite son" vote for him on the first ballot.*

On Tuesday, July 12, the California delegation *caucused*, or met together, for three hours. According to Lawrence Davies, writing for *The New York Times:*

"So persistent were the Stevenson delegates at the caucus, along with their allies from the camps of senators Stuart Symington and Lyndon B. Johnson, that they forced an immediate poll of the Californians over the objections of the Kennedy strategists.

"The roaring voice votes, the cheers and boos made it difficult at times for Senator Clair Engle, the delegation chairman, to keep his fellow delegates in line. . . .

"The California roll call, taken at the end of the uproarious meeting in the National Broadcasting Company studios in Hollywood, gave these results: Stevenson, 31½ votes; Kennedy, 30½; Symington, 9; Johnson, 6½; Governor Edmund G. Brown, 2½; Representative Chester Bowles of Connecticut, ½. One delegate with one-half vote abstained. . . .

"Five of the delegates with one-half vote each persisted in voting for Governor Brown as this state's favorite son candidate for the Presidency, despite the fact that the Governor announced he had asked that his name not be placed in nomination."†

*"Brown Declares for Kennedy Bid," *The New York Times*, July 11, 1960, p. 18.
†Lawrence Davies, "Stevenson Wins Double Triumph," *The New York Times*, July 13, 1960, pp. 1, 18.

23 The Role of Interest Groups

The American who does not belong to some identifiable group is rare. Churches, bowling leagues, labor unions, and discussion clubs are all groups that unite people on the basis of a common interest. Such groups may or may not be politically active.

An organized group may become a force in the political process when it decides that its objectives might best be served by gaining support for them from the larger community and by implementing these objectives through political action. When labor unions want the legislature to pass minimum wage laws, they must convince both the legislators and the larger community that such laws are desirable. Labor unions want to create a good feeling toward labor in the community so that the community supports legislators who are also sympathetic to labor. After all, it takes a majority of the community to elect a legislator, not just the members of one interest group.

Businessmen, too, unite in organizations and support legislation and candidates favoring their interests. The Chamber of Commerce is a nationwide organization of businessmen who have united in the interest of maintaining the strength of the American business community. Doctors, teachers, parents, and veterans all have organizations which can become politically active when an issue or candidate affects their group's shared interest.

There are still other interest groups which become politically active, but which are not organized on a permanent basis. These are groups which unite either to fight or support one particular candidate or issue. They generally disband after the election or issue is settled. Some of the interest groups which you will study later in this reading are examples of this temporary kind of interest group.

Interest groups exert political pressure in a number of ways. Over one thousand interest groups maintain lobbyists in Washington today. A *lobbyist* is a professional representative of an interest group. The function of a lobbyist is to watch proposed legislation. Whenever bills come up that affect the interest that he represents, he studies the bill carefully and follows its progress closely. If his group considers the bill harmful to its interests, the lobbyist attempts to influence congressmen to vote against it. He may try to influence them through personal contact, acquainting them with his interest group's point of view. Or he may prepare his objections in printed form and send it to the congressmen.

Interest groups can also exert political pressure by having their members go out and ring doorbells or make phone calls to acquaint other voters with their views on particular issues or candidates. Their attempts to influence voting may also take the form of writing letters or sending telegrams to congressmen to persuade them to see things as the interest groups see them.

On the American political scene, interest groups have generally chosen to participate in the election process through existing political parties. On occasion, interest groups do form a political party with a slate of candidates who are supporters of their interests. Prohibitionists, Vegetarians, and Socialists have all tried to further their interests through their own parties and candidates. In general, however, interest groups have been unaffiliated, throwing their support behind those candidates and issues they find in keeping with their interests. Sometimes an entire interest group formally endorses a candidate, but more frequently prominent officials or members of the group publicly endorse a candidate.

Reading 23 will acquaint you further with the activities of interest groups as they involve themselves in an election. As you read, think about the following questions:

1. What groups interested themselves in this election? What was the basis of their interest?
2. How important do you think the activities of the interest groups were in affecting the outcome of the election? Why?
3. What do you think were the underlying factors that made one interest group more politically effective than another?

The Special Case of Public Education

ALAN ROSENTHAL

The interest groups described in this reading were concerned with a bond-issue referendum. Bonds are certificates issued by a borrower to a lender as a promise to repay a loan of money. Often a government wants to pay for a certain project by borrowing money and issuing bonds to the lenders. Since the citizens of the community are the ones who will have to pay off the bonds, often through an increase in their taxes, they may be called on to make the decision on whether or not a bond issue will be permitted. Alan Rosenthal, "The Special Case of Public Education" in Cases in State and Local Government, *edited by Richard T. Frost, © 1961. By permission of Prentice-Hall, Inc. Englewood Cliffs, New Jersey.*

Events leading up to the bond-issue referendum of 1957 began eight years before when Dr. Roger Snow was hired by the Parkside Board of Education to be the new superintendent of schools. . . .

It soon became apparent that Snow was less interested in developing new curricula than in improving and expanding the physical plant. . . . Snow waited until . . . 1952 . . . before embarking upon what he described as "my active push for a new building program." . . .

Snow had no difficulty convincing board members of the merits of his plans for physical expansion. Morton Fishbein, then president of the board, was especially sympathetic. . . .

During the first three months of 1956, Snow and his staff . . . met together to determine exactly what was needed. The educators decided not only on an addition to the high school but also on an addition to one of the elementary schools in the town. Everything was to be lumped together and paid for by one large bond issue. . . .

By the end of July, estimates of plans and costs were almost completed. . . .

On August 24, at a special meeting attended by the entire board . . . the architect presented complete plans and cost figures . . .

The board officially adopted the program, and . . . a [bond-issue] referendum was scheduled for January 22, 1957.

In October 1956, Roger Snow left Parkside for a higher-paying job as school superintendent in a neighboring county. The task of leadership then fell to Fishbein. . .

By the end of 1956, not only had no organized opposition to the bond issue developed, but municipal agencies and officials also seemed to favor the proposal. . . .

[But] suddenly opposition developed. At its January 10 meeting, the [town] planning board voted against the bond-issue proposal on the grounds that "the school board had not kept it fully informed of contemplated land uses" and because the amount requested was "excessive." . . .

Since the [school] board had foreseen no organized opposition, it had formulated no campaign plan. But as Mrs. Harrison [vice-president of the school board] said, "Fortunately, we had an explanatory pamphlet ready, and the day after the planning board decided against us, we put our case before the town." On January 11 and 12, student volunteers from the high school distributed the school board brochure to every home in the community.

On January 14, a public meeting, sponsored by the board of education and the high school P.T.A., was held. Over three hundred persons attended, apparently evenly divided on the building proposal. At this meeting a new threat was announced. The mayor and several councilmen, speaking, they maintained, as individual citizens rather than as town officials, questioned the school board's expenditure program. Admitting that existing educational facilities were inadequate, they suggested that the board's program was excessive. . . .

Encouraged by the coolness of the town officials to the bond issue, organized opposition developed. Several Parkside residents formed a local taxpayers association specifically to campaign against the school board program. . . . All the organizers were relatively wealthy, and their incomes, either through rents, commissions, or salaries, were directly dependent on real estate. They, of course, had no desire to see property taxes rise [to pay off the bond issue] in a state where such taxes were already among the highest in the nation.

During the final week of what by then had become a vigorous campaign, members of the group made telephone calls to people who they believed were sympathetic to their cause. They emphasized "the disasterous effects of an ever-increasing tax rate," . . . Two days before the referendum, the association mailed an eight-page pamphlet to every household in Parkside. . . . Admitting . . . that certain renovations and additions . . . were . . . necessary, the association declared that "at this time, additions could be made, and standards of education maintained with an expenditure of about half the presently proposed bond issue." Other communities had gotten by for less, the pamphlet declared. . . .

At about the same time the taxpayers association organized, the president of the school board recruited assistance from other members of the community. If the bond issue were to pass, help was needed. Several members of local P.T.A.'s, all of whom were personal friends of school board members, met together and formally offered their services. . . . Led by a local clergyman, a member of the local League of Woman Voters, a P.T.A. activist, and a university professor, the Parkside Citizens Committee for Better Schools took on the job of publicizing the bond-issue program.

The pro-school board citizens committee aimed its appeals at members of four local P.T.A.'s primarily. Members were called by phone and asked to tell their friends and neighbors to vote "yes" in the approaching referendum. Advertisements were inserted in the local newspaper, and a spot-announcement program was put on the radio station. . . .

As soon as the taxpayers association pamphlet came to the attention of members of the citizens committee, they decided to reply with their own flyer. . . . Principal [of the high school] Sheen was asked to provide factual information to counter the taxpayers' assertions about lower building costs in other communities. . . .

Sheen phoned the administrators of seven school districts that had been cited in the taxpayers association brochure and discovered that cost estimates for building programs had been distorted by the association. He forwarded the information to the citizens committee, and a flyer was then mimeographed for general distribution. To deliver the message to Parkside, the committee provided cars and chauffeurs, the school guidance counsellor and the athletic director plotted distribution routes, and the student council supplied pupil volunteers to hand out the flyers early in the morning before school opened. . . .

On January 22, 1957 — the day of the bond-issue referendum — both sides worked hard to bring their voters to the polls. Representatives of the taxpayers association . . . went from door to door, offered to drive citizens to the polling place at the elementary school, and warned once again of the serious threat to all taxpayers. Members of the citizens committee, P.T.A. volunteers, and school teachers telephoned, visited homes, offered to baby-sit while residents voted, and warned that the future of public education in Parkside hinged on this election.

When the ballots were counted that evening, more people had voted in the 1957 referendum than in any other school election ever held in the town. But only 2,720 citizens voted. Only two out of five registered voters took the trouble to cast a ballot for or against the bond issue. . . . The educators, board members, and citizens committee had won. By the slim margin of fifty-four votes, the pro-bond-issue groups were authorized to expand educational facilities and thereby increase local tax levies for the next thirty years.

24 Transfer of Leadership in the American Political System

The way in which the citizen participates in the selection of his political leaders provides one measure of how democratic a political system is. The way in which positions of leadership pass from one man to another provides a second measure. Reading 24 is concerned with this second measure.

The Constitution states that when a member of the United States House of Representatives vacates his seat for any reason, the governor of the state involved is authorized to issue a writ calling for a special election to fill that vacancy. In the case of a vacancy in the United States Senate, the governor is authorized to issue a writ for a special election unless the state legislature has empowered him to make a temporary appointment until the next election.

According to Article II, Section 1 of the Constitution, when the office of the President is unexpectedly vacated, the Vice-President, an elected official, becomes President. This transfer of leadership of course leaves the office of the Vice-President vacant. Therefore, the Twenty-fifth Amendment has been enacted. It empowers the new President to nominate a man for the vacant Vice-Presidency. Congress must then confirm the nomination by a majority vote of both houses.

On November 22, 1963, the office of the President was unexpectedly vacated when President John F. Kennedy was assassinated. A shocked and grief-stricken nation listened to the news of his death. A short while later came the news that Vice-President Lyndon B. Johnson had been sworn in and had assumed the Presidency.

Reading 24 describes how the transfer of Presidential power took place. As you read, consider the following questions:

1. What are the constitutional provisions for transferring the powers of the President to the Vice-President upon the death of the President?
2. What procedures were followed in transferring these powers from President Kennedy to President Johnson? How smooth was the transfer?
3. How do these provisions and procedures reflect the ideology upon which the Constitution was based?

The Day Kennedy Died

NEWSWEEK

Copyright, Newsweek, Inc., December, 1963.

In one sudden, swift, awful convulsion of history . . . the majesty and the burdens of the Presidency of the United States shifted from one man to another.

In a shattering moment, at once random and calculated, John Fitzgerald Kennedy was cut down in his forty-seventh year by an assassin's bullet in Dallas, Texas. . . .

Reflexively, the President's Secret Service driver started the car and roared off toward Parkland Memorial Hospital, three and a quarter miles away. . . . The seventy-seven-block dash to the emergency entrance of the tan, thirteen-story hospital took nine minutes. . . .

Newsmen clustered in a nurse's classroom to wait for official word. At 1:33 P.M., assistant White House press secretary Malcolm Kilduff pushed into the room . . . he read: "President John F. Kennedy died at approximately 1 P.M., Central Standard Time, today here in Dallas. He died of a gunshot wound in the brain."

The President was dead.

. . . What counted most now was the continuity of government, the constitutional rite reuniting the abruptly broken past with the uncertain future.

The Constitution dictated that the mantle of the Presidency pass to the Vice-President, to the towering, folksy, politically wise Texan who seemed so unlikely a running mate for Mr. Kennedy in 1960. . .

. . . Lyndon Baines Johnson—under heavy guard—sped unannounced back to Love Field, climbed aboard Air Force One, and stepped into the 12- by 15-foot Presidential conference room. The federal judge who would swear him in—his old friend Sarah T. Hughes, a tiny woman of sixty-seven—had been summoned. Waiting

for Mrs. Kennedy, Johnson whispered gravely for a moment with some Texas congressional friends. He spotted Mr. Kennedy's secretary, Mrs. Evelyn Lincoln, and kissed her hand.

At 2:18 P.M., the hearse drew up, and the coffin was carried up the rear ramp, Mrs. Kennedy . . . close behind. The gold-upholstered conference room was already crowded and sweltering after three hours in the hot Dallas sun. Larry O'Brien, Mr. Kennedy's legislative liaison man, handed Mr. Johnson the small leather-bound Bible the former President had kept in his aft sleeping compartment. Lady Bird Johnson took a place at his right elbow, Mrs. Kennedy at his left. Among the twenty-seven spectators behind them was Admiral George Burkley, Mr. Kennedy's personal physician, his shirt cuffs still bloodstained.

Her words barely audible above the whine of the fan-jet engines, Judge Hughes read the oath:

"I do solemnly swear that I will faithfully execute the office of the President of the United States and will to the best of my ability preserve, protect, and defend the Constitution of the United States."

Softly, the new President repeated the words, adding at the close: "So help me God." He turned to Lady Bird—her eyes brimming—and kissed her on the forehead. Mrs. Johnson took Mrs. Kennedy's hand in turn and told her, "The whole nation mourns your husband." . . .

At 2:41 P.M., Mr. Johnson made his last good-bys and gave his first order as President: "Now let's get airborne." As the jet roared aloft and headed home to Washington at 635 miles per hour, he set to work composing a statement:

"This is a sad time . . . We have suffered a loss that cannot be weighed. For me it is a deep personal tragedy. I know the world shares the sorrow that Mrs. Kennedy and her family bear. I will do my best. That is all I can do. I ask for your help—and God's."

Washington—set reeling by the first news, was already at work bridging the change in Presidents. . .

At the White House, Mr. Kennedy's national security adviser, McGeorge Bundy, took charge. A plane carrying Secretary of State Dean Rusk and five other cabinet members to Japan was called back via Honolulu to Washington for a meeting Saturday morning. Staffers laid out pads and pencils around the White House cabinet table and moved Mr. Johnson's chair around to the President's spot.

The order was changing.

At 6:00 P.M. that bewildering night—a bare four hours after John Kennedy died—Air Force One touched down at Andrews Air Force Base outside Washington. The floodlights were doused; in the pale glow of a quarter-moon, the plane taxied like a gray ghost to the landing apron. A catering truck, mounted on top with a hydraulic lift platform, rumbled to the back door. The President's brother, Attorney General Robert Kennedy, bounded aboard. An all-service honor guard carried the bronze casket onto the lift, to be taken first to Bethesda Naval Hospital for embalming and finally—in the deep stillness at 4:30 A.M.—home to the White House.

Coatless and bareheaded, Mr. Johnson stepped out, his wife beside him. Soberly, government officials surged forward to shake hands and wish him well. He paused long enough to read the statement, invoking the help of his countrymen and his God. Then the Johnsons boarded an Army helicopter with Bundy, Defense Secretary Robert McNamara, Under Secretary of State George Ball, and a few staff men.

A crowd watched the helicopter disappear into the dark and started scattering, each alone with a sense of loss. . . .

. . . Perhaps better prepared by experience than any previous Vice-President succeeding to the top job, Mr. Johnson took charge in remarkably brisk order.

The President was still talking defense with McNamara, Bundy, and Ball as he alighted on the White House lawn. On the spot, he asked Bundy to stay on. Then, instead of turning off at the carefully prepared Cabinet Room, he strode through the West Wing, across Executive Avenue to his own second-floor office in the Executive Office Building.

First, he called former Presidents Truman and Eisenhower to discuss funeral plans. He ordered dinner; a Filipino steward brought it on a tray, and Mr. Johnson ate at his desk. The congressional leaders of both parties—summoned by White House staffers—straggled in. Gravely, Mr. Johnson told them he wanted their "united support." With equal gravity, they pledged themselves behind him.

Next came Mr. Johnson's own staff for a quick conference. Afterward, he checked by phone with FBI director J. Edgar Hoover about the hunt for the assassin. At 3:24 A.M., the new President headed home. . . .

On a busy first morning in office, Lyndon Johnson paused to issue a proclamation declaring Monday a day of national mourning. He made his last silent good-bys to Mr. Kennedy. He and Mrs. Johnson spent twenty minutes upstairs at the White House with Mrs. Kennedy.

Otherwise, he spent a long day breaking into the world's most difficult job.

Checking in at the White House just after 9, he talked with Robert Kennedy over a coffee table across the oval office from the empty Presidential desk. Bundy took him from there to the situation room for a briefing by CIA director John McCone. Then came conferences with Rusk, McNamara, and—once again—the legislative leaders.

He discussed world trouble spots with General Eisenhower over lunch in his old Vice-Presidential office across the street; later he spent a half-hour with Harry Truman. He made pro forma phone calls to the AFL-CIO's George Meany and American Telephone and Telegraph's Frederick Kappel. Always he spoke of the need for unity. . . .

. . . At 2:30 P.M., he called together the late President's cabinet for a brief, to-the-point twenty-five-minute meeting. "I need your help in the time ahead," Mr. Johnson said. Treasury Secretary C. Douglas Dillon, responded first, then Adlai Stevenson. They pledged the support of the full cabinet; all were "prepared to serve as long as the President wanted them to serve."

On Wednesday, Mr. Johnson planned to address a joint session of Congress.

And so, in a moment of high tragedy, the link between the past and the future of the nation—this "old but youthful union," Mr. Kennedy had called it—was forged anew. The loss was momentous. Americans everywhere—those who liked John F. Kennedy and those who despised him—felt the void, and it hurt.

But the fabric was preserved. . . .

Chapter 7

Personal Characteristics of Soviet Leaders

STATING THE ISSUE   In Chapters 5 and 6, four types of American political leaders were identified: elected officials, appointed officeholders, political theorists, and behind-the-scenes manipulators. The readings concentrated on the elected officials, for although all types of leaders influence political decisions, the elected official is the center of the democratic process. Democracy has been defined as a device by which the general electorate is allowed to choose, in free and relatively frequent elections, the group that will establish the policy by which the government will be run.

Day-by-day administrative decisions in the American government are made by millions of government employees who reached decision-making positions by appointment. But the basic policy on which they base their decisions is set by elected officials. It is the elected officials, Congress and the President, who make the guidelines within which appointed administrators operate.

In the first half of this unit on leadership, you looked at the American political system in operation and searched for clues to characteristics of its leaders. In this chapter, you will reverse the process and look at personal and social characteristics of Soviet leaders in search of clues to how the Soviet political system operates.

You can find clues concerning the operation of a political system if you look closely at its leaders. In Reading 20 you saw that Senator Edmund Ross was not reelected when he went against the wishes of his electorate. From that fact, you could theorize that in the American political system, an elected official must remain responsive to the will of his voters if he is to stay in office. As you read about Soviet political leaders, look for similar clues. What are the characteristics of Soviet political leaders? What sort of backgrounds do they have? What personal characteristics seem to have helped them to come to power in the Soviet system? What do these characteristics tell you about the Soviet political system?

25 Characteristics of a Local Soviet Leader (Part One)

In analyzing American political leadership, you concentrated primarily on the characteristics of national elected officials. In the readings in Chapters 5 and 6, you did not study political party officials, nor did you study local government officials. In American politics, the power to make major policy decisions affecting everybody in the United States is held by national elected officials. State and local officials set policy in their areas. Their decisions are important and may sometimes even have national impact, but these decisions still must stay within the guidelines set by the Constitution and federal laws.

In Reading 25, you will start a series of readings that focus on political leadership in the Soviet Union. You will investigate various facets of leadership. What individuals have sufficient power to make major policy decisions? What offices do they hold? What groups are influential in helping them get power?

In the early 1950's, Harvard University organized a project to analyze the ways in which the social system of the Soviet Union was organized. Members of the project read widely and interviewed refugees to determine how the Soviet social system worked. In 1955, Raymond Bauer, a member of the Harvard staff, wrote nine sketches in which he attempted to portray the lives of nine typical Soviet citizens. His sketches are based on the data compiled by the project. Each figure is, of course, fictional, a composite of the characteristics of many individuals. The characteristics he included were those that the Soviet refugees who were interviewed described most frequently.

Reading 25 is part of Bauer's account of Antip Trofimovitch Teplove, referred to in the article below as Teplov. Teplov is a "typical" Communist Party secretary at the district, or raion, level. As secretary, he is responsible for the administration of all the social, political, and economic affairs of his district. As you read, think about the following questions:

1. What are Teplov's personal characteristics? Do they differ from the personal characteristics of such an American politician as Wes Uhlman? If you think that they do, in what ways do they differ?
2. What does Teplov's story tell you about how Soviet party officials are recruited? the way in which they are trained? the way in which tasks are assigned to them?
3. What clues to the operation of the Soviet political system do Teplov's characteristics offer?

The Party Secretary (Part One)

RAYMOND BAUER

Joseph V. Stalin had dominated the Communist Party in the Soviet Union for twenty-five years. His death in 1953 set off a chain of events that was felt at every level of the party's organization—from the highest officials in Moscow to farm workers in the far corners of Russia. First, a "collective leadership" replaced a single ruler. Then, L. P. Beria, who had been Stalin's Minister of Internal Affairs and right-hand man, tried to establish himself as dictator in Stalin's place. He was convicted of high treason December 23, 1953, and executed the same day. While G. M. Malenkov was serving as head of the government, a great power struggle developed in which Nikita S. Khrushchev eventually emerged victorious.

The following portrait is based upon the daily activities of a party secretary in an administrative district during the period immediately after Stalin's death. It is the party secretary's duty to see that all affairs in his district are running according to the party's designs. Though his main concern is the industrial or agricultural production of his region, he must also be a combination administrative expert and trouble shooter. Reprinted from Nine Soviet Portraits *by Raymond Bauer by permission of The M.I.T. Press, Cambridge, Massachusetts. Copyright, 1955 by The Massachusetts Institute of Technology.*

Teplov rubbed his eyes to keep awake. It was midnight, and he wanted to go home to bed, but years of service in the party apparatus had taught him the necessity of careful paper work. He was preparing an agenda for the meeting of the executive committee of the raion [district] party committee in the morning, and this was no time to make mistakes. It was one of those periods in which any action could have the profoundest political ramifications. Teplov was a technician first, and a politician second, but in a time of crisis, politics inevitably saturated all of life.

Stalin's picture still hanging on the wall symbolized the instability of Teplov's world, which would not be peaceful until another picture hung in its place. But whose picture would it be? And when would it happen? It was risky to take sides, and it was risky not to take sides.

Kornetsky, the sardonic second secretary, had chanced into the office one day as Teplov was putting a picture of Malenkov in his desk drawer. "We must be prepared for any eventuality, eh, Antip Trofimovitch? One must also be careful that he does not put in the same drawer the picture of two incompatible persons. This might prove to be a very serious business," Kornetsky had commented.

Teplov had looked up, angered. But he did not know how to respond to Kornetsky. He searched the second secretary's face for some trace of expression that would give him a clue as to what was on his mind. Kornetsky's teeth were fastened firmly on the huge pipe which he seldom smoked, but which was as fixed a feature of his face as his nose and ears.

Many times in the course of the day, he looked at the door of the office and his name in reverse through the glass, "A. T. Teplov, First Secretary, Baltinsk Raion Committee." When he did, the same unspoken question came to his mind that came when he looked at Stalin's picture. The sign painters weren't very skillful, but it took very little effort to scrape a name off the door and replace it with another—no harder than changing Stalin's picture on the wall.

But worrying about such things was a luxury a busy man could not afford. The life of the raion was dependent on Teplov, and Teplov was dependent on the life of the raion. If the raion did not develop, flourish, and produce, he would have failed, and his career would be over. There was little he could do about the fight that was raging among the big shots, but his responsibilities to the raion were many and immediate. He returned to his desk and was working furiously when he heard a tap at his door. It was Shvartz, the third secretary, young, thin-faced, bookish-looking. . . .

"Well, Antip Trofimovitch," Shvartz said, "I see you're still working."

Teplov gestured silently, drawing his hands across the pile of work on his desk with a single sweeping motion. "How about you?" he asked.

Shvartz grimaced. "I had a class for the four new party candidates. I'm leading them patiently by the hand through the *Short History of the Communist Party*. A lazy bunch—I thought they'd go to sleep."

"Well, keep them at it," Teplov answered and returned to the work on his desk.

Shvartz seemed unperturbed by being cut off so shortly by his chief. He said, "Good night. I'll see you in the morning," closed the door behind him, and turned to leave the building. On the way out he noticed a small light bulb burning in one of the offices—and right in the middle of the campaign to save electricity; he groaned as he stepped inside for a moment to turn it off.

"A funny chap, the old man," Shvartz mused as he left the building. "You'd think he'd be more interested in the job I'm doing. Political education is an important part of the party's work." . . .

Teplov was interested in political education, but not in the way that Shvartz was. Teplov wanted the party and Komsomol [Young Communist League] members in the raion to be sufficiently literate in the political classics and sufficiently up-to-date on the party line so that they would not commit embarrassing errors. And he wanted Shvartz to keep the general populace at a sufficient level of apparent enthusiasm so that there should be no unfavorable reports going into [Communist Party headquarters] about morale in the raion.

The Soviet state was built on deeds, not on words, but even a practical man had to have a proper respect for the role of persuasion. It took years of experience and a long process of ripening to appreciate the delicate balance to be maintained between persuasion and coercion. . . .

But some young party workers never realized how this balance of coercion and persuasion worked. On Teplov's desk lay a note which read simply, "New partorg [party organizer] for shoe factory." If Shvartz tended slightly to overestimate the importance of words, the former partorg at the shoe factory had underestimated it badly. He was assigned the task of securing a 10 per cent voluntary contribution to the state loan from the workers of the plant. With guileless naiveté he had posted an announcement that 10 per cent would be deducted from their pay énvelopes . . . without an agitation program in the shop to explain the need of the state for the funds, . . . without calling a factory meeting at which the activists among the workers could pledge the required amount. His action caused a furor in the raion committee. At Teplov's direction the head of the industrial section called the young man in, gave him a good dressing down, and returned him full-time to his job of running a stitching machine in the factory. Now they would have to select a new partorg—one with a greater sense of delicacy and of proper form. . . .

He worked his way patiently through the pile of notes. There were a few production problems in several of the small factories in the raion, but thank God, not many. Nikitin, as head of the agricultural sector, would have to give them a report on the progress of the crops. Also a general propaganda and agitation program would have to be worked out in connection with the recent arrest of Beria. The editor of the raion newspaper had taken his cue quietly, and of course printed the editorial that had been broadcast from Moscow. But the entire resources of the raion would have to be mobilized.

Finally, about one-thirty, he finished. It was a warm July evening. Teplov wore a light coat as he walked home. His house was less than a quarter-mile from the office. Baltinsk, after which the raion took its name, was a small provincial settlement. The streets were unpaved. There was a crude telephone connection with the nearest city. Electricity had been introduced only in the years after the war. As Teplov strolled along under the night sky, he was surveying his capital, for indeed this rural town was the center of the area over which he held sway.

But, now that he was no longer working, his feeling of uneasiness returned. The decision to seek a career in the party apparatus was a risky one, although it hadn't seemed so to Teplov at the time. He was an engineering student, son of a foreman in a textile plant. His mother was a peasant who had come to the city to work in the same factory in which she met his father. It had seemed quite natural for him to enter the Komsomol, and quite natural for him to accept the assignments which were given him. Before he realized it, shortly after graduation he was no longer an engineer, but an *apparatchik*, a member of the party apparatus. First he was party secretary of the plant in which he had shortly before been a junior engineer; then head of the industrial sector in a raion committee; an interruption for the war, when he served as a political officer to a regiment and was wounded; and then he returned to be second, and, finally, first secretary of the Baltinsk Raion. Teplov had not been a very distinguished youth. He was a little more energetic than average, a little above average in intelligence, and below average in imagination. He was very little concerned with politics, but quite intent on making a career for himself, and was entirely content to do what was asked of him in order to attain that goal. He was a technician-bureaucrat in a world of politics. As much as possible, he tried to stay apart from factional struggles within the party . . . he managed to survive a full dozen years in the party without becoming identified as anybody's man.

But tonight he was worried. It was comforting that he was not involved in any of the contending factions in the party. He could be sure that he would not automatically . . . [lose his job] if the wrong faction won. But, at the same time, he could not be sure of the support of any of the factions either . . . and even though he had no one group of enemies, he did have individual enemies. Particularly he knew that he had enemies in some of the agencies in Moscow and in some of the central party offices. . . .

Perhaps his worst enemy was V. N. Rashevsky, now a fairly high official in the Kremlin. Rashevsky had been head of the oblast industrial sector [an oblast is a large provincial unit of which a raion is but a segment] when Teplov was appointed to head the raion industrial sector. They had a number of arguments, an act of rare audacity on Teplov's part since he was little given to open displays of resistance.

While Teplov was away at war, he heard that Rashevsky had been appointed first secretary for the oblast. Fortunately for Teplov, Rashevsky moved on to Moscow before he returned. There was little doubt that if Rashevsky had been oblast secretary at the time of Teplov's appointment, it would not have gone through.

Teplov rose in the raion on the basis of his energetic work. But he continued to have his brushes with Rashevsky, who was now in the agricultural sector of the Central Committee.

On one occasion a division of troops was moved into Teplov's raion. They were authorized to draw on raion food resources for subsistence. It was quickly clear that the raion's resources were inadequate. . . . There would have been rebellion on all the kolkhozes [collective farms, which are made up of many small farms worked together under government supervision], and the workers in the towns would have been short of food. Teplov carried the fight to the oblast committee, insisting that the regular deliveries be reduced accordingly, and the new oblast secretary took the matter up to Moscow. It was only later, after the matter had been settled in his favor, that Teplov heard that his old antagonist, Rashevsky, had been behind the original order. Incidents like these preyed on his mind. . . .

26 Characteristics of a Local Soviet Leader (Part Two)

Reading 25 helped you to identify the personal and social characteristics of Teplov, a "typical" district leader of the Communist Party in the Soviet Union. Teplov did not have to appeal to the voters for support. He was appointed district leader by his superiors in the Communist Party. He came to power by performing acceptably in previous assignments and pleasing his superiors. He stayed in power by continuing to please them. You can gain insight into the operation of a political system by learning which individuals and groups one must appeal to if he is to become a political decision-maker. Such knowledge tells you how a person becomes a leader.

An American elected official must keep in touch with the voters. He makes speeches. He writes reports of his activities and sends them to his constituents. He supports bills that benefit the people of the district he represents. His efforts are reported in the local press, and he makes himself accessible to his electorate in a number of ways.

Teplov's situation is different from an American official's, and he has a different role to play. Consequently, he behaves differently. Reading 26 concludes Bauer's sketch of Teplov, and in this segment you will concentrate on discovering the things that Teplov did in order to remain in power. As you read the account, think about these questions:

1. What political position did Teplov hold? What were his tasks?
2. What personal characteristics would he need to do these tasks effectively?
3. Who appears to have the authority to decide whether Teplov will have political power? What does the answer to this question tell you about the political system in which he operates?

The Party Secretary (Part Two)

RAYMOND BAUER

Reprinted from Nine Soviet Portraits *by Raymond Bauer by permission of The M.I.T. Press, Cambridge, Massachusetts. Copyright, 1955 by The Massachusetts Institute of Technology.*

Still in an uneasy reverie, he arrived at his house, a small, four-room structure with two bedrooms, a kitchen, and a living room. His wife was sleeping in one bedroom and his two boys in the other. It was typical that he should return home after the family was asleep. He occasionally lamented how little he saw his family. But, except for being deprived of his company, they were well provided for. They were well dressed, housed, and fed. You could tell them by their more prosperous appearance if you saw them in any gathering. . . .

Teplov knew nothing from the time he hit the bed until his wife shook him awake at eight o'clock in the morning. . . .

His driver was waiting outside the house sitting in the car and reading the copy of the raion newspaper which he picked up regularly for Teplov every morning. They exchanged good-mornings, and Teplov got into the back seat. The driver handed Teplov the newspaper.

Teplov was doubly interested in the paper. On one hand, he was responsible for virtually everything that happened in the raion. Therefore, he was anxious to see that it carried out policy properly. On the other hand, it told him of what was happening in the world outside the raion. Of special interest were the items which Moscow sent out by radio to be printed verbatim. Occasionally, when he had an evening to himself, he would sit at home and listen to news stories and editorials being dictated at slow speed over the radio. Particularly in recent months, the ponderous voice of the announcer would frequently intone statements reflecting the tremendous changes which were taking place: ". . . *comma* who has repeatedly committed antistate activities, *comma* has been taken into custody *period*" . . . "the doctrine of one-man rule *comma* which is completely contrary to the principles of the party *comma* must be replaced by . . . [collective] decisions". . . "a series of benefits *colon* lowered food prices *semicolon* an ever-increasing standard of living *semicolon* . . ." These dispatches were like the acts of some unknown being who would suddenly and violently intervene in Teplov's life, sometimes doing good and sometimes doing evil. . . .

As the car pulled up in front of the raion headquarters, Teplov noticed an automobile sitting in front of the building. He recognized one of the chauffeurs from the shoe factory waiting in the car. For a brief moment he was puzzled; then he remembered that an inspector from the chief administration was expected. . . .

The inspector, Boris Aleksandrovitch Davidenkov, was waiting in Teplov's office. A round-faced, stocky man, his clothes marked him for a member of the Moscow bureaucracy, but their disheveled condition also showed the effects of his trip. He jumped up smiling and pumped Teplov's arm warmly. "Just came in to see how the plastic soles are working out in the shoes, Antip Trofimovitch!" he said.

. . .The inspector was a good fellow who caused no difficulty for the raion, . . . He brought Teplov many juicy bits of gossip from Moscow. For this Teplov was grateful. . . .

"Good morning, Boris . . . I'm delighted to see you," Teplov replied. "I understand things are going fairly well with the plastic soles out at the shoe factory. They had a little trouble with the stitching machines at first, but I think that's pretty well in hand now. . . . But you can see for yourself when you visit the plant. Tell me, how are things in the ministry?"

"So-so. Looks like they're going to ease up on the pressure. At least you don't hear people going around [talking] about raising the production quotas. . . ."

"What's happening to my old friend Rashevsky?" Teplov asked.

"Oh, is he an old friend of yours?"—Davidenkov had missed the irony in Teplov's tone.—"Well, I guess you're in luck. The rumor is he's going to be head of the cadres division [trainer of key personnel] of the central committee. . . .

Teplov's head swam. There was no worse place to have an enemy . . . unless it was in the secret police itself, and even they were under attack these days. There was no worse place. But his face and voice showed little of his feelings. The more you revealed about yourself and your weaknesses, the more weapons you put into the hands of your enemies. He rose and shook hands with Davidenkov: "I suppose you're in a hurry to get to the factory. I hope you will drop in here afterward and let me know what you think of how things are going here. I hate to rush you out, but you'll miss the director if you don't hurry. He's due here for a meeting of the executive committee at ten o'clock."

Davidenkov shook hands, and left. Teplov took care of several bits of routine business, but the threat of Rashevsky lay in the back of his mind, and as time for the meeting came closer, he found himself ever less able to concentrate on the problems immediately before him. . . .

At five minutes after ten, Kornetsky and Voronsky [director of the shoe factory] arrived together. . . .

"Sorry to delay things, Antip Trofimovitch," Voronsky said. "But Davidenkov got to my office at twenty to ten, and I couldn't get away sooner. Comrade Kornetsky was with me at the time, and we were both held up. That Davidenkov is too . . . talkative. We couldn't get away from him. He had to give us all the Moscow gossip before he would let us leave." . . .

Kornetsky's flat voice came from between clenched teeth. "Yes, he told us the news about your old friend, Rashevsky. Big things are happening."

. . .For a moment [Teplov] had no feeling. There could be no doubt but that Kornetsky's use of the phrase "old friend" was deliberate irony. . . . [Teplov] glanced up at Kornetsky, but again the second secretary's face was a mask, with the huge pipe sticking out from his mouth. . . .

"Yes," Teplov answered, "Rashevsky is a very excellent man. He will do a very good job. However, I believe we had better get on with the meeting, since Comrade Blonsky will be delayed for a few minutes."

Teplov turned to the chief of the cadres section. He was not a member of the committee and ordinarily would not be attending the meeting, but since there were so many personnel decisions to be made, he was sitting in. Teplov asked him to present his recommendations. He began with the job of the partorg in the shoe factory. He suggested a young foreman who had been a member of the party for about three years. He had a good party record, was an excellent worker, and seemed to be ambitious to move ahead in the party.

Kornetsky objected: "He is a valuable worker. The shoe factory is one of the pilot plants developing the use of synthetic soles for the entire country. It cannot spare the services of so valuable a workman."

Teplov was dumbfounded. What was behind Kornetsky's protest? The job of partorg in the shoe factory was not sufficiently important to take the man off his regular job more than part time. If it were a big factory with hundreds of party members, Kornetsky's objection might make sense. Then there might be a full-time party secretary, and he would have to be pulled off production. What, Teplov wondered, can Kornetsky be up to. Ordinarily he would have given Kornetsky a thorough dressing down for such stupidity. But maybe this time there was more behind his protest than met the eye. Teplov turned his eyes questioningly toward Voronsky, the factory director.

Voronsky was flustered. He stammered and could not answer immediately. Kornetsky cut in and continued: "We must be extremely careful with our personnel decisions. At the present time even such an appointment as this may be reviewed by the cadres division of the central committee. But, of course, I defer to the judgment of Antip Trofimovitch."

Teplov began to perspire. So this is the game, he said to himself; he's going to make enough of a protest to get himself on the record, let me push the appointment through, and then use this as a lever to get me out by going to Rashevsky with it. Teplov fumbled for words, but before any could come to his lips, there was a noise in the hall, the door flew open, and Blonsky, the editor of the paper, bustled in. . . . He was flourishing a sheaf of papers. "Sorry, sorry, gentlemen," he said. "Big news from Moscow. I had to wait around to make sure the stenographer got it off the radio correctly. Here it is, Antip Trofimovitch." He tossed the papers down on Teplov's desk.

Teplov glanced at the dispatch. . . . The men in the room watched him, waiting for some comment.

Teplov read the dispatch aloud:

"A group of enemies of the Soviet state have been arrested for a plot to capture key positions in the Central Committee of the party itself. These scoundrels, supporters of Lavrenty Beria in his antistate activities, had wormed their way into influential posts in the party apparatus. They planned to effect their dominance over the party by securing positions from which they could influence the appointments of personnel. A major step in this plan was to promote to the position of chief in the cadres section. . . ."

Teplov paused and stole a glance at Kornetsky. Kornetsky's pipe was not in its accustomed position. He had it in his hand and was stuffing it energetically with tobacco. Teplov continued:

". . . V. N. Rashevsky. Rashevsky, knowing that he could not escape from Soviet socialist justice, took his own life yesterday evening. All other members of this bandit clique are in custody."

Teplov put the dispatch down. "The rest," he said, "just gives some details. Well"—he paused—"I suppose we had better get on."

He turned back to the chief of the cadres section. "I think we can take that man as partorg. Now, how about the rest of the list?"

27 Characteristics of Top Soviet Leaders (Part One)

The personal characteristics of a leader can give you insight into the role he plays in a political system. A successful leader's characteristics illustrate qualities needed to function effectively in the position he holds. The characteristics of a man who fails to hold a political office often indicate his shortcomings for the role. These shortcomings, in turn, tell you what characteristics he should have had to keep political power.

An American President must have qualities that enable him to win his political party's nomination, to beat his opponent in an election, and to convince enough members of Congress and the voting public to support the policies he advocates. You have studied some of these characteristics in previous readings.

A top Soviet leader needs some of these same qualities, although not in the same order of importance, or to the same degree. Readings 25 and 26 indicated that Teplov was concerned about keeping the personal support of his political superiors. He also worried about how acceptable his policies might be to them. In future readings you will examine the extent to which Soviet political leaders concern themselves with the reactions of other groups.

In 1964 Nikita Khrushchev was removed from two major positions of power in the Soviet Union: Premier of the Soviet government and First Secretary of the Communist Party. As holder of these two offices, Khrushchev spoke for the Soviet Union for ten years. The account which follows was written in October 1964, shortly after his fall from his lofty position in the Soviet Union. It analyzes his character and gives you information about how one becomes a leader in the Soviet political system. It also suggests some of the things a leader must do to stay in power. As you read, think about these questions:

1. What were Khrushchev's most important personal characteristics? List them in your notes.
2. How does the author explain Khrushchev's fall from power? In what ways did his personal characteristics contribute to his downfall?
3. Using your answers to the last two questions as evidence, list the personal characteristics you think might have helped Khrushchev to stay in power.

As Moscow Slept, a New Era Began
NEWSWEEK

Early in this account, Anastas Mikoyan is mentioned as the Soviet President. The Soviet President is the Chairman of the Presidium of the Supreme Soviet. Two important Soviet newspapers are also mentioned in this account. Izvestia *is the official paper of the Soviet government, and* Pravda *is the official paper of the Communist Party. Copyright, Newsweek, Inc., October, 1964.*

A heavy autumn mist hung low over the slick cobblestones on Red Square, shrouding the incandescent ruby stars atop the Kremlin towers. From time to time, a black Chaika government limousine, its rear windows curtained off from public view, sped by on some unknown mission. The brick walls of the sprawling fortress were already hung with the fifteen giant crimson and gold banners of the fifteen Soviet republics, ready for the celebrations welcoming the three-man team of Russian cosmonauts that had circled the earth a few days earlier. And within the Kremlin, the ultramodern Palace of Congresses, Soviet President Anastas Mikoyan and visiting Cuban President Osvaldo Dorticos were listening attentively to a concert of Russian folk music. By all outward appearances, it was a quiet, gloomy, chilly but normal October night in Moscow.

Except for two curious occurrences. The regular evening edition of the government newspaper *Izvestia*, edited by Aleksei Adzhubei, the rambunctious son-in-law of Premier Khrushchev, had not yet appeared, though it generally goes on sale between 5 and 6 P.M. More ominous, for those used to reading such devious portents, was another disappearance: a huge, smiling portrait of the Premier, raised to its usual perch above the Moskva Hotel adjacent to the Kremlin, had been hurriedly hauled down and carted away sometime before 10 P.M. At that moment, as the world soon learned, abruptly, incredibly and awesomely, the era of Nikita Sergeyevich Krushchev came to an end—not with a bang but with the quiet removal of his image in the night.

. . .When Western correspondents rushed to Moscow's central telegraph office on Gorky Street to flash the news abroad, they found that there, too, an eight-foot high portrait of Khrushchev was no longer in view. "When did it happen?" one newsman asked the blond Russian girl at the reception desk. "During the night when we were sleeping," she shrugged. . . . Perhaps most mysterious was the unexpectedly commonplace fashion in which the prodigious power now possessed by the ruler of the Soviet Union was transferred and the apparent indifference of most Muscovites [residents of Moscow] to the change. Over their radios and in their morning newspapers, Russians were told that Khrushchev had "resigned" because of poor health and that his dual responsibilities as party and state leader were now to be divided between his two chief lieutenants, Leonid I. Brezhnev, a party secretary, had taken over as First Secretary of the Communist Party Central Committee, and Aleksei N. Kosygin, a First Deputy Premier, had moved up to Premier. To this transparent palace revolution, the Soviet people reacted with traditional Russian passivity and a studied prudence. . . .

At a newspaper stand near GUM, the giant Soviet department store on Red Square, a collective farmer fresh in from the country, dressed in felt boots and padded jacket, scanned *Pravda's* front-page announcements, then shook his head sadly, and said: "That's right. Khrushchev is probably too old now." A bearded old man standing in line outside Lenin's tomb told *Newsweek's* Moscow bureau chief Robert J. Korengold: "This is not our business. It's their business over in the Kremlin." A waitress, a bookseller, a translator, all improvised various careful variations on the "we'll just have to wait and see" theme. . . .

. . . The world—East and West—reacted with shock and incredulity at the news of Khrushchev's fall. The New York Stock Exchange was hit by the heaviest selling since the assassination of President Kennedy, as fitting a symbol as any of the fact that since November 22, 1963, no event had taken the world with such utter surprise. For the truth was that before last week, outside of a handful of Kremlin politicians, few statesmen, diplomats, or even Sovietologists [experts on the Soviet system] believed that Khrushchev's position as supreme leader of the Soviet Union was in any serious jeopardy.

In hindsight, to be sure, there were abundant explanations and theories. It was known, for example, that for years Khrushchev had carried on a running fight with the Soviet military, seeking to cut army appropriations — particularly for conventional ground forces — in order to invest more heavily in the production of consumer goods [such goods as cars, clothing, television sets, which directly satisfy human wants]. Then, too, Khrushchev's consistent failure to maintain a steady economic growth rate — after an initial burst of energy which ended in 1961 — involved him in disaster after disaster, culminating in the most humiliating of all, the need to go begging for wheat in the capitalist West.

In foreign policy, Khrushchev's "adventurist" installation and subsequent withdrawal of missiles from Cuba in October 1962 must have come as a severe blow to his colleagues in the Kremlin. Nor was his handling of the monumental dispute with Communist China calculated to gain him admirers. No single man was more responsible for the disintegration of the world Communist movement. His dogged determination to bring Communist China to its knees at all costs paradoxically only succeeded in raising Peking to the status of a true ideological rival to Moscow. At the same time, and equally important, it allowed the East European bloc and Communist parties around the world to begin to disengage themselves from the once complete hegemony [authority] of Russia.

Beyond all this, there was Khrushchev's ever volatile personality and peculiar ruling style. The peasant from Kalinovka was always unpredictable — thumping his shoe in the United Nations, threatening to "bury" capitalism in one breath and praising Western restraint in another, always spontaneous, sometimes reckless and heedlessly daring. Time after time, he switched signals at home, decentralizing, then recentralizing control, seeking the one all-purpose nostrum to cure Russia's economic ills — the virgin lands project of 1954 [cultivation of wastelands for grain], the intense corn campaign of 1961, the present all-out emphasis on chemical fertilizers, the possible reintroduction of the profit incentive. In his dealings abroad, especially in the past two years, he seemed more stable; but even here, most notably in his heavy-handed treatment of China and Eastern Europe, Khrushchev had shown himself willfull and impetuous.

And it was Khrushchev's character, if his successors' testimony can be trusted, that in the end proved to be his undoing. The first official word out of Moscow, as the inevitable — and yet still somehow unbelievable — de-Khrushchevization campaign began last week, indirectly accused Khrushchev of the very same charge he had leveled at Joseph Stalin eight years ago: fostering a "cult" of his own personality. A long editorial in *Pravda* amassed a formidable list of personal sins: "harebrained scheming, . . . hasty decisions and actions divorced from reality, bragging and phrasemongering, . . . armchair methods." And to emphasize the point that it was Khrushchev's methods, rather than his goals, that were intolerable, the new government promptly fired his entire kitchen cabinet [personal advisors] and dismissed from his post the one man most closely associated with Khrushchev's mercurial working style—Aleksei Adzhubei. . . .

The full story of Khruschchev's disgrace may not be known for months, or years—or, if the past is any precedent, perhaps forever. But as reports began to seep out of Moscow last week—aided by the Russians themselves, who were anxious to demonstrate that the change of government implied no basic change of policy toward the West—observers were able to piece together at least a partial chronology of events.

Of late, Russian sources emphasized, Khrushchev's rule had grown increasingly autocratic and capricious. Against the better judgment of a number of his colleagues, he insisted on going ahead with his plans for a December meeting of world Communist parties, though his efforts to isolate China seemed doomed to failure and likely to antagonize East European leaders even further. Despite opposition, too, Khrushchev was determined to pay an official visit to West Germany early next year; this alarmed not only conservative Russian leaders such as Foreign Minister Andrei Gromyko but also his East German allies, who feared that a Moscow-Bonn rapprochement [establishment of relations between the states] would be made at their expense.

Domestically as well, Khrushchev was showing little patience with opponents of his economic policies. Three weeks ago he insisted on publishing a controversial speech stressing the need for a sharp increase in consumer goods. He had also toured the provinces, hammering home the same theme to the Communist Party rank and file and to the masses. He even threatened to thrash out the whole vital issue of economic allocations [government spending] at the meeting of the Central Committee which was scheduled for next month.

Confronted with Khrushchev's stubbornness, the story continues, his ten colleagues on the Presidium of the party Central Committee—the Soviet Union's highest decision-making body—feared additional domestic disasters and foreign setbacks were imminent and decided they had to act quickly. Late last month, one of its members told a U.S. diplomat the Presidium ordered Khrushchev to go take a rest at Pitsunda, his villa on the Black Sea—ostensibly out of concern for his health. On October 1, Khrushchev dutifully headed south. Adzhubei joined him; two other close aides were also providentially away from Moscow on independent missions. The way was clear for the plotters, who then proceeded to round up support.

For twelve days Khrushchev rested at Pitsunda, playing badminton, swimming, seeing occasional guests, conducting little official business except for a congratulatory radio conversation with the orbiting cosmonauts. On October 3, he confided, rather obscurely, to a visiting Japanese: "Politicians shouldn't be responsible for the distant future. Stalin should have died earlier." Ten days later, the same subject was still very much on his mind when he told Gaston Palewski, the French Minister of Scientific Research, that "a political leader should never leave power of his own free will."

The latter dictum proved to be prophetic. While talking to Palewski, Khrushchev abruptly cut the interview short, saying he had to return to the capital. That night—Tuesday, October 13—he was back in Moscow and reportedly attended an eight-hour Presidium meeting. Though he was permitted to defend himself verbally, his colleagues presented him with a virtual *fait accompli* [accomplished fact]; they were unanimous in voting him out of his most important job as First Secretary of the party Central Committee.

Once before, in 1957, Khrushchev had been voted out by the Presidium. But he was able to recoup by calling together the full 330-man party Central Committee, in which he had the backing of the majority. On that occasion, what really turned the trick was the help of Marshal Georgi Zhukov, whose planes flew Khrushchev supporters into Moscow for the meeting—and whom Khrushchev later ignominiously fired. But Khrushchev had also been given a major assist by Mikhail Suslov, an old Stalinist hand and ranking party ideologist, who joined the assault in the Central Committee on Khrushchev's opponents, Georgi Malenkov and Vyacheslav Molotov.

This time, however, there was to be no reversal. The day after the Presidium meeting, the full Central Committee did in fact meet in its gray office building near the Kremlin. But instead of heading up the defense, Mikhail Suslov was now leading the attack against Khrushchev, accusing him of everything from nepotism [favoritism to relatives] and agricultural mismanagement to bungled relations with foreign Communist parties. Again, Khrushchev tried briefly to defend himself. But when half a dozen speakers rose to attack him, he finally acknowledged defeat and accepted the majority vote. Later, the pro-Khrushchev minority in the Central Committee agreed to make the decision unanimous. And the following day, with Khrushchev's wily old colleague Anastas Mikoyan presiding, the Presidium of the Supreme Soviet formally removed him as Premier and appointed Kosygin in his place. . . .

28 Characteristics of Top Soviet Leaders (Part Two)

Within the Soviet political system, Khrushchev, the fiery, impulsive son of a miner and former peasant, became both Premier of the Soviet government and First Secretary of the Communist Party. His personal characteristics were important in helping him rise to power. They helped him perform as head of the Soviet government. But they also contributed to his downfall from power.

In the Cheyenne political system, when a man became a leader, he was a leader for life. Most of the decisions he made were made within the guidelines set by the traditions of his society. Little change had to occur. But in modern industrialized societies, change is rapid, and the political systems reflect these changes. Within a few years, or even a few months, political leaders may be called upon to make dozens of decisions for which there are no precedents. The political climate in which these decisions are made may also change.

When Khrushchev rose to power, international political attention focused on the problem of uniting East and West Germany. By the time he fell from power, attention had shifted to the problems of Southeast Asia. As world political forces shift, political leaders must be capable of responding and adjusting. Characteristics that spelled success in one decade may predict failure in the next.

When Khrushchev fell from power, the positions he held were filled by Leonid Brezhnev and Aleksei Kosygin. These men shared some of Khrushchev's characteristics, but in many ways they differed from him and from each other. Reading 28 describes these two men. As you read, think about the following questions:

1. What characteristics do Brezhnev and Kosygin appear to share? Did Khrushchev share these characteristics?
2. Do the characteristics of Brezhnev and Kosygin, as compared with the characteristics of Khrushchev, indicate that changes have taken place in the Soviet political system since the Russian revolution?

Two for One: After K, the Gray-Flannel Men Move In
NEWSWEEK

Copyright, Newsweek, Inc., October, 1964.

Leonid Ilyich Brezhnev, the new First Secretary of the Soviet Communist Party, is a ruggedly handsome, seemingly straightforward man who moves with the gait of an ex-athlete, nowadays just a bit out of shape. Some of Brezhnev's Communist colleagues profess to find him too straightforward. Yugoslav officials who have dealt with him dismiss him as a predictable man lacking in mental resourcefulness. But most Western diplomats who know Brezhnev disagree. He is, they say, a man of intelligence and authority who will make a popular and formidable leader.

Though he owes his career to Khrushchev's favor, Brezhnev is very different from his ex-boss. He is neither as garrulous as Khrushchev nor as impulsive. His outlook, says a Westerner who has known him well for a decade, "is that of an engineer. He analyzes problems like an engineer in a practical and precise way—not so much on speculation but on facts." Unlike Khrushchev again, Brezhnev is, by Soviet standards, a careful dresser with a fondness for Western suits, Italian neckties, and silk shirts. Sometimes he even manicures his nails, and occasionally he uses tonic on his graying, bushy hair.

Tough, ascetic, and businesslike on his frequent trips abroad, Brezhnev at home is a gregarious, fun-loving man who likes to slap people on the back and speak off the cuff for as long as anyone will listen. He is not without social graces; at the annual Kremlin ball on November 7, he is always among the first out on the polished parquet dance floor, and recently when he was called upon to meet Frau Ulbricht, wife of East German Communist boss Walter Ulbricht, at the Moscow airport, he distinguished himself by kissing her hand.

In Communist circles, in fact, Brezhnev has something of a reputation for high living. At diplomatic receptions, he has frequently been observed to take his fair share of the drinks and fall into a mellow mood.

In staider moments, Brezhnev relaxes by hunting, swimming, and watching soccer. He also collects antique watches and is an ardent amateur ornithologist who is believed to have one of the finest collections of live birds in Moscow. The softest spot in his heart, however, belongs to his daughter Galina, who frequently accompanies him on his foreign trips and who would dearly love to become a movie actress —an ambition she is considerably more likely to realize now than she was a week ago.

All this is a far cry from Leonid Brezhnev's impeccably proletarian origins. Born of working-class parents in the small Ukrainian town of Kamenskoe in 1906, he went to work in a steel mill at fifteen, then developed an interest in farming, attending agricultural school, and became an official of the Ural Provincial Land Board.

These, however, were the days of the first five-year plan, the agonizing era when Stalin set out to industrialize Russia at whatever cost, and shrewd Leonid Brezhnev decided to move with the times. Returning to his home town, he took a degree in metallurgical engineering and began to rise slowly in the party hierarchy. In 1938, he was named a member of the Dnepropetrovsk regional committee —where his boss proved to be Nikita Sergeyevich Khrushchev, then head of the Ukrainian Communist Party.

From that moment on, Brezhnev's wagon was firmly hitched to Khrushchev's star. During World War II, Lieutenant General Khrushchev kept Brezhnev at his side as a political commissar [one who attempts to control public opinion]. And after Khrushchev rose to supreme power and decided to launch his much-opposed virgin lands scheme, it was the efficient Brezhnev he chose to administer the program. Thanks to abundant rain, Brezhnev temporarily coaxed bumper crops from the virgin lands, and after two years Khrushchev recalled him to Moscow in triumph and installed him first as a Communist Party secretary and, the next year, as a Presidium member.

In Moscow, too, Brezhnev did Khrushchev good service. In 1957 when the army grew restive over the firing of Marshal Georgi Zhukov, Russia's greatest World War II hero, it was Brezhnev, trading on his popularity in military circles, who managed to pacify the generals. And again he was richly rewarded, first with appointment in 1960 to the titular post of President of the U.S.S.R. and then with promotion to the rank of heir apparent to Khrushchev himself.

On the surface, Brezhnev is an amiable, relaxed man. And in fact, he does represent a new breed of Soviet leader—the "gray-flannel Communist." He is the organization man par excellence, the technocrat bred by the revolution who survived the purges of Stalin's era* to flower under the comparative freedom inaugurated by Khrushchev. But though he is clearly too civilized a man to permit any reversion to Stalinist terror, Leonid Brezhnev was not too civilized to destroy politically the man who raised him from obscurity. In the power struggles that almost certainly rage in the Kremlin, he can be counted on in months to come to maneuver ruthlessly and with consummate mastery of the devious ways of Soviet bureaucracy.

"There are no amusing anecdotes about Aleksei Nikolayevich Kosygin," a Soviet diplomat once remarked. Quiet, shy, and colorless, the U.S.S.R.'s new Premier is the epitome of managerial professionalism—a man who weighs his words, calculates costs, and is far more interested in getting the job done than in political intrigue or flights of imagination. When a U.S. businessman once reminded him of President Kennedy's proposal that the U.S. and Russia cooperate in getting to the moon, Kosygin earnestly replied: "Let's not waste time on that; let's concentrate on getting along together here on earth."

Dour and weatherbeaten in appearance, the sixty-year-old Kosygin has impressed Westerners by his cordiality; but, at bottom, he is a humorless, ascetic man whose only interest, apart from his wife and two children, appears to be his work. All his mature life, he has spent fourteen to sixteen hours a day in his office. His health has held up, his friends say, only because, unlike many Russians, he does not overindulge in food and drink and because he keeps fit with skating and volleyball.

*In the 1930's, Stalin brought many of his political enemies to trial and made them confess to acts of treason and espionage. He then had them executed. These purges were carried out on a mass scale and gave to the Stalinist era its peculiar terrorist character.

The son of a Leningrad lathe operator, Kosygin joined the Red Army at fifteen to fight in the civil war. What formal education he has, he got at the Leningrad Textile Institute. Thanks largely to Stalin's purges, which wiped out a whole generation of Soviet administrator-technicians, he became mayor of Leningrad at thirty-four and in that job caught Stalin's eye.

Thereafter, the dictator promoted him through a series of important economic posts, and even when the so-called "Leningrad gang" was purged in the late 1940's Kosygin was spared—reportedly because his meekness convinced Stalin that he was harmless. And although he was knocked off the party Presidium, his government career hardly faltered. He took on one top ministry after another —finance, light industry, consumer goods, then planning chief. In 1960, Nikita Khrushchev readmitted him to the Presidium and promoted him to First Deputy Premier.

Today, both his admirers and detractors argue that Kosygin's apparent meekness is deceptive. His critics claim that he is the complete product of the Stalin era who knows that under communism only winners survive. (In the 1930's he accepted the exile of his brother without a word of protest.) More friendly commentators insist that he is, as the Muscovites called him, a *solidny chelovek*—a solid man. And his defenders include some surprising people. "I know him very well," said new British Prime Minister Harold Wilson last week. "He's very tough."

Chapter 8

The Process of Becoming a Soviet Leader

STATING THE ISSUE   Political leaders in the United States and the Soviet Union hold varying degrees of power. Local leaders like Wes Uhlman and Teplov had limited political power. National leaders like President Kennedy and Premier Khrushchev had very extensive political power, for they made many of the major policy decisions in their political systems.

Wes Uhlman and John Kennedy both got their political power through general elections. Aleksei Kosygin did not gain his power as Premier of the Soviet Union through general election. It is true that he was elected a *deputy,* or delegate, to the Supreme Soviet in 1938. But all of the offices he held from 1939 on, leading up to the Premiership, were appointive. These positions ranged from People's Commissar to the Textile Industry (1939) to Minister of Finance (1948) to First Deputy Chairman of the Council of Ministers in 1964, after which he replaced Khrushchev as Premier.

Leonid Brezhnev rose to his present position as First Secretary of the Communist Party through a similar series of appointments. The Soviet Union also has four types of important political leaders — elected officials, appointed officeholders, political theorists, and behind-the-scenes manipulators — but the appointed officeholder there has much greater access to political power than his counterpart in the United States has.

In Chapter 6 you analyzed the processes by which political leaders came to power in the United States. Elections, the manipulations of political parties, and public opinion all proved instrumental in moving men into positions where they were empowered to make political decisions.

Elections also take place in the Soviet Union. Your job now becomes one of comparing the election process in the Soviet Union with that of the United States. You will try to determine whether elections play the same role in the Soviet political system that they do in the American system. What officials come to power through elections? How much power do they hold? What groups are instrumental in influencing elections?

29 The Selection of Candidates for Political Office

Wes Uhlman won the right to run for office by winning a primary election. John Kennedy became a candidate for President by convincing the delegates at a national party convention that he should be their choice.

Since, within constitutional limits, each state is authorized to specify its time, place, and manner of elections, the rules governing elections vary. In almost every state, a voter must register before he can vote. Qualifications for registration differ, however. Most states limit requirements to a certain period of residence within that state.

The way in which a candidate gets his name on the ballot also varies. In almost all states, candidates for office, other than that of President and Vice-President, are chosen by direct primary. To get on a primary ballot, candidates must file petitions signed by a required number of voters. Some states also ask their voters to indicate their preference for Presidential candidates, but each party's candidate for President is actually chosen at the party's convention.

After candidates have filed their petitions, primary elections are held. In most states, voters must publicly declare themselves members of a particular political party to vote in its primary. They become members of a particular party simply by stating that they are members when they register to vote, or by voting in the primary of the party of their choice. In a few states, primarily in the South, voters must swear they supported a party's candidate in the last election before they can vote in that party's current primary.

In the primary elections, voters choose the candidates who will represent the contending political parties in elections for office.

Reading 29 describes the process by which candidates for election are chosen in the Soviet Union. The account, written by P. Tumanov, a Communist Party official, was published in *Izvestia*, the official newspaper of the Soviet government. It was translated by the Joint Committee on Slavic Studies at Columbia University.

As you read this account consider the following questions:

1. How are candidates chosen to run for office in the Soviet Union?
2. How does this process differ from the way in which candidates are chosen in the United States?
3. What is the significance of this difference?

Guarantees of Democratism
P. TUMANOV

The following article was published on May 13, 1966.
The election which is referred to early in this article took place in the Soviet

Union early in 1966. Translation from The Current Digest of the Soviet Press, *published weekly at Columbia University by the Joint Committee on Slavic Studies, appointed by the American Council of Learned Societies and the Social Science Research Council. Copyright 1966, the Joint Committee on Slavic Studies. Reprinted by permission.*

In the election campaign for elections to the U.S.S.R. Supreme Soviet, three highly important stages are clearly distinguished.

The first stage is preparatory . . . the creation of election districts . . . and the formation of election commissions. The second stage is the nomination and registration of candidates for deputy. The third stage is the holding of the balloting and the determination of its results.

The first stage of the election campaign has already been completed. A total of 1,517 election districts have been created, including 767 for elections to the Council of the Union and 750 for elections to the Council of Nationalities. Election sectors have been formed. The work of forming election commissions is finished. Voting lists have been drawn up, which are to be offered for general familiarization. In past elections more than 140 million Soviet citizens were included in the voting lists. This number is now growing substantially.

The second stage of the election campaign has also been completed —the nomination and registration of candidates. This is a very important measure. The formation of the Supreme Soviet, the highest agency of state authority in our country, begins with the nomination of candidates for deputy.

Many voters want to know not only the norms for representation in the Supreme Soviet established by the constitution but also how the nomination and registration of candidates takes place. In particular, voters ask why it is that in each election district only one candidate is registered and listed on the election ballot.

The U.S.S.R. constitution and the law on elections to the U.S.S.R. Supreme Soviet not only proclaim the right of the working people to nominate candidates and elect as deputies people in whom they have confidence but also guarantee them this opportunity. The right to nominate candidates for deputy is granted to public organizations, societies, and general meetings of working people. Experience shows that candidates are usually nominated by meetings of working people. This guarantees the broadest participation of Soviet people in the nomination and consideration of candidates. Candidates for consideration are proposed to the meeting by the public organizations of enterprises, collective farms, and institutions after a preliminary study of the views of the collective in question. This procedure makes it possible to submit for consideration by the general meeting those candidacies that actually enjoy the confidence of the majority of the collective.

The participants in the meeting discuss the candidates named by the public organizations from every aspect. Anyone may challenge a candidate and propose another.

In practice it happens that the collective of workers and employees of one enterprise or collective farm, learning that the meeting of another collective has already nominated a candidate for deputy and that this candidate, in the general opinion, is fully worthy of being its choice, does not nominate its own candidate but decides to support the candidate already named by the other collective, although according to the election law every collective has the right to nominate its own candidate as well.

Free and comprehensive discussion and selection of the best of the best are the main principles in nominating candidates for deputy in our country. Thus, Soviet people have the opportunity to choose as deputies to the soviets those who are really the most worthy of their representatives, people capable of fulfilling the will of the voters.

The procedure by which the district election commissions register candidates for deputy is very simple. The meeting, which has proposed a candidate, presents the district election commission with a statement drawn up according to established form. The candidate must submit his written consent to be placed on the ballot in the given election district. District election commissions must register all candidates proposed for deputy no later than thirty days before the elections. Any citizen of the U.S.S.R. who has reached the age of twenty-three may be a candidate.

The U.S.S.R. constitution (Article 125) and the law on elections (Article 70) grant every organization and every citizen of the U.S.S.R. the right to unimpeded agitation for candidates registered with the district election commissions at meetings, in the press, and by other means. All the agencies of the socialist state are called upon to ensure the real and practical implementation of this right. Printing facilities, supplies of paper, the press, meeting space, radio, and television—in our country all this is in the hands of our state, in the hands of our people, which also provided real opportunities for free agitation for candidates.

We see another picture in bourgeois countries. There all the material means of agitation are in the hands of capitalists. Public buildings, newspapers, printing facilities, radio, and television —everything belongs to them or is controlled by them. V. I. Lenin, in his theses and report "On Bourgeois Democracy and the Dictatorship of the Proletariat," said that "freedom of assembly" is an empty phrase if the bourgeoisie has at its disposal all the best public and private buildings and the machinery of ruling authority, which it uses for its own purposes.

In capitalist countries the practice exists of putting up a monetary deposit, which is forfeited if the candidate does not get a fixed number of votes. [Such practice occurs to some degree in England and France, not in the United States.] There the state does not assume the costs of elections. All this makes it difficult and sometimes simply impossible for the working people to nominate their own candidates.

Almost 100 per cent of the voters in our country participate in the elections, and they unanimously cast their votes for candidates proposed by the working people themselves.

During the nomination of candidates for deputy, many meetings name several candidates. Why does only one candidate's name remain on the ballot? Back in 1937 M. I. Kalinin, speaking at a pre-election rally in Leningrad, said: "If, in our country in a number of places, candidates withdraw their names in favor of a single candidate, this is the consequence of their social kinship and the community of their political goals. After thorough discussion, tens and hundreds of thousands of voters have agreed on a single candidate. This is also a hallmark of socialism, a sign that there is no and cannot be any discord that exists with bourgeois society."

There are no antagonistic classes in our country. Workers, peasants, and the intelligentsia have common interests and common goals, which are expressed in the policy of the Communist Party. All the public organizations of working people in our country work under the leadership of the Communist Party, which has no other purpose than to serve the people. This is why all Soviet people have recognized the Communist Party as the guiding force of our society, the directing nucleus of all state and public organizations. This is written in Article 126 of the U.S.S.R. constitution, the basic law of our state. . . .

30 The Role of Soviet Elections

In the United States, once the candidates for political office have been selected to run, voting procedures are fairly uniform throughout the country. Areas do vary in that some use Australian, or paper, ballots, while others use voting machines.

Under the Australian ballot system, the government prints uniform ballots listing the names of all candidates. Near the names of the candidates, space is provided where the voters mark their selections. The ballots are printed on good-quality paper so that once the ballots are marked and folded, the voters' marks cannot be seen by unauthorized eyes.

Voters who use voting machines indicate their choices by depressing the levers positioned by the candidates' names. When they have made their selections, they throw a master lever which registers their votes and clears the machines for the next voter.

Whether Americans use paper ballots or voting machines, they cast their votes in the privacy of closed booths. If they use paper ballots, they deposit their folded ballots in sealed boxes. If they use voting machines, their votes are registered and erased from view.

In the Soviet Union since 1936, everyone over the age of eighteen, regardless of race, creed, social origin, or occupation, has been allowed to vote. At Soviet elections, over 99 per cent of the eligible voters actually do vote. The procedure by which Soviet citizens cast their votes is somewhat different from that practiced in the United States. Reading 30 describes this procedure. As you read, think about the following questions:

1. What positions were being filled by the election described?
2. In what significant ways do elections in the Soviet Union differ from elections in the United States?

Premier Votes in Soviet Election
THEODORE SHABAD

This article appeared in The New York Times *on March 19, 1960. ©1960 by The New York Times Company. Reprinted by permission.*

Moscow, March 18 [1960] — Today was Election Day in the Soviet Union, with a single slate of Communist-approved candidates placed before the voters. Election Day, which began at 6 A.M., was snowy and overcast in Moscow. But the gloom caused by the weather was partly dispelled by red flags and bunting and music blaring from loudspeakers. Premier Khrushchev cast his ballot in midmorning in Precinct 52 of the Frunze Election District, a block from the Kremlin wall. A correspondent for Reuters News Agency was the only foreign newsman invited to be present.

Others who were observed voting in the precinct near the Kremlin were Mikhail. A. Suslov and Dmitri S. Polyansky, two other members of the present Soviet leadership group, and Vyacheslav M. Molotov, a former member now in disgrace.

Other Moscow voters went to the city's 2,600 polling places singly or in family groups. Before voting, the citizens identified themselves to election workers and received printed ballots. They dropped the ballots into waist-high wooden boxes.

Some voters inserted the ballots in the slit with scarcely a glance at the papers. Others stopped briefly and perused the contents. Still others disappeared with their ballots into curtained booths.

The significance of the booths, of which there were four or five in each polling place visited, was explained in varying ways by election officials. Vasily A. Meretskov, chairman of the Electoral Commission of Precinct 3 of the Kuibyshev Election District, said:

"Voters who know their candidates drop the ballots directly into the boxes. Others use the booths to familiarize themselves with the names of the people for whom they are casting votes."

Irina B. Usharenko, who presided over Precinct 9 in the Sverdlov District, said:

"Some use the booths to vote against a candidate by crossing out the name and writing in another. Others use the booths to write messages or greetings to the Communist Party and the government."

Whatever the reasons, the booths were being used by voters without apparent embarassment or furtiveness.

Although the polls were scheduled to stay open until midnight, most of the votes were being cast between 10 A.M. and noon.

By 2 P.M. according to election officials, more than 90 per cent of Muscovites had voted.

The polling places ranged from ceremonious, quiet premises resembling funeral parlors to noisy, businesslike, and crowded rooms.

In Precinct 9, in the Central House of Artistic Workers, a social club, voters cast their ballots in a room that was almost bare except for a large bust of Lenin.

Both the bust and the ballot boxes were guarded by uniformed schoolchildren.

A bustle of activity greeted the visitor at Precinct 130 in the Lomonosov District in southwest Moscow.

Election workers had set up their equipment in the lobby of a dormitory of the Institute of the Petrochemical and Gas Industry. Young men and women arrived from their rooms in informal dress and crowded around the registration desks, wishing one another a "happy holiday."

After the closing of the polls, precinct commissions were scheduled to meet to open the ballot boxes and count the votes.

The results of the election for the Supreme Soviet are expected to be announced in two days.

[*When the results were announced, all of the candidates, who had been uncontested, were, of course, elected. Of the 139,947,206 persons entitled to vote 99.95 per cent actually voted. Of the ballots cast, only 2,000,000 voters registered disapproval or, in any way, spoiled their ballots.*]

31 Interest Groups and the Selection of Leaders

When Wes Uhlman decided to become a political leader, he turned to the public for support. He and his wife rang doorbells and introduced themselves to the voters. Those who were active in his campaign put stickers on their car bumpers to advertise their candidate. Leaflets were printed and distributed.

When John Kennedy decided to run for office, he went on television to convince the people that they should choose him as their President. He traveled coast to coast stopping at key areas to speak to local political leaders and to their constituents.

Throughout political campaigns in the United States, the activities and views of major party candidates are reported and commented on by local and national news analysts. Newspapers, radio, and television are all forces that a candidate must consider as he runs for office. In the American political system, the winner of an election has succeeded in capturing more support from political parties, interest groups, and unorganized voters than his opponent has.

Generalizations concerning how victory is achieved cannot be made easily. Every campaign has different candidates and different issues. Different issues move different people and different groups to political activity. The Parkside referendum stimulated activity on the part of educators and real estate owners. Political analysts still debate the importance of the Roman Catholic vote in electing John Kennedy as President of the United States. While the impact of specific interest groups on particular elections still cannot be predicted or precisely measured, all students of the American political scene agree that interest groups do have a significant impact on the selection of political leaders in the United States.

In the Soviet Union, candidates for political office are selected by the Communist Party. Elections offer the voters no choice of candidates. On the surface it would appear that Soviet politics has no place for interest groups. In recent years, however, political analysts have suggested that interest groups do indeed play a part in the selection of Soviet political leaders. These analysts suggest that since there is but one political party in the Soviet Union, the real struggle for power takes place behind the scenes rather than in front of a television camera. It is their thought that these struggles are not necessarily personal struggles for power but the interaction of groups with different ideas about how the country should be run. The theorists suggest that the *apparatchiki,* or state bureaucrats, might be considered a political interest group ready to support the leader who promises to look out for their interests. Economic managers and technicians, scientists, intellectuals, and nationality groups are all seen as possible forces that operate quietly and behind the scenes to influence the selection of political leaders.

One group that has, in recent years, been somewhat outspoken in its political opinions has been the intellectuals. Prior to Khrushchev's downfall, Soviet intellectuals had spoken out in criticism of some of his policies. You have already seen that a number of forces contributed to his loss of political power, and surely this criticism has to be counted among those forces. Reading 31 is an example of the type of criticism to which Khrushchev was subjected. It is an exchange between the Soviet poet Yevtushenko and Khrushchev.

In December 1962, Khrushchev paid a visit to an art exhibit, "Thirty Years of Moscow Art." The exhibit included a group of modern paintings and sculptures that displeased Khrushchev. In addition to some very uncomplimentary remarks about the works of art, he said, "As long as I am President of the Council of Ministers, we are going to support a genuine art. We aren't going to give a kopek for pictures painted by jackasses."

Following this incident, a series of meetings was called to explain Soviet policy on the arts. On December 17, 1962, this exchange took place at a meeting at which four hundred artists, writers, film workers, and composers were present. As you read, consider the following questions:

1. What were the interests of the group for whom Yevtushenko spoke?
2. Why were they concerned about the stand that Khrushchev had taken?
3. How important do you think such an exchange was in weakening Khrushchev's position as political leader? How important do you think such an exchange might be in the United States?

The Poet and the Commissar
PRISCILLA JOHNSON

This exchange deals with two topics: anti-Semitism and art. The first topic is raised because the Soviet Union has been accused quite frequently of having within it hostility and discrimination toward its approximately three million Jews. The second topic is raised because traditionally Soviet policy has favored realistic art—paintings which are almost like photographs in their presentation. Only fairly recently have Soviet artists begun to show more "modern" works of art. Many of these are far removed from the cameralike reproductions of former times and are abstract rather than realistic. Quoted from "Russian Art & Anti-Semitism," from Commentary, *by permission; copyright © 1963 by the American Jewish Committee.*

YEVTUSHENKO: First of all I want to thank the leaders of the party and the government for kindly making it possible for me to speak here. Permit me to begin my speech with a verse which I wrote not so long ago which I consider very timely. [Recites the last two lines of his poem "Babi Yar," which deals with anti-Semitism.]

COMRADE KHRUSHCHEV: Comrade Yevtushenko, this poem has no place here.

YEVTUSHENKO: Respected Nikita Sergeyevich, I especially selected this poem and with the following purpose in mind. We all know that no one has done more than you in the liquidation of the negative consequences of the Stalin cult of personality, and we are all very grateful to you for this. However, one problem yet remains which is also a negative consequence of those times, but which today has not yet been resolved. This is the problem of anti-Semitism.

COMRADE KHRUSHCHEV: That is not a problem.

YEVTUSHENKO: It is a problem, Nikita Sergeyevich. It cannot be denied, and it cannot be suppressed. It is necessary to come to grips with it time and again. It has a place. I myself was a witness to such things. Moreover, it came from people who occupy official posts, and thus it assumed an official character. We cannot go forward to communism with such a heavy load as Judophobia [fear of Jews]. And here there can be neither silence nor denial. The problem must be resolved and we hope that it will be resolved. The whole progressive world is watching us, and the resolution of this problem will even more greatly enhance the authority of our country. By resolution of the problem I mean the cessation of anti-Semitism—[translation not clear] along with instituting criminal proceedings against the anti-Semites. This positive measure will give many people of Jewish nationality the opportunity to take heart and will lead us to even greater success in all areas of Communist construction.

I would like to say a few words about abstract painting and our artists. I think that our young artists have acted incorrectly in organizing the "underground exhibition" and inviting foreign correspondents to it. [Yevtushenko refers to a semiprivate exhibit of young artists organized on November 26, 1962, at the studio of Eli Belyutin, an art teacher. A number of Western correspondents were invited to view it, as well as some Soviet cultural officials and a couple of hundred of Soviet citizens. This exhibit was closed after a few hours and then summoned to be hung at the Manezh (a public art gallery).] This was done without forethought and deserves widespread censure. We also cannot permit our artists to sell their works abroad. This can only be a blow to our prestige and to our art. But I want to say that we must have great patience with this abstract trend in our art and not rush to suppress it, for the result may be the opposite. I know the artists in question, I know their work, and I can emphasize that side by side with the abstract aspect, they are attracted to the realistic manner of expression. I am convinced that several formalistic tendencies in their work will be straightened out in time.

COMRADE KHRUSHCHEV: The grave straightens out the hump-backed.

YEVTUSHENKO: Nikita Sergeyevich, we have come a long way since the time when only the grave straightened out hump-backs. Really, there are other ways. I think that the best way is to display patience and tact and give examples of how to work at our art. I think that we should permit the existence of various schools in painting and let art, our Soviet art, progress in the arguments among them. Artists, like writers and musicians, are most sensitive to any pressure. Therefore, it is best not to resort to it. Everything will remain in its place.

COMRADE KHRUSHCHEV: I don't believe that you personally like abstract art.

YEVTUSHENKO: Nikita Sergeyevich, there are all kinds of abstractionism. What is important is that it should not be charlatanism [fraudulence]. I submit that a situation can occur when it would not be possible to convey the newest trends of our epoch in the old manner of writing. I must openly admit that I do not like our portrait painting although it is realistic. I very much respect those comrades who are depicted in these portraits, but the portraits themselves seem to me to be ordinary color photographs incapable of stirring the viewer. I cannot permit the idea, Nikolai [sic] Sergeyevich, that you can like the tastelessly drawn picture *N. S. Khrushchev Among the Workers*. The latest period of my life has been closely linked up with Cuba. I like Cuban abstract art very much. It would be good if we would organize an exhibition of Cuban art. Cuban abstract art is very popular among the Cuban people and their leaders. Fidel Castro is attracted to it. Cuban abstract art is helping the Cuban revolution and is walking in step with it. I think that our art, including the abstractionists, is also going in one straight line of fighters for communism. I appeal not for appeasement, but I call for self-restraint, for the deepened study of the theory and practice of modern art, and in the final analysis, a consolidation of the forces of literary and artistic workers for the good of our country.

Thank you for your attention.

32 A Summary Exercise

At the end of Unit One, you made a list of five concepts. Political leadership was among them. Take out your original list, and add to it new analytical questions about political leadership which have occurred to you as you studied this unit. Remember that a good analytical question can be used to analyze any political system at any time or place. For this reason, a question which asks about the Communist Party, for example, would not be very useful because most countries at most times have not had a Communist Party within them.

Bring your list of questions to class tomorrow. You will use these questions as the basis for discussion of political leadership in the United States and in the Soviet Union.

SUGGESTED READINGS

ALSOP, STEWART, "The New President," *Politics, U.S.A.*, pp. 430–37.
Question: How does Stewart Alsop characterize President Johnson?

AMERICAN POLITICAL SCIENCE ASSOCIATIONS, "The Need for More Responsible Political Parties," *Political Institutions*, pp. 129–33.
Question: What is the advantage of having political parties that are responsive to the public?

BAILEY, STEPHEN K., "Leadership in Local Government," *Capitol, Courthouse and City Hall*, pp. 352–56.
Question: What type of individual does the author suggest is needed for local leadership positions? Do you agree?

BAIN, R. NISBET, "The Rule of Peter the Great," *The USSR and Communism*, pp. 66–72.
Question: How was Peter prepared for his role as political leader?

BARGHOORN, FREDERICK C., "Portrait of Joseph Stalin," *The USSR and Communism*, pp. 165–68.
Question: As portrayed by Frederick Barghoorn, what type of man was Joseph Stalin? How might his personal characteristics have influenced the role he played as a political leader?

BELL, JACK, "Fire from the Right," *Democracy in Action*, pp. 186–90.
Question: According to the author, what personal characteristic limited President Eisenhower as a political leader? Do you agree with this evaluation?

BROWN, JOHN MASON, "Dwight D. Eisenhower: A Lesson in Coalitions," *Democracy in Action*, pp. 41–44.
Question: How does the author describe General Eisenhower? Would the characteristics that were important to his success as a general be equally important to his success as a President?

BROWNLOW, LOUIS, "What We Expect the President to Do," *Political Institutions*, pp. 221–24.
Question: According to Louis Brownlow, what are the functions of a President?

BURKE, EDMUND, "The Proper Role of a Legislator," *Political Institutions*, 181–82.
Question: Would Edmund Ross have agreed with the point of view expressed by Edmund Burke? Do you?

CATER, DOUGLAS, "Atlanta, Smart Politics and Good Race Relations," *Democracy in Action*, pp. 405–14.
Question: What leadership characteristics appear to have contributed to Mayor Hartsfield's success in handling a difficult political situation?

"The Contentious Lords of the Senate," *Politics, U.S.A.*, pp. 357–63.
Question: How would you describe the role of Senate majority leader as played by Mike Mansfield? As played by Lyndon Johnson?

COURTLANDT, CANBY, "Who Is this Lincoln?" *Democracy in Action*, pp. 15–20.
Question: Which of Lincoln's characteristics helped him to fulfill his role as President?

CUNEO, ERNEST, "The Quick Change: The Little Flower Blooms," *Democracy in Action*, pp. 401–04.

Question: How did LaGuardia get things done?

DESMOND, THOMAS C., "To Help Governors Govern," *Profile of American Politics*, pp. 325–28.

Question: What does Thomas Desmond mean by his statement that under present conditions "election to a governorship does not earn a man the right to govern, only the right to struggle to govern"?

FORTUNE MAGAZINE, "New Strength in City Hall," *Capitol, Courthouse and City Hall*, pp. 202–06.

Question: In what ways have big cities changed in the past half-century? How have these changes affected the governing of cities?

FISCHER, JOHN, "A Defense of American Political Parties," *Political Institutions*, pp. 127–29.

Question: How do political parties serve the interest groups within the American political system?

GREENFIELD, MEG, "Everett Dirksen's Newest Role," *Politics, U.S.A.*, pp. 363–70.

Question: How would you describe the role of Senate minority leader as played by Everett Dirksen?

HYMAN, SIDNEY, "The Art of the Presidency," *Profiles of American Politics*, pp. 178–81.

Question: What does the author mean by a Buchanan? a Lincoln? a Cleveland? Which of these types do you feel is called for at the present time in the United States?

JOHNSON, GERALD W., "Gaiety in Peril: Laughter Among the Trumpets," *Democracy in Action*, pp. 154–58.

Question: What trait of President Roosevelt's does Gerald Johnson cite as being an important one in gaining the confidence of the American people?

KELLEN, KONRAD, "Filling Stalin's Shoes," *The USSR and Communism*, pp. 168–76.

Question: Who were the contenders for leadership after Stalin's death? How were they eliminated?

KHRUSHCHEV, NIKITA S., "The Secret Speech of Nikita Khrushchev," *The USSR and Communism*, pp. 128–33.

Question: What characteristics of Josef Stalin did Khrushchev condemn? What is the significance of this condemnation?

LONG, CLARENCE D., "Observations of a Freshman in Congress," *Politics, U.S.A.*, pp. 350–57.

Question: According to Representative Long, what are the goals of an effective Congress? How could Congress be helped to reach these goals?

LYFORD, JOSEPH P., "John M. Bailey, the State Chairman," *Democracy in Action*, pp. 44–48.

Question: What is the job of the state chairman? What characteristics appear to have helped John Bailey perform well in this job?

MARTIN, RALPH G. and ED PLAUT, "The Horse Race: Photo Finish," *Democracy in Action,* pp. 75–91.

Question: How does the role played by Kennedy in his bid for the Vice-Presidential candidacy in 1956 differ from that of Nixon as described in Earl Mazo's "Ike and Dick"?

MAZO, EARL, "The Great National Climax: The Conventions, Ike and Dick," *Democracy in Action,* pp. 65–74.

Question: What events influenced the choice of Nixon as a running mate for General Eisenhower?

MILLER, CLEM, "Letters of a Congressman," *Politics, U.S.A.,* pp. 344–50.

Question: What are the tasks of a congressman, as described by Clem Miller?

MILLER, WILLIAM LEE, "Can Government Be Merchandised?", *Politics, U.S.A.,* pp. 297–303.

Question: What devices must a candidate for national office resort to in order to get elected?

MORLAN, ROBERT L., "City Politics: Free Style," *Capitol, Courthouse and City Hall,* pp. 289–92.

Question: How does a political leader come to power in Minneapolis?

NEUBERGER, RICHARD L., "Who Should Pay for Political Campaigns?" *Profile of American Politics,* pp. 128–32.

Question: Why does Senator Neuberger think the government should pay for political campaigns? Do you agree with him?

NEUSTADT, RICHARD E., "The Presidency at Mid-Century," *Political Institutions,* pp. 225–29.

Question: What is a President expected to do?

PATMAN, WRIGHT, "Letter from a Congressman to a Constituent," *Political Institutions,* pp. 182–84.

Question: Up to what point is a congressman responsible to his constituents? Were the demands made by Marshall, Bud, and Kenneth upon Wright Patman reasonable?

ROSSITER, CLINTON, "Democrats or Republicans: What Difference Does It Make," *Politics, U.S.A.,* pp. 254–75.

Question: What is the role of the Democratic and Republican parties in the American political system?

SCHWARTZ, HARRY, "Khrushchev: The Practical Marxist," *Communism in Theory and Practice,* pp. 26–29.

Question: How did Khrushchev's approach to political leadership differ from that of his predecessors?

SHUB, DAVID, "Nicolai Lenin, Organizer of Revolution," *The USSR and Communism,* pp. 121–23.

Question: What were Lenin's personal characteristics? How did these fit him for the role he was to play in the history of the Soviet Union?

STEVENSON, ADLAI E., "The Ordeal of a Presidential Campaign," *Profile of American Politics*, pp. 125–28.
  Question: What did Adlai Stevenson see as the responsibility of political candidates?
TROTSKY, LEON, "Stalin Takes Control," *The USSR and Communism*, pp. 156–59.
  Question: How did Stalin gain control of the Soviet Union in 1927?
TRUMAN, HARRY S., "A Defense of Presidential Powers," *Profile of American Politics*, pp. 181–85.
  Question: How does former President Truman define the job of the President?

Unit Four

Political Decision-Making: The U.S. and the U.S.S.R.

A POLITICAL SYSTEM exists to make decisions. Political institutions are both the ways of handling political decision-making and the organizations in which decisions are made. In Unit Two you studied some of the institutions that the United States and the Soviet Union have developed to make political decisions. The Congress of the United States is an institution for making decisions that become laws. Federalism is an institution for deciding where the responsibility for decision-making will lie. The Communist Party is an important political institution for decision-making in the Soviet Union.

In Unit Three you studied the characteristics of American and Soviet leaders, the men who make the decisions within the political systems. But neither of these two aspects of a political system — institutions or leadership — would need to exist if political decisions did not have to be made.

Political decisions must be made in all branches of government — executive, legislative, and judicial. They must also be made at all levels of government — national, state, and local. Finally, political decisions must be made by all types of government — from those highly democratic to those highly totalitarian. The kinds of problems that a government deals with and the ways it makes its decisions in dealing with them will give you many clues to the nature of the political system of which that government is a part.

In Unit Four you will concentrate on the decision-making process in the United States and the Soviet Union. You will analyze the heart of the political process — the way a government makes up its mind.

Chapter 9

Decision-Making in the American Political System (I

STATING THE ISSUE   Thousands of political decisions are made every day in the United States. Every time that a city council, a state legislature, or the Congress of the United States passes a law, a political decision has been made. Similarly, every order given by a mayor, a governor, the President, or any official appointed by these executives represents a political decision. Every court case, whether it is heard in a local court of common pleas or in the Supreme Court of the United States, also involves a political decision.

Understanding political decision-making in the United States requires background in the ideology, institutions, and patterns of leadership in American society. Democratic ideology implies that no one person and no one political body has complete control over political decisions. Hence, the United States has built a scheme of checks and balances into its political system. Each of the three major branches of government—the executive, legislative, and judicial —has some measure of control over what the other two divisions do. The United States has also developed a system by which leaders are chosen by the people and are responsible to them. In addition, the power to make decisions is divided among three levels of government—local, state, and national. A feature of democracy is that the power to make decisions is widely distributed.

The variety of political decisions which must be made seems endless. The variety of circumstances in which they must be made seems endless, too. For example, in a foreign affairs crisis, political decisions must be made quickly. At other times—such as when a man's life is at stake in a court trial—speed is not nearly so important as is the careful weighing of the evidence. American society has tried to take these different circumstances into account by setting up a variety of decision-making bodies.

Chapter 9 deals with decision-making in American government. What is the decision-making process of a democratic government? How are decisions made in the executive, legislative, and judicial branches of the national government? These are the major questions with which you will be concerned in this chapter.

33 The Decision-Making Process

Decision-making is the core of the political process. If there were no need to make decisions regulating relations among people, there would be no need to have political systems. In a complex society, issues arise daily that require decisions. Government often makes the decision when the problem involves people who are not all in the same private group, like a labor union or a business firm or a fraternal organization.

Political decisions involve the interaction of many forces. Often it is impossible to identify all of the factors that influence a political decision. Frequently the decision-maker himself cannot identify all of these influences, for he may not even be consciously aware of all of them himself. However, if you study decisions carefully, you can find clues to the people and events that influenced the decision-maker to choose one alternative over another.

In October 1962, President John F. Kennedy faced one of the most serious decisions of his career. He was advised that Soviet weapons capable of mounting an offensive against the United States were being installed by Soviet technicians in Cuba. An account of how the President decided what to do about these missiles follows. As you read, keep the following questions in mind:

1. What steps did the President take in reaching his decision? Make a list of these steps in your notebook.
2. Was each step necessary? Why or why not?
3. What does Kennedy's decision-making process tell you about executive decision-making in the American political system?

The Cuban Crisis Decision of October 1962

This account was prepared by the Carnegie Tech Curriculum Development Center.

On Sunday afternoon, October 14, 1962, an American Air Force U–2 reconnaissance plane in flight over San Cristobal, Cuba, took pictures of Soviet medium-range missiles. Immediately, these photographs went to Washington, where they were developed and analyzed by intelligence officers. By 5:30 P.M. Monday, these officers had decided that Soviet weapons of a type designed for offensive warfare existed in Cuba. . . .

After the photographs had been further analyzed to make sure that no mistake had been made, telephone calls began to spread the word to key people in the government. Among these were McGeorge Bundy, the President's Special Advisor on National Security Affairs; Lieutenant General Joseph F. Carroll, Director of the Defense

Intelligence Agency; Roswell L. Gilpatric, Deputy Secretary of Defense; U. Alexis Johnson, Deputy Under Secretary of State for Political Affairs; General Maxwell D. Taylor, Chairman of the Joint Chiefs of Staff; and Roger Hilsman, Director of Intelligence and Research at the State Department. . . .

Throughout the night, a team of intelligence experts worked on a report for the President. Mr. Bundy took this report to him in his bedroom about 8:45 the next morning. Within ten minutes the President had given general directions about how the decision-making was to proceed and who was to be called in.

At 11:45 A.M., this group assembled in the cabinet room; it was composed of the President, the Vice-President, the Secretary of State and two of his assistants, the Secretary of Defense and one of his assistants, the Secretary of the Treasury, the Attorney General, a deputy director of the Central Intelligence Agency, the Chairman of the Joint Chiefs of Staff, and two of the President's special assistants. A few people were to be added to this group later in the week, and many people were to be asked to do special assignments for it. . . .

At the first meeting of the planning group, four alternatives were discussed. The United States might (1) do nothing, (2) bomb the bases, (3) invade Cuba, or (4) blockade the ports. If the United States were to do nothing, the Soviet Union would win a big political and a big military victory, and our allies would cease to believe that we would defend them. If the United States bombed the bases or invaded Cuba, the neutrals and the European allies would cry that our moral position had been tarnished, and the Russians would have an excuse for counteraction elsewhere. If the United States blockaded Cuba, the European allies might be irritated because of interferences with their shipping. The Russians might again have an excuse for retaliation. . . .

There was some feeling that the second, third, and fourth alternatives might worsen the situation, but to make no response at all was the worst course to take. The first alternative was virtually dropped at this meeting. It was also decided that the flights of the U–2's over Cuba were to be continued and that action should await better knowledge of the situation in Cuba. Finally, it was decided that all planning should take place in absolute secrecy in order to be able to take the Russians by surprise, whatever the response would be.

Meanwhile, much staff work had to be done. In order for the planners to make intelligent choices, the Pentagon had to produce long studies of the time, the kinds of equipment, and the number of men needed for each of the alternatives that had been considered. The State Department had to explore chances of support from our allies in Latin America and in Europe.

On Wednesday the planning group met in very informal session at the State Department through most of the day and the night. . . .

During this day there was some support for a "surgical operation," that is, an air strike to bomb the missiles out of Cuba. There was also support for a blockade. Invasion was considered impossible as a first step for these reasons: it would take too long to mount, and surprise would be impossible; the effect on world opinion would be unfavorable; and the Soviet Union might respond with nuclear warfare. Meanwhile, new photographs of more missile sites were adding urgency to the situation.

The President did not attend the planning session on Wednesday, and he was present only at short intervals during the rest of the week. Secretary of State Rusk and Secretary of Defense McNamara also stayed away many times during the week. . . .

On Thursday, thinking among the planners moved away from a possible air strike and toward a blockade. At nine o'clock in the evening, nine members of the group went to the White House to confer with the President. There they found that he also was moving toward the alternative of the blockade. From the White House, Attorney General Robert Kennedy called his assistant, Nicholas deB. Katzenbach, and asked him to begin work on a legal basis for a blockade. Leonard Meeker, Deputy Legal Advisor at the State Department, also began work on the same problem that night.

For some time, Friday had been scheduled for the President as the day for campaigning in the Middle West. It was midterm election time. All of the House and one third of the Senate was up for election. The President and his advisors decided that he should meet these appointments for speeches if only to avoid arousing suspicions that a crisis was brewing in Washington. Thus far, the secret had been maintained rather well.

On Friday, the planners decided that the President should make a speech to the nation on Monday evening to explain the crisis to the American people and to announce the response that he would make to the Russian threat. . . .

During the day there was some renewed interest in an air strike when a paper was read which explained in detail the possible consequences of a blockade. The Attorney General, however, argued against the air strike on moral grounds. He reasoned that an attack on Cuba without warning could easily be compared to the sneak Japanese attack on Pearl Harbor, and would hurt not only our reputation in the world but also our own conscience. [The attack on Pearl Harbor in Hawaii in December 1941 severely damaged the United States Navy and brought the United States into World War II.]

This argument was effective, and by the end of the afternoon, the thinkers had nearly agreed that the choice they would advise the President to make would be the blockade. Nevertheless, they had thorough staff work done on the alternatives so that the President could have everything before him when he made a final decision.

The President returned to Washington at 1:30 P.M. on Saturday, was brought up to date by Mr. Bundy, and read a first draft of a speech for Monday evening prepared overnight by Theodore Sorensen. (Eventually five drafts of this speech were to be written before it was delivered.) Then he ordered the army and the navy to prepare for blockade action subject only to final orders the next day. . . .

. . . At the Pentagon, the main points of a blockade proclamation were finished. At the State Department, the approach to the allies was being prepared. A "master scenario" showing everything that would have to be done before the President's speech, that is, orders to embassies, briefings, and ship movements, was prepared.

About noon on Sunday, the President gave the all-clear signal on the decision for blockade. However, he changed the name to *quarantine* in order to make the action sound less warlike.

Now it was necessary to implement the decision. First it had to be made known. At the State Department, forty-three versions of a letter were drafted before one was sent to Willy Brandt, Mayor of West Berlin. . . . West Berlin might possibly be the scene of some Soviet counteraction in retaliation for our Cuban quarantine. A letter to Premier Khrushchev was drafted to be delivered with a copy of the Monday evening speech. Instructions were drafted to sixty United States embassies abroad, and all embassies and consulates were warned to take precautions against demonstrations and riots.

On Monday morning, twenty congressional leaders of both political parties were called to Washington. At five o'clock in the afternoon, the President and Secretary Rusk informed them of the crisis and the intended action. . . .

At 6:00 P.M., Ambassador Dobrynin of the Soviet Union came by request to Secretary of State Rusk's office, where he was informed of our knowledge of Soviet offensive weapons in Cuba and of our intended reaction to this Soviet move. . . . Ambassador Dobrynin seemed very surprised.

The President began his speech to the nation at 7:00 P.M. He began by presenting evidence of the missile sites, and he blamed the Soviets for violating their most solemn assurances that they were sending only defensive weapons to Cuba. He reported that he had ordered a quarantine for all such offensive weapons headed for Cuba and that ships carrying them would be turned back. The work on the missile sites must cease, he said, or else the United States would have to take "further action."

Forty-five minutes before the speech, forty-six allied ambassadors had been briefed on the situation. After the speech the Latin American allied ambassadors were given further briefing. The ambassadors of the neutral nations were briefed at 8:00 P.M.

On Tuesday, the reaction from the rest of the world began to come in. . . . The European leaders sent letters and telephone calls of support. The Latin American allies, meeting together in the Organization of American States, unanimously passed a resolution, 10 to 0, approving the use of force by the United States to enforce the blockade. The Soviet Union, of course, was not so pleased. But its reaction betrayed an uncertainty that convinced officials in Washington that the Kremlin had been caught off guard and was now playing for time in which to make a decision.

The quarantine was proclaimed Tuesday evening, to go into effect at 10:00 A.M. Wednesday. It prohibited the importation of offensive missiles, their warheads, their electronic equipment, and bomber aircraft. It ordered the navy to stop and to search any vessels suspected of carrying these items and to take them into custody if they insisted upon continuing their journey to Cuba.

As the quarantine went into effect, twenty-five Soviet ships were on their way to Cuba, but there was no contact between Soviet and American ships that day. Then it became known that twelve of the twenty-five ships had turned around. . . .

At about 9:00 P.M. on Friday, a letter arrived from Moscow. In it Premier Khrushchev implied that he would be willing to remove the offensive missiles from Cuba under United Nations supervision if the United States would lift the blockade and would promise that neither it nor any other American nation would invade Cuba. This was a private letter.

The next morning a second letter came. This time a public one, it offered to trade the Soviet bases in Cuba for American bases in Turkey. . . . The planners took a gamble. They drafted a note to Moscow, all but ignoring the Turkey note. It said in effect that if the United States understood Khrushchev's private offer correctly, then it was a deal.

On Sunday, October 28, exactly two weeks after the first missiles were photographed at San Cristobal, Khrushchev returned a letter to Washington stating that he had ordered work on the missile bases stopped and the missiles crated and returned home. . . .

34 Executive Decision-Making

The President plays many roles; in each role he makes important decisions. As chief executive, he administers a government employing two million people. While he delegates much of this job to others, he is the one who must decide on crucial policy-making matters. As chief legislator, he must decide what legislation he will recommend to Congress, and once Congress has passed legislation, he must decide which bills he will approve and which he will reject. As a politician, he decides on the national policies that his political party will follow. As chief of state, he directs foreign-policy decisions.

In all his roles, the President is a decision-maker of great influence and power. Theodore Sorensen, an intimate advisor of President Kennedy, wrote that a "President's entire existence is a continuous process of decision—including decisions not to decide and decisions not to take action—decisions on what to say, whom to see, what to sign, whom to name, and what to do. . . ."

The President, however, is not free to make any decision he wants to in any of these areas. His decision-making powers are limited by the Constitution, by custom, by the resources available to him, by public opinion, and by previous commitments. Read Article II of the Constitution of the United States of America (page 279). It defines the President's responsibilities and the limits set on his decision-making powers.

Reading 34 describes an unsuccessful decision made by President Kennedy. Shortly after becoming President (in 1961), he learned that a plan to invade Cuba had been underway for some time. The plan involved attacking Cuba with a small band of Cuban refugees who had been trained and equipped by the United States. Kennedy had to decide whether the plan should be continued, revised, or abandoned. As you examine Reading 34, answer these questions:

1. What were the steps involved in the decision-making process described in this reading. Make a list of the steps in your notebook. Are they the same as the ones in the case of the Cuban missile crisis?
2. Who besides the President was involved in making this decision?
3. What limits were there on the President's power to make any decision he chose?

The Lessons of the Cuban Disaster
STEWART ALSOP

The events which Mr. Alsop describes in this account took place in 1961, about a year and a half before the Cuban missile crisis described in Reading 33. Copyright 1961 by Stewart Alsop, reprinted from an article in The Saturday Evening Post.

. . . Now consider President Kennedy's position, when, after his election, he found on his desk the top secret plan for a Cuban landing operation evolved under the administration of his predecessor. . . . He finds that all the professionals in this secret business, without a single exception, favor an operation which, if it succeeds, will greatly alter the situation in the Western Hemisphere in favor of the United States. He finds that nearly 3,000 Cubans have been trained by the U.S. government to liberate their homeland from a Communist tyrant.

The President is told, moreover, that time is running out. Soviet jet fighters are arriving in crates in Cuba, Czech-trained Cuban pilots are due there soon, and the Guatemalan government had given notice that the Cuban training camps in Guatemala must soon be evacuated. . . .

On one point all witnesses agree. From the start Kennedy's instinct was to kill the operation. . . . But with all the old pros favoring the operation, it is not hard to understand why Kennedy did not follow his own instincts and cancel the operation.

What he did instead was to turn from the old pros—the CIA [Central Intelligence Agency, the agency that planned the invasion] professionals and the military—to the new boys, the men he himself had brought into the government. He turned especially to Dean Rusk, his Secretary of State, and to his able special assistant, Mc-George Bundy. . . .

What actually happened, when the President weighed the views of the new boys against those of the old pros, was that a peculiar, progressive watering-down process occurred. In the end, as a result of this process, the Cuban plan that was put into operation was different in essential ways from the plan Kennedy had inherited from Eisenhower.

That plan, like the final Kennedy plan, was based on the assumption that there would be widespread anti-Castro uprisings and defections. It was hoped that these would make any overt American military intervention unnecessary . . . to maintain control over the beachhead and prevent destruction of the anti-Castro forces.

From the very first, this was the aspect of the Cuban plan which Kennedy and most of his new boys disliked most heartily. By early March, on Kennedy's insistence, an alternative plan had been devised. This plan called for air strikes against Castro's air force. The air strikes were to be billed for world consumption as the work of defectors from the Castro air force, but were actually to be mounted from Guatemalan bases and piloted by Cuban refugee pilots. These air strikes were to knock out the Castro air force, pathetically small by Pentagon standards, and thus obviate any need for American intervention. The new plan had been [examined] and approved by the Pentagon and the CIA. But the final decisions were taken at two crucial meetings, on April 4 and April 5.

The April 4 meeting, which must have been a rather dramatic occasion, took place in a crowded conference room in the vast new wing of the State Department Building. The President presided, and those present included Rusk, Secretary of Defense Robert McNamara, Secretary of the Treasury Douglas Dillon, Allen Dulles [Director of the CIA], General Lemnitzer [Chairman of the Joint Chiefs of Staff, who had approved the plans], former Assistant Secretary of State Thomas Mann, Assistant Secretary of Defense Paul Netize, South American expert Adolf Berle, Bundy, [Presidential assistant Arthur] Schlesinger, and [Richard M.] Bissell [CIA deputy in charge of the day-by-day planning of the invasion]. And there was a new face, that of Senator William Fulbright of Arkansas, who had been invited in his capacity as Chairman of the Senate Foreign Relations Committee.

Bissell outlined the proposed operation, being careful to point out that he strongly favored the plan and that his arguments ought to be weighed accordingly. Dulles commented briefly on the operation's purposes and chances of success. Then Fulbright spoke, launching into an eloquent and obviously deeply felt denunciation of the whole operation. This sort of oblique attack on another government, however abhorrent that government, was inherently immoral, Fulbright argued. It was not the sort of thing the United States did well, and therefore it was not the sort of thing the United States ought to try to do at all.

Kennedy then went round the table, pointing his finger in a typical gesture, and asking those present in turn whether they favored or opposed the operation. He never did get all the way round the table, and thus Schlesinger and one or two others—doubtless to their relief—were never exposed to the pointing finger. But all those Kennedy asked—including Rusk—gave explicit approval of the scheme, reluctant or enthusiastic as the case might be. . . .

Presumably the President slept on the whole matter that night. The next day he called a smaller meeting in his office, attended by Rusk, McNamara, and Allen Dulles. At this meeting Kennedy made his final decision to go ahead with the operation. But, he ruled, under no circumstances whatever would American forces become involved. Moreover, the Cuban leaders must be categorically warned in advance of this decision. . . .

. . . A few days before the invasion took place, the President said flatly at a press conference . . . that the United States would under no circumstances intervene with force in Cuba. . . .

. . . An essential part of the Kennedy plan was the knocking out of Castro's tiny air force by the sixteen Guatemala-based B-26 bombers supplied to the rebels by the CIA. The first air strike occurred on April 15, two days before the landings. According to plan, it was billed as a spontaneous act by pilots defecting from Castro's air force.

The President had given orders that nothing should be done to "impair the credibility" of [the] American Ambassador to the United Nations, Adlai Stevenson. In other words, Stevenson should not be lied to, and should not be asked to lie. Stevenson was aware of these orders. Thus when he heard from the State Department that the pilots of the April 15 air strike actually were defectors, he believed it. The Cubans, who, of course, knew that the defection story was a phony, charged American aggression and challenged Stevenson to produce one of the B-26 pilots, who had landed in Florida, for questioning by the UN.

Stevenson thereupon arose [in the United Nations], passionately protested American innocence, and even produced a photograph of the plane which had landed in Florida, showing Cuban air force markings (which had, of course, been painted on by the CIA). When he heard, too late, that a State Department underling had been stupid, and that the defection story was in fact a lie, Stevenson was understandably furious and demanded that there should be no more of this sort of thing. He was supported by Rusk in this demand, and the President ordered that the second planned B-26 strike against the Castro air force, which was to take place just before the landings, be called off.

By this time the invasion force was already at sea. The April 15 air strike had knocked out most of the Castro air force. As the invaders were soon tragically to learn, three armed T-33 jet trainers . . . had survived. The comparatively lumbering B-26's of the invading forces were sitting ducks for the jets. The invaders' ammunition ship, the *Rio Escondido*, was sunk, and the invaders soon lost what all the planners had recognized as essential—control of the air over the battlefield. When that was lost, all was lost.

35 Legislative Decision-Making

Congress—the Senate and the House of Representatives—passes the laws that govern the nation. In the process of passing laws, congressmen make many kinds of decisions. A congressman probably makes some of his most important decisions in his work as a member of one or more congressional committees. These committees do the main legislative work of both houses of Congress. Although the number of committees varies from time to time, the House of Representatives has about twenty standing, or permanent, committees, and the Senate has about fifteen. These committees range in influence from the House Appropriations Committee, which controls the money needed to carry out the programs approved by Congress, to the District of Columbia Committee, which governs the city of Washington, D.C.

As committee members, congressmen decide whether or not bills should be brought to Congress for its consideration. They hold hearings on bills at which witnesses testify. They amend, or change, bills after they have studied them. They can recommend bills for congressional consideration, or they can kill bills either by rejecting them outright or by refusing to consider them in committee.

A congressman makes decisions about the legislation proposed by committees. Should he support or oppose these measures? He must decide which bills need amending and whether or not he should participate in debate over one bill or another. He must decide whether to vote for or against a bill, knowing that his vote will be recorded for all to see.

A congressman also makes decisions about the voters who elected him and about the political party of which he is a member. Should he vote for a particular bill that he favors despite the fact that he knows many of his constituents oppose it? Should he vote as his party leaders recommend? These questions require decisions.

Reading 35 traces a series of events that influenced a particular congressional decision. In March 1964, President Lyndon B. Johnson urged Congress to join him in waging a war against poverty. The President delivered a message to Congress appealing for support. In his message he outlined the problem and indicated the kind of legislation that would be needed to eliminate the causes of poverty. After the President delivered his message, Congress prepared to hold hearings. The hearings were to be held by the House Committee on Education and Labor. Reading 35 consists of excerpts from *The New York Times* that give clues to some of the things that influenced the decisions ultimately reached by that committee. As you read, keep the following questions in mind:

1. What steps had to be taken before President Johnson's request for antipoverty legislation could become law? Make a list of these steps in your notebook.
2. What groups or individuals attempted to influence the Committee on Education and Labor while it was holding its hearings? What groups or individuals tried to influence the decisions of the congressmen who were to vote on the proposed law? What methods did they use?
3. What do your answers to the two previous questions tell you about the legislative decision-making process in the United States?

A Bill Becomes a Law
THE NEW YORK TIMES

A Supreme Court decision of 1954 marked the end of lawful segregation in the public schools and the beginning of an active struggle among American Negroes for total equality. Demonstrations were held for equal rights in voting, public accommodations, and housing, and sometimes violence ensued. The movement gathered momentum and drew support from every corner of the country. On August 28, 1963, some 200,000 demonstrators marched peacefully into Washington, D.C., in an effort to convince

*Congress, as well as the rest of the nation, that more legislation was needed
if the Negro was to take his rightful place in a free society.*

*Such leaders as Dr. Martin Luther King, Jr., President of the Southern
Christian Leadership Conference, and Roy Wilkins, Executive Director of the
National Association for the Advancement of Colored People, pressed
for civil rights. Other prominent Negro citizens like Whitney Young, Jr., of
the National Urban League, believed that a strong antipoverty program was
needed if civil rights laws were to have any practical benefit for a majority
of Negroes. The President responded with a speech in which he recommended the passage of legislation to attack the problem of poverty. © 1964
by The New York Times Company. Reprinted by permission.*

March 18, 1964, page 31

[When the special subcommittee of the House Committee on
Education and Labor opened hearings on the antipoverty bill today],
Republicans centered their attacks on three points:
   (1) They said the bill would give too much power to the director
       of the program.
   (2) They said the government already had programs to carry out
       many of the proposals in the bill.
   (3) And they said it was unwise to put all the proposals into a
       single bill covering everything from education to agricul-
       ture. . . .

April 15, 1964, page 20

A civil rights leader told Congress today that the time had come for
America to say to the Negro, "We believe in you."

Pleading for passage of the administration's antipoverty bill,
Whitney M. Young, Jr., Executive Director of the National Urban
League, said, "the demonstrations that we are seeing in the streets
today are the ones fostered by despair and hopelessness."

Responsible Negro leadership, he continued, "desperately needs
some tangible evidence of the intentions of this country to right a
historic wrong."

Without some victories to show to his people, Mr. Young declared,
"the next march on Washington won't be led by the Martin Luther
Kings, the Roy Wilkinses and the Whitney Youngs. This isn't a
threat: It's a reality of a desperate people."

Testifying without notes in a hushed hearing room, Mr. Young told
members of the special House subcommittee that is handling the
antipoverty bill:

"I think Negro citizens, in the face of the . . . historic abuse, have
shown an amazing . . . loyalty. . . . They have said to America, 'I
believe in you.'" . . .

While the nation must have the civil rights legislation, Mr. Young
said, it needs the antipoverty program, too.

"Today, some of those most difficult problems we face are in those cities and states like New York," he said. "We are afraid that we might end up here with a mouthful of civil rights and an empty stomach, living in a hovel." . . .

In asking for passage of the antipoverty legislation, Mr. Young said that it was not enough, but it was a beginning.

Earlier, the committee received a prepared statement from spokesmen for the United States Chamber of Commerce, opposing the antipoverty legislation.

The federal government should not set up new programs, chamber officials contended. Antipoverty programs — such as manpower development and training, vocational education, work relief for those on welfare rolls — are already available to help eliminate poverty, they noted.

The chamber suggested that vocational education be extended to encourage training of adults; that migrant workers be helped to get to places where jobs are available; that the compulsory school age be raised from sixteen to eighteen; that states train youths rejected by Selective Service; and that a voluntary group be created to provide loans for adult education.

Most of the work to alleviate poverty, the chamber argued, should be through state, community, and private action.

April 24, 1964, page 16

The National Association of Manufacturers opposed President Johnson's antipoverty program today and offered instead what it called a "genuine antipoverty program."

Heading the business group's list of proposals was a suggestion for a further tax cut to stimulate business. . . .

April 9, 1964, page 13

Secretary of the Interior Stewart L. Udall said today the government's antipoverty program could help wipe out the $15 billion to $20 billion backlog in "urgently needed" conservation work. . . .

Testifying in support of the administration's program, Mr. Udall disclosed that his department had "fully developed plans to establish and operate" 170 conservation camps in 35 states. . . . He presented figures showing that billions of dollars worth of timber were being lost. The Interior and Agriculture Departments alone, he said, could use 41,000 men annually in the national forests and 45,000 annually in parks [and] refuges. . . .

April 1, 1964 page 17

A nation eager to be heard is having its say about the great American dream of prosperity — and its accompanying nightmare of poverty. . . .

Their letters, scribbled in pencil and neatly typed on business stationary, now number in the tens of thousands. They continue to arrive daily at the already overcrowded offices set aside for the antipoverty planning staff. . .

May 8, 1964, page 15

Republicans took up "squatters' rights" today outside a locked committee room where Democrats noisily thrashed out their differences over antipoverty legislation. . . .

. . . It appeared that there was just one question still to be resolved by the Democrats: whether to amend the legislation to allow federal aid to parochial schools with programs to help wipe out poverty.

The Republican protest came in late afternoon. Sitting primly on folding chairs in the marble corridor, Republican members of the House Education and Labor Committee held up an improvised sign saying: "Open the Door, Adam."

The Republicans contend they have been "locked out" of their own committee by the Democratic chairman, Representative Adam Clayton Powell of Manhattan.

The committee's Democrats have been holding what they term caucuses for nearly a week, seeking to reconcile differences over certain features of the $962.5 million antipoverty bill President Johnson sent to Congress last March.

To protest their exclusion from the sessions, the Republicans took to the House floor yesterday and accused Mr. Johnson and the Democrats of playing partisan politics with the nation's poor. . . .

May 14, 1964, page 1

President Johnson called in Democratic members of the House Rules Committee last night for what was described as a pep talk on his legislative program. Word of the secret meeting leaked out at the Capitol today, but the White House would not acknowledge that it had taken place. . . .

All ten of the committee Democrats were invited, and seven attended. Also present were Representative John W. McCormack of Massachusetts, Speaker of the House, and Carl Albert of Oklahoma, the Majority Leader. . . .

The Rules Committee is of particular concern to the administration because major legislation from all other committees must ordinarily pass through it to reach the floor. . . .

May 13, 1964, page 26

. . . The House Education and Labor Committee . . . began work today on the . . . antipoverty legislation sought by President Johnson.

Seventeen amendments were proposed, and eight were adopted. The only far-reaching change agreed upon was to open the Job Corps, a youth training program, to young women. . . .

May 27, 1964, page 1

The administration's $962.5 million antipoverty program was approved today by the House Education and Labor Committee.

The 19-to-12 vote was on straight party lines. The committee's Republicans opposed the measure.

The committee bill, basically the same as President Johnson's proposal of March 16, will go to the House Rules Committee in about ten days after a formal report is prepared. . . .

June 26, 1964, page 10

The administration still hopes to get clearance of its $962.5 million antipoverty bill from the House Rules Committee next week, but prospects appear dim.

In three days of hearings last week, the committee heard from just two witnesses, Representative Phil M. Landrum, Democrat of Georgia, sponsor of the bill; and Representative Peter H. B. Frelinghuysen, Republican of New Jersey, the most outspoken critic of the measure.

Mr. Landrum said that the Democrats do not intend to offer any more witnesses. The Republicans, however, have said they have a long list of those who wish to be heard in opposition.

Asked today when he plans to resume the hearings, Representative Howard W. Smith, the Virginia Democrat who heads the committee, replied:

"I'm not making any plans at the moment."

July 8, 1964, page 1

President Johnson's $962.5 million program to combat poverty was sent to the Senate floor virtually intact today.

The omnibus Economic Opportunity Act, which is stalled in the House Rules Committee was reported favorably [endorsed] by the Senate Labor Committee. . . .

The administration may now shift its strategy and move to pass the antipoverty bill in the Senate first. . . .

July 24, 1964, page 1

President Johnson's antipoverty bill passed the Senate tonight virtually intact after nearly ten hours of often bitter debate. The vote was 62 to 33.

Ten liberal Republicans joined with 52 Democrats in voting for the bill. Voting against were 11 Democrats, most of them Southerners, and 22 Republicans, including Senator Barry Goldwater, the Republican candidate for President.

If the President had failed to get some southern and Republican support, the bill would have failed.

The bill now goes to the House for action possibly late next week. Its fate there is uncertain, but the relatively wide margin of Senate passage may influence the outcome in the House, for it indicates that a far larger amount of southern support can be counted on than had been expected.

The bill did not escape unscathed. Several rural programs were eliminated. The original $962.5 million price-tag was cut to $947.5. A states' rights amendment giving governors veto power over certain projects in their states was adopted. . . .

July 29, 1964, page 1

. . . Representative Howard W. Smith, chairman of the House Rules Committee, announced the bill's clearance through his committee today by saying:

"This crazy bill was reported out of committee, and I don't care if you say I called it that."

The committee placed a six-hour limit on floor debate, the largest amount of time allotted to any measure since the civil rights bill on which a ten-hour limit was placed. . . .

August 6, 1964, page 36

The American Federation of Labor and Congress of Industrial Organizations called today for additional government measures to stimulate the economy and create more jobs. . . .

The [AFL-CIO] Council, alarmed by reports that the administration's antipoverty bill might be defeated in the House, also telegraphed all House members urging them to vote for the measure. . . .

August 7, 1964, page 4

President Johnson faces one of the most crucial tests of his political career as his antipoverty bill heads for a showdown on the House floor tomorrow.

The outcome, still in doubt tonight, could have a far-reaching effect on the Presidential campaign this fall, for the antipoverty program has already become a highly partisan issue.

While a handful of Democrats and Republicans angrily exchanged words on the House floor today, there was feverish activity behind the scenes as both sides sought to line up votes. . . .

Attention centered on a small number of uncommitted southern Democrats, whose votes could either defeat or pass the bill.

Leaders on both sides met with the uncommitted in back corridors and private offices and party cloakrooms. . . .

The North Carolinians, most of them uncommitted, were called to a top-level conference in Speaker John W. McCormick's office. There, they met with the House leadership, White House aides, and Sargent Shriver, who would direct the antipoverty program.

Uncommitted Southerners from other delegations also were summoned to the Speaker's office from time to time during the day.

President Johnson, too, had gotten into the fray personally yesterday when he posed for pictures with individual members of Congress. Uncommitted members reported later that the President, while posing with them, had asked them to support the bill. . . .

August 8, 1964, page 1

President Johnson's antipoverty bill won an all-but-final victory in the House tonight by a surprisingly wide margin of 38 votes.

However, opponents succeeded in delaying final action until tomorrow. . . .

. . . Opponents delayed a final vote by demanding an engrossed bill—a printed copy of the measure and all its amendments. This demand automatically put off final action until the printers could prepare the document.

The delaying maneuver was viewed as a temporary setback for the administration, which had pressed for quick passage while the votes were in hand.

Many members usually go home for the weekend. It could prove difficult to keep the supporters, particularly those who reluctantly backed the administration, in town for the final vote scheduled for tomorrow. The House will meet at noon. . . .

August 9, 1964, page 1

President Johnson won a major victory today when the House passed his $947.5 million antipoverty bill by a 42-vote margin. . . .

While praising the House action, administration leaders are worried that the bill may run into trouble in the Senate.

The Senate passed the bill 61 to 34 on July 23, but the measure now goes back to the Senate for action on House amendments.

The biggest possible block in the Senate is expected to be a House amendment requiring written disclaimers of belief in or membership in any organization seeking to overthrow the government by force.

Such written disclaimers—violently opposed by liberals and in many academic circles—would be required of all persons . . . receiving federal funds under the antipoverty program.

The disclaimer amendment . . . was adopted by the House last night during a boisterous session in which opponents proposed many changes in the antipoverty bill. . . .

Before passing the bill today, the House defeated a proposal by Representative Peter H. B. Frelinghuysen, Republican of New Jersey, to shelve the administration bill in favor of one of his own. The proposal lost by a vote of 295 to 117.

The Frelinghuysen measure would have set up a $1.5 billion, three-year program, utilizing existing agencies — such as the Labor Department and the Department of Health, Education, and Welfare — already seeking to combat poverty and unemployment. . . .

August 12, 1964, page 1

President Johnson's $947.5 million antipoverty bill smoothly cleared its final congressional hurdle today.

It was a strangely quiet climax to what had been one of the most partisan political battles waged in Congress in recent years.

Only a dozen of the 100 senators were present for the final action, and the galleries were sparsely filled.

House amendments to the Senate-passed bill were approved by voice vote, marking the end of nearly a five-month legislative journey for the measure that President Johnson had called the opening gun in his "total war on poverty."

The bill will reach the President's desk sometime tomorrow, after the usual clerical processing on Capitol Hill.

President Johnson is expected to sign it into law immediately, clearing the way for the program to go into operation and show results before the fall election. . . .

36 Judicial Decision-Making

The most primitive way to resolve conflict is to fight it out. Even savage tribes, however, find this method unsatisfactory in the long run. As conflicts arise, combatants turn to leaders for rulings. These rulings eventually become accepted guides for behavior; they become "the law." As a body of laws grows, a group must develop a way to interpret and apply general laws to specific cases. Eventually, these interpretations and applications become a society's judicial system.

A judicial system can act simply as a mechanism for carrying out political decisions made by the executive or legislative branches of the government. On the other hand, a judicial system can participate in making political decisions. The limitations placed on the power that the courts in a judicial system have to interpret and apply law regulates the extent of the system's influence.

There are two sets of courts in the American judicial system—the federal courts and the state and local courts. Federal courts interpret and apply laws passed by the national government and settle disputes between citizens of different states. State and local courts concern themselves mainly with enforcing the laws of their particular locality.

There are three levels of federal courts. At the first level are the District Courts—eighty-eight of them in the United States. At the next level are the Courts of Appeals; the United States is divided into eleven "circuits," each of which has a federal Court of Appeals. A person who has lost a case in the District Court can appeal to the Circuit Court of Appeals to review the lower court's ruling, provided he has new evidence or thinks that a rule has been broken in the handling of his trial. At the highest level in the federal court system is the United States Supreme Court, the final judge on questions of federal law. It has the last word in disputes over the proper inter-

THE UNITED STATES FEDERAL COURTS

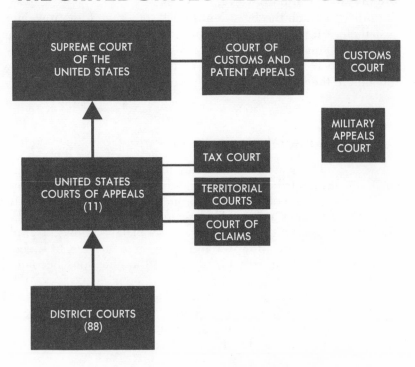

pretation of the Constitution, and it is through this function that the Supreme Court exercises its greatest influence as a political decision-maker.

Although states differ, their court systems generally parallel the organization of the federal courts. At the first level there are trial courts, and at the highest level in each state there is the state supreme court.

The account which follows concerns a Supreme Court decision that became a landmark in American history. In 1954, the United States Supreme Court ruled that laws providing for school segregation violated the Fourteenth Amendment of the Constitution. It ordered schools to desegregate. As you read the details concerning this case, consider the following questions:

1. How did the federal courts become involved in the problem of desegregation?
2. What were some of the reactions to the court's decision on *Brown vs. the Board of Education*? How have these reactions affected the impact of the Court's decision?
3. To what extent did this judicial decision affect political decision-making in the United States?

Ten Years After the Ruling
RELMAN MORIN

Reprinted with the permission of The Macmillan Company from Politics U.S.A. *by Andrew M. Scott and Earle Wallace. Copyright © The Macmillan Company, 1965, 2nd edition.*

On a spring day in 1951, a Negro clergyman in Topeka, Kansas, went to school with his nine-year-old daughter.

Linda Brown attended Monroe Elementary, an all-Negro school, twenty blocks from her home. She rode the school bus most of the way.

But on that day, the Reverend Oliver Brown did not take his daughter to Monroe. Holding Linda's hand, he led her to an all-white school, Sumner Elementary. It was four blocks away. They walked.

In the building, the Reverend Mr. Brown attempted to enroll Linda. The request was denied. He told her to wait in the hallway. Then he took his request to the principal of the school. Again, it was denied.

This brief sequence was soon to go into American legal and social history as part of the monumental decision by the U.S. Supreme Court in the case of *Brown vs. the Board of Education*.

On May 17, 1954 – just ten years ago – the court ruled that segregation in the schools is unconstitutional.

In seventeen states, segregation was mandatory. Kansas, New Mexico, Arizona, and Wyoming had laws that permitted, but did not require, segregated schools. (Wyoming never exercised the laws.)

All this, of course, was beyond the understanding of a nine-year-old girl. Nor did Linda Brown understand why her father had taken her, that day, to the school for white children.

Today she says, "My father felt strongly for the whole Negro race. And he was upset because I had to go so far to school. He felt that we paid taxes the same as anyone else, and there was no reason for this inconvenience."

Linda Brown's father could have told her that much more than "inconvenience" to Negroes was involved in his action.

Segregated public schools had been a fact of American life for a century before Linda Brown's father and other Negro parents challenged it in 1951.

It began in the North, in Boston, in 1848 and lasted there until 1855. In San Francisco in the early 1900's, Oriental children for a time were assigned to a separate school.

The Supreme Court, in its ruling of May 17, 1954, said, "It is apparent that such segregation has long been a nationwide problem, not merely one of sectional concern."

The scene in Sumner Elementary was one Negro's protest about a school.

But what followed, as a result of the Court's decision, was a social upheaval involving much more than the public schools. From this was to come the great drive for full equality for the Negro – voting rights, job opportunities, housing, public accommodations, the right to enter a public park, the right to read a book in a public library.

Every corner of America would feel it. . . .

Five Negro parents in Topeka brought the lawsuits against the board of education. Similar actions had been initiated in South Carolina, Virginia, Delaware, and the District of Columbia.

Eventually, they all came to the Supreme Court and were considered together as *Brown vs. the Board of Education.*

"These cases . . . are premised on different facts and different local conditions," the Court said, "but a common legal question justifies their consideration together in this consolidated opinion."

The question——

"Does segregation of children in public schools solely on the basis of race, even though the physical facilities and other 'tangible' factors may be equal, deprive the children of the minority group of equal educational opportunity? We believe that it does."

And at the heart of the decision——

"We conclude that in the field of public education, the doctrine of separate-but-equal has no place. Separate educational facilities are inherently unequal."

The decision was unanimous.

It was read by Chief Justice Earl Warren of California. The associate justices were Hugo L. Black of Alabama; Harold H. Burton of Massachusetts; Tom C. Clark of Texas; William O. Douglas of Minnesota; Felix Frankfurter, born in Vienna with a New York and Massachusetts background; Robert H. Jackson of New York; Sherman Minton of Indiana; and Stanley F. Reed of Kentucky.

Legal precedent collided with a new concept of public education —and people—in the hearings on *Brown vs. the Board of Education*.

In 1896, the Supreme Court had handed down another historic decision pertaining to segregation, *Plessy vs. Ferguson*. This did not involve schools. It concerned a state law requiring that white and Negro passengers on railways be carried on separate cars. The Court refused to declare the law unconstitutional.

Thus, for fifty-eight years, "separate-but-equal" remained clothed in legality.

John W. Davis, Democratic nominee for President in 1924, was one of the leading advocates for the South in the 1954 hearings. He cited *Plessy* and other precedents, one as late as 1927. Based on these, he argued that segregation in the public schools had been "many times decided to be within the constitutional power of the states to settle without intervention of the federal courts under the federal Constitution."

The Court also referred to *Plessy*. But it said:

"We cannot turn the clock back to 1896. We must consider public education in the light of . . . its present place in American life throughout the nation."

It emphasized that education is vastly more important today than it was in 1896. "In these days," it said, "it is doubtful that any child may reasonably be expected to succeed in life if he is denied the opportunity of an education."

Then came the new concept.

The Topeka parents had not contended that the Negro schools were inferior to the white schools. They acknowledged that the facilities for their children were, in tangible aspects, equal to those provided for white children.

The question was: Did segregation, per se, create difficulties for the Negro child and put him at a disadvantage in acquiring an education?

In *American Rights,* Walter Gellhorn, Betts professor of law at Columbia University, wrote:

> *Brown vs. the Board of Education* brought before the court for the very first time in a clear and unmistakable form the question of whether isolation in education on racial grounds was in itself objectionable. . . .

The high court cited the language in a Kansas case:

> A sense of inferiority affects the motivation of a child to learn. Segregation with the sanction of law, therefore, has a tendency to retard the educational and mental development of Negro children and to deprive them of some of the benefits they would receive in a racially integrated system.

Further, referring to an Oklahoma case, the Court said:

> To separate them [school children] from others of similar age and qualification simply because of their race generates a feeling of inferiority as to their status in the community that may affect their hearts and minds in a way unlikely ever to be undone.

The Court indicated its reliance on a number of psychological and sociological studies, along with others related to the development of public education.

Thus after fifty-eight years of legally segregated schools, the Court overturned *Plessy* and declared *Brown* the law of the land.

"When the social needs demand one settlement rather than another," Justice Benjamin Cardozo had written long before, "there are times when we must bend symmetry, ignore history, and sacrifice custom in the pursuit of other and larger ends."

The next decade would show that it is not easy to "ignore history" and "sacrifice custom."

Words of shock, jubilation, anger, satisfaction, bewilderment, and warning studded the nation's newspapers in the wake of the Supreme Court decision.

To the Negro and his white sympathizers, it seemed to herald the dawn of a bright new day.

To many southern whites, it appeared as the work of a politically motivated court, based on unproven sociological premises rather than the law.

The potential effect on the North, now so apparent, could scarcely be imagined ten years ago.

But the magnitude of the decision and its place in the history of race relations in the United States was apparent to everyone.

The Voice of America poured out the story of the world, hour after hour, in thirty-four languages. It zeroed in especially on Communist countries. Toward Red China alone, it beamed the news in the principal languages, Mandarin and Cantonese, and in several widely spoken dialects.

Editorial comment filled columns in American newspapers.

It is acceptance of a process that has been going on a long time. —*Louisville Courier-Journal.*

This milestone in our history means that we will struggle successfully toward our own ideals. —*Hartford Courant.*

We believe that Negroes have earned the right to be treated as first-rate citizens and earned it the hard way. —*Cleveland Plain Dealer.*

Let no one minimize the task that lies ahead for the southern states. —*Des Moines Register.*

Acceptance of the decision does not mean that we are stopped from taking such honorable and legal steps as may be indicated to avoid difficulties it presents to both races. —*Birmingham Post-Herald.*

This is a time for calm and unhysterical appraisal of the situation. —*Richmond Times-Dispatch.*

It is no time to indulge demagogues on either side or those who are always ready to incite violence and hatred. Our best minds must be put to work, not to destroy, but to arrive at constructive conclusions. —*Atlanta Constitution.*

Some of the later developments were clearly foreshadowed in the immediate reaction.

"The South will not abide by nor obey this legislative decision by a political court," said Senator James Eastland of Mississippi. Violence, foot-dragging, and resistance were soon to come.

The National Association for the Advancement of Colored People (NAACP) announced that it would now broaden its objectives. Its new goals, officers said, would be to eliminate discrimination in housing and jobs. These are two main friction points in the North today.

Thurgood Marshall, Negro lawyer and one of the attorneys who argued the plaintiff's case before the Supreme Court, looked into the future. *The New York Times* asked him how long he thought it would be before segregated schools would be eliminated. He replied it might be "up to five years."

The *Times* reported, further, that Marshall predicted that by 1963 —the 100th anniversary of the Emancipation Proclamation—segregation in all its forms would be gone from America. . . .

Less than two months after the Supreme Court outlawed school segregation, the NAACP chairman in Sulphur Springs, Texas, petitioned the school board to admit Negroes. On July 18, 1954, two shotgun blasts and seven pistol slugs were fired into his empty home.

So quickly did racial violence begin.

In the ten years thereafter, all seventeen southern and border states and the District of Columbia—the areas most affected by the Court ruling—witnessed racial incidents. In some instances they arose from white resistance to desegregation. In others from Negro efforts to speed up the process.

159

The publication *Southern School News* today lists sixty-five major incidents of violence or protests related to the schools in the last ten years. It says they occurred in every school year except the 1961–62 term. . . .

The frustration of the Negro today, ten years after the precedent-setting Supreme Court decision, can be explained in part by a statistic——

Less than 10 per cent of the Negro children of elementary and high school age are attending schools with white students in the southern and border states.

The precise figure is given as 9.3 per cent.

It was announced by *Southern School News* in a special edition marking the tenth anniversary of the Court's ruling. The publication regularly compiles figures on desegregation in the seventeen southern and border states and the District of Columbia.

In the whole region, the publication says, 315,481 Negro students out of a total of 3,408,688 are in school with whites.

The great majority of these—281,731—are in the border states, the paper says. The remainder—34,110—are in the southern states. This represents 1.18 per cent of the total in these states. . . .

The racial picture in the United States today is mottled. It is a montage of sunlight and shadow.

For example, the Justice Department maintains figures on what has taken place in 556 cities in southern and border states. Statistics cover almost nine months.

They show that desegregation of some public facilities, or formation of biracial committees, went from 36 per cent of the 566 cities as of June 21, 1963, to 69 per cent as of February 11, 1964, when the last report was compiled.

In the field of Negro voting rights, the report cites Baker County, Georgia, where the department worked for two years to induce local officials to voluntarily change a long-standing pattern of discrimination.

"Until last spring, no Negro was registered to vote," the report says. "Finally, last April, the county board of registrars permitted Negroes to register. Of 243 Negroes who applied, 200 were found qualified and were registered. They voted in a local election later the same month."

Similarly, the report says, in Macon County, Alabama, Negro registration went from 13 to 42 per cent in 1963; in Bullock County, Alabama, from 1 per cent to 27.6 per cent; and in Washington Parish, Louisiana, from 4.6 per cent to 23.9 per cent.

These are barometers. Whether they are encouraging or discouraging depends on your point of view. . . .

160

Chapter 10

Decision-Making in the American Political System (II)

STATING THE ISSUE The major policy rulings of national decision-makers tend to monopolize the news. Almost everybody wants to know what Congress intends to do about fighting crime or sending men into space. When senators and representatives express their opinions on controversial subjects, their views receive widespread attention. They are reported on radio and television and in the newspapers. A Presidential press conference draws hundreds of reporters and cameramen who examine and analyze everything that is said. Even the Supreme Court is good front-page copy. But most political decisions are made quietly in the process of carrying out laws already passed by Congress. They are made in the offices of officials appointed by the executive branch of government.

As American society has become more complex, Congress has passed thousands of laws which deal with complicated issues. The legislators cannot possibly anticipate all of the circumstances which will arise as each law is put into effect. They cannot write specific instructions for the handling of each case that the law covers. Therefore, to give laws flexibility over the years, legislators deliberately write them in general terms. Then agencies, bureaus, and commissions are established to carry out the provisions of the laws and to apply general laws to specific situations. Administrative officials are appointed to head these agencies, and civil service examinations are given so that lawyers, typists, clerks, and investigators can be selected to staff the bureaus. Through this establishment of agencies, bureaus, and commissions, decision-making powers are given to many appointed officials.

Neither congressmen nor the officials who are appointed to carry out the laws congressmen pass make all of the political decisions in the United States. Political decisions are also made in local areas by local leaders. These decisions are never considered in the halls of

Congress, and they rarely come to the attention of those who live outside a particular geographic area. Yet they are vitally important to many people, and they require the attention of some governmental body. Such problems as eliminating air pollution, fighting fires, and building schools occupy the time of decision-makers at the state and local level. The Constitution leaves to the states and their local units of government power to deal with any matters not specifically assigned to the national government.

Chapter 10 concentrates on the activities of American decision-makers in appointed offices at the national level and in offices of state and local governments. How do appointed officials make political decisions? What is the nature of the political decisions made by state and local governments? What decision-making process do they use? These are the questions you will try to answer in Chapter 10.

37 Decision-Making by Appointed Officials

The executive branch of the federal government includes twelve executive departments, forty-six independent agencies, and over two thousand bureaus, divisions, and branches. All of these groups have the job of carrying out laws passed by Congress.

Ninety per cent of the work of executive bureaus and administrative agencies is done by civil service appointees who are subject to the rules and regulations of the Civil Service Commission. These civil servants have technical proficiencies which range from skills required to do the job of a maintenance man to skills needed to design a nuclear-powered space platform. The heads of these agencies and departments are appointed by the President and approved by the Senate. Their tasks vary from getting the mail delivered to regulating business practices. They are frequently called upon to gather information for the President and to give him advice. Think back to the decisions that President Kennedy made in the Cuban missile crisis and in the invasion of Cuba. To what extent were appointed officials involved in making those decisions?

In Reading 37 you will see a group of appointed officials as they face a decision. The officials are members of an independent federal agency, the Federal Communications Commission, or FCC. This commission was established as a result of a nationwide problem which began in the 1920's when hundreds of radio stations were set up throughout the United States. Broadcasters used the same wavelengths and jammed each other's programs. The situation was chaotic. In 1927, Congress took action by passing the Radio Act. This act set up the Federal Radio Commission, authorized to police the radio industry. In 1934 the Federal Radio Commission was replaced by

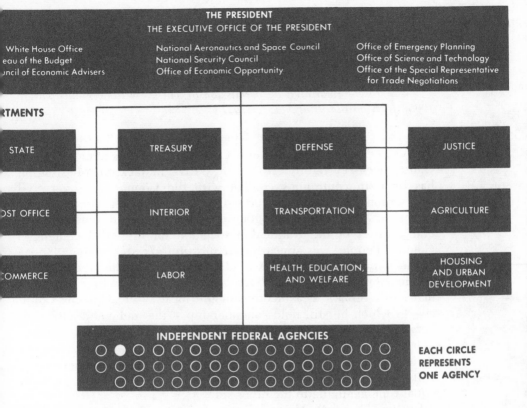

THE PRESIDENT
THE EXECUTIVE OFFICE OF THE PRESIDENT

White House Office	National Aeronautics and Space Council	Office of Emergency Planning
eau of the Budget	National Security Council	Office of Science and Technology
ncil of Economic Advisers	Office of Economic Opportunity	Office of the Special Representative for Trade Negotiations

RTMENTS

STATE · TREASURY · DEFENSE · JUSTICE

OST OFFICE · INTERIOR · TRANSPORTATION · AGRICULTURE

COMMERCE · LABOR · HEALTH, EDUCATION, AND WELFARE · HOUSING AND URBAN DEVELOPMENT

INDEPENDENT FEDERAL AGENCIES

EACH CIRCLE REPRESENTS ONE AGENCY

the Federal Communications Commission which had broader authority to regulate all interstate communication by wire or radio. Before anyone could set up a broadcasting station, he had to get a license from the FCC. He was assigned a wavelength over which he alone could broadcast and therefore would not interfere with the operation of other broadcasters. He had to demonstrate that his station would operate in the public interest. By the time television came along, the place of the Federal Communications Commission was established. From the start, television stations had to be licensed. Reading 37 considers the deliberations of the FCC over the licensing of a television station in Jackson, Mississippi. As you read, think about the following questions:

1. What were the points of disagreement between the station owners and the FCC officials? Was the FCC operating within its authority?
2. What are the dangers involved in giving a government agency the authority to rule on licensing requirements? What are the dangers involved in not giving an agency this authority?
3. Do you think that laws should be written more specifically, to avoid leaving important decisions in the hands of appointed officials? Why or why not?

Discriminating Television
in Jackson, Mississippi
WALTER PINCUS

Reprinted by permission of The New Republic, *copyright 1965, Harrison-Blaine of New Jersey, Inc.*

For most television station owners, license renewal by the Federal Communications Commission comes after a bureaucratic once-over lightly. However, WLBT in Jackson, Mississippi, has been in continuous conflict with the Commission over civil rights programming since 1955. That year, the station deliberately cut off an NBC network program in which Thurgood Marshall, general counsel of the National Association for the Advancement of Colored People, was appearing. It substituted a sign saying, "Sorry, Cable Trouble." The NAACP filed a complaint and included an article from the *Jackson State Times* reporting WLBT's general manager's remark at a meeting of the local White Citizens Council—in which he still holds membership—"that radio and television networks were overloading the circuits with Negro propaganda." Marshall was blanked out, said WLBT, because "it has been our policy not to permit local or network propaganda on either side. . . . If it had been telecast, then we would have been obligated to make equal time available to the other side."

In 1957, the late Medgar Evers, field secretary of the NAACP, unsuccessfully sought equal time on WLBT after telecast of a program in which elected Mississippi officials discussed "The Little Rock Crisis." The program participants, according to Evers, "included only persons of the Caucasian race and expressed only the segregationist point of view and thereby did not express the views of Negroes on this very vital issue." WLBT'S owners answered that "time was not given for a reply [by Evers] to these elected officials as we did not consider the matters presented as being controversial but a report from our duly elected officials to the people of Mississippi." At the same time, the letter stressed a continuation of the policy of not presenting local programs dealing with racial integration. WLBT's 1958 renewal was delayed a year by the FCC and only granted after the Commission directed the station to be certain that "authorized facilities are not used to misinform the viewing public."

During the fall of 1962, at the time James Meredith enrolled at the University of Mississippi, complaints against the station reached such a pitch that the FCC began a special inquiry. The station by letter was asked to submit a report on its telecasts dealing with racial integration along with its efforts to present contrasting views on that issue. Among the programs the station reported it carried were a series of editorials opposing Meredith's entry into "Ole Miss." Their tone was indicated by excerpts from one broadcast of September 12, 1962: "Mississippi is facing the final hour in its official fight to maintain segregation in all its public schools. . . . Mississippi is fortunate in having men at its leadership who have vowed to prevent integration of our schools. . . ."

About the same time, the FCC found, WLBT presented a series of commercial announcements, paid for by the Jackson Citizens' Council, showing "published proof that the Communists are behind the racial agitation now going on in Mississippi."

Responding to the Commission's questions about applicability to these telecasts of the fairness doctrine—which requires a station to make equal time available for the "other side"—WLBT said "it had no understanding that the fairness doctrine extended to commercial spot announcements." As to the anti-Meredith editorials, they did not deal with "racial integration as such" but rather with "states' rights" in a "constitutional crisis."

While the FCC was trying to decide what to do about WLBT— and several other apparently less culpable Mississippi stations—license renewal time again came around. The United Church of Christ, along with two Mississippi civil rights leaders—Aaron Henry, president of the state's NAACP, and Reverend Robert L. T. Smith of the Mississippi Freedom Democratic Party—petitioned the Commission to deny renewal on the grounds that WLBT failed to serve its Negro audience, which made up 45 per cent of the service area's population, and did not give a fair presentation of race relations.

With regard to religious programming, WLBT was found to carry four hours of church services each Sunday. But though half the city's churches are Negro, the only program telecast for them was 15 minutes of spirituals at 6:45 A.M. Negroes were not permitted to participate in live talent programs carried by WLBT—specifically cited was a one-hour dance program called "Teen Tempo" which allegedly invited only whites to appear.

Several individual affidavits attached to the church petition alleged that WLBT at times introduced NBC network news broadcasts on the morning *Today Show* with a local voice saying "What you are about to see is an example of biased, managed, Northern news. Be sure to stay tuned at 7:25 to hear your local newscast."

The WLBT reply was unusually abrupt: ". . . Apparently [the church group] feels that 45 per cent of programming on station WLBT should be Negro programming simply because it is their understanding that this is the population percentage in the area. It appears immaterial to them that many of these Negroes may not desire to appear on the station, may not have anything to say, may not have any talent, and to date have not been able to take advantage of the offers of time made to them by the station." As to civil rights programs: "[The FCC] must . . . allow a station to decide how an inflammatory issue should be handled on a local basis. It is clear that the public interest may require that a certain issue not be presented."

As the Commission took up WLBT's renewal early this year, one further issue—actual ownership of the station—was added to the matters under consideration. Mississippi law prevented the Lamar Life Insurance Company from owning a television outlet, and so Lamar Life Broadcasting was formed to operate WLBT with ownership vested in five of its officers and employees. The insurance company put up the money to build the station and received an option—which has been periodically renewed—to purchase this multimillion dollar property for $10,000.

On April 9, while license renewal was under active FCC consideration, Lamar Life Insurance Company announced to the Commission it wanted to exercise its option and take direct control of WLBT.

Finally, the Commission decided by a 4-to-2 vote on May 20, to renew WLBT's license for one year, rather than the normal three years, during which time the station will be given an opportunity to "demonstrate and carry out its stated willingness to serve fully and fairly the needs and interests of its entire area." Chairman E. William Henry strongly dissented from the one-year approval and was joined by Commissioner Kenneth Cox. The issue was not civil rights, Henry contended, but "the integrity of the public interest standard and the Commission's renewal process."

The fight is far from over. Should Lamar Life Insurance follow through and exercise its option, the Commission will review the transfer of control. In addition, WLBT's next renewal application must be filed in nine months; at that time outside parties will again have a chance to comment.

Meanwhile other stations across the South must take into account the Commission's general feeling that broadcasters "can make a most worthwhile contribution to the resolution of [race relations] problems. . . . That contribution is needed now—and should not be put off for the future." Those are good words, but unless the Commission is willing to use its licensing power to back them up, they are meaningless.

38 Decision-Making at the State Level

States reproduce in miniature the decision-making apparatus of the national government. Governors head the executive branch of government at the state level. They recommend legislation, approve or veto laws passed by the legislature, lead the political parties within their states, and supervise their executive bureaus.

The state legislators pass laws binding on the citizens of the state, and the state judicial system interprets and enforces these laws.

Each state operates under its own constitution. Consequently, states vary considerably in their approach to government. But all states in the American political system are responsible for making political decisions in those areas which the federal Constitution does not specifically assign to the federal government. In Reading 38 Richard Neuberger gives some idea of the variety of decisions a state legislature must make. As you read "I Go to the Legislature," consider the following questions:

1. How would you classify the types of decisions Richard Neuberger describes as characteristic of those made by the Oregon state legislature?
2. How do these decisions differ from decisions made by the national legislature? Does the process of decision-making appear to differ at these two levels?
3. Are decisions made at the state level completely independent of decisions made at the national level? Why or why not?

I Go to the Legislature
RICHARD L. NEUBERGER

The late U.S. Senator Richard L. Neuberger was first elected to office in 1941 and served as a Democrat in the Oregon State House of Representatives until 1942. It was a time when President Franklin D. Roosevelt's New Deal, a government program designed during the 1930's to promote economic recovery, was making way for the high cost of World War II. Richard L. Neuberger was U.S. Senator from Oregon from 1955 to 1960.

. . . In the six months I have been a member of Oregon's house of representatives, I have learned more about the people and government of my native state than in four years at its university. I am taking a practical course in American democracy.

At the desk ahead of mine in the fir-paneled legislative chamber sits a piano salesman. Next to him is a haberdasher. To my right is a prominent lawyer, to my left a longshoreman. . . . We are a cross section of our state, and the issues we decide upon, ranging from the length of passenger trains to the test for pure milk, touch the personal lives of every man, woman, and child in Oregon.

Any American who is free and twenty-one may do what we are doing. Without . . . permission from high authority, he can submit to other Americans like himself his candidacy for public office. . . .

West Point trains our generals, and Annapolis prepares men to command the fleet. For half a century Americans have proposed an academy which would equip citizens for careers in public life. To date, membership in the various legislatures has been most nearly the equivalent of this. . . . A few win their epaulets and go on to Congress or the governorship, and the rest gradually fall by the wayside.

What is membership like in one of these . . . academies that offer embryo American politicians their first practical experience?

I arrived at our new marble Capitol expecting to spend most of my time considering momentous issues — social security, taxes, conservation, civil liberties. Instead we have devoted long hours to the discussion of regulations for the labeling of eggs. We have argued about the alignment of irrigation ditches, the speed of motorboats on mountain lakes, the salaries of justices of the peace, and whether or not barbers and beauty parlor attendants should be high school graduates. . . .

None of these questions concerns large numbers of people. Yet each question concerns a few people vitally. Two or three poultry raisers told me that a change in the labeling of fresh and cold-storage eggs would put them out of business. . . . More mail has come to my desk about what high-powered speedboats would do to the tranquility of Diamond Lake than about a series of antisabotage bills in which the issue of free speech is said to be involved. . . . In common with most other states, Oregon has antiquated county governments. The state must undertake innumerable functions that are purely local. These things may be fundamentally unimportant, but the people directly concerned do not think so. A farmer cares whether his livestock can cross a state highway. Jewelers are deeply interested in regulations governing the sale of watches. Residents quickly protest an unreasonable speed limit in their suburb. After five months in the legislature, I am convinced that the position taken on these many questions of comparatively slight significance has a lasting effect on a political career.

A few doors from me lives a prominent manufacturer. . . . We have argued violently about free trade *vs.* tariffs. . . . the New Deal *vs.* rugged individualism. Not long ago I received a letter from him. Looking at the envelope, I was sure another clash of political philosophies was impending. But he was writing me, as his representative in the legislature, seeking support of a bill to prevent canneries from gutting Oregon's streams of trout and salmon. If I voted for the bill, my neighbor's devotion to fishing would overcome his Republicanism and "all would be forgiven."

Here my neighbor and I were in ready agreement. I not only voted for the bill but made a speech for it. My anti-New Deal neighbor is one of my backers now. . . .

Mail is highly important. Letters unanswered are votes thrown away. This is particularly true of personal mail which some man or woman has taken the bother to write in longhand. . . . A citizen interested enough to write his legislator is also interested enough to tell his neighbors and friends and relatives his estimate of that legislator. This is why, if necessary, we miss a session of the house to turn out the morning mail.

I am a newspaperman. Before going to the legislature, I heard my fellow newspapermen criticizing the trades and compromises customary in lawmaking. I resolved to have no part of this. Through thick and thin I would stick to every original promise. I would not yield an inch. . . .

I am older and wiser now. My newspaper friends were partially correct, but they also were downright wrong. The legislature is as full of compromises as the Pacific Ocean is of water. Yet I wonder how else laws could be enacted at all. There are sixty of us in the house of representatives. Thirty-eight are Republicans; twenty-two are Democrats. Some of us think Franklin D. Roosevelt is the greatest President since Lincoln; others are sure he is the worst. A few blame the world crisis on labor; a few others attribute it to big business. Some of us are from metropolitan Portland; others are from the wilderness of the Cascade Mountains. On a multitude of issues, the area of disagreement among us seems as vast as the universe.

We include many professions and occupations. Among us are lawyers, real estate agents, editors, prune growers, schoolteachers, storekeepers, mechanics, and men who are out of jobs. Each of us has prejudices . . . which others consider unreasonable. . . . Three or four legislators belong to the Associated Farmers, an organization bitterly fighting labor unions. One legislator is president of the largest labor union in the state. A member from Portland is proud of his pet police dogs, which he rents to movie companies. A member from a woodland district forty miles from Portland insists that police dogs have been killing his sheep.

Yet all of us represent the people of Oregon. They have sent us to their Capitol to make laws regarding medicine, agriculture, roads, taxation, schools, and a huge variety of other subjects. We have to agree somewhere, or government will break down. We must give and take. . . .

Democracy is the fusing together of many ideas and that is what we are doing in the legislature. I introduced a measure making it mandatory for public power districts to recognize the collective bargaining rights of their employees. The bill also gave the state commissioner of labor the right to fix the wages paid by those districts. Republicans on the Utilities Committee were against the bill entirely. They wanted to table it. The Democrats sought its passage unchanged. At last both sides gave in. The Republicans agreed to allow the bill to come out on the floor. We agreed to eliminate the provision permitting the labor commissioner to stipulate wages.

Was this a compromise with principle? I do not think so. The wage clause in the bill was important, to be sure. Yet insistence on it would have meant adoption of no bill at all. Now, at least, an act is on the statute books calling for the recognition of collective bargaining. Perhaps a future session of the legislature will add the clause which we had to abandon. After the settlement one of the Republicans wryly said to me, "Well, neither one of us seems very satisfied. I guess that means we've got a pretty fair bill, huh?" . . .

Despite the chasms of disagreement, there is a certain comradery among us which not the most savage debate can stifle or discourage. I think this stems largely from the fact that we in the legislature are not responsible to each other. Our only masters are those unseen folks back home, those folks whose letters are piled on our desks in neat stacks every morning. If Representative French assails my resolution for the construction of the Umatilla reclamation project, I tell myself that irrigation farmers in the 22nd District will take care of him at the next election. He, I am sure, is equally positive that taxpayers in the 5th District will deal sternly with me.

No matter how contentiously we may argue, we invariably refer to each other as "My illustrious colleague from the picturesque Willamette Valley" or as "The worthy and honored member whose historic district occupies so warm a spot in the hearts of our people." We can be locked in desperate verbal combat one hour, and then eat lunch at the same table in the Capitol restaurant the next. Not only are we independent of our fellow members but also of the executive department officials and functionaries who swarm through the state house. We have only to make our peace with God and the voters back home who elect us. . . .

Some men and women despair of democracy because it is cumbersome and works slowly. In the legislature I have had the experience of sitting with men of many faiths, of many political creeds. Somehow, out of all our quarrels and differences, we have produced the laws under which the people of a great Pacific Coast state will live. Some of those laws I voted against; others I supported. Yet only a few of them are very bad, and a lot of them are pretty good. Whatever failure there has been in the legislature has been the failure of the human machine, and that failure, I suppose, occurs in armies, factories, chancellories, and everywhere else on earth. . . .

39 Decision-Making at the Local Level

There are many different ways of making political decisions at the local level. Some cities are governed by an elected mayor and city council who make and carry out the local laws. The mayor, like the President of the United States or the governor of a state, is an elected official. He comes to office, having been selected by those who chose to vote. He is the chief executive of the area he governs. He administers the local laws and, in general, is responsible for keeping a city in operating condition. If public transportation breaks down as the result of a strike, the mayor must step in and use his office to get the city moving again. If riots break out, the mayor must act as mediator to help find solutions that will calm both sides of the dispute and restore peace to his community. The mayor heads an economic and social unit, the city. It is his job to keep it operating as smoothly as possible.

Not all cities have mayors. Operating a city has become so complex that some students of government feel the job can be best handled by men who have been specially trained for the job. Communities that support this view hire professional city managers rather than elect mayors. Still other communities are reluctant to entrust the operation of their community to a single person. In these communities commissions are selected. Members of a commission make joint decisions by which their locality is governed.

No matter what institutional setup a town or a city or a county has chosen to govern itself, the officials must make political decisions. Many choices which come before these officials involve the personal lives of their friends and neighbors, who can often become thoroughly aroused over what seems to be a routine matter to an outsider. Issues which affect citizens personally are the lifeblood of local politics. Local politicians are physically accessible to the voters. The pressures of close personal contact are easily brought to bear on them. The necessity of reaching a compromise in which there is something for everybody is easily seen. As you read "The Case of the Crowded Corral," look for evidence that supports these generalizations. Think about the following questions as you read this account:

1. What were the facts of the case? What was the problem that confronted the city?
2. Who were the parties to this dispute? What role did interest groups play? What influences were exerted on government officials?
3. What were the steps in the decision-making process? Do they parallel the steps in national decision-making which you studied in Chapter 9?
4. To what degree did the final decision represent the interests of the general public? To what degree did the final decision represent the interests of the individual who owned the restaurant involved in the dispute?

The Case of the Crowded Corral

WARNER E. MILLS, JR., AND HARRY R. DAVIS

The events you will read about in this case took place in Beloit, Wisconsin. At the time they occurred, Beloit was a city of about 35,000. Condensed from Small City Government: Seven Cases in Decision-Making *by Warner E. Mills, Jr. and Harry R. Davis. © Copyright 1962 by Random House, Inc. Reprinted by permission.*

. . . In the northeastern section of Beloit is located Michael Bonafede's restaurant, known as The Corral. Just a few years ago The Corral was a mere tavern. Mike, a handsome young Italian with a flair for business, altered the character of the establishment. He modernized it, hired a good chef, and made it one of the fine eating places—and one of the show pieces—of the city. . . .

One of Mike's problems as his business expanded has been parking for his patrons. The Corral is located at the corner of two of the busiest streets on the east side: Park and Henry avenues. . . .

The amount of on-street parking near The Corral has always been limited. . . Only a fraction of the numbers Mike wants to feed each day can find on-street parking within a reasonable distance of his front door. . . .

If parking has been worrisome to Bonafede, the traffic which is related to parking has been bothersome to the city of Beloit. On both its west and north sides The Corral is built very close to the street. It partially obscures vision at the corner and thus makes the intersection hazardous for automobile traffic. Though now heavily traveled, Henry Avenue reflects its origin as a residential street in its narrow width. When cars park on both sides of the street, traffic is virtually throttled down to a single-lane trickle. The corner has been the scene of a number of relatively minor accidents, even though the city has long since made the corner a four-way stop.

Late in 1958 the city made a further effort to solve the traffic problem: it forbade parking on one side of Henry and Park avenues within a block of the Park-Henry corner. This had the intended effect, as accidents were sharply reduced in number. In a special report to the city council, Traffic Lieutenant Donald Lightfoot noted that in the first half of 1958, there had been six accidents at the intersection; in the same period of 1959, only one accident occurred. But however justified from the point of view of public safety, this restricting of parking made Bonafede's problem more acute.

Even before parking on Park and Henry avenues was limited, however, Mike had determined on developing . . . off-street parking. He arrived at this conclusion partly through the urging of members of Beloit's city council with whom he talked over the problem. The city council had consistently urged businessmen afflicted with inadequate parking to develop off-street lots. This suggestion was interpreted by the businessmen as a promise that the council would cooperate in making such projects possible. In the fall of 1958, Mike went so far as to propose to the council that he build a parking lot on Harrison Avenue, which parallels Park one block to the east. But the council members were not enthusiastic, for the lots Bonafede wanted for parking were residential properties bounded by residential streets.

The parking restriction on Park and Henry prompted Mike to look once more for land which might be made into parking areas. After some search and negotiation he was able to obtain options to buy two properties lying parallel to and on Henry but fronting on Harrison Avenue. . . . With the options in hand and a plan developed. Bonafede had only to get the city's permission to use the properties for parking.

Every piece of land in Beloit is zoned, or classified, according to the use or uses deemed proper for it in the light of overall community planning. The properties Bonafede took an option to purchase were zoned for residences. Before turning the properties into parking lots, Bonafede had to persuade the city to change their classification.

Administration of the zoning ordinances is in the hands of the city plan commission and the city council. The city plan commission is an advisory body to the council and is composed of the city manager, the city engineer, one councilman, and four other citizens appointed by the manager and council. The plan commission hears petitions for rezoning in the first instance and makes recommendations on them, but its actions are not binding. The city council receives and acts on the petitions, and at its discretion may accept or reject the recommendations of the plan commission. The council's decisions are final, subject only to appeal to the courts.

To help him present his case to the plan commission and the council, Mike hired attorney George Blakely. . . .

Blakely and Bonafede worked out their strategy. They agreed that Mike petition the plan commission and council to change the classification on the properties from "Residential" to "First Business, Class I." As First Business, Class I, the properties might be used for parking. At a future date they might also be used for other business purposes. . . .

The drafting and presenting of the first petition alerted property owners in the area. Those residing to the north and south along Park and Harrison avenues felt that the construction of the parking lots would render the area more commercial and, hence, less desirable as a place in which to live and raise their children. . . .

Property owners in the vicinity felt, moreover, that the building of the parking areas would reduce the value of their lands and homes. . . .

The petitions to rezone the three properties came before the plan commission and were acted upon at its meeting of May 6. According to procedure, the plan commission held a hearing and listened to arguments on both sides. The members of the commission viewed Mike's request as a petition for "spot zoning." Spot zoning is antithetical to the whole concept of planning. The members of the commission, their minds focused on the development of a rational plan for the city's development, very naturally took a jaundiced view of petitions which tended to destroy this pattern. Furthermore, the one member of the plan commission who also sits on the city council, canny, white-haired Herman Schultz, was opposed to the granting of the petitions. Schultz's position on the council gives his voice a good deal of weight in plan commission decisions.

The plan commission made its recommendation to the city council that the petitions be denied. But it evidenced a certain awareness of and sympathy for Bonafede's parking problem by coupling its recommendation with a suggestion that parking be restored on both Park and Henry avenues near The Corral, except during the daylight hours of very heavy traffic.

The question came before the city council for the first time at its meeting of Monday, May 18, when Bonafede's petitions, together with the recommendation of the plan commission, were laid before it. Almost immediately, several persons who resided near The Corral made known their presence and asked to speak in opposition to the rezoning. Kevin Keenan, the short but formidable lawyer who is president of the council, lectured this group on council procedure. He informed them that the council would not and in law could not act upon petitions until it had held a formal hearing for which due notice had been given to all interested parties. . . . It was duly moved, seconded, and passed that the city clerk be authorized to advertise the petitions, and that the hearing be held on the night of June 1. . . .

In the two-week interval between council meetings, a certain amount of minor skirmishing took place. A law partner of Blakely called on one of the councilmen, a close friend both socially and politically—the two men also attend the same Beloit church—and induced the councilman to drive with him through the area around The Corral. While the attorney did not formally ask for a commitment, and none was given, the general nature of his visit was clear. At the same time, a letter protesting the zoning change and addressed to the council was circulated for signatures among the residents of the area. Over two dozen homeowners put their names on the document. . . .

On June 1 the council met in its regular session. On its agenda was the hearing on the Bonafede petitions. Blakely opened up the subject with a rather long presentation of his client's case. . . .

174

In the ensuing questioning of Blakely by the council . . . he was asked why Bonafede was petitioning for a change of classification from Residential to First Business, Class I, when he could accomplish the same end by asking for a straight "Parking" classification. The council noted that, were the properties to be zoned Parking, they may not be used at a later date for other commercial purposes without further council action; moreover, if they were ever discontinued as parking lots, their classification would automatically revert to Residential. Blakely artfully dodged the question by saying his client had no immediate plans for further commercial use of lots, "though, of course, that might change at any time." He hinted that his client would settle for the Parking classification, but he stated his preference for the broader category.

Burton C. Peters was chief spokesman for the property owners. . . . Peters first called the attention of the council to the fact that over two dozen residents of the area had signed a letter to the council protesting the change. He made sure in his rather slow drawling way that the councilmen understood that these signers were not merely property owners but voters as well.

Peters argued that the granting of the Bonafede request would reduce the value of the properties of those living nearby. . . .

When all who wished to do so had spoken, Council President Keenan worried the problem a bit. Keenan first discussed the alternatives and sternly admonished the audience that the council intended "to be fair with everybody." The he moved that Bonafede's request for the zoning change for 1806 Harrison be tabled and, thus, defeated. . . . On the vote the Keenan motion passed unanimously.

At this point Keenan proposed to Blakely, who was standing nearby, that Bonafede amend his petitions to ask for the Parking classification instead of the First Business, Class I. Blakely bowed to the request and indicated to City Clerk Richard Calland by a nod that he so read the petitions. With this point cleared away, Councilman John Falco moved that the petitions be granted, and the motion was seconded. . . .

On June 15 the episode came to an end. When the council met again, Councilman Falco moved that the ordinance embodying the zoning change as adopted the fortnight before be numbered 423 and that it pass finally. No debate occurred; no protests were heard. The issue was put to a vote and passed. . . .

40 A Summary Exercise

You have now begun to study the process of decision-making in the American political system. At this point, you have only a beginner's knowledge of this complicated process. Thousands of books and articles have been written about it, and political scientists continue to suggest new interpretations of what they see. Still, you have made a beginning. Your knowledge of the American political process will grow and change as you become conscious of the political decisions constantly being made around you and more skilled in interpreting the implications of these decisions.

Suppose you wanted to investigate an instance of political decision-making which you had not studied before. How would you go about it? If your sources of information consisted only of the records of a legislature and its committees and of the reports of their decisions reported in a newspaper, how would you figure out how these decisions were reached?

One good beginning point for such an investigation consists of posing a few analytical questions that will help you know what to look for. Since you began this course, you have been compiling lists of analytical questions related to five political science concepts. For tomorrow, write down in the order of their importance no more than five analytical questions which you think will be useful in analyzing how and why the following political decision was made:

> During the first month of its new session, the state legislature appropriated five million dollars to be used in the state's seven largest cities. The money is to be used to improve the quality of education in sections inhabited primarily by the poor. As reported in your local newspaper, debate was heated, and the vote was close. Support for the bill seemed to come mainly from civil rights groups and from groups which have a history of supporting measures that aim to improve the lot of the underprivileged. Opposition came from representatives of rural areas and groups which have a history of feeling grave concern over the extent to which government expenditures have increased over the years. Of the forty-nine legislators who voted for the bill, thirty-nine were Democrats and ten were Republicans. Of those thirty-seven legislators who were opposed, thirty-five were Republicans and two were Democrats.

Chapter 11

Decision-Making in the Soviet Political System (I)

STATING THE ISSUE How did President Kennedy reach the decision that Cuba had to be quarantined? Was his decision in any way affected by the fact that a political campaign was under way? To what extent was he affected by the support of the Latin-American nations? Did he share his brother's moral objections to an air strike? None of·us can be certain of the answers to these questions. Identifying the extent to which a particular force has influenced a political decision is very difficult no matter how much information is available.

The study of Soviet decision-making is more difficult than the study of American decision-making because there is very little information published about the handling of political affairs. If Khrushchev met with advisors while he planned his responses to the Kennedy decisions on the Cuban crisis, his daily movements were not recorded and published for the world to see. He did not go on television to explain to his people what he was doing and why he was doing it. Soviet leaders prefer not to publicize political controversy. When decisions are made in the Soviet Union, it is difficult to learn who made them or the circumstances under which they were made. For this reason, it is not at all unusual to find reputable scholars disagreeing about how political decisions are made in the Soviet Union.

In Chapter 11 you will begin your study of decision-making in the Soviet Union. You will look at legislators, bureaucrats, and Communist Party officials in the process of making decisions. You will ask many questions. What role does the Supreme Soviet play in the making of laws? What is the role of the Council of Ministers? How influential are appointed government officials? What is the relationship between the Communist Party and the government? These are the questions you will try to answer as you work with Chapter 11.

41 The Supreme Soviet of the U.S.S.R.

Reading 41 attempts to answer the question, "Who makes political decisions in the Soviet Union?" According to the Soviet constitution, "The legislative power of the U.S.S.R. is exercised *exclusively* by the Supreme Soviet of the U.S.S.R." But other sources imply that the Supreme Soviet has no significant role in making Soviet legislative decisions. Chapter 11 attempts to evaluate these conflicting views.

The Supreme Soviet of the U.S.S.R. is an elective body having two chambers, the Council of Union and the Council of Nationalities. Deputies to the Supreme Soviet are elected directly by the people. Meetings are normally held every six to eight months, and generally they last three or four days. The Supreme Soviet selects from its membership a small group called the Presidium. The Presidium acts for the Supreme Soviet when it is not in session.

In addition to the Presidium, the Supreme Soviet also selects from its membership the Council of Ministers, who serve as the heads of the executive departments of the government. As Premier, the Chairman of the Council of Ministers holds the highest office in the Soviet government. When the Supreme Soviet is in session, the Council of Ministers and the Presidium present reports and legislation for its approval. The Supreme Soviet is also called upon to approve the appropriation of funds needed to run the government.

Each of the fifteen union republics joined in the Union of Soviet Socialist Republics has a similar supreme soviet of four hundred to five hundred members, who are elected for four-year terms. Each supreme soviet has its own presidium and its own council of ministers responsible for the day-by-day handling of the affairs of the republic.

The republics, in turn, are subdivided into administrative units called territories, regions, areas, districts, towns, and villages. Each subdivision has its own soviet. At all levels, soviets are not in permanent session; each meets when called together by the executive committee chosen to run its affairs. Local soviets meet quite frequently. They are responsible for administering local affairs and carrying out policy decisions made at the national level.

Deputies to all soviets, from the Supreme Soviet of the U.S.S.R. down to the smallest village soviet, are elected directly by adult citizens in the area to be governed. The deputies to the soviets need not be members of the Communist Party. At the national level, over 75 per cent of the members of the 1962 Supreme Soviet were Communist Party members. At the local level, the percentage of party members varies with the republic. The Russian Republic tends to have an overwhelming percentage of Communist Party members in its soviets. Such republics as the Armenian Republic have had soviets in which fewer than 40 per cent of the delegates were members of the Communist Party.

Reading 41 is a report of the December 1965 meeting of the Supreme Soviet of the U.S.S.R. The details reported here are those considered important by a Soviet observer of the meeting. The account represents a Soviet point of view of legislative decision-making. As you read, look for clues to help you answer these questions:

1. For how many days did the Supreme Soviet meet?
2. What decisions were made during this period of time? Make a list of them in your notebook. How were they made?
3. How large a role did the members of the Supreme Soviet appear to play in shaping the legislation that they passed?

Supreme Soviet Meets;
Podgorny Replaces Mikoyan

IZVESTIA

The excerpts in this reading are translated from communiqués which appeared in Izvestia *on December 8, 9, and 10, 1965. Translation from* The Current Digest of the Soviet Press, *published weekly at Columbia University by the Joint Committee on Slavic Studies, appointed by the American Council of Learned Societies and the Social Science Research Council. Copyright 1965, the Joint Committee on Slavic Studies. Reprinted by permission.*

The seventh session of the Sixth U.S.S.R. Supreme Soviet opened December 7, 1965, at 10 A.M.

A meeting of the Council of the Union . . . was held in the Great Kremlin Palace.

A meeting of the Council of Nationalities . . . was held in the Kremlin Theater. . . .

At the separate meetings of the chambers, the agenda and the order in which the questions were to be considered were approved. . . .

The agenda consists of the following questions:
1. On the state plan for development of the U.S.S.R. national economy in 1966.
2. On the U.S.S.R. state budget for 1966 and on fulfillment of the U.S.S.R. state budget for 1964 [that is, whether or not the 1964 budget went according to plan].
3. On ratification of decrees of the Presidium of the U.S.S.R. Supreme Soviet.

At 11 A.M. a joint meeting of the Council of Nationalities and the Council of the Union . . . opened in the Great Kremlin Palace.

The U.S.S.R. Supreme Soviet heard a report . . . on the state plan for development of the U.S.S.R. national economy in 1966 and a report . . . on the U.S.S.R. state budget for 1966 and on fulfillment of the U.S.S.R. state budget for 1964.

Then the chairman of the meeting announced the inquiries put by a group of deputies to the U.S.S.R. Foreign Minister:

On the course of the Twentieth Session of the UN General Assembly and its review of the Soviet Union's proposals for the nonproliferation of nuclear weapons and noninterference in the internal affairs of states . . . on the second conference of Asian and African countries and the Soviet Union's possible participation in it.

The chairman of the meeting stated that the inquiries would be transmitted to the U.S.S.R. Minister of Foreign Affairs for a reply. . . The second meeting of the Council of Nationalities . . . was held in the Great Kremlin Palace.

At the meeting Deputy M. A. Yasnov, Chairman of the Budget Committee of the Council of Nationalities, delivered the co-report of the Budget Committee on the state plan for development of the U.S.S.R. national economy in 1966, on the U.S.S.R. state budget for 1966, and on fulfillment of the U.S.S.R. state budget for 1964. . . .

The second meeting of the Council of the Union . . . was held in the Kremlin Theater.

At the meeting Deputy I. V. Kapitovov, member of the Budget Committee of the Council of the Union, gave the co-report of the Budget Committee on the state plan for development of the U.S.S.R. national economy in 1966, on the U.S.S.R. state budget for 1966, and on fulfillment of the U.S.S.R. state budget for 1964. . . .

The seventh session of the Sixth U.S.S.R. Supreme Soviet continued on December 8 in the Kremlin. . . .

Discussion of the reports on the state plan for development of the U.S.S.R. national economy in 1966, on the U.S.S.R. state budget for 1966, and on fulfillment of the U.S.S.R. state budget for 1964 continued at the meeting. . . .

The seventh session of the Sixth U.S.S.R. Supreme Soviet continued its work December 9 in the Kremlin. . . .

A second joint meeting of the Council of the Union and the Council of Nationalities, under the chairmanship of Deputy J. V. Peive, Chairman of the Council of Nationalities, was held at 12:40 P.M. in the Great Kremlin Palace.

Comrade N. K. Baibakov, Vice-Chairman of the U.S.S.R. Council of Ministers and Chairman of the U.S.S.R. State Planning Committee, delivered concluding remarks on the report on the state plan for development of the U.S.S.R. national economy in 1966. In a separate vote by chambers, the U.S.S.R. Supreme Soviet unanimously adopted the Law on the State Plan for Development of the U.S.S.R. National Economy in 1966.

The U.S.S.R. Supreme Soviet heard concluding remarks by Comrade V. F. Garbuzov, U.S.S.R. Minister of Finance, on the report on the U.S.S.R. state budget in 1966, and on fulfillment of the U.S.S.R. state budget for 1964. In a separate vote by chambers, the . . . Supreme Soviet unanimously adopted the Law on the U.S.S.R. State Budget for 1966 and approved the report on fulfillment of the U.S.S.R. state budget for 1964.

Deputy M. P. Georgadze, Secretary of the Presidium of the U.S.S.R. Supreme Soviet, gave a report on the decrees submitted by the Presidium of the U.S.S.R. Supreme Soviet for ratification by the U.S.S.R. Supreme Soviet.

The U.S.S.R. Supreme Soviet ratified the decrees of the Presidium of the U.S.S.R. Supreme Soviet and adopted the corresponding laws and resolutions.

The U.S.S.R. Supreme Soviet elected Comrade G. V. Kaznin a member of the U.S.S.R. Supreme Court. . . .

On the representation of Comrade A. N. Kosygin, Chairman of the U.S.S.R. Council of Ministers, the U.S.S.R. Supreme Soviet appointed Comrade P. V. Kovanov Chairman of the U.S.S.R. People's Control Committee.

Because the C.P.S.U. [Communist Party of the Soviet Union] Central Committee has considered it essential that Comrade A. N. Shelepin, as Secretary of the C.P.S.U. Central Committee, should concentrate on the work in the C.P.S.U. Central Committee, the U.S.S.R. Council of Ministers submitted a proposal that he be relieved of the duties of Vice-Chairman of the U.S.S.R. Council of Ministers.

The U.S.S.R. Supreme Soviet adopted a resolution relieving Comrade A. N. Shelepin of the duties of Vice-Chairman of the U.S.S.R. Council of Ministers.

A third joint meeting of the Council of the Union and the Council of Nationalities . . . was held at 4 P.M. in the Great Kremlin Palace.

Deputy A. A. Gromyko, U.S.S.R. Minister of Foreign Affairs, delivered a report in connection with the inquiries of deputies. . . .

On behalf of the foreign affairs committees of the Council of the Union and the Council of Nationalities, Deputy B. Ye. Paton submitted a draft declaration by the U.S.S.R. Supreme Soviet on U.S. aggression in Vietnam.

The U.S.S.R. Supreme Soviet unanimously adopted a resolution on the report of the U.S.S.R. Minister of Foreign Affairs in reply to the deputies' inquiries and also the declaration on U.S. aggression in Vietnam.

The chairman reported that government delegations from the Democratic Republic of Vietnam, the Mongolian People's Republic, and the Republic of Ghana were present at the meeting of the U.S.S.R. Supreme Soviet. The deputies warmly greeted the guests.

Then the floor was given to Deputy A. I. Mikoyan, who asked the U.S.S.R. Supreme Soviet to relieve him of the duties of Chairman of the Presidium of the U.S.S.R. Supreme Soviet.

Comrade L. I. Brezhnev, First Secretary of the C.P.S.U. Central Committee, took note of Comrade A. I. Mikoyan's distinguished services to the Communist Party and the Soviet state and on behalf of the C.P.S.U. Central Committee recommended that Comrade A. I. Mikoyan's request be satisfied; he also moved that he be elected a member of the Presidium of the U.S.S.R. Supreme Soviet.

On behalf of the C.P.S.U. Central Committee, Comrade L. I. Brezhnev moved that Deputy N. V. Podgorny be elected to the post of Chairman of the Presidium of the U.S.S.R. Supreme Soviet.

The U.S.S.R. Supreme Soviet complied with Deputy A. I. Mikoyan's request that he be relieved of the duties of Chairman of the Presidium of the U.S.S.R. Supreme Soviet and elected him a member of the Presidium of the U.S.S.R. Supreme Soviet.

The U.S.S.R. Supreme Soviet elected Deputy N. V. Podgorny Chairman of the Presidium of the U.S.S.R. Supreme Soviet. . . .

Comrade N. V. Podgorny in his statement thanked the U.S.S.R. Supreme Soviet for its high trust.

The seventh session of the U.S.S.R. Supreme Soviet has ended its work.

42 The Council of Ministers of the U.S.S.R.

In Reading 41 you read that the Supreme Soviet of the U.S.S.R. is said to have the exclusive right to make the laws of the Soviet Union. At the December 1965 meeting, however, it was called upon to do little more than approve the legislative decisions recommended by members of the Council of Ministers, of the Presidium of the Supreme Soviet, and of the Communist Party. In Readings 42, 43, and 44, you will continue to examine both legislative and executive decision-making in the Soviet Union in an attempt to identify more clearly the role played by each of these institutions.

Article 56 of the Soviet constitution refers to the Council of Ministers of the U.S.S.R. The Council includes the heads of the ministries and agencies that operate the government departments. In Reading 41 you learned that Comrade N. K. Baibakov, Chairman of the U.S.S.R. State Planning Committee and Vice-Chairman of the U.S.S.R. Council of Ministers, submitted a report on the state plan for development of the national economy which was unanimously adopted as law by the two chambers of the Supreme Soviet. His report was followed by a report from Comrade V. F. Garbuzov, U.S.S.R. Minister of Finance, which was also adopted into law. These Soviet ministers appear to have the authority to formulate and shape laws. The Council of Ministers also has the authority to issue edicts without approval of the Supreme Soviet. In practice, these edicts have the force of law.

The Chairman of the Council of Ministers is sometimes referred to as the "head of government," or the Premier. When Khrushchev was at the peak of his career, he was First Secretary of the Communist Party and a member of the party Presidium. He was also Chairman of the Council of Ministers of the Soviet government. When he was removed from power, he was replaced by Aleksei Kosygin as Chairman of the Council of Ministers. Leonid Brezhnev became First Secretary of the Communist Party.

In general, ministries can be divided into two categories: those that deal with economic matters and those that do not. There are ministries of communications, foreign affairs, agriculture, defense, and many others. These ministries differ from their American coun-

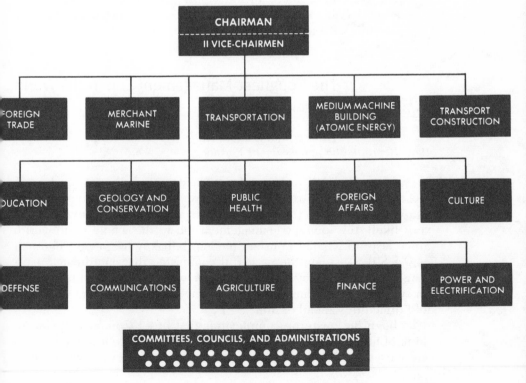

COUNCIL OF MINISTERS OF THE U.S.S.R.

CHAIRMAN

II VICE-CHAIRMEN

FOREIGN TRADE — MERCHANT MARINE — TRANSPORTATION — MEDIUM MACHINE BUILDING (ATOMIC ENERGY) — TRANSPORT CONSTRUCTION

EDUCATION — GEOLOGY AND CONSERVATION — PUBLIC HEALTH — FOREIGN AFFAIRS — CULTURE

DEFENSE — COMMUNICATIONS — AGRICULTURE — FINANCE — POWER AND ELECTRIFICATION

COMMITTEES, COUNCILS, AND ADMINISTRATIONS

terparts in that they run industries as well as regulate them. In the United States the Federal Communications Commission has the authority to regulate the licensing of television stations. But the FCC does not have the authority to operate stations. In the Soviet Union, the Ministry of Communications not only regulates the television industry; it runs it.

Since the Soviet Union takes responsibility for operating and regulating activities that range all the way from making steel to producing an opera, the man who heads the State Planning Committee is very influential. His committee plans how Soviet resources can be used to best advantage. Should more labor be given to the steel industry? How much steel is needed to build a new factory? These are but a few of the decisions that he and his committee must make. As you know from Reading 41, Nikolai Konstantinovich Baibakov has served as the Chairman of Gosplan, the Soviet Union's State Planning Committee. Reading 42 describes his job. As you read, consider the following questions:

1. What kinds of decisions do Comrade Baibakov and the State Planning Committee have the authority to make?
2. To what extent do these decisions affect the average Soviet citizen?
3. Do you think there are any limits on Comrade Baibakov's authority to make decisions on state planning? If so, what do you think these limits might be?

The Toughest Management Job in the World

GILBERT BURCK

This account is excerpted from Fortune *Magazine of July 1, 1966. Reprinted by permission of* Fortune.

High in a dun fourteen-story building at the foot of Moscow's Gorky Street, a genial, round-faced fifty-five-year-old man from Azerbaijan [one of the union republics] holds down what is very likely the toughest management job in the whole wide world. Since last fall Nikolai Konstantinovich Baibakov has been Chairman of U.S.S.R. Gosplan, the powerful committee that coordinates planning for the entire Soviet Union. As one who has been in the business for twenty years, Comrade Baibakov has no illusions about the manifold difficulties ahead of him. . . .

To begin to grasp the complexities that beset Comrade Baibakov, think of him as a kind of staff executive vice-president of the biggest and most diversified . . . monopoly the world has ever seen—one in which all the problems of running a great . . . corporation are raised to the nth power. General Electric, which is commonly regarded as the most diversified of all large corporations, conducts about a hundred identifiably different businesses, makes 500 different products in 242 plants in twenty-one countries, and employs over 300,000 people. The U.S.S.R. turns out perhaps 20,000 different classes of products, each of which may be divided into dozens and even hundreds of categories; it runs more than 3 million different organizations, of which 200,000 are industrial plants or "enterprises" ranging from small to immense, and it directly employs some 93 million people.

What is more, Comrade Baibakov and his colleagues in the vast managerial bureaucracy of the U.S.S.R. Inc. are deep in the toils of an appropriately titanic reorganization. . . . In a colossal way, their problem is similar to that confronting Alfred Sloan and General Motors in the early 1920's. Precisely because the managers at the center have been trying to discharge too much responsibility, they have vitiated [weakened] their control of their far-flung complex. The task ahead of them is to strengthen their control, and to do it by finding ways of giving local managers the kind of autonomy [independence] that will drive them to work harder and more efficiently toward a national goal.

But such an undertaking, which was hard enough for managers of so homogeneous a company as General Motors [that is, a company that has a uniform structure throughout] and in an environment so hospitable to change as the United States, is infinitely more complex for the managers of the U.S.S.R. As practical industrialists looking for efficient ways to get things done, they are constantly inhibited [held back] by a highly impractical as well as hidebound ideology. Nothing is further from their minds, at least right now, than turning over any part of their economy to private ownership, as Yugoslavia and other eastern European countries have done. But they are heeding Lenin's admonition to learn from capitalism. And they are painfully rediscovering fundamental and neutral economic laws that they have unfortunately been taught to identify with the "evils" of capitalism—that true prices reflect scarcity as well as costs, that rent and interest on capital are useful and desirable.

So the "great" Soviet economic reform movement is under way. After more than a decade of remarkably open discussion and contention by practically all the first-rate economic talent in the land, after years of administrative reshufflings, Premier Aleksei Kosygin and some of his colleagues are cautiously experimenting with various changes that may well turn out to be a practical decentralization policy. But everybody who knows anything in the Soviet Union knows the days ahead will be arduous [difficult]. . . .

. . . What makes planning for the Soviet monopoly so much harder than planning for even the most conglomerate Western corporation [that is, a corporation made up of many different elements], what makes decentralization of Soviet management harder still, is the enormous void between what planners and managers know and what they need to know. They are drowning in data; according to almost incredible estimates in two economic journals, more than 10 million Soviet citizens were engaged in collecting and processing data back in 1962, and the number has probably grown a lot since. Yet the planners lack the information they need. . . .

By the estimates of leading Soviet economists themselves, 25 to 50 per cent of the country's potential output has been lost in fulty planning. Right at the birth of a plant or "enterprise," the planners have been handicapped by their inability to evaluate their investment. For each proposed new plant they issue an impressive document called a *proiekt* — an extraordinarily thorough set of builders' instructions, complete not only with cost estimates but with blueprints of everything down to the location of each water tap. The *proiekt* for the Novo Lipetsk steel mill in 1962, for example, contained 70,000 pages in ninety-one volumes. The trouble, as both *Izvestia* and the *Economic Gazette* complained at the time, was that "only one aspect of the project is not considered at all: its economic effectiveness." The reason for this lapse was that nobody really knew whether the resources spent on it could have been put to better use elsewhere. If the Soviet press is to be believed, many such uneconomic plants have been put up. . . .

It was in the year-to-year planning for the 200,000-odd existing industrial enterprises that the whole business was most frustrating. Each enterprise usually began a preliminary draft of its annual operating plan for the next year in April or May. Meantime the planners in Moscow and in division offices were drawing up preliminary schemes and sending out preliminary directives to the enterprises. There ensued much haggling. Then the enterprise prepared a draft operating plan together with a statement of its requirements. More haggling; mutual agreement might not be reached until the end of August and after as many as a hundred changes in the plan.

About this time Gosplan would begin to draw up a colossal balance sheet with all the supplies for the economy entered on one side and the planned uses on the other. After weeks of heroic juggling, animated by a patriotic determination to get the most production out of the available resources, the planners achieved a rough balance between supply and output. But they did not and could not have enough information to balance things perfectly, or even well. The only thing they could be sure of was that plant or enterprise directors were asking for more resources than they needed. So to be on the safe side, the planners allocated fewer resources to nonpriority enterprises than they asked for. Thus, they found themselves consistently misallocating the nation's resources. . . .

Nobody has been more painfully aware of their mistakes and shortcomings than the Soviet authorities themselves. For years, eminent contributors to the country's journals and newspapers have spared neither fervor nor candor [frankness] in their analysis and criticism of their economy's defects and in their prescription for reform. Their essays and reports have provided American Sovietologists with gold mines of information. . . .

43 The President of the Soviet Union

When the Supreme Soviet of the U.S.S.R. is not in session—which is most of the time—its business is carried on by its Presidium. The constitution lists a number of functions that the Presidium is authorized to perform. It can call sessions of the Supreme Soviet and adjourn them. In between sessions, it can act in the name of the Supreme Soviet. It can recommend legislation for approval by the Supreme Soviet, and as you saw in Reading 41, it does. It can present awards and confer honors. It can appoint foreign ministers and assign personnel to foreign embassies. It has been called the collective head of state.

The Presidium has a chairman who speaks in its name. He is sometimes referred to as the head of state, or President of the Soviet Union. In the United States, the office of the President is itself imbued with power. The man who becomes the American President will control national executive decision-making power. In the Soviet Union this is not the case. The Soviet President performs the ceremonial duties of the head of state—conferring honors, welcoming foreign dignitaries, and so on. Men of power, have, on occasion, been Chairmen of the Presidium of the Supreme Soviet, but more often the Chairman, or President, has been an accepted elder statesman.

At the December 1965 session of the Supreme Soviet, Deputy M. P. Georgadze, Secretary of the Presidium of the Supreme Soviet of the U.S.S.R., gave a report on the decrees submitted by the Presidium to the Supreme Soviet for ratification. The Supreme Soviet ratified the decrees and adopted the corresponding laws and resolutions. The report of that session reveals that the Presidium does use its authority to make laws and must have some influence on political decision-making within the Soviet Union. The question is, "How much influence does it have?"

You would assume that as President, the Chairman of the Presidium of the Supreme Soviet of the U.S.S.R., would be its most influential member. Reading 43 evaluates the power held by the President. It describes the appointment of Anastas Mikoyan as President of the Soviet Union in July 1964. As you re. l, consider the following questions:

1. Who nominated Mikoyan for the job of President? What were the circumstances under which he was nominated and elected?
2. Whom did Mikoyan replace?
3. Which job is considered to have more power, that of President or that of deputy secretary in the Communist Party Secretariat? How would you evaluate the power of the Soviet President as compared with that of party Secretary? with that of Chairman of the Council of Ministers?

Mikoyan Is Named Soviet President; Brezhnev Shifted
THE NEW YORK TIMES

The following article appeared in The New York Times *on July 16, 1964. The events described occurred three months before Khrushchev's ouster.* © *1964 by The New York Times Company. Reprinted by permission.*

Anastas I. Mikoyan became President of the Soviet Union today.

Leonid I. Brezhnev, who had held the post since 1960, stepped aside to devote himself full-time to his duties as Premier Khrushchev's deputy in the Secretariat of the Communist Party, the center of power in the Soviet Union.

Western analysts drew the following conclusions from the change.

Mr. Brezhnev's chances of becoming Mr. Khrushchev's eventual successor have been substantially enhanced.

Mr. Khrushchev's own power has been increased, since his two closest associates now occupy the key posts of titular head of state and deputy party leader.

The Presidency—technically the post is the chairmanship of the Presidium of the Supreme Soviet (Parliament)—is likely to gain in importance. Mr. Mikoyan, while assuming the representative functions of his new post, is expected to continue many of his activities in the field of foreign relations.

Some analysts saw today's move as the first step in a long-range program to assure an orderly transition from Mr. Khrushchev to Mr. Brezhnev.

The analysts thought that the change raised a possibility that Mr. Khrushchev, when he felt the time had come, might decide to turn over the party leadership to Mr. Brezhnev and take over the Presidency from Mr. Mikoyan.

Mr. Mikoyan's rise to the Presidency came at a short and surprisingly matter-of-fact meeting of the Supreme Soviet.

Mr. Khrushchev rose and in the name of the Central Committee of the Communist Party nominated Mr. Mikoyan.

He praised Mr. Mikoyan as a "true Leninist" and a "fighter for peace" and declared that the Central Committee felt he deserved to be entrusted with the post.

Premier Khrushchev thanked Mr. Brezhnev for the "fruitful work" he had done and wished Mr. Mikoyan good luck in the position.

Mr. Khrushchev prefaced these remarks by saying that perhaps he spoke too soon since the deputies [to the Supreme Soviet] had yet to vote. But he was sure, he added, that they would accept the Central Committee's recommendation.

The Premier was right. The Supreme Soviet, which is not in the habit of turning down recommendations from the leadership, agreed in a lightning vote.

There was no debate. None of the 1,443 deputies raised his hand when the presiding chairman asked who was against the nomination. There was not a sound when he asked whether there were any abstentions.

But there was a roar of approval and loud handclapping when the chairman declared that the nomination had been carried.

Mr. Mikoyan made a short acceptance speech, thanking the deputies and the Central Committee for their trust. Then the session was adjourned until next December.

The brevity and the perfunctory nature of the election were in sharp contrast with the situation a little more than four years ago when Mr. Brezhnev succeeded Marshal Kliment Y. Voroshilov as President.

At that time there was an emotional scene in which Mr. Khrushchev, Mr. Brezhnev, and Marshal Voroshilov hugged and kissed each other.

A non-Communist diplomat attributed this contrast to the personality of Marshal Voroshilov. He said that the marshal was an emotional man of the old school, while the two main figures in today's change were "Communists in gray flannel suits," crisp and businesslike.

Mr. Mikoyan is the sixth man in the post. His predecessors were, in chronological order, Yakov M. Sverdlov [first President], Mikhail I. Kalinin [President from 1919 until his death in 1946] and Nikolai M. Shvernik [1946 until Stalin's death in 1953], followed by Marshal Voroshilov [1953–1960] and Mr. Brezhnev [1960–1964].

Mr. Mikoyan was born in 1895 at the village of Sanain, Armenia. His father was a carpenter. He was educated in the Armenian Theological Seminary in Tiflis, Georgia, but after graduation he decided against becoming a priest. . . .

Soon after graduation he became a member of the Bolshevik faction of the Social Democratic Party. He was active in the Baku region during the 1917 revolution and was wounded in the civil war that followed.

Mr. Mikoyan emerged near the center of national power in 1926 when he became People's Commissar of Foreign and Domestic Trade. He has been associated with foreign economic relations ever since.

Informed Soviet sources said today that Mr. Mikoyan could be expected to turn the Presidency into a more powerful position than it had been under Mr. Brezhnev, at least for the last fourteen months.

During this period, Mr. Brezhnev divided his attention between the Presidency and his other post as a key member of the Secretariat of the party.

His interest in the Presidency seemed to wane as time went on, and an increasing number of his protocol and other functions were turned over to the deputy chairmen of the Supreme Soviet.

By contrast, Mr. Mikoyan has long had a vital personal interest in foreign policy, with which the Presidency is intimately connected.

Unlike Mr. Brezhnev, who never took an active role in the conduct of foreign relations, Mr. Mikoyan is expected to deal personally with foreign representatives and to conduct key negotiations as well as carrying out the protocol functions.

Western diplomats were unanimous tonight in saying that Mr. Brezhnev, in giving up the Presidency, had not lost but gained power and had enhanced his position in the hierarchy.

Mr. Khrushchev in his short speech specified what everybody knew — namely, that Mr. Brezhnev had been freed of his Presidential duties to permit him to give undivided attention to his duties in the party Secretariat.

44 The Communist Party and Decision-Making

The Soviet constitution refers to the Communist Party only once. Article 126 guarantees citizens of the U.S.S.R. the right to unite in the Communist Party, "the vanguard of the working people in their struggle to build a communist society." No clear role is defined for the party. It is assigned no political function. It is given no authority to make political decisions. Yet, when the Supreme Soviet of the U.S.S.R. met in December 1965, several key appointments were made on the recommendation of the Communist Party.

If you think of the government of the Soviet Union as a giant corporation, as suggested in Reading 42, the Communist Party might be described as its board of directors. The party sets the policy. The government manages the "corporation" in line with this policy. Alfred G. Meyer, former Assistant Director of Harvard University's Russian Research Center, has said, "The party owns the Soviet Union. It does not, of course, have legal title to the country and does not claim it. But it acts as if it owned it; and since it gets away with acting in this fashion, it does in fact own it." In practice, it is the party that sets the rules, not the constitution.

The way in which decisions are transmitted by the party varies. Sometimes the party makes its will known through recommendations to the Supreme Soviet. Sometimes the Communist Party Presidium issues formal decrees. Sometimes party policy is made public through editorials in the newspaper *Pravda* or even through casual statements made by top party leaders.

Reading 44 describes the decision-making role of the Communist Party. As you read, consider the following questions:

1. Who are the decision-makers within the Communist Party?
2. Is there any evidence that indicates how they get the authority to make decisions?
3. What decisions do they make? Are there any known limits to the decisions that can be made by leaders of the Communist Party?

The Communist Party Is the Rear Guard of Russia
PETER GROSE

This article appeared in The New York Times Magazine *on March 27, 1966.* © *1966 by The New York Times Company. Reprinted by permission.*

. . . The Communist Party of the Soviet Union is holding its Twenty-third Party Congress this week, starting Tuesday. Against the background of the epic revolution led by this presumptuous political organization forty-eight years ago, the judgment of today is ironic: the Communist Party has fallen behind the society it created. The Soviet society the Communists built is exciting and awesome; inside it, the least exciting, the least inspiring, the least promising element is the Communist Party itself. Its work as the vanguard of the twentieth-century revolution finished, the Communist Party goes into its Twenty-third Congress desperately searching for a new role.

Article 126 of the Soviet Constitution says, "The most active and politically conscious citizens in the ranks of the working class, working peasants, and working intelligentsia voluntarily unite in the

Communist Party of the Soviet Union, which . . . constitutes the core of all organizations of the working people, both public and state." But this (like several other sections of the constitution) fails to correspond with reality. As the core of political power in the country, the Communist Party is unchallenged — this goes without question — but in the society at large, the party seems to have lost its creative and driving force. The motivating power has passed elsewhere: to the professional organizations, to special interest groups, and to individuals kindred through their geographic, economic, and social positions. In the changing Soviet society, the party is following, not leading. . . .

As Soviet society evolves, the Communist Party becomes middle-aged and fat. On January 1, 1965, total party membership was 11,758,169 — an increase of nearly 25 per cent over five years ago. This means that about one out of every twenty Soviet citizens is a party member.

According to the statistics, the composition of the party looks hopeful. The percentage of members with higher education has risen from 13.7 to 15 per cent in the past three years. Those with secondary education rose from 27.2 per cent to 30.1 per cent, while those with only elementary education fell from 27.8 per cent to 24.4 per cent.

Though their proportion is gradually decreasing, white-collar workers still account for almost half the total party membership: 46.2 per cent at the start of 1965. Factory workers rose to 37 per cent, and peasants declined to 16.5 per cent. Of the white-collar employees, scientists, engineers, teachers, and other intellectuals showed the largest increases in proportion of membership. About 10 per cent of the total membership is composed of professionals — the *apparatchiki* — who hold full-time jobs in the party bureaucracy. . . .

Party leaders are clearly aware that the census figures tell only a part of the story, and in the countless declarations building up to this week's Party Congress, Communist officials took every opportunity to warn that members are not doing everything they should for the party.

Typical was the speech of Nikolai G. Yegorychev, First Secretary of the Moscow City Party Committee. "The concept of 'leadership by the party in all the life of society' presupposes that each party member . . . actively works in a party organization," he said. "The overwhelming majority of Communists set examples and are initiators of everything new and progressive. . . . Unfortunately, in the party organizations there are still members who pay insufficient attention to the requirements of the party. . . . The task is to show much greater concern for drawing into the party the best people.". . .

The mechanism for creating and executing policy in the Communist Party is one of the most elusive aspects of modern Soviet society. An outsider's attempts to probe this sphere seldom achieve enlightenment. How, for instance, did the two "people's assessors" (roughly, jurymen) — to say nothing of the supreme court judge — arrive at their sentence of hard labor for the writer Sinyavsky and his codefendant Yuli M. Daniel (pseudonym: Nikolai Arzhak)? [The trial of these two men is described in Reading 45.] It is fatuous to suppose that a decision of this international importance was weighed and reached by two or three ordinary party members. Yet knowledgeable observers question whether anything so unsubtle as a specific message — "You will sentence them thusly. . ." — ever reached the members of the court.

"It would seem that these people just knew what was expected of them," was the way one long-time student of Communist Party affairs described the process. They knew what was expected of them from the cumulative effect of dozens of party statements and innuendoes — in this way if in no other, the minor party *apparatchik* is as subtle, imaginative, and sensitive as any person on earth. Sometimes, of course, there are mistakes. The party journals are full of remarks about erring party workers and local officials who have been replaced for wrongdoing. The *apparatchik*'s life is not an easy one.

If in sociological terms the Communist Party's politics and power are dwindling, the party, nonetheless, retains an absolute monopoly and absolute authority.

On paper, the party hierarchy is straightforward. The supreme organ is the Party Congress, a general meeting called to lay down the guidelines of national policy. In theory, this is to be convened every four years; in practice, there have been long gaps — Stalin seldom bothered with Party Congresses after his rule was secure, and even the present leadership has postponed its first Congress beyond the statutory period (this Congress should have been held last fall).

Between Congresses it is the Central Committee of about 170 members which ostensibly directs party affairs. The two chief organs of this committee are the twelve-man Presidium and the Secretariat, headed by First Secretary Leonid I. Brezhnev. From the Central Committee downward extend the party lines, both functionally (the Ideological Commission, the Control Commission, and so on) and geographically (the republics' party organizations, subdivided into districts, all the way down to village or collective farm committees).

Party workers or agents sit in all government offices, in social organizations, and in professional societies. They all should know what is expected of them; their word is either heeded when it comes to an issue, or an "incorrect" decision is adjusted at the next higher level where the word will be heeded. Realities of power are constantly changing inside this hierarchy, and the workers down the line become ultrasensitive to these realities, hedging their decisions in time of doubt if they intend to keep their jobs.

Stalin built the post of First Secretary (or General Secretary) into a position of unchallengeable power. Khrushchev could never operate so freely, but on occasion he went to the entire Central Committee for support, bypassing a hostile Presidium. Now it is the Presidium which dominates, making Central Committee meetings short and perfunctory affairs.

Unlike other national Communist parties, the Soviet [Party] Presidium has no chairman. It is as head of the Secretariat that Brezhnev is acknowledged as leader of the Communist Party of the Soviet Union. As the Presidium acts between meetings of the Central Committee, the Secretariat acts between meetings of the Presidium. Significant light could be shed on the center of party power today if it were known how often the Presidium meets. This is a secret closely guarded from outsiders, but all the indications are that the Presidium meets frequently — at least once a week.

With a strong Presidium, Brezhnev and his Secretariat are far from free in their management of the party. With Brezhnev on the Presidium sit the head of government, Premier Aleksei N. Kosygin; the head of state, President Nikolai V. Podgorny; three young contenders for high posts — Aleksandr N. Shelepin, Dmitri S. Polyansky, and Kirill T. Mazurov; the durable ideological specialist Mikhail A. Suslov; the retired head of state, Anastas I. Mikoyan, and others. Suslov and Shelepin are also in the Secretariat; Mazurov and Polyansky are first deputy premiers in the government.

This is the core of the collective leadership, unchanged in its essentials since the ouster of Khrushchev. . .

In government, it is Kosygin's ministries and the social and professional organizations which go about their tasks in their specialized ways — subject to review by the party *apparat* but not to detailed instruction. Only on certain major issues will the party take direct control: Vietnam, for instance, is a policy question on which diplomats have been given to understand that decisions rest clearly with the Presidium, not with the Foreign Ministry or Prime Minister. And a cultural question affecting ideology and social discipline — such as the Sinyavsky-Daniel trial — is not something to be trusted to the Union of Writers or to impartial courts. Here the party's guidance will prevail.

This is the present leadership's understanding of the role which the Communist Party should play in a mature communist society: Instead of allowing its energies and stature to be dissipated in details, the party must return to its historical role as an inspirational and ideological force of creation and motivation. . . .

Chapter 12

Decision-Making in the Soviet Political System (II)

STATING THE ISSUE In Chapter 11 you looked at the Supreme Soviet of the U.S.S.R. to analyze its role in political decision-making in the Soviet Union. You found that its role was not significant. A more significant role was played in both executive and legislative decision-making by the Presidium of the Supreme Soviet, and the most significant roles were played by the Council of Ministers and the leaders of the Communist Party.

In studying political decision-making in the United States, you learned that executive and legislative decisions can be checked by judicial interpretation. In this chapter you will take a look at the judicial system of the Soviet Union and see one of its courts in action, the Supreme Court of the Russian Republic. Do Soviet courts act as checks on executive and legislative decision-makers? Are they concerned with interpreting the law, or are they simply mechanisms for carrying out executive and legislative decisions?

Many observers of the Soviet political scene feel that significant changes have been taking place in the Soviet Union. They point to Khrushchev's replacement by Kosygin and Brezhnev as evidence of these changes. As you work with this chapter, you will evaluate this theory. Do Brezhnev and Kosygin represent a new approach to political decision-making? Are new and different groups involved in making political decisions? Has a "cult of impersonality" replaced the "cult of personality" which developed under Stalin and later Khrushchev? Did Khrushchev represent the end of an era?

Chapter 12 concludes with a review and a summary, but the conclusions you draw from them and from the rest of your study of Soviet decision-making cannot be final. One's knowledge of the Soviet decision-making process must remain inconclusive. The most serious Soviet scholars reevaluate their judgments constantly as new evidence becomes available. Will you predict any changes over the next few years in the political decision-making process in the Soviet Union?

45 The Soviet Judicial System

The court system of the Soviet Union has undergone many changes since the 1917 revolution. The first decree issued by the revolutionary leaders contained provisions for establishing "revolutionary tribunals" whose task it was to see that the new government stayed in power. Under these provisions, police courts were used to rid the government of persons considered politically undesirable. During the regimes of both Lenin and Stalin, the police could make arrests and bring their prisoners to trial before police courts. But ever since the death of Stalin, the Soviet court system has been undergoing radical changes. Police courts were abolished in 1953. Professional lawyers have been trained. Trial procedures have been improved, and a number of new procedures have been adopted to protect the rights of defendants.

The Supreme Court of the U.S.S.R. is the Soviet Union's highest court. It serves as a court of appeal and review. Each union republic also has a supreme court that reviews judgments reached by the republic's lower courts. Below the supreme courts of the republics are the provincial courts. At the lowest level are the people's courts.

In most Soviet courts, cases are heard by a judge and two non-professionals called *people's assessors.* These people's assessors are

THE SOVIET COURT SYSTEM

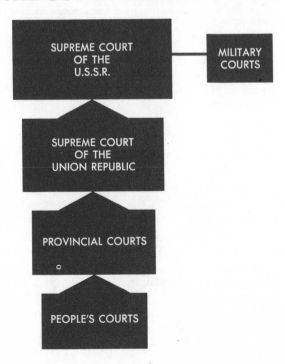

SUPREME COURT OF THE U.S.S.R.

MILITARY COURTS

SUPREME COURT OF THE UNION REPUBLIC

PROVINCIAL COURTS

PEOPLE'S COURTS

elected by the citizenry. In theory, they share equal power with the judge, but in practice, they almost never disagree with the judge's decision.

Due to a shortage of trained professionals, Soviet judges are not required to have legal training, although most of them are trained to some extent. The higher the level of court, the better the qualifications of the judges are likely to be.

Reading 45 describes a case heard by the Supreme Court of the Russian Republic in 1966. The case involves two Soviet authors, A. D. Sinyavsky and Y. M. Daniel. They were tried in a small courtroom before a preselected audience. Only Soviet newsmen who had been invited were admitted. The Soviet press carried brief accounts noting the crimes the defendants were accused of and the action taken. They carried no details of the testimony. This reading is taken from a transcript of the trial, alleged to have been recorded in the courtroom, which was published in the Paris-based Polish magazine *Kultura*. This transcript was translated and republished in *The New York Times*. As you read, keep the following questions in mind:

1. What was the basis for the charges brought against Sinyavsky and Daniel?
2. On what did Sinyavsky and Daniel base their defense?
3. Do you think that Sinyavsky and Daniel had a "fair trial"? Why or why not?

Trial of Sinyavsky and Daniel

MAX HAYWARD

From On Trial: Soviet State Versus "Abram Tertz" and "Nikolai Arzhak." *Translated and edited by Max Hayward as it appeared in* The New York Times Magazine, *and reprinted by permission of Harper & Row Publishers, Inc. Copyright © 1966 by Harper & Row Publishers, Inc.*

The trial opened on February 10 at 10 A.M. in the Moscow Oblast (province) Court, in a small hall seating 150 – 160 persons. The Russian Supreme Court – under the chairmanship of L. N. Smirnov, sitting with N. A. Chechina and P. V. Sokolov, people's assessors – heard the case of A. D. Sinyavsky and Y. M. Daniel, accused under Section 1 of Article 70 of the Criminal Code of the Russian Republic, which says: "Agitation or propaganda, conducted with a view to subverting or weakening the Soviet regime or committing dangerous state crimes; the distribution for the said purposes of slanderous inventions maligning the Soviet political and social system, and also the distribution or preparation or harboring, for the said purposes, of literature of similar content are punishable by imprisonment from six months to seven years and exile from two to five years. . ."

The audience consists almost entirely of men. Entry is by special invitation cards (a different color used for each court session), which are checked twice, once at the building entrance, and again at the foot of the stairway leading to the courtroom. . . .

The accused are led in. They look as they would in everyday life, with no traces of their five-month detainment for investigation. Sinyavsky is thin, short, with a reddish, unkempt beard. He wears a snow-white nylon shirt under a black woolen sweater with a round collar. He looks like a gnome, or rather like a good-natured goblin. Daniel is tall, dark-haired, but growing bald, with a large, strong mouth, nervous lips, dressed in a cowboy shirt and a worn jacket. Behind each accused is an unarmed guard.

The prosecutor and counsel for the defense enter.

The court clerk says: "Please stand" and, after a short interval, adds loudly, with stress on the first word, "The court is in session."

The members of the court enter. First, Chechina, a thin woman wearing glasses, dressed in a simple dark suit; behind her, Smirnov, a big man of fifty-eight, who walks with his head thrust forward in a bull-like manner, purposeful, like a man who is accustomed to exercise authority. Finally, Sokolov, a well-built, good-looking man of forty. . . .

The secretary of the court reads out the indictment accusing Sinyavsky and Daniel. The content of the indictment is briefly as follows:

The writings of a so-called Soviet literary underground have been widely distributed in the United States, Britain, and other capitalist countries to discredit the Soviet people, our government, the Communist Party of the U.S.S.R. and its policies. Slanderous works of underground writers are being passed off by hostile propaganda as truthful accounts about the Soviet Union. Such works include the novels *The Trial Begins* and *Lyubimov* and the article "On Socialist Realism" by Abram Tertz; and the works *This Is Moscow Speaking,* "Hands," "Atonement," and "The Man from Minap" by Nikolai Arzhak. The state security organs have established that Sinyavsky concealed his identity behind the pseudonym Abram Tertz, and Daniel behind that of Nikolai Arzhak. They were arrested in September 1965.

The investigation showed that Sinyavsky and Daniel, having adopted a position hostile to the Soviet state on a number of questions, sent their writings abroad starting in 1956. In the novel *The Trial Begins,* Sinyavsky, under the guise of criticism of the personality cult, maligned the Soviet system and the principles of Marxism-

Leninism. [Sinyavsky felt that a new "cult of personality" was grow-
up around Khrushchev.]

In 1956, the indictment continues, Sinyavsky wrote the article "On
Socialist Realism," in which he tried to revise Marxist principles
from an anti-Soviet point of view. That article was directed against
the guiding role of the Soviet Communist Party in Soviet culture. . . .

[*The indictment goes on to accuse first Sinyavsky and then Daniel of
sending their writings abroad through Helene Peltier-Zamoyska, the daughter
of a former French naval attaché in Moscow. Following the reading of the
indictment, the court went on to examine Sinyavsky and Daniel on the
reasons for their actions and to hear their final pleas.*]

Excerpts from the Four-Day Proceedings

JUDGE: Defendant Sinyavsky, do you plead guilty to the charges,
in full or in part?

SINYAVSKY: No, I don't, either in full or in part.

JUDGE: Defendant Daniel, do you plead guilty to the charges, in
full or in part?

DANIEL: No, I don't, either in full or in part.

*(The prosecutor asks the court to adopt the following procedure:
examination of Daniel, examination of Sinyavsky, followed by
testimony of witnesses and experts in the order listed in the indictment.)*

The Examination of Daniel

PROSECUTOR: What was the nature of your literary activity in the
U.S.S.R.?

DANIEL: I worked as a translator and wrote articles. The Children's
Publishing House printed a story of mine called "Escape"; however,
this was not released for sale.

JUDGE: Your story is part of the evidence. *(He holds up the book.)*

PROSECUTOR: In other words, as a poet-translator and writer, you
worked under your own name in the U.S.S.R.?

DANIEL: Yes

PROSECUTOR: And you did not use any pseudonyms?

DANIEL: No.

PROSECUTOR: Which of your works were written under a pseudonym and when?

DANIEL: Works are not written under a pseudonym; they are
published under a pseudonym.

PROSECUTOR: All right, then, what was published under a pseudonym?

DANIEL: Under a pseudonym I published "Hands," *This is Moscow Speaking*, "The Man from Minap," and "Atonement.". . .

PROSECUTOR: If you saw nothing anti-Soviet in your writings, why
didn't you submit them to Soviet publishers?

DANIEL: I knew very well that the editors would not publish anything on such controversial topics. My writings have a political tinge, and they would not have printed them on political grounds. What I mean is that the editors and publishers have their own policies.

PROSECUTOR: In other words, Daniel, you knew there was something in your writings that stood in the way of their publication in the Soviet Union.

DANIEL *(irritated):* I am simply talking about the practice of our publishers who are afraid to print anything on a controversial topic. . . .

PROSECUTOR: Why did you write works that could be interpreted as anti-Soviet?

DANIEL: Are you asking about them all, or about any one in particular?

PROSECUTOR: You can tell us about any one of them.

DANIEL: I'll talk about "Hands." I know I don't have the right to put questions to the court. But can the prosecution point to a single sentence, a single word, a single letter that could be interpreted as anti-Soviet? This story is a literary version of an actual event that was recounted to me. There is nothing in the story to justify the charges against me. The indictment contradicts itself when it talks about this story. The indictment contends that the Soviet regime has never used force. But such a point of view is not scientific, it is not Marxist, it is not Leninist. According to Lenin, revolution is coercion, and the state is coercive, and [in a revolutionary state there is] coercion of the minority by the majority. The indictment charges that I wrote that "the Soviet regime coerced the Soviet people." There is nothing of this sort in the story, which is about the execution of counterrevolutionaries. There is nothing in the story about retribution. It cannot be interpreted as in the indictment. . . .

JUDGE: Why did you select "Hands" as your first work to be sent abroad for publication? ["Hands" is a story told in the first person by an old member of the Cheka, the secret police, to explain why his hands shake uncontrollably. As a young man in the early days of the revolution, he was a member of a firing squad that executed counterrevolutionaries. One day he is executing a group of priests—but, as a joke, his comrades have loaded his gun with blanks, so that the priests seem immune to his bullets. This ruins his nerves, and he has to leave the service.]

DANIEL: Because I could assume that this story would not be published here; it is about a forbidden subject that has not been dealt with in our literature since the 1930's. . .

JUDGE: Why was the subject of the shooting of the priests so important to you at this time? Why did you have to revive that theme at this time?

DANIEL: I had no political purpose when I wrote the story. *(Laughter in the courtroom.)*

PROSECUTOR: Let us assume that you did not understand the political character of the story. Why, then, did you send it abroad under a pseudonym and by illegal means?

DANIEL: I sent it out to be published; that was an adequate reason for me. If I had been a physician or an engineer, I would have published it under my own name. But I am a translator. Getting work for a translator of my class depends on good relations with publishing houses. If it had become known that I was being published abroad, I would have lost my translation work. When I gave these things to Peltier, I did not know where, when, and in what country they would be published. The final stage of any literary work is publication. You can interpret this as you wish, as vanity, as excessive pride. But if I had been a physician or engineer, I would not have used a pseudonym. I have already said that I thought it unethical.

PROSECUTOR: You wanted to be published. But didn't you think about our enemies, about the fact that these writings could be used for anti-Soviet propaganda?

DANIEL: I did not think about it.

PROSECUTOR: And when did you start thinking about it?

DANIEL: After 1963 when I first saw two of my books, one with a foreword by Filippov [an ex-Soviet citizen, now publishing in Washington, D.C.]. Then I realized what construction was being put on them. Despite my doubts, I sent one more manuscript abroad. But since 1963 I have written nothing more and sent nothing more abroad. . . .

Final Plea of Sinyavsky

It will be rather difficult for me to speak, since I had not expected that I should be called upon to make my final plea so soon. I had been told that it would be on Monday, and I have not had time to prepare. It will be even more difficult in view of the specific atmosphere that one can feel here fairly keenly. I am not convinced by the arguments of the prosecution, and I stand by my previous attitude. The arguments of the prosecution give one the feeling of being up against a blank wall, against which one batters one's head in vain, and through which one cannot penetrate in order to get to some kind of truth.

The arguments of the prosecutor are the same as those of the indictment, and I heard them many times during the preliminary investigation. It is always the same quotations over and over again. . . . It is always the same hair-raising quotations from the indictment, repeated dozens of times and mounting up to create a monstrous atmosphere that no longer bears any relations to any kind of reality.

It is an artistic device to keep on repeating the same phrases over and over again, and it is a powerful one. It creates a kind of shroud, a peculiar kind of electrified atmosphere in which the boundary between the real and the grotesque becomes blurred. . . .

It is the atmosphere of a murky anti-Soviet underground hidden behind the bright faces of the doctor of philosophy Sinyavsky and the poet-translator Daniel, who hatch plots, nurture plans for putsches [uprisings], terrorist acts, pogroms [massacres of helpless people], assassinations, assassinations, assassinations . . . with only two actors: Daniel and myself. . . .

Final Plea of Daniel

In the final plea of my comrade Sinyavsky, there was a note of despair about the impossibility of breaking through a blank wall of incomprehension and unwillingness to listen. I am not so pessimistic. I wish to go over the arguments of the prosecution and the defense once again.

Throughout the trial, I kept asking myself: what is the purpose of cross-questioning? The answer is obvious and simple: to hear our replies and then put the next question; to conduct the hearing in such a way as finally to arrive at the truth.

This has not happened. . . .

How did they try to prove the anti-Soviet nature of Sinyavsky and myself? Several procedures have been used. The simplest and most head-on form of attack has been to attribute to the author the ideas of his characters. One can do all kinds of things by this method. . . . I, Yuli Markovich Daniel, a Jew, am [declared] an anti-Semite—all this by virtue of the fact that one of my characters, an old waiter, says something about the Jews, and so the following entry goes down in my dossier [record]: "Nikolai Arzhak [Daniel] is a consummate and convinced anti-Semite.". . .

Then there is still another very simple, but extremely effective way of "proving" anti-Soviet intent: this is to invent something on the author's behalf and say that a work has anti-Soviet passages, even though there are none. Take my story "Hands." My defense lawyer, Kisenishsky, gave a well-argued proof that the basic idea of the story is not anti-Soviet, in whichever way you care to interpret it. In her reply to Kisenishsky, Kedrina [a public accuser] said: "Just look with what expressiveness and vividness, which are otherwise uncharacteristic of him, Daniel has described the episode of the execution!". . .

What other methods are used to accuse us? Criticism of a certain period is made out to be criticism of a whole epoch; criticism of a five-year period is passed off as criticism of fifty years; even if you write about as short a space of time as two or three years, we are accused of writing about the whole Soviet era. . . .

202

Finally I should mention one last procedure—the assertion that criticism of the part applies to the whole, so that disagreement with certain things is made out to be a rejection of the system as a whole.

These in brief, are the ways and means by which our guilt has been "proved.". . .

All I have said should not be taken to mean that I regard myself and Sinyavsky as shining and impeccable paragons of virtue and that the court should release us from detention immediately after the trial and send us home in a taxi at its own expense. We are guilty—not for what we have written, but for having sent our works abroad. There are many political indiscretions, exaggerations, and jibes in our books. But isn't twelve years of Sinyavsky's life and nine years of mine a rather excessive payment for our frivolity, thoughtlessness, and misjudgment? . . .

As we both said under preliminary investigation and here, we deeply regret that our works have been detrimentally exploited by reactionary forces and that thereby we have caused harm to our country. We did not wish this. We had no ill intentions, and I ask the court to take this into consideration.

I wish to ask forgiveness of all my near ones and friends, to whom we have caused distress.

I also wish to say that no articles of any criminal code nor any accusations against us will deter Sinyavsky and me from feeling that we are persons who love our country and our people.

That is all I have to say.

I am ready to hear the sentence.

[*Daniel was found guilty and sentenced to five years imprisonment, and Sinyavsky was found guilty and sentenced to seven years.*]

46 Changes in Soviet Decision-Making

Since the death of Stalin, there has been some change in the way Soviet political decisions are made. Those capable of influencing major decisions are still few in number, but more appear to be involved in the decision-making process than in the days of the "cult of personality." The theory of control through terror appears to have fewer supporters. Khrushchev was overthrown, but he did not have to face a firing squad. Reading 31 shows that such poets as Yevtushenko can disagree with their leaders without being sent to Siberia. But the fate of Daniel and Sinyavsky seems to indicate that the extent to which Soviet citizens can disagree is very limited. While changes have occurred, much has remained the same. Information available to the Soviet community is strictly censored. Debate among the leaders is not carried on in public. Power still appears to be centered around men rather than institutions. Changes can be observed, but how much they have basically affected the system is still questionable.

In the opinion of Hadley Cantril, Chairman of the Board and Senior Counselor of the Institute for International Social Research, "There is apparently an increasing realization that the individual sense of dignity and freedom can no longer be so completely and easily violated and throttled; there is a restricted humanism seen most clearly in Soviet literature. There seems little doubt that a liberalizing tendency has begun in the Soviet Union and that it may be an irreversible tendency. All observers who visit the Soviet Union now and compare it to the society they had known earlier are impressed by the increased frankness of the people in admitting their problems and by the increased relaxation of individuals both in their appearance and in their behavior, and their apparent freedom to live somewhat more by their own rules."

A change in leadership within the Soviet Union replaced the volatile Mr. Khrushchev with the restrained Kosygin and Brezhnev. Reading 46 is concerned with the effect of this change on the Soviet decision-making process. As you read, consider these questions:

1. What evidence is there that the way in which political decisions are made in the Soviet Union changed after Brezhnev and Kosygin came into power?
2. What appears to have created this change?
3. How far-reaching do you think the effects of this change might be?

The Cult of Impersonality
PETER GROSE

This account appeared in The New York Times Magazine *on October 9, 1966.* © *1966 by The New York Times Company. Reprinted by permission.*

. . . Brezhnev and Kosygin govern the society in which two highly imaginative writers were convicted as criminals because the way they chose to write differed somewhat from the way the government said they could write.

Theirs is the society that took ancient tribal peoples of Central Asia and turned them into a productive, industrial proletariat, with a living standard far higher than that in the Middle Eastern lands across the Soviet frontiers.

Mid-century Soviet society has produced . . . artists who can portray reality just the way photographers do. It may be the first society to place a man on the moon. It may be the last to place a dinner that is hot before a patron in a restaurant.

At the head of this society now is a regime of men aware of the contradictions they are facing, dealing with each problem as it arises, trying to find a middle course with the widest acceptability. Their style is not to ride roughshod. In principle, they are neither forging ahead into some new conception of communism, nor seeking refuge in the comfort of the Stalinist past—a time when things political may not have been good, but at least were clear-cut. In practice, they are doing a little of both.

The policies of Brezhnev and Kosygin have reflected the belief that the Soviet Union needed to settle down within itself; that the last thing needed was any more of the dynamic leadership gushing forth in fits and starts from Nikita S. Khrushchev—toward what end not even Khrushchev seemed to know. Theirs has not been leadership; it has been management. . .

From the start Brezhnev and Kosygin displayed a remarkable confidence in themselves and in each other. They did not act as if they feared being overthrown. There was no pressure for rapid results, for vivid accomplishments to justify their seizure of power—a move so startling, and so efficiently brought off, that even the Grand Master of Kremlin-style chess, Khrushchev himself, did not recognize the checkmate until it had happened. Their programs for agriculture and industry (they had none for foreign policy) were long-term, and the effects would be felt only gradually over the years to come. They were not men in a hurry.

From the perspective of two years, it is evident that the new men in the Kremlin could agree on more than just the need to depose Khrushchev. The evidence, scanty though it is even now, suggests that neither Brezhnev nor Kosygin nor any other one man dominated the plot. It was a collegial [collective] decision by the Communist Party Presidium, meeting in Khrushchev's absence. . .

It would be contrary to all political logic to suppose that unanimity of views exists among the men in the Kremlin, but evidence of factions within the leadership is hard to come by these days. Some experienced observers of Soviet politics concede—and they express amazement—that this leadership seems to have established a noteworthy balance among widely differing views. "The most serious policy disputes are not among the top members of the leadership," says one diplomat. "Rather, they are between the leadership group as a group, and the amorphous force of bureaucrats, *apparatchiki* and low-level people who have the power to prevent implementation of policy but not to make another policy."

As party leader, and thus number one man in the Soviet Union, Brezhnev is neither despotic, as was Stalin, nor domineering, as was Khrushchev. There is nothing in his manner or his background to suggest that his ambition reached any higher than to be an efficient and businesslike head of a vast apparatus. And this is what he is.

Still less ruled by ambition for personal power is Brezhnev's partner, Aleksei Nikolayevich Kosygin, sixty-two, the Prime Minister. Probably against his inclinations, Kosygin has had to take on the role of spokesman and representative of the Soviet Union in public. He is the man to greet foreign visitors and to travel abroad to spread Soviet good will. . . .

Apart from his shyness when exposed to the public, Kosygin displays a warmer personality than Brezhnev. Through sad blue eyes he peers straight at his listeners, speaking with gentle insistence and conviction. His speeches are models of dullness, but he is a quick man in conversation, making witty or ironical remarks with almost boyish anticipation. In his element when probing through exhibits of factory machinery or examining new products, Kosygin seems to wish he did not have to epitomize Soviet power in person. At a British trade fair in Moscow, he tried to test the upholstery in a new British double-decker bus, but jumped up quickly when he saw that photographers were maneuvering to take him in the pose of a London commuter.

Kosygin is clearly working himself into exhaustion on the job. Though his skill in managing the unwieldy Soviet economic system came as no surprise, his success in the field of diplomacy was unexpected. . . .

In public appearances together, Kosygin invariably gives way to Brezhnev; the party still holds pride of place over the government. The relationship between them seems to be something like that of the chairman of the board and the chief executive officer of the corporation. There are no signs of personal tensions between them; they do not act like rivals, but like partners.

Under Brezhnev, the Communist Party is withdrawing from the operational role it assumed under Khrushchev. Kosygin's government machinery is increasingly running the country, following guidelines laid down by the party.

Cutting across the division between their functional positions, the two men have agreed on clearly divided personal responsibilities regarding policy-making and implementation of policy in two crucial spheres of activity: agricultural and industrial organization. These are the two broad planks in the platform of the post-Khrushchev leadership.

Brezhnev's program for agriculture was the first major undertaking of the new regime, announced in March 1965. It promised the vast sum of $78 billion for carefully phased investment in farming over the years to 1970. Farmers were offered the security of knowing exactly what was expected of them, and how much money they could receive as a minimum for five years to come (previously the planning had been on a year-to-year basis). Further security came in the form of guaranteed minimum wages for collective farmers. A land reclamation program [a program to make wasteland farmable] was drawn up, having as its basis not any new gimmickry but simply the application of time-proven techniques of good estate management. . . .

Kosygin's project is the widely discussed industrial reform plan, in which pragmatism [practical measures] and local initiative are emphasized, instead of theoretical planning from the center. . . . To the extent that there will be no large-scale private ownership, this is certainly not capitalism. But with increasing reliance on techniques that capitalists call their own — material incentives, production governed by supply-and-demand factors — the communist economy is pulling back from the radical model of early Marxists and seeking a middle ground of economic organization. . . .

The projects of Brezhnev and Kosygin are profound in their implications for the future of communist society; yet their bases are technical, not inspirational. They are adjustments of the existing society designed to make it more efficient; this is as far as the vision of the post-Khrushchev leadership seems to extend. If any of these men have articulated to themselves how the communism they say they are guiding will really look or feel in ten or twenty-five years, such deep thoughts are not expressed in public. . . .

47 A Review of Soviet Decision-Making

Chapters 11 and 12 have introduced the subject of political decision-making in the Soviet Union. The political system of the Soviet Union is very complex. Lines of authority are not clearly drawn, and they frequently overlap. Groups with no formal authority make laws. Groups with clearly defined constitutional authority to legislate appear not to use their authority.

The lack of clarity with which the Soviet system is defined may make the study of Soviet decision-making difficult for American students. The student's lack of background and information when he approaches the subject complicates the confusion. As Americans, you have lived with the American political system. On your television sets, you have seen conventions in the process of selecting political leaders. You have seen Presidents and watched them conduct press conferences. You may even have been to Washington and visited sessions of Congress. But what is a presidium or soviet? Can you visualize the Council of Ministers in the process of performing its job? How does the President of the Soviet Union act when he is interviewed?

Because the information concerning the Soviet political system is so new and strange, Reading 47 is a review. It is written by Harrison Salisbury, who has served as assistant managing editor of *The New York Times* and as that paper's Moscow correspondent. At the end of his explanation, Mr. Salisbury draws some conclusions about the Soviet political system. As you read, think about these questions:

1. What is meant by the principle of "democratic centralism?" How would this principle affect the political decision-making process?
2. Do you agree with Mr. Salisbury that the fatal flaw in the Soviet system is its inability to handle succession of leaders in an orderly fashion? Why or why not?

How the Soviet Union Is Ruled
HARRISON E. SALISBURY

This review is an excerpted version of Chapter III of Russia *by Harrison E. Salisbury, A* New York Times *Byline Book, published by Atheneum, 1965. Copyright © 1965 by The New York Times Company. Reprinted by permission of the author and Atheneum.*

. . . In the Soviet Union the problems of political change are handled secretively and mysteriously, for in the Soviet Union, power is vested in what constitutes a cabal or oligarchy with no clear-cut institutional, traditional, or constitutional method of transferring or conferring authority.

The fact is that Russia has never had a democratic apparatus. The constitutional underpinnings of the Russian monarchy were primitive. The czars regarded themselves as despots in which all power was vested. And until the nineteenth century, more often than not, a change in rulership was accomplished by intrigue, murder, or revolt. . . .

Lenin was as firm a believer in concentrated authority as the czars. He believed in what he called "dictatorship of the proletariat," which meant dictatorship by the Communist Party — or, in real fact, dictatorship by the leader of that party.

The Soviet Union has a constitution, filled with fine phraseology, guarantees of free speech, freedom of religion, and so on. It has a parliament, called the Supreme Soviet, which is elected by universal suffrage. The parliament names a cabinet [the Council of Ministers] and a Premier, approves the budget, and passes all legislation. On paper it differs only in detail from the processes of Western democracies.

The nation is divided into fifteen so-called constituent or union republics, each of which has its own government, capital, and legislature, somewhat after the manner of an American state . . .

The largest is the Russian Republic, with its capital at Moscow. It embraces almost 6.6 million square miles, and its population (as of 1963) is 123.4 million. Second in importance and population is the Ukraine, whose capital is Kiev. Its population is 44.1 million.

The other union republics are Kazakhstan (population 11.3 million), Uzbekistan (9.5 million), Byelorussia (8.4 million), Georgia (4.3 million), Azerbaijan (4.2 million), Moldavia (3.2 million), Lithuania (2.9 million), Kirghizia (2.4 million), Tadjikstan (2.3 million), Latvia (2.2 million), Armenia (2 million), Turkmenia (1.7 million), and Estonia (1.2 million).

Each of these units has its own budget, national language, laws, and courts. However, the laws follow closely the Soviet national statutes, and the legislatures in general confine their deliberations to purely local matters. . . .

The important difference between the Soviet governmental system and those with which we are familiar is the fact that only one party, the Communist Party, is permitted. Only one candidate's name (almost always a Communist) appears on the ballot for each elective post. The parliament, the cabinet, the constitution—all are a facade. The actual power is firmly vested in the party.

There are roughly 8 or 9 million Communist Party members in a total population of 230 million. These members elect their own delegates to the Party Congress, which is the supreme governing body of the party. The Congress names the Central Committee, which in turn names the Presidium (formerly Politburo) and the party secretaries.

But here, too, reality is just the opposite of what is written on paper. Since the time of Stalin, the Presidium or Politburo has been the ruling oligarchy. Stalin named his own oligarchy and ruled it with an iron hand. The oligarchy, in turn, named the Central Committee, the party secretaries, the lower party organs, and so on, right down to the individual party members.

A nation can be ruled by a one-man dictatorship. This has been common enough throughout the world. The difficulty arises when a shift must be made—because of death, because of failure of policy, because of any of the normal hazards of government.

In the United States when a President dies, his place is taken by the Vice-President, designated specifically for that purpose. Similar arrangements prevail in other Western countries. The continuity of government is maintained. Authority passes from man to man smoothly and without crisis. If controversy arises over policy, the difference of opinion is reflected in Congress or Parliament. At the next general election the issue is decided by the people at the ballot box. If they wish a new policy or a new man, they make the change according to law and custom. The decision is accepted as binding.

Not so in the Soviet Union. Lenin set up his Communist Party as a conspiratorial organization with a [military-like] discipline. Orders came down from the top and were not to be challenged. He permitted debate — often very free debate — before a decision was made. But, once taken, the decision was binding on all. Regardless of reservations, all were required to support it under what he called the principle of "democratic centralism."

Because Lenin himself tolerated fairly wide differences of opinion within the party and was not [vengeful] to those who disagreed with him, the system did not work too badly so long as he lived. But it was made to order for a cunning manipulator like Stalin, who brooked no opposition and no rivals. Under Stalin, pure tyranny prevailed. He methodically killed or imprisoned any possible rival or opponent. The mere expression of a differing viewpoint could cost a man his life. As Khrushchev once remarked: "When you were summoned to the Kremlin, you did not know whether or not you would come out alive." Stalin encouraged rivalry among his lieutenants and stimulated feuds in a manner reminiscent of the Borgias.

When Stalin died, the stage was set for a struggle for power among his successors. First a triumvirate sought to rule. This was made up of Premier Georgi M. Malenkov, Police Chief Lavrenti P. Beria, and Foreign Minister Vyacheslav M. Molotov. It quickly disintegrated. Beria was arrested in June 1953 by his colleagues and shot in December 1953. Malenkov was displaced as Premier by Marshal Nikolai A. Bulganin in 1955, and Molotov was ousted as Foreign Minister. Power flowed to Nikita Khrushchev — a man who had not even been mentioned as a possible successor to Stalin, a man who held no official or party post of prominence at the time of Stalin's death.

But Khrushchev proved superior in the deadly game of Kremlin politics. He ousted his rivals and, with the aid of Marshal Georgi K. Zhukov, turned back an attempt which was made in June 1957 to depose him through a coup d'état.

The plotters, including Khrushchev's best friend, Bulganin, had lined up eight of the eleven votes in the party Presidium against him. When he and Bulganin returned from a brief official trip to Finland, Khrushchev was confronted by a meeting of the Presidium at which he was voted out of office. He refused to accept the decision and demanded a meeting of the Central Committee — a body of about 125 members. Khrushchev's opponents barred the Kremlin to the Khrushchev supporters. But the party chief had an invaluable ally — Zhukov, the Minister of Defense. Zhukov put army planes at the disposal of loyal Khrushchev men and flew them into Moscow. He smuggled them into the Kremlin, and in a dramatic scene Khrushchev turned the tables on his enemies, won the backing of the Central Committee, and threw his opponents out of the party.

It was a classic example of the Soviet struggle for power. Once he had won, Khrushchev promptly deposed Marshal Zhukov in October 1957. If Zhukov was strong enough to save Khrushchev in his hour of need, he was strong enough to oust him, too—if he so desired. Khrushchev was taking no chances.

In reality, Khrushchev's ouster of Zhukov may have been his fatal error. Khrushchev never achieved the kind of iron control possessed by Stalin. He ruled the Kremlin by balancing one faction against another. The threat to him in 1957 arose when a half dozen different factions joined forces against him. The possibility of another such coalition was always present.

Seven years passed. Khrushchev weathered several serious crises, particularly one which followed the Cuban debacle of November 1962. When he was forced by President Kennedy to withdraw his missiles, he suffered tremendous loss of face. His enemies within the [party Presidium] struck quickly. Khrushchev survived that time. In the autumn of 1963, failure of the Soviet grain crop brought another crisis. But Khrushchev managed to get through that also.

Then, in October 1964, the bell tolled again. The circumstances were almost exactly those of June 1957. Once again Khrushchev was out of town, this time at his summer villa on the Black Sea. His chief lieutenants were also out of Moscow. Just as his old friend Bulganin had been at his side on the trip to Finland, so, now, his old friend Anastas I. Mikoyan was with him at the villa. A Soviet cosmonaut flight was in progress. Khrushchev talked to the spacemen on a national television hookup. Nothing could have been more normal, more peaceful. He wished them: *"Do svidaniya"* — "Till we meet again." Those were the last words the Soviet public was to hear him speak as Premier.

This time the plotters had profited by the experience of the abortive June 1957 coup. The lines were laid carefully. A virtually unanimous Presidium vote was assured to oppose Khrushchev. He was kept out of the way until the action had been taken. The Central Committee was primed to act against him — not with him. And, most important, when Khrushchev was finally flown back to Moscow to confront a fait accompli, he could no longer turn to his friend Zhukov. The army this time lined up against, not with, Khrushchev.

The ouster of Khrushchev put into power Aleksei Kosygin as Premier and Leonid Brezhnev as party chief. . .

By the ouster of Khrushchev, did these men become the masters of the Kremlin? Not exactly. When Lenin died, a triumvirate — Trotsky, Kamenev, and Zinoviev — came to power. But Stalin ousted them and ruled in his own name. When Stalin died, a triumvirate — Malenkov, Beria, and Molotov — came to power. But Beria was executed, and Khrushchev thrust Malenkov and Molotov aside.

The Soviet system is not made for collective rule. Power tends to flow into the hands of one able, ruthless man. In the interim between single rulers, the struggle goes on. To become master of the Kremlin, a man must win the support of all the big power groupings—the army, the secret police, the key party secretaries, the industrial bosses, the important foreign Communist parties.

During the struggle for power, Soviet policy inevitably becomes enmeshed in the intrigue. The dangers are obvious. In a nuclear age they menace the world. Ambitious men in the Kremlin may play politics with intercontinental missiles in order to advance a personal drive for absolute power. They may employ the thunderbolt of nuclear retaliation as a pawn in the game of communist political chess.

Thoughtful Russians have become increasingly aware of the anachronism of a world superpower's being ruled by the methods of medieval Florentine princes. They have sought to propel the Soviet Union onto the path of constitutionalism, to lay the foundations of orderly succession, to substitute some precept for the primitive law of the jungle still prevailing in the Kremlin.

A little progress has been made. No longer are Soviet statesmen shot when they are removed from office. Malenkov was given a job running a power station in Ust-Kamenogorsk. Molotov was sent to Mongolia as ambassador. Bulganin was given a big state farm to administer. Zhukov was sent to retirement on an estate outside Moscow.

Khrushchev was removed with meticulous regard for at least the forms of the statutes. He was placed in protective custody, but, by Soviet standards, the public recriminations, denunciations, and [condemnation] were mild.

Yet the fatal flaw of the Soviet dictatorship, its inability to handle [the succession of men in power] in orderly fashion, persists. The day may be coming, as some Russians have begun to suggest, when two candidates for a post may be listed on the election ballot. Legalism and constitutionalism may be gaining some ground. But the distance to be covered before the cruel power struggle within the Kremlin is eliminated is vast. Meanwhile, Moscow's outmoded system of oligarchy is as dangerous—to the Soviet Union and the world—as it would be to put an Elizabethan coachman at the controls of a modern jetliner.

48 A Summary Exercise

At the end of Unit One, you prepared a list of analytical questions to help you find information about the political systems of the Cheyenne Indians and the Stoerpenberg prisoners. You started by identifying five basic concepts: political leadership, decision-making, institutions, ideology, and the role of the citizen. For each concept you thought of analytical questions to help you recognize evidence related to that concept. You evaluated your questions in terms of how much they helped you to find specific information that helped you to understand how politics worked.

Now you are ready to evaluate your analytical questions. How helpful were they in giving you insights into the political systems of the Soviet Union and the United States? Did they make you see relationships between specific events and the concepts you were exploring? How sharp is the cutting edge of each question? Does it tell you enough to help you distinguish clearly between events that are relevant and those that are not? Reading 48 presents a problem that conceivably could turn up in either the United States or the Soviet Union. Read this imaginary case carefully, then answer the questions posed at the end:

> Simultaneously, the political leaders of both the United States and the Soviet Union decide that the demands of modern technology are so great that it is impossible to train properly all the technicians, engineers, and economists that are needed to maintain their respective positions as "first in space." Both nations pass laws making it compulsory for everybody between the ages of six and eighteen to go to school ten hours a day, six days a week. Students are shocked; they talk of nothing else. In both countries there are rumors that a student strike is being planned. It is said that on a particular day, at a specified hour, all students will march from their classrooms and refuse to return until the laws are repealed.

On the basis of what you now know about political decisionmaking in both the Soviet Union and the United States, what do you think the leaders of each country will decide to do if these rumors prove true? How will they go about making these decisions? What questions must you ask about decision-making to test your theories?

SUGGESTED READINGS

ALSOP, STEWART and CHARLES BARTLETT, "In Time of Crisis," *Politics, U.S.A.*, pp. 526–35.
    Question: In reaching each decision of the Cuban crisis, how much consideration was given to possible Soviet reaction?
ANDERSON, DILLON, "The National Security Council—A Super Cabinet," *Political Institutions*, 230–34.
    Question: What are the functions of the National Security Council?
ARMSTRONG, JOHN A., "The Apparatus," *Ideology, Politics, and Government in the Soviet Union*, pp. 65–82.

Question: What role does the apparatus play in Soviet political decision-making?

"The Party," *Ideology, Politics, and Government in the Soviet Union,* pp. 47–61.

Question: How does the way in which the Communist Party is organized help it maintain dominance over all Soviet affairs?

BRYCE, JAMES, "The Values of Local Self-Government," *Capitol, Courthouse and City Hall,* pp. 1–3.

Question: Why does Mr. Bryce consider it important for local areas to retain self-government?

BUDGET BUREAU, 1958, "The Budget Bureau," *Political Institutions,* pp. 234–36.

Question: How does the Budget Bureau influence political decision-making?

BURNS, JAMES M., "Memo to the Next President: Political Party Reform," *Political Institutions,* pp. 123–27.

Question: How would the reorganization of the major political parties, as suggested by Mr. Burns, affect national political decision-making?

CASE, SENATOR CLIFFORD, "A Republican Prescribes for His Party," *Profile of American Politics,* pp. 117–22.

Question: What does Senator Case see as the proper role of political parties in the American political system?

CATER, DOUGLAS, "Government by Publicity," *Politics, U.S.A.,* pp. 164–82.

Question: How is the press used as an instrument of government? How does the press influence government?

"Just the Facts, Ma'am: What is Straight News," *Democracy in Action,* pp. 296–98.

Question: To what extent can the press influence political decisions?

CLARK, TOM C., "Inside the Court," *Politics, U.S.A.,* pp. 440–44.

Question: How does the Supreme Court function?

DEPARTMENT OF EDUCATION AND RESEARCH, CIO, "Government by Minority," *Political Institutions,* pp. 185–90.

Question: What groups would resist attempts to reapportion political power in the state of Maryland?

DESMOND, THOMAS C., "The States Eclipse the Cities," *Capitol, Courthouse and City Hall,* pp. 36–39.

Question: How does Thomas Desmond think the relationship between states and the cities within them can be improved?

"To Help Governors Govern," *Capitol, Courthouse and City Hall,* pp. 131–33.

Question: As described by Desmond, what functions is a state governor expected to perform?

DOUGLAS, WILLIAM O., "Misconceptions of the Judicial Function," *Profile of American Politics,* pp. 202–05.

Question: What is the philosophy upon which the American court system is based? What is the relationship between the Constitution and decisions handed down by the courts?

FARMERS' UNION, 1959, "It Pays to Fight," *Political Institutions,* 94–96.

Question: What methods does the Farmers' Union use to influence legislative decisions?

HEARINGS BEFORE THE SUBCOMMITTEE ON APPROPRIATIONS, "A Million Dollars for Cocktails," *Political Institutions,* pp. 251–52.

Question: What influence does the congressional committee on appropriations have over State Department decisions?

HYMAN, SIDNEY, "Inquiry into the Decline of Congress," *Political Institutions,* pp. 201–05.

Question: Why has congressional decision-making power declined in relation to that of the President, according to Mr. Hyman? Do you think his analysis is correct?

KELLEY, STANLEY, "Medical Economics and Doctor Politics," *Politics, U.S.A.,* pp. 189–95.

Question: What methods did the American Medical Association use to present their point of view to the public?

KERR, BRENTON W., "The Efficiency of the Russian Supreme Soviet," *Political Institutions,* pp. 214–15.

Question: Why does it take the British House of Commons three quarters of a year to transact the legislative business that is completed by the Supreme Soviet in about two weeks?

KOENIG, LOUIS W., "The Power Behind the Throne," *Politics, U.S.A.,* pp. 402–12.

Question: What is the function of "The Assistant to the President"? As the role was played by Sherman Adams, how much power does an assistant have to influence Presidential decisions?

LEWIS, R. CRAGIN, "New Power at the Polls: The Doctors," *Politics, U.S.A.,* pp. 303–10.

Question: How did doctors organize to influence congressional voting on compulsory health insurance?

LINDSAY, JOHN V., "An Inquiry into the Darkness of the Cloak, the Sharpness of the Dagger," *Politics, U.S.A.,* pp. 535–44.

Question: According to Mr. Lindsay, what has the role of the CIA been in the making of foreign policy decisions?

MAGRATH, C. PETER, "Nine Deliberative Bodies—A Profile of the Warren Court," *Politics, U.S.A.,* pp. 444–56.

Question: What did Justice Robert H. Jackson mean when he said the United States Supreme Court "functions less as one deliberative body than as nine." How does this affect the role of the court in the American political system?

MCGILL, RALPH, "If the Southern Negro Got To Vote," *Political Institutions,* pp. 137–40.

Question: How has the southern Negro been limited in his ability to influence political decisions?

MEDINA, HAROLD R., "The Ordeal of Judge Medina," *Politics, U.S.A.,* pp. 456–63.

Question: How did Judge Medina conduct himself throughout the trial of the American Communist Party leaders? What does his attitude tell you about the way in which he sees the role of the judge in the American political system?

NATIONAL MUNICIPAL LEAGUE, "Forms of Municipal Government—How Have They Worked?", *Capitol, Courthouse and City Hall,* pp. 176–84.

Question: What do you consider the most desirable form of city government? Why?

NEUSTADT, RICHARD E., "The Case of the Reluctant Leader," *Politics, U.S.A.*, pp. 394–401.

Question: What groups actively attempted to influence President Eisenhower's decision concerning support for the 1958 budget submitted to Congress?

NEWSWEEK MAGAZINE, "A Surprising Decision: Cheers, 806 and OK," *Democracy in Action*, pp. 93–96.

Question: What considerations appear to have influenced the decision that resulted in Lyndon Johnson's becoming the Vice-Presidential candidate in 1960?

OSBORN, JOHN, "One Supreme Court," *Profile of American Politics*, pp. 34–41.

Question: Has the Supreme Court abandoned the traditional practice of law for the "rule of reason"?

PARKINSON, C. NORTHCOTE, "How Seven Employees Can Be Made To Do the Work of One," *Profile of American Politics*, pp. 196–200.

Question: What is the implication of Parkinson's law?

POLLOCK, JAMES K., "An Appraisal of the Initiative and Referendum," *Political Institutions*, pp. 145–47.

Question: According to the author, what is the value of allowing voters to participate directly in the making of legislative decisions? Do you agree?

PRESS, CHARLES AND CHARLES ADRIAN, "Why Our State Governments Are Sick," *Capitol, Courthouse and City Hall*, pp. 13–19.

Question: What are the problems of state governments as seen by Charles Press and Charles Adrian?

SHULMAN, MARSHALL D., "Has the Soviet System Changed Since Stalin?", *The USSR and Communism*, pp. 176–79.

Question: How did political decision-making change under Khrushchev?

TRUMAN, HARRY S. and DOUGLAS MACARTHUR, "A Change of Command," *Democracy in Action*, pp. 197–210.

Question: With whom did President Truman confer before reaching a decision concerning the release of General MacArthur? What factors appear to have entered into his decision?

VANDERBILT, ARTHUR T., "The Essentials of a Sound Judicial System," *Capitol, Courthouse and City Hall*, pp. 169–75.

Question: What does Arthur Vanderbilt consider the essentials of a sound judicial system?

WALSH, JOHN, "Appropriations," *Politics, U.S.A.*, pp. 381–87.

Question: What is the function of the House Appropriations Committee? How does this committee influence legislative decision-making?

WASHINGTON POST, "The Gas Lobby—A Case Study," *Profile of American Politics*, pp. 82–87.

Question: What pressure-group methods were used to influence the decision of the Senate?

YARMOLINSKY, ADAM, "The Kennedy Talent Hunt," *Politics, U.S.A.*, pp. 412–18.

Question: How did President Kennedy go about staffing the top administrative posts in the federal government? How much influence do these administrators have over political decision-making?

Unit Five

The Role of the Citizen: The U.S. and the U.S.S.R.

POLITICAL LEADERS have the greatest amount of influence over the decisions made within a political system. Other citizens participate in the decision-making process to varying degrees. The degree to which citizens who are not leaders influence their government helps us to separate one type of political system from another.

In simple societies it is sometimes difficult to tell who is playing the role of a political leader and who is being led. In Reading 7 you saw that when Red Robe's sons were killed by the Crows, Cheyenne warriors went to talk to him. After their discussion, all swore vengeance against the Crows. A political decision had been made without the leaders playing a more important role than the other citizens.

In more complex societies the role of the political leader is more distinct. Ordinary citizens sometimes have a part to play, and they play it by bringing influence to bear on their leaders. Democracy has been defined as a political system in which the general public influences the selection of leaders and the decisions they make. Totalitarianism, on the other hand, can be defined as a political system in which the citizen has no real influence on decisions. In Unit Five, you will examine the role played by the citizen in the political systems of the United States and the Soviet Union.

Chapter 13

The Role of the Citizen in the United States

STATING THE ISSUE   As President of the United States, John F. Kennedy played the role of a leader. When he made decisions concerning the Cuban crisis, he was playing this role. But when he voted in an election, he was once again a private citizen, playing his role as a voter. No matter what other roles an individual plays in his life, he is also a citizen within a political system, governed by the system's leaders.

Even though the individual citizen is not directly involved in the process of making major political decisions, it does not necessarily follow that he cannot influence them. In Reading 23 you saw individuals working in interest groups to influence an election. In Reading 31 you witnessed Yevtushenko's attempt to influence a decision that Nikita Khrushchev was to make.

In Chapter 13 you will concentrate on analyzing the role played by the individual citizen in the American political system. You will approach this analysis in a number of ways. First, you will take a closer look at elections. To what extent do American citizens participate in the political process of voting? How does the citizen who votes differ from the one who does not? Second, you will examine the American's access to political information. What conditions limit the role that the citizen can play in politics? How much information can he get about political issues? How reliable is this information? Finally, you will investigate the American citizen's right to disagree with political decisions. Through what channels can he express his opinion? To what extent is he encouraged to express them? These are the questions that you will examine.

49 Voter Behavior

Since democracy implies "government by the people," it assumes that citizens will be interested in politics. Yet many people who have both the right and the opportunity to influence political decisions fail to do so. Without citizen interest, "government by the people" is impossible. A surprising number of citizens of the United States play no role at all in the political process in their country.

In 1950 Julian Woodward and Elmo Roper surveyed the political activities of eight thousand Americans. The results of this survey were published in *The American Political Science Review* of December 1950. These results indicated that while 75 per cent of those interviewed had voted once or more in the preceding four years, a very small percentage were active politically in any other way. Of those interviewed, 21 per cent said they discussed public issues with others, 31 per cent belonged to one or more organizations that took stands on public issues, 13 per cent communicated with public officials to express an opinion on a public issue, and 11 per cent actively worked in campaigns for the election of particular political candidates.

Many political scientists have studied voter behavior to identify why some citizens are politically active while others are willing to take no part in the making of decisions that vitally concern them. Reading 49 is concerned with the results of some of these studies. As you examine the statistics in the three tables which follow, consider these questions:

1. How politically active are citizens in the American political system?
2. What appears to influence the extent to which a citizen participates in the political process?
3. How serious a problem is political inactivity?

1. Relation of Degree of Interest in Campaign to Voting Turnout, 1956

A. CAMPBELL, *et al.*

The citizens whose answers are recorded in this table responded to these questions: "Some people don't pay much attention to the political campaigns. How about you? Would you say that you have been very much interested, somewhat interested, or not much interested in following the political campaigns so far this year?" From The American Voter, *1960. Reprinted by permission of John Wiley & Sons, Inc.*

DEGREE OF INTEREST IN CAMPAIGN

	Not Much Interested	Somewhat Interested	Very Much Interested
Voted	58%	72%	87%
Did Not Vote	42	28	13%
	100%	100%	100%
Number of Cases	540	695	520

2. Relation of Degree of Concern About Election Outcome to Voting Turnout, 1956

A. CAMPBELL, et al.

The citizens reported here answered the question: "Generally speaking, would you say that you personally care a good deal which party wins the Presidential election this fall, or that you don't care very much which party wins?" From The American Voter, 1960. Reprinted by permission of John Wiley & Sons, Inc.

DEGREE OF CONCERN OVER ELECTION OUTCOME

	Don't Care at All	Don't Care Very Much	Care Somewhat	Care Very Much
Voted	52%	69%	76%	84%
Did Not Vote	48	31	24	16
	100%	100%	100%	100%
Number of Cases	230	367	627	459

3. Relation of Political Participation to Level of Issue Familiarity, 1956

V. O. KEY, JR.

What relation does a citizen's familiarity with the issues important in an election have to his participation in it? How familiar with the issues were the persons who reported low participation? those who reported medium participation? those who reported high participation? Use the data in this table to answer these questions. Reprinted from Public Opinion and American Democracy *by V. O. Key, Jr.* © *Copyright 1961 by V. O. Key, Jr. Reprinted by permission.*

ISSUE FAMILIARITY		LEVEL OF PARTICIPATION		
		Low	Medium	High
High	4	16%	30%	45%
	3	17	27	27
	2	18	19	16
Low	1	49	24	12
		100%	100%	100%
Number of Cases		394	770	515

50 The Individual's Access to Political Information

To be effective politically, an individual must know what is happening. If a citizen has no information about a crisis in Cuba, he cannot express an opinion about how it should be handled. If he knows nothing about the circumstances surrounding the crisis, his opinion will not be of much value.

Americans are bombarded with political information. In 1965, 1,751 daily newspapers printed political stories. Thousands of magazines, some of which sell millions of copies of a single issue, carry news about national and local government. Radio and television stations beam broadcasts into the home of virtually every American. Interest groups mail leaflets to potential voters; civic groups send representatives to speak at meetings of citizens; neighbors talk politics with each other. Information on controversial political questions can scarcely be avoided. Moreover, the wide diversity of sources of information helps to assure that all sides of an issue will be heard.

Newspaper editors, television and radio commentators, and public speakers, however, all have to decide what political information they will present. Limited space or time compels selection. The editor of a daily newspaper cannot print everything; he picks out a few stories and rejects others. Then he must decide which item to headline and which to bury on an inside page. The news commentator similarly selects incidents to discuss. He probably has only fifteen minutes or a half-hour of valuable air time allotted to him. Should he talk about what happened in Washington or in his own city? Is his audience more interested in politics, sports, or murders? Editors of trade papers, periodicals, and the newsletters of interest groups all face this same problem of selection. The way they select information and the way they present it reflect their point of view.

Reading 50 presents two cases that illustrate some of the questions a newspaper editor must answer as he decides what political information to make available to his readers. In considering the problems confronting a single editor of a single newspaper, think about the following questions:

1. What are some of the political issues that were given broad coverage in *The Toledo Blade*? How would you classify these issues? As a result of this coverage, how effective does the *Blade* appear to be in getting its readers to support a particular point of view? On these issues, what other sources of information might have been available to *Blade* readers?
2. What type of question do you think the editors of *The New York Times* asked themselves before reaching a decision about whether they should publish their exclusive story on the Cuban crisis? Through what other communications media might this information have come to the attention of the American public?
3. To what extent does the United States government appear to control the individual's access to political information?

1. The Power of the Press: The Case of the *Toledo Blade*

REO M. CHRISTENSON

Reprinted from Midwest Journal of Political Science *Vol. III, No. 3 (August, 1959) by Reo M. Christenson by permission of the Wayne State University Press.*

Ever since Franklin D. Roosevelt and Harry S. Truman overcame the massed opposition of the nation's newspapers, observers have wagged their heads over the political impotence of the press. The dominant position of the *Toledo Blade* in Toledo politics, however, suggests that the power of the press has other dimensions besides that of electing Presidents. . . .

The press renders an invaluable service to self-government by reporting upon men and organizations who possess political influence and power, and by passing judgment on them. On the other hand, the press exercises power of its own which is largely unreported and unexamined. . . .

Although Publisher Paul Block, Jr. (who also owns the only other newspaper in town, the morning *Times*), would win no popularity contest in Toledo, the *Blade* is by all odds the most potent political force in Toledo. It certainly does not run the city in arbitrary, single-handed fashion. No newspaper could. But it wields immense influence. It has made, broken, and chastened many a politician. It has pushed through or blocked many a public policy. When it gives the word and applies the heat, [city] council is normally quick to respond. When it adopts a Sphinx-like pose, council squirms uneasily. Day in and day out, council acts with one eye cocked on the *Blade*.

Editor Mike Bradshaw, no man to boast, put the *Blade's* position in these words a few years ago. "[I would] shudder to think what the responsibility [of the editorial page] must have been if [its influence] was ever greater . . . the political influence of our independent newspaper in our independent community is so strong that we are not so much concerned with the power of the press as with our responsibility to use it wisely."

Bradshaw added that ". . . unavoidably, the editorial page has become the arbiter of community affairs in many of our single owner-ship cities. When Democrats and Republicans have at each other, it is our responsibility to say which party has offered the better candidates—to choose between them.

"But the same thing happens in a less measurable way in other civic controversies. If the chamber of commerce and the CIO get into a hassle, if the milk drivers strike for higher wages, if the judge of our domestic relations court insists that a building for the Child Study Institute and his chambers, should cost a million dollars and the real estate board contends that $750,000 will be enough, we are supposed to weigh the arguments and say which side is right. The newspaper is to be the referee.". . .

So far as national politics and policies are concerned, Toledo residents are of course exposed to the reports and interpretations of a wide variety of sources—national television and radio networks, news magazines, journals of opinion, and syndicated newspaper columnists, for example. In this hotly competitive field, the *Blade's* news and editorial columns must contend with numerous other voices.

But about the only picture most Toledoans get of Toledo is that supplied by the *Blade*. . . .

If the *Blade* chooses to promote or discredit or simply call commu-nity attention to a development or proposal in which it is interested, it may detail a reporter to do a special story, or series of stories, on that subject. For example, it was able to arouse community support for a more vigorous enforcement of the city's housing regulations by printing a series of reports describing the squalid conditions existing in certain rental units, naming the owners and spelling out their resistance to previous law-enforcement pressures. . . .

Again, when the Conant report on secondary schools made

twenty-one recommendations for achieving sound high school programs, the *Blade* commissioned a reporter to see how well Toledo's schools measured up to the Conant criteria. The feature articles which followed undoubtedly helped stimulate a reappraisal of Toledo schools by its educational leaders, and there are indications that this reappraisal will bear fruit.

On the other hand, like every other newspaper, the *Blade* may play down developments it frowns upon, or which do not contribute to the community picture it prefers to reflect. Because of the lack of reader sophistication in these matters, selectivity and emphasis in reporting the news can be employed quite freely to help shape desired community attitudes without unduly arousing community suspicions. . . .

. . . The *Blade*, which keeps a sharp eye on persons or groups which may be seeking a larger leadership role than it thinks proper, keeps its guns perpetually trained on the Toledo Municipal League. The league, a perfectly respectable, responsible, and useful research and "good government" body, has been exposed to a prolonged succession of withering attacks by the *Blade*. The latter has repeatedly gone out of its way to belittle the league, all too often by distorting its position or by attributing improper motives or chicanery to it which the paper is able to sustain only by innuendo. . . .

A brief rundown on some of the *Blade*'s major activities will help illustrate the paper's dominant place in Toledo.

Although its performance was less striking in the last election, the *Blade* has a notable long-run record of supporting local candidates who turn out to be winners. In 1950, displeased with the candidates for Congress offered by both political parties, the *Blade* backed an independent, Frazier Reams (openly labeled "the *Blade* candidate"), and was probably responsible for his election. . . .

Four years later, either because Block thought Toledo would be better served by a congressman associated with one of the major parties, or because he was nettled by Reams' wishy-washy attitude toward the Oppenheimer case [the case involving the security clearance of J. Robert Oppenheimer], the *Blade* disowned Reams, supported an almost unknown young Democrat, Ludlow Ashley, and saw him elected by a comfortable margin. . . .

. . . . While some political veterans can undoubtedly win without *Blade* support, more obscure political figures, including younger men trying to get a foothold on the city's political ladder, are critically dependent on the *Blade*'s favor. An editorial or two lambasting or lauding a relatively unknown man can affect his fortunes crucially. And if the *Blade* makes a really determined effort to defeat a councilman who won by a narrow margin in the previous election, it is more than likely to succeed. . . .

The *Blade*'s control over council has occasioned both wry amuse-

224

ment and considerable irritation among those who follow municipal affairs closely. . . .

Council normally shrinks from taking a firm stand on any major civic measure until the *Blade* has tipped its hand. Once the latter has given its marching orders, council knows the path of safety and the path of peril and almost invariably chooses the former. A number of occasions could be cited, in fact, in which council, after voting one way in committee of the whole, reversed itself in regular session following an editorial blast by the *Blade*. . . .

If the *Blade*'s power for weal and woe has impressive local dimensions, the *Blade* would be the first to concede the limitations of its influence. Although it favored the substitution of the strong-mayor for the city-manager form of municipal government in 1957, it made only a feeble pitch for the former because it sensed the deep-rooted community opposition which later erupted at the polls. When a property tax boost to provide capital improvement funds was proposed on the heels of a reassessment which had raised property taxes considerably, *Blade* pleas for its passage were met by a negative avalanche of tax-weary votes. A second try in the spring of 1958, with the increased levies limited to financing expressways, was also beaten despite *Blade* support.

Thus, even a shrewd and generally respected monopoly newspaper appears unable to shape local opinion when voters are strongly predisposed to favor a given course of action or inaction. But where they are closely divided, or more commonly, apathetic, the *Blade*'s experience suggests that a newspaper which knows what it's about can often carry the day.

Although the power of the press in local affairs is a largely unexplored area of America's political anatomy, the writer is under no illusion that the power of the *Blade* in municipal affairs is typical of the power of the press on the local scene. Possibly a majority of publishers look upon the newpaper as a strictly commercial enterprise and make little or no serious effort to convert it into a vehicle for acquiring and exercising the maximum political power. Many of them lack the instinct to do battle, shrink from giving offense to any important group in the city, or lack the political finesse which effective leadership demands. Some newspapers apparently have a negative political impact—their endorsement of a candidate or a proposal constitutes the kiss of death.

But if the *Blade*'s power is not representative of American newspapers, the role of papers like the *Milwaukee Journal*, the *Louisville Courier-Journal*, the *Cleveland Press*, the *Akron Beacon-Journal*, and the *Los Angeles Times* suggests that the *Blade*'s experience is by no means unique. Thus, even if the press can't elect Presidents at will, it is time to challenge the notion that its political influence has largely withered away. . . .

2. Bay of Pigs Avoidance Seen
If Story Was Told

ASSOCIATED PRESS

St. Paul, Minnesota, June 1—The late President Kennedy told a *New York Times* executive that if the *Times* had printed all it knew about the pending Bay of Pigs invasion of Cuba, the United States would have been saved from a "colossal mistake," a *Times* editor disclosed here today.

Managing Editor Clifton Daniel revealed—for the first time, he said—some painful decision-making at the *Times* before both the Bay of Pigs invasion and the later Cuban missile crisis. . . .

Daniel traced in detail some strong differences of opinion among *Times* executives leading to the toning down of a *Times* dispatch on April 7, 1961, which described Cuban invasion plans. [The invasion did not take place until April 17.]

Daniel painted a picture of a President apparently torn in two directions by the course the *Times* took during the Bay of Pigs buildup.

At one point, meeting with a group of editors after the incident, President Kennedy "ran down a list of what he called premature disclosures of security information," mostly from the *Times,* Daniel said.

"While he scolded *The New York Times*," Daniel went on, "the President said in an aside to Mr. Catledge [then the managing editor of the *Times*] 'If you had printed more about the operation, you would have saved us from a colossal mistake.'". . .

Daniel told of detailed and heated exchanges among top *Times* executives before the decision was made to give the controversial dispatch a lesser headline, eliminate reference to the "imminent" invasion, and drop reference to participation of the Central Intelligence Agency in invasion preparations.

Daniel said his own view today is that the Bay of Pigs operation "might well have been canceled, and the country would have been saved enormous embarrassment if *The New York Times* and other newspapers had been more diligent in the performance of their duty."

By contrast, Daniel added, when the crisis of Russian missiles in Cuba came to a head, the *Times,* at the personal request of President Kennedy, withheld its exclusive story until the government had had an opportunity to complete plans to counter it. . . .

51 The Right to Disagree: Dissent

In both the United States and the Soviet Union, individuals sometimes disagree with the decisions made by their political leaders. Yevtushenko disagreed with Khrushchev's decision to limit artistic expression. Governor Faubus disagreed with the Supreme Court's decision that called for the integration of Little Rock schools. One way to compare political systems is to evaluate the freedom individuals have to express their opinions when they think decisions made by political leaders are unwise.

Dissent is the term used to describe the disagreement of individuals with decisions made by political leaders. Dissent arises around specific issues. The Mothers' League of Central High School in Little Rock, Arkansas, disagreed with the 1954 decision of the Supreme Court. The members expressed their dissent by calling upon Governor Faubus "to prevent forcible integration of the Little Rock schools because it would be contrary to an act passed by the state legislature." Others expressed their dissent by surrounding the high school on the day Negro students were to enroll. Dissent has been demonstrated through marches, picketing, and protest meetings. It is expressed through letters to the editor and telegrams to congressmen. It is verbalized in conversation and public speeches. To be politically effective, however, dissenters must have an audience who can influence key decision-makers.

In 1965, a group of dissenters devised an unusual technique for getting their views heard. A group of university professors questioned decisions the government had made about the war in Vietnam. They wanted to present the "facts" surrounding the problem and to look at conflicting views of its solution. They devised a technique called a *teach-in*.

On March 24, 1965, some two hundred members of the University of Michigan's faculty and two thousand students attended a night-long rally to discuss and debate United States policy in Vietnam. Within weeks the teach-in movement had spread to campuses all over the country. Hundreds of professors and students participated in all-night discussions. On May 15 a national teach-in took place at a Washington hotel with closed-circuit radio relaying the debate to 110 campuses. Over 100,000 persons heard the program, and after the formal presentation they continued with all-night sessions of their own.

The teach-in, conceived as a forum for both sides of the controversy, invited top-level government officials to engage in debate with college professors, some of whom disagreed violently with government policy. McGeorge Bundy, the President's Special Assistant for National Security Affairs, was scheduled to represent the government's position. Bundy cancelled his appearance on the day of the debate because he had to leave on an unexpected mission to the Dominican Republic, where a sudden crisis had erupted. But he sent a prepared message that was read for him. Other government officials did participate in a debate with academic authorities on Asian affairs in an effort to put before the American public the difficulties involved in reaching consensus on complex, value-laden problems.

Webster Schott, a writer for the *St. Louis Post-Dispatch,* listened to the national teach-in broadcast at Washington University in St. Louis. His account of the experience is recorded in "The Teach-In—New Forum for Reason." As you read, keep these questions in mind:

1. Who participated in the teach-in at Washington University?
2. How did the professors involved explain their reasons for participating? What do you think of their reasons?
3. To what extent is dissent limited in the United States? Is the teach-in an effective way to express dissent?

The Teach-In—New Forum for Reason
WEBSTER SCHOTT

In 1965, controversy raged over the United States' involvement in the war in Vietnam. The article below appeared in The Nation Magazine *on May 31, 1965, and describes one of the many manifestations of this controversy. From* The Nation Magazine, *May 31, 1965. Reprinted by permission.*

. . . Affiliated with the national teach-in at Washington that failed to produce McGeorge Bundy, some one hundred teach-ins were held at colleges and universities across the country on May 15. At Washington University in St. Louis, the teach-in began at 1:00 P.M., with radio-telephone hookup to the Washington debate; it ended the next morning at 1:30. Professors and students then swept up cigarette butts, paper plates, leftover French fries, and rearranged chairs and tables for breakfast in Wohl Student Center cafeteria.

I attended the Washington University teach-in because the Ad Hoc Committee on Foreign Policy there had placed the public needle in McGeorge Bundy, Presidential adviser, that led to his accepting an invitation to appear at the national teach-in held by the Inter-University Committee for a Public Hearing on Vietnam.

Earlier, Bundy had rejected the Washington University committee's letter of April 10, inviting him to come to St. Louis for a teach-in debate. "I find strange your assumption that a public official is somehow accountable to the profession in which he worked before coming to the government. . . ." He closed by saying that if the letter, which raised questions about American policy in Vietnam, "came to me for grading as a professor of government, I would not be able to give it high marks." The exchange of correspondence became national news. The professors' letter, signed by 127 Washington University faculty members, was transmitted by Robert Buckhout, secretary of the ad hoc committee. A twenty-nine-year-old assistant professor of psychology, Buckhout was chairman of the Washington University teach-in.

For three hours, students and faculty intermittently listened, hissed, applauded, read, wandered, took notes, tape recorded, and ate to the debates taking place 750 miles away. If there was a hero in these Washington exchanges, brought to St. Louis at a cost of $200, paid by faculty contributions, he was Hans Morgenthau. Cheers arose when he demanded "full and honest answers" from the government about Vietnam instead of "contradictions, half truths, and double talk." If there was a villain, he was McGeorge Bundy, who canceled his appearance shortly before air time because of "important national business."

In the absence of Mr. Bundy, the Washington teach-in became a three-hour version of "Meet the Academics," but the crowd grew in the ground-floor northwest bay of Wohl Center, and soon Dr. Buckhout took the debate upstairs to the cafeteria, where there was room for several hundred more.

Academia was to be seen in profile: Beatle haircuts and beards; barefoot girls with elbow-length hair and Daisy Mae shorts; little old ladies in hair nets; professors pulling on their pipes; a man in overalls; middle-aged "adult education" women who might have been on their way to the A & P; and outside Wohl the inevitable baby carriages. . . .

The repetitiousness of the panelists' arguments combined with the marvel of electronic technology somehow managed to render boring the life-and-death issues being argued at the Sheraton Park Hotel in Washington. In St. Louis, the good guys and bad guys had been identified by the location of their names on the wall. The audience fidgeted, reflexed, and stared as if waiting for a bull to appear and take the place of Bundy, who was assumed to be in hiding. It also waited, somewhat lovingly, for pickets from the Young Americans for Freedom who never showed up.

Everything except the sandwiches, Cokes, and smoke changed when the "live" teach-in started late Saturday afternoon. Ideas took on vitality because they came from identifiable personalities. Faculty and students from Washington University, St. Louis University, Flat River Junior College, the University of Missouri at St. Louis, Maryville College, Eden Theological Seminary, and elsewhere delivered papers, made extemporaneous speeches, questioned, and answered from the floor as the rotating panel rolled through the night. The interplay among panelists, faculty, and students revealed the teach-in as more than a phenomenon of protest and dissent. Could it become a permanent new technique of interdiscipline education or a means of achieving a consensus of intellectuals on issues of national concern?

By the time the teach-in had taught itself out, approximately thirty panelists (some unscheduled and improvising hastily) and perhaps one hundred five-minute speakers from the audience had discussed the State Department White Paper on Vietnam, national liberation movements in America and Asia, the Vietcong, Leninism, U.S. intervention in the Dominican Republic, Maoism, international law, the bankruptcy of liberal ideology, the Monroe Doctrine, Madison Avenue, civil rights, racism, capital punishment, Austria and Czechoslovakia, the French underground in World War II, social democracy and capitalism, Algeria, Walter Lippmann and James Reston, creeping involvement, managed news, Mussolini and Ethiopia, the nationalization of British industry, the student-professor relationship, dominoes and checkers, salami and baloney. I took sixty-one pages of notes. . .

There were no good guys and bad guys during the live teach-in. Continuously changing as some two thousand students came and went for eight hours, the audience of five hundred to six hundred responded unpredictably. Both defenders and opponents of government foreign policy found support. The only speakers left hanging on threads of applause were those who lacked facts, took vague positions, or droned abstractions. Around midnight, Buckhout asked whether someone didn't want to heckle, and someone did. Students came to the teach-in because they wanted to know.

The largest ovation of the day or night followed a long, detailed account of Indo-Chinese social and political history by Father Francis Corley, a Jesuit professor of Asian studies at St. Louis University. Students took notes on French colonialism, Bao Dai, the Geneva accords of 1954, the Diem family government, changes in Vietnamese regimes, the formation of the National Liberation Front and the Vietcong. . . . The enthusiasm for this painstaking presentation supported a point made at the start of the teach-in by Dr. Bernard Baumrin, associate professor of philosophy and one of the teach-in organizers.

"There is nothing improper in what we are doing here," he said. "We are just covering up for, or updating, a poorly designed curriculum. We forgot to have courses on Southeast Asia politics in the curriculum this year. The academic community failed in Germany during the 1930's. We are not going to let it happen here.". . .

Successive academicians probed, attacked, and illuminated. The audience listened, applauded, ate, and lined up for questions. There was no typical speech. They ranged through history and, it seemed, through eternity:

Theodore H. Von Laue, professor of history at Washington University:

The national teach-in movement has tried to force an experiment in direct democracy. The great disappointment of the Johnson administration is that it is committed to a program of economic and social development at home and has found itself wrapped up in a war it cannot end. We are striving for a "negotiable position." Everyone seems to agree: get out of Vietnam. The question is how. . . .

Joseph Summers, professor of English at Washington University:

Dean Rusk's anger at the academic community is that it "dares to violate established bureaucratic procedures." Professors "don't believe Rusk's handouts because we've been lied to too often." First the political chaos in South Vietnam was due to Diem, then to the Buddhists, now to the Vietcong. Which is it? The truth is the U.S. has been willing to risk a world war rather than admit its own defeat. . . .

Earl Reeves, professor of political science at the University of Missouri in St. Louis:

Academicians can speak more freely than those in government. The crucial matter is the issues discussed during the national teach-in, not the insult of the government's failure to produce Mr. Bundy or refusing to provide panelists for the Washington University teach-in. Government does not contribute to the satisfactory discussion of issues; that is up to the electorate. . . .

And so it went. The professors argued: Richard Yang, an associate professor of Asian studies . . . demanded that the United States behave like a real tiger and stop the Communists. Stanley Spector, Yang's chief at Washington University, insisted otherwise . . .

. . . The teach-in carries the fervor, the grind, the provocation, and even a name derived from the civil rights movement. But the teach-in is different. This revolt against the existing power structure in the United States must have faculty leadership, organization, and participation. The physical requirements demand at least tacit administration approval. Thomas H. Eliot, Chancellor of Washington University, who rose to his post from the Political Science Department, was unavailable for comment on the teach-in. On several other occasions, however, he has defended academic freedom. The provost, George E. Pake, declined to comment on the teach-in directly, saying the university was neither for nor against it. However, he said, "the university is in favor of anything which brings about a free and open discussion of national issues.". . .

52 The Right to Disagree: Alienation

Dissent is a vital part of the democratic process. It is a link between the people and their government. It is a means of communication, a way in which voters can tell their leaders what they want. Disagreement and the balancing of conflicting interests is the base upon which a democratic political system is built. But even a democracy must limit dissension, or chaos may result.

Dissenters may disagree with the decisions their leaders make, but they do not challenge the government's authority to make decisions. They may disagree with the Supreme Court's judgment that separate school facilities cannot be equal, but they do not stand in the way of officials authorized to enforce this judgment. They may disagree about the wisdom of the government's policy in Vietnam, but they do not deny the government's right to make foreign policy. They are dissenters, but they are not alienated from the entire system.

The term *alienation* has been used to describe many different phenomena. Citizens who do not vote and play no role in the political process are said to be alienated. In a system built around the belief that control of the government should lie in the hands of citizens, the nonvoter challenges the existence of the system itself. He is acting in a way that is contrary to the system, a way that, if generally adopted, would destroy it.

Not all alienated people are passive. Some decide to act out their dissatisfaction with the system. Such a man was Frederick John Kasper. Reading 52 describes an incident involving him that occurred in Clinton, Tennessee. As you read consider the following questions:

1. What happened in Clinton, Tennessee? Why did Kasper get involved? What did he do?
2. At what point can Kasper's actions no longer be considered legitimate dissent?
3. How do the alienated threaten the political system?

The Town That Became "Everybody's Test Tube"

DAVID HALBERSTAM

From The Reporter, *January 10, 1957. By permission of the publisher and the author.*

Clinton, Tennessee, a small rural community built around a courthouse in the eastern coal-mining hills of the state, seems in many respects more like a northern town than a southern one. There are, for instance, few Negroes on the streets; one sees whites at janitorial duties; and last November the most conspicuous political headquarters housed Republicans. Clinton has frequently elected Republicans to local offices and the state legislature. . . .

. . . Five years ago its Negroes decided they were tired of sending their children twenty miles away to a segregated high school in Knoxville. So they started a long course of litigation for admission to Clinton High, in the middle of which the Supreme Court handed down its school decision. Federal Judge Robert L. Taylor then ordered integration of the high school to get under way in the fall of 1956.

Given the court order, Clinton prepared peacefully—if not voluntarily—to carry it out. . . . "There's been no trouble here at all," high school principal D. J. Brittain, Jr., told me on the eve of registration. "The people may not like this by choice, but they realize it's a court order, and it's what we have to do. I'm not expecting any trouble." Looking back after four months, the principal's optimistic prediction has proved drastically wrong. Twice in that period Clinton has verged on the brink of a complete breakdown of law and order. . . .

Enter Kasper

When he operated a Greenwich Village bookstore a few years ago, a young man named Frederick John Kasper liked to talk with his Negro friends about a man's role in history. In each great man's life, he said, comes a moment when he seizes greatness. "The strong Negroes must lead the weaker ones. If I were a Negro, I'd lead a march on Washington to get something done for my people." He told one Negro friend, an artist named Ted Joans: "Why don't you hang one of your paintings in the Museum of Modern Art? Everyone steals paintings, but no one hangs them. Think of the publicity you'll get."

Joans never hung that painting, but on August 25, 1956, the weekend before school started in Clinton, John Kasper, now executive secretary of the Seaboard White Citizens' Council of Washington, D. C., seized the moment he thought would bring his own moment of greatness. Kasper came to Clinton unannounced, sleeping in his car the night before like a seedy traveling salesman. Then Saturday and Sunday he canvassed the town, looking for dissent. No less an authority on Kasper than Kasper himself gave this account of his purpose: "I'm a rabble-rouser. The people of Clinton needed a leader, so I went there to lead them."

Leo Burnett, an accountant at the local Magnet Mills, was washing his car that Saturday afternoon when a tall young stranger cut through his backyard. Without introducing himself, the stranger asked Burnett what he thought about Negroes going to the high school.

"Well, I'm like most of the people here," Burnett answered. "I'm not for it, but my personal feelings don't enter into it. It's inevitable. The Court ordered it."

Then Kasper introduced himself and discussed his purpose. "You don't have to obey the law," he said. "The will of the people is supreme.

"Will your wife picket the high school Monday?" he went on. "I've talked to a lot of other people who said they would." Burnett said she wouldn't, and they argued about it for awhile. "If our forefathers took your attitude," Kasper said, "we'd still be ruled by England."

"I'm not interested in starting a revolution," was Burnett's answer.

Kasper continued his house-to-house campaign, telling the people they didn't have to obey the law if they didn't want to. By the end of the week, Clinton was a battleground. There were riots, cars were rocked, citizens and travelers molested. The following Saturday, a week after Kasper's arrival, the mob seemed to take over, and only a hastily organized home guard of the town's leaders throwing tear gas could keep it down until a hundred state troopers arrived, followed soon by six hundred National Guardsmen, who had been ordered in by Governor Frank Clement. . . . On August 31, Kasper was convicted of violating a federal injunction against interfering with racial integration in the Clinton high school. . . .

"John'll Show 'Em"

The alliance between the mob and its leader is an unusual one: Kasper, the New Jersey-born Columbia graduate in his neat gray suit, his brooding eyes accusing the whole world of persecution, will suddenly brighten as he is surrounded by his followers, reaching out to shake hands with him or just to touch him, whispering in his ear or getting his autograph; then he smiles benignly, a liberator of the downtrodden and oppressed.

Kasper is a study in irony: a twenty-seven-year-old firebrand overpowered by a sense of history and his own relation to it but still going against one of its strongest currents; the militant anti-Communist writing a tragedy that can give complete satisfaction only to the Communists; the political crusader with a states' rights pin on his lapel who interrupts his pleas for local sovereignty with prolonged attacks on Tennessee's governor and all of Clinton's elected officials.

"There are a few sincere segregationists in his group," says Buford Lewallen, the mayor's son, "but I'm afraid that they're mostly people opposed to anyone who has achieved a little material success. I guess this is latent in any community, and it just took an anarchist to bring it out. These people aren't so much for segregation as they are *against* something. It happens to be integration, but they're against authority and looking for excitement.

"Kasper talks to them about Blackstone's *Commentaries*, about Ezra Pound, and about his own interpretation of the Constitution, and they love it, even though they never heard of the first two and don't understand the third." . . .

Building Utopia

On the night of November 5, Kasper spoke to his followers on temperance, since . . . there was to be a liquor referendum the next day. Kasper said he favored temperance because alcohol was a part of the Communist conspiracy. "If you scan some of the lesser known writings of the top Communist officials, you find that youth should be encouraged to wealth and luxury and alcohol so that they can be easily manipulated and enslaved." Kasper went on to attack Buford Lewallen for drunkenness and to charge that Lewallen had an interest in setting up a liquor store 150 feet from a church. . . .

Then came the peroration [ending of a speech]: "I want to tell you people that you have made history here, that people all over the world are watching what you do and applauding it, and that you have built a great record and a great history. But I don't want you to stop. I want you to make Anderson County the leader for the entire Southland. You have the best people in the world to do it. People would come from all over the world just to see Anderson County as a tourist attraction just because they have heard what a Utopia it is. This is not a pipe dream. This can be done."

Mr. Lewallen's Views

When you ask Buford Lewallen what Kasper has done to his life, he says: "I'm no different from anyone else here. He's shattered it. You start up the street and you don't know whether you'll get there or not. He's set up animosity between people and groups, and thrown the whole town off its center."

Lewallen is typical of those whom Kasper's group resents most bitterly . . .

"I'm for segregation," Lewallen told me one day, "just as a way of life, and something I grew up with . . . I fought the integration suit because I thought it was the right thing to do. But when we received the court order to desegregate. I never had any doubt about what I would do. I've been practicing law for ten years, and I've never told a client to violate an order yet, and that's what this would have meant—the school board was my client."

For these views Lewallen and a few others such as Principal Brittain have been singled out for constant abuse and a concerted campaign of intimidation—telephone threats, burning crosses, and economic pressure. Recently a Kasper follower refused to shake hands [with] . . . and took a swing at Lewallen, who in his exasperation reached for a gun. He faces trial on this charge in the near future. Although Lewallen says that the majority of the white community is for law and order (as evidenced by the normal attendance figures at the high school and the 4-to-1 defeat of a slate of candidates backed by the [White] Citizens' Council in a December mayoralty election), the split in the community over so tense and emotional an issue drove most of the law-abiding citizens of Clinton into a fearful silence. The effect of this silence was to further undermine law and order, since the segregationists were so conspicuous by contrast that those of more moderate views seemed to have no support in the community.

[*Kasper was arrested for the first time on August 31. Among the charges brought against him was sedition, which according to an old Tennessee law is "a revolt against constituted authority." Kasper was brought to trial for sedition on November 5, 1956.*]

When Kasper was acquitted after his sedition trial in November, the wounds were reopened, and Kasper's followers began talking tougher than ever. . . . A chapter of White Youth for America was formed to start an anti-Negro campaign within the school, where up to then racial incidents had been infrequent. It was this campaign that put Principal Brittain in his most difficult position. How does a man who does not have official backing discipline or expel some forty students? . . . Egg-throwing and pushing kept increasing until the Negroes refused to go to school. Pressure also increased against Brittain.

"We wonder how long the people of Clinton," wrote H. V. Wells, Jr., editor of the local weekly, "are going to continue to sit idly by and see their elected officials kicked around merely because they believe in law and order and because they insist that peace be maintained."

"We Need Help"

But how do you support a man completely at this point? Give him power to expel the students and get himself beaten up? Since the school was under a federal order and there was an injunction preventing anyone from violating that order, the board met and asked for federal aid. . . .

[U.S. Attorney General Herbert] Brownell answered that the federal government would arrest "all persons" who blocked integration at Clinton, although at the same time he said that primary responsibility for the protection of students rested with local and state officers. . . .

. . . The normal number of students has returned quietly to Clinton High. But beneath the surface, the savage forces John Kasper tried to release and men like Buford Lewallen and D. J. Brittain tried to restrain are still seething . . .

Chapter 14

The Role
of the Citizen
in the Soviet Union

STATING THE ISSUE Chapter 13 indicated that American citizens can exercise considerable influence on the political system. There are frequent elections in which a citizen can vote and influence the choice of leaders. In many states, he can become involved in the primary process and affect the choice of candidates. He is flooded by political information representing many different points of view and can express his own views freely. He is limited by the extent to which he uses the tools of influence available to him and by the provision that he cannot render the system powerless through the use of force.

The individual in the Soviet political system also votes. At recent elections, more than 99 per cent of all Soviet adults have voted. But despite the large number of votes cast, the individual has little impact on the political system. Election Day is a holiday, not a vital part of the political process. Voters approve candidates that the Communist Party has already selected to govern the people.

Chapter 14 contains an analysis of the role of the citizen in the Soviet political system. While you know that the Soviet citizen has little influence as a voter, he appears capable of exerting some influence through other channels. You have no way of knowing the extent to which Yevtushenko influenced Khrushchev's decisions concerning the freedom of artists, but you do know that he felt free to comment and apparently was not punished for stating his views. It seems that certain citizens may have some impact upon the political decisions made in the Soviet Union.

To influence decisions, the citizen must have information about decisions being made. He must also be able to get his opinions heard. Chapter 14 will attempt to answer questions that probe the extent to which both of these conditions are met in the Soviet Union. To what extent is individual influence limited by a lack of political information? Can the individual make himself heard?

53 The Individual's Access to Political Information

In 1917 the Bolsheviks became the political leaders of millions of individuals who had no understanding of communist ideology. Hence, the Communist Party had to educate the people to its way of thinking. The rules of the party state that "the principal objects of the Communist Party of the Soviet Union today are to build a communist society through gradual transition from socialism to communism, continuously to raise the living and cultural standards of society, to educate the members of society in the spirit of internationalism and fraternal ties with the working people of all countries, and to strengthen to the utmost the active defense of the Soviet motherland against aggressive actions on the part of its enemies." To achieve its goals, Soviet leaders took control of all media of communication.

Over 10,000 newspapers are published in the Soviet Union in eighty-one different languages. All are controlled by the government. The Soviet citizen has his newspaper, which he is likely to read on a public bulletin board, and he is also likely to have a radio. Many citizens have television sets. The studios for both radio and television transmission are owned and operated by the government. Programs are planned by the government. News commentators are employed by the government. In the Soviet Union, all political information is censored before it gets to the individual. Even mimeograph machines are publicly owned, and everything duplicated on them must be approved.

Organized groups in the Soviet Union do have publications that meet their needs for specialized information. Artists, writers, economists, electrical engineers, educators, industrial managers, Armenians, Russians, and many other groups have their special-interest publications, and differences of opinion are found among them. But all are published by the government.

Reading 53 examines the impact that government control of information has on the role of the citizen in the Soviet political system. As you read, keep the following questions in mind:

1. What were citizens in the Soviet political system told about the Berlin crisis? What information was suppressed? What were they told about the India-China dispute? What was suppressed? What did they know of the Cuban crisis? What did they not know?
2. How would you describe the role of the press in the Soviet political system?
3. How would government control of news affect the role of the citizen in the Soviet political system?

The Role of the Press

LEO GRUILIOW

From Problems of Communism, *1963. Reprinted by permission of the United States Information Agency Press and Publications Service.*

From Lenin's time to ours, the Soviet leaders have regarded the press purely as a tool for manipulating the public mind and never as an objective reporter of information. . . .

As long as the facts can be used in accord with the regime's purposes and as long as they can be explained in a manner consonant with its ideology, even awkward information can be presented in the Soviet press. . . It is when the facts shatter the regime's public image and do not lend themselves to any explanation within the ideological framework that the big curtain descends.

We have had three . . . conspicuous examples: the erection of the Berlin wall in the autumn of 1961, the story of the Soviet bases in Cuba in the autumn of 1962, and the Chinese attack upon India in the same period. Each one was a test case, and each is instructive in its own way.

The central element in the story of the Berlin wall was the purpose of the wall — namely, to prevent the further flight of East Germans. This so flatly contradicted the whole Communist thesis that it could not be tolerated. As far as Soviet newspapers were concerned, no one fled from East Germany except a handful of thieves and spies; the border was closed solely to prevent the entry of spies from West Germany; Soviet troops were not in the vicinity; tanks and guns were not deployed, statements from the West, such as U.S. Secretary of State Rusk's offer to submit the Berlin question to the United Nations, were suppressed; criticism by neutrals, such as Indian Prime Minister Nehru, was not reported; in fact, for a long time Soviet citizens were not even told that there was a wall. It was only a month after the wall had been erected that a single Soviet daily, *Izvestia,* made brief mention of a barrier of barbed wire, bricks, and cement. Until that time it had been treated merely as a peaceable closing of the border by an indignant and aroused East German populace.

. . . The fighting on the Chinese-Indian frontier was a more difficult story for Agitprop [the Communist Party's division for Agitation and Propaganda] to handle. Here, too, the facts contradicted a basic ideological claim — namely, that the Communist countries were united in the pursuit of peace. For five days after both sides had announced the outbreak of hostilities, the Soviet press suppressed the news. On the sixth day two papers alone, out of the whole Soviet press, carried the text of a Chinese statement declaring that armed clashes had occurred and proposing a truce on Chinese terms. Editorials in the two papers backed the proposal. . . .

Two weeks of warfare went unreported; then *Pravda* (November 5, 1962) carried another editorial urging a truce, but not describing the state of affairs; and that was the extent of the information offered to the Soviet public until the cease fire, one month after the fighting had broken out. . . .

President Kennedy's initial disclosure of the presence of long-range Soviet missiles in Cuba was never published in the U.S.S.R. The Soviet government statement breaking the news of the quarantine to the Soviet people spoke only of "weapons defined by the United States as offensive weapons." It did not identify them as long-range missiles or as Soviet weapons. The press broke into denunciations of U.S. "piracy" and "aggression" and accused the United States of "strangling" Cuban women and children by cutting off supplies. Protest meetings went on all over the Soviet Union for three days. U.S. aerial photos of weapons installations in Cuba were derided as fakes.

The first indication to the Soviet public of the nature of the weapons in question did not come until the height of this period of protests and demonstrations, and it was accompanied by denials of the American charges. Even then the exact nature of the weapons was concealed. After three days of meetings protesting against the "farce" of the American charges, it must have come as a shock to the Soviet people to read in Premier Khrushchev's October 28 [1962] message to Kennedy:

> I regard with great understanding your concern and the concern of the people of the United States of America in connection with the fact that the weapons which you describe as offensive are indeed formidable. . . Both you and we understand what kind of weapons these are.

Within a week "nonoffensive" weapons changed, in the Soviet press, into menacing ones; they ceased to be Cuban and became Soviet; and their removal became a victory for peace (the question of what their installation had been was left unanswered). The Soviet public was not told that Soviet vessels carrying peaceful cargoes had been passed by the U.S. quarantine forces, nor that other vessels had turned back at sea; it was not told that word on the missile installations had first proceeded after the announcement of the quarantine and then stopped; it was not told of the negotiations over inspection of the weapons' removal or of differences between the Soviet stand on this matter and the position that Cuba took.

These are three case histories of the Soviet suppression of major news. The instances could be multiplied; there are a host of lesser cases. Suppression of information, however, is only part of the picture. In any consideration of the Soviet press, it is equally significant to note the regimented unanimity with which it swings into action at the slightest signal from above. . . .

Soviet treatment of crime news runs in "waves" depending upon what campaign has currently been decreed. When the campaign fever is running against speculation [buying something for the purpose of reselling it at a profit], almost all the crime reports are on speculation. The same is true when the favored target is "hooliganism" [lawless, disorderly conduct; vandalism] or embezzlement. In short, what is printed is less news than it is "advertising" for drives ordered from above. Then there are periods when crime news disappears. This, too, is a campaign, of a kind. . . .

What are we to make of this Soviet press? The question is crucial to the whole discussion of the "democratization" of Soviet society, for there can hardly be a trend toward more democratic practices without an informed public.

Certainly [today's] press is a great improvement over Stalin's. Just as certainly, it is not a free press. All of the controls and all of the dictation from above remain. The difference is in how the controls are applied. . .

54 The Right to Disagree: Dissent

By 1967, when the Soviet Union celebrated the fiftieth anniversary of the Russian Revolution, Soviet ideology was generally accepted by the Soviet people. But the government was still maintaining strict control over the individual's access to political information. Yet, as the exchange between Yevtushenko and Khrushchev indicated, some differences of opinion existed and were being expressed.

In Reading 51 you learned that on the night of March 24, 1965, over two thousand Americans participated in a teach-in at the University of Michigan. Some of the participants voiced fervent disagreement with the government's decision to wage war in Vietnam. The dissenters accepted American ideology; they were not advocating that the system be overthrown. They were openly disagreeing with a decision made by their political leaders. Their views were heard by those who attended the teach-in. These views were published in a magazine circulated nationally. They were repeated by radio and television commentators. The right of these dissenters to express their views is protected by the First Amendment to the Constitution.

Although Article 125 of the Soviet constitution guarantees individuals in the Soviet Union freedom of speech and freedom of assembly, Soviet citizens do not, in fact, have these rights. But they do have ways to voice disagreement. Yevtushenko's exchange with Khrushchev expressed disagreement. Other poets and authors have published literary works critical of the leaders. Soviet literature has become one of the principal means for expressing political discontent. In 1956 the Soviet poet Kirsanov wrote:

> I long for audacity
>   in thought
>   sound
>   color
> I long for an idea
>   born out of exaggeration
> I want that everything
>   should seem
>   like first love
> that we should
>   be satiated
> with faith and trust
> so that we should
>   no longer live
>   like petitioners
>   behind numb doors.
>   (*S. Kirsanov, "Seven Days of the Week,"*
>   *published in* Novii Mir, *1956*)

Because of the role poets play as social and political critics, a poetry reading by a recognized poet in the Soviet Union may attract thousands of people. A new book by such a poet as Yevtushenko may sell 100,000 copies on the first day it is issued.

Reading 54 tells of Bulat Okudzava, a popular Soviet balladeer. The government refuses to record his songs, but he travels around the country singing and accompanying himself on a guitar. His songs are picked up and sung by those who hear them, and they have spread throughout the nation. As you read about Okudzava, keep these questions in mind:

1. What are the subjects of Okudzava's protests? Is he protesting against the ideology of the Soviet Union?
2. How effective do you think his type of dissent is in spreading a point of view?
3. How easy do you think it would be to convert support for his type of dissent into political pressure?

Unperson Sings to the Russians
MIHAJLO MIHAJLOV

This article appeared in The New York Times Magazine *on May 15, 1966. Its author is a Yugoslav teacher and writer who wrote an essay in 1965 which was so controversial that he was fired from his teaching job and was temporarily jailed.* © *1966 by The New York Times Company. Reprinted by permission.*

Okudzava could be called the most popular man in Russia. He is a poet, a novelist, but above all a writer and singer of songs. His ballads, which he sings in a pleasant if untrained voice and which he accompanies on a guitar, have made a tremendous impact on the people of the Soviet Union, especially on the younger generation. His songs are not allowed to be recorded, but they are spread throughout the nation by tape recorder and by mouth and are sung by heart by the entire country . . .

According to the official Soviet press, Bulat Okudzava barely exists. . . . Okudzava's stanzas are printed occasionally, to be sure, and even a few collections of his poems have been published. But the main thing—his lyrics, his songs—can almost be said not to exist. . . .

Bulat Okudzava was born in Moscow in 1924. His father, a high party functionary, was shot during the mass purges of the thirties; his mother, also a party member, spent nineteen years in a Siberian concentration camp. In 1942, when he was eighteen, Okudzava went to war, an experience which had an imperishable effect upon him.

After graduating from the Pedagogic Institute and teaching in a village school, he started writing verses and published his first collection of poems, *Lyrical Poetry*, in 1956. The second collection, *The Islands*, appeared in 1959, but in an edition of just two thousand copies; his third collection, *The Happy Drummer*, was published in 1964, but only after prolonged harassment and an open letter to L. F. Ilyichev, the ideological chief of the party. . . .

Okudzava published his first novel, *Good Luck to You, My Pupil*, in 1961 in the now-banned magazine *Tarusskye Stranitsy*, to which most eminent Russian literati [writers] also contributed. In it, Okudzava discarded the previously standard, paper-thin profile of the soldier-hero who fearlessly marches to his death "for Stalin and the fatherland," and presented a real, human soldier. This raised a tumultuous reaction from the official critics because it "removed the halo of heroism" from the Soviet soldier. . . .

The novel is autobiographical, describing the wartime life of a youngster who goes to the front lines straight from the schoolroom. In comparison with contemporary Soviet prose, it is written in a very modern style of brief, condensed sentences. Okudzava has avoided the pathos customary in works of this kind in Soviet literature and has created instead a living character—a simple man who is terror-stricken by death, wounds, and frost, notwithstanding his voluntary arrival at the front. The young soldier feels no sense of heroism in the chaos of war, but rather an element of senselessness:

> "What happened: we were all swept up, carried on, and mixed up. . . . Pupils are crawling in trenches, they die of wounds, and without their arms and legs, they return home. . . . A girl is the sergeant. . . . What is happening?"

In contrast to the frightened young men who still volunteer to go to war, there are the soldiers whose ideas of "patriotism" and "heroic fighting" mean staying in the rear. One of these haughtily asks the principal hero of the novel: "Do you love your fatherland?"

"'Yes I do,' I replied. 'I was taught to, while I was still in the first grade.'"

Later, when it turns out that the first soldier did not go to the front because he had a document showing he was "irreplaceable in the rear," he tells the young man: "That's how it goes. Who likes to die, anyway?"

. . . Okudzava was smeared by the official critics. But if the novel alone were involved, they would not have been so severe—the book would not be published anymore, and that would be that.

Something much worse had happened: Okudzava's songs had become known and had proved enormously popular. And a miracle had taken place. Though the U.S.S.R. spreads over one sixth of the mainland of the world and has over 220 million people, Okudzava's songs permeated the entire territory . . . without any assistance from the radio or press.

Okudzava had become a genuinely popular artist, in the best sense of the word. . . The government could do nothing about it—neither by ignoring him nor even by publicly attacking him. The songs of Bulat Okudzava had become the property of the young spirited people of the vast land.

In his songs Okudzava is even more candid than in his novel. Most of them deal with the war—or, rather, with the tragedy and the senselessness of war. But unlike the official Soviet "peacemakers" who shift all guilt to the other side. Okudzava assumes an equally disgusted attitude toward "our heroic Soviet army" as well.

One of his most popular songs is entitled "On a Soldier". . .

> And if something is as it shouldn't be—we don't
>   worry!
> As the saying goes, "The fatherland has ordered it!"
> How nice it is not to be blamed for anything,
> To be an ordinary soldier, an ordinary soldier.

In a country where, for half a century now, the public lie has become a normal thing, and where speaking the truth is not only dangerous but also in a sense indecent, Okudzava sings that the most important thing in life is not to be involved with any sort of lie:

> Oh, that your hands should only remain clean,
> And all the rest will come by itself.

It is for such sentiments that Okudzava has become so popular, and so distasteful to the authorities. And for his dozen allegorical songs which, with a specific, satiric note and yet a thread of melancholy, have sought to embody this credo. These allegories, though gentle and controlled, enraged the "responsible comrades." The most popular of them are "The Paper Soldier"—about a soldier who wishes to make the world happy but is not aware that he is made of paper—"The Fools," and "The Black Cat.". . .

"The Black Cat" [the black cat is meant to symbolize Communist authority] goes:

> From the yard one comes to a familiar staircase
> Called the black passage.
> On this staircase, as though it were his own estate,
> Lives the black cat.
>
> He hides a smile beneath his whiskers,
> Darkness is his shield.
> All tomcats sing and cry
> But only the black cat keeps silent.
>
> He has not hunted mice for years,
> He smiles with his whiskers,
> He seizes upon our word of honor,
> Upon a slice of sausage.
>
> He does not run, and does not pray,
> His yellow eye gleams;
> Everyone feeds him
> And on top of that says thanks.
>
> The cat himself does not make a sound.
> He only eats and only sleeps.
> If he were to claw the staircase—
> It's as if he would claw our throat.
>
> That is why the house
> Where we live is joyless. . .
> We should install a lamp,
> But in no way can we raise the money.

55 The Right to Disagree: Alienation

Frederick John Kasper's activities in Clinton, Tennessee, challenged the ideology of the American political system. He replaced law and order with terror and violence. American ideology stresses respect for each individual and the views he holds. The system cannot tolerate men who turn to violence to impose their opinions on others.

In the Soviet political system, the individual is less important than the group. Collective welfare is the goal of Soviet ideology. The Soviet system is based on the conviction that the institution of private property turns men against each other; the interests of those who "have" inevitably conflict with the interests of those who "have not." According to the Communists, conflict between men will cease only when the institution of private property is abolished, and man's greed for individual profit ends. These are the teachings of Karl Marx.

In Reading 52, you learned that political alienation threatens the political system itself. Like the United States, the Soviet Union has dissenters, and it, too, has individuals who are alienated from the system. In Reading 55 you will read about such an individual, a Russian construction worker who openly challenged the philosophy upon which the system is built. The account was written by an American studying as a cultural exchange student at a Russian university. It is based on the proceedings at the trial of the worker. As you read about the worker Zaitsov, keep the following questions in mind:

1. Why can Zaitsov's crime be considered political alienation? How great a threat to the Soviet political system was it?
2. In what ways would Soviet political alienation differ from American political alienation? Give specific examples.

Moscow: A Day in the People's Court

GEORGE FEIFER

This account appeared in The Reporter *of May 21, 1964. Copyright 1964 by The Reporter Magazine Co.*

People's Court, Leninskii District, City of Moscow. The room is small, sagging, stuffy. The gray of late afternoon in late December seeps through two double-paned windows. One light bulb is burning. Three spectators wander in. Behind the desk, the tieless judge slowly puts down his glasses.

"Defendant Zaitsov, stand. Do you understand the charge against you?"

A small voice, matching the boyish face and faintly dandyish blond hair that go with it, searches for a convincing tone.

"Yes, Comrade Judge, I understand."

"And do you admit your guilt as charged in the indictment?"

No answer. The defendant wrinkles his brow.

"Zaitsov!"

"Of course, I know I acted wrong. Yes, I admit I'm guilty, and I'm ashamed of myself. But the indictment is wrong, too. All wrong. I can't admit to all of that."

"So you do not admit your guilt fully?" The judge makes a fleeting, obviously unconscious grimace of impatience. "Exactly what do you admit, and what do you deny? Tell us the whole story. The court wants to hear everything you know about the charge."

The defendant assumes a pose, the picture of innocence. His gestures and features are younger than his thirty-three years. He is —the judge has established—Russian, a bachelor, a construction worker earning 105 rubles a month; he was born in a village north of Moscow, received five years' schooling, is not a party member, has never been convicted of a criminal charge. Under his overcoat he sports the only white shirt and tie in the courtroom.

"I admit I let him into line, Comrade Judge. I'm sorry about that—though, you know, everybody does it. But I took no money; there was never any talk about money. I only did it as a favor, to. . . ."

"There was no talk about money? Did you take three rubles from him or did you not?"

"Comrade Judge . . . [pause] . . . yes. I took them. Just to have a drink after he said that. . . ."

"You took the money. You admit that. Three rubles from the victim. And in spite of that you deny your guilt? Defendant Zaitsov, we want the whole story. Start at the beginning and explain exactly what happened."

"It was on the twenty-first. I had just got through working. . . ."

"The twenty-first of what month?"

"Of October, Comrade Judge."

"Go on. What happened on the twenty-first?"

"On the twentieth, I'd worked a double shift on our construction site—you know, we're building apartments. Then I went to my sister's. Just for a little relaxation after the week's work. I stayed overnight. In the morning I told my sister I was going to the *yarmarka* [an outdoor bazaar of stalls and booths] to buy a raincoat.". . .

. . . I stood in line for a few hours for a raincoat. . . . They were selling these new belted Polish raincoats, and you can imagine that the line was pretty long. . . Plus lots of people who were butting in. You know how it works. Well, I'm standing there pretty near the front finally, and suddenly this man comes up to me, this stranger, and says he's in a terrific hurry. He says he's got a car waiting for him—to go south, on vacation. He's been to the *yarmarka* three days in a row, he tells me, but couldn't get a coat, and it looks like another day is going to be shot because he's number 465 back on my line, and he doubts that he'll *ever* get to the booth. He tells me all this, and I feel sorry for him. So I let him in—in my place. That's the whole story. It's just that he was in a hurry to go on vacation."

"And the socks?"

"Yes, the socks, Comrade Judge. That's simple. After he gets his belted raincoat, he suggests we go buy some socks, his supply of socks is running out. So he gives me ten rubles and goes to tell his car to wait, and I find that line and ask a girl to let me in; I tell her I'll return her kindness. Then I buy a few pair of socks."

"What size?"

"Twenty-five."

"And what's your size?"

"Twenty-three."

"So the socks were no good *for you*. You couldn't use them *yourself*." (To prove speculation, it must be shown that the accused bought an article intending to resell it for profit, not to use it himself.)

"I gave one pair of socks — they were good ones, with elastic tops — to the girl and offered two pairs to that man. He agreed to buy them. And that's all there was to it, Comrade Judge. Then we separated, and he thanked me warmly. He said, 'I'm very grateful; you helped me with my shopping a lot.'"

"How much change did you give him?"

"Er . . . [pause] . . . I . . . forget."

The judge fumbles with his glasses again and glances at the dossier. "You gave him four rubles, isn't that right? When you had just bought the socks for two rubles and fifty kopecks a pair the minute before. That makes five rubles, but you charged six. You made a ruble profit on the deal. Is that or is it not correct?"

"Er . . . yes." Zaitsov hangs his head.

"Plus three rubles for selling your place in line. Disgusting! You know it's disgusting. You deliberately milked a stranger, a Soviet citizen, a workingman just like yourself, of four rubles. Just like that. It's a plain case of intentional cheating. And you had it all planned, Zaitsov. Isn't that right?"

"Absolutely not, Comrade Judge. Oh no, I didn't mean to sell him anything." Zaitsov fairly trembles with conviction. "It just happened that way. When we separated, he said, 'I must thank you, I'd be happy to drink with you properly. But I'm in a great hurry. So take this instead' — he handed me three rubles — 'and drink on it as a token of thanks.' At that moment a citizen rushes up to us shouting. 'I'm an *operatif*, give me your passport and come with me.' That whole *yarmarka* is crawling with detectives, snooping around, just waiting for anyone to make one false move. So this guy arrests me and takes me to the station house. That's how it happened: the rubles were pressed on me, I didn't even want to take them."

"Then what made you?"

"Can you insult a man who offers you a drink?"

The judge clears his throat, surveys his shabby courtoom and sighs ". . . Now, Zaitsov, this is not the first time with this same thing, is it? It's the third time, at least. You have been warned. Good people — the authorities — have tried to reform you. The third time. The same disgraceful business. Why did you do it again? Why? How can you, a Soviet worker, allow yourself to decay into a rotten little swindler, a petty speculator? Do you know what you're forcing us to do with you?

". . . on October 6, just two weeks before – what happened then?"

"*Oi*, Comrade Judge . . . that was a mistake. Honest." It turns out that on October 6, the defendant was fined twenty rubles for selling his place in line to buy Czech woolen underwear. . . .

Aside from October 6, did you ever before engage in petty speculation?"

"No, Comrade Judge. Just two mistakes."

"Never?"

No answer.

"There is no point in hiding the truth from us."

"Maybe something very minor – long ago."

"When?"

"In 1959. May first."

The judge sighs. "Tell us about that."

. . . Zaitsov stammers through a lengthy narrative, obviously embellished during scores of tellings. The court learns that at one time, Zaitsov had worked in a construction crew that won the title Brigade of Communist Labor. The award was an expense-paid May Day trip to Leningrad, on which he sold his place for thirty rubles to a worker from another brigade.

"And this was in 1959?"

"I don't remember, Comrade Judge. My memory is bad."

"1959. Now strain your poor memory and tell the court about the other incidents."

"I can't remember. I don't think there were any more."

"None? Think! In 1959, a few months later – do you remember that?"

. . . In 1959, he bought a camera and resold it almost immediately, pocketing a 25 per cent profit. Then he sold a rug. Then he dealt in jazz records.

"Don't you understand that there have been too many of these incidents? It's no longer a joke. You're on your way to becoming a dangerous criminal. Why? What makes you cheat like this?"

"Comrade Judge, I don't even know how it happens. I'm sorry."

"Was it necessary for you to cheat? Was there something you needed? Something lacking? Were you in difficult straits? We want to hear your motive."

No answer. The defendant rests his head on his chest and covers his eyes.

"Maybe you'll think it over and tell the court how those three rubles *really* changed hands. Your story is weak. Don't think I'm talking you into anything. But we'll give you a chance to think it over. If you've made mistakes in life, you yourself must be the first to recognize and correct them. You must judge yourself honestly; then things will be better for you. Your job is to reform yourself, to make yourself an honest, upright Soviet citizen. Young man, you simply cannot go on like this, cheating like a bourgeois money-lender, scavenging for profits, filling your pockets with filthy money squeezed from the toilers, living like a parasite, a fungus, a blemish on our Soviet society. A society building communism cannot tolerate a piece of rust like you. We must scrape it away. But unless you reform, unless *you* see the folly of your ways, the punishment won't do you any good. You've got a skill: 'a construction worker' is a proud title in our land. And you go around dreaming only of rotten little profits. Disgusting! Intolerable! Are you a son of the working class, or some capitalist scum? Your greed will only destroy you. We are trying to help you stop it, but first you must tell the whole truth and explain *why* you continue with this ugly cheating."

No answer. Finally the defendant looks at the judge. "I'm truly sorry, Comrade Judge. I swear it will never happen again. Give me a chance to show I can be a useful member of Soviet society."

. . . The hearing has lasted an hour, and writing the verdict takes another half. When the trial is resumed, there are no surprises. "In the name of the Russian Soviet Federated Socialist Republic" it was found that the defendant Zaitsov, Viktor Mikhailovich, committed the acts charged in the indictment; that is, crimes specified by Article 154 (III) of the criminal code: petty speculation, committed repeatedly. In appointing measures of punishment, the court took into consideration the defendant's long history of speculative activity and obvious unwillingness to learn from administrative warnings, and also his apparently genuine promise to reform. The sentence is a year of "corrective labor" without deprivation of freedom. Zaitsov must continue to work at his construction job and forfeit 20 per cent of his wages to the state. . . .

56 A Summary Exercise

You have now compared the political systems of the United States and the Soviet Union on the basis of five major political science concepts: political institutions, ideology, leadership, decision-making, and the role of the citizen. For each concept, you have developed a list of analytical questions that proved helpful in analyzing these two political systems. Part of your purpose in developing these questions was to help you learn about the Soviet and American systems. A much broader purpose was to give you a set of tools with which you might analyze any political system.

In the years ahead you will probably be called upon to study the political systems of a number of nations: England, France, India, South Africa, and many more. To understand and analyze these governments, you will have to ask analytical questions: What kinds of political institutions do these people have? What is their political ideology? What kind of leaders do they have? How do they go about making political decisions? What role does the citizen play in this society?

Reading 56 contains three excerpts used in a course in the history of Western civilization. The three selections concern the court of Louis XIV, King of France. The first selection was written by Louis XIV himself, the second and third by a noble of his court, Saint-Simon. Use the analytical questions you have developed to investigate political systems to help you gather information to answer the following questions:

1. What do these readings tell you about the institutions and ideology of the political system within which Louis XIV ruled?
2. What do they tell you about its leadership and the way political decisions were made?
3. What theories can you form about the role the citizen was likely to have played in this political system?

1. Louis XIV's Description of Kingship

In 1666 Louis wrote a memorandum to his son describing how a king ought to act. The following selection is an excerpt from that memorandum. From Memoires pour l'instruction du dauphin *in Oeuvres de Louis XIV, (Paris, 1806), Vol. I, pp. 19–25 passim. (Translated by John M. Good.)*

Without any doubt, two things were absolutely necessary for ruling: very hard work on my part and a wise choice of persons who were capable of carrying out my work.

As for work, my son, you will probably read these lines when you dread work far more than you love it. You will have finished your schooling and will be happy to be free of lengthy study. Yet it is toil by which one reigns and for which one reigns. . . .

I set a rule for myself to work regularly twice each day for two or three hours at a time. Each time I worked with different persons. This regular work does not include the hours which I spend privately working on matters of state, nor the time I was able to give on particular occasions when special problems arose. I permitted people to talk to me about problems at any time, provided they were urgent. . . .

I cannot tell you how important my resolution to work was. I felt myself, as it were, uplifted in thought and courage. I found that I was a new man, and joyfully scolded myself for not having been aware of work's importance earlier. My timidity, especially on occasions when I had to speak in public, disappeared in no time. I felt that I was

King and born to be one. I experienced a delicious feeling which you will not know until you are King. You must not think, my son, that the affairs of state are like some obscure and thorny philosophical problem with which the mind struggles, often arriving at no conclusion. . . . A king must first of all be guided by his own good sense, which is natural and effortless. . . . A king, however skillful and enlightened his ministers are, is the principal cause of good work being done. He cannot act without seeing his effect on the state. Success, even in small matters, gratifies us as well as success in great affairs. And there is no satisfaction equal to that of noting every day some progress you have made in glorious and lofty enterprises and in the happiness of your people which comes from the work you have done yourself.

My son, the work of a king is agreeable. One must have his eyes open to the whole earth. He must endeavor to learn each hour the news concerning every province and every nation, the secrets of every court, the moods and weaknesses of every prince and every foreign minister. He must be well informed on all matters from commerce and science to art and philosophy. He must find out the secrets of our subjects and discover the selfish interests of those who approach us trying to disguise their real motives. I do not know of any other pleasure that I would take in place of the work of a king.

2. A Noble's Appraisal of Louis XIV

DUC DE SAINT-SIMON

The Duc de Saint-Simon was born into one of the most prominent noble families of France. His memoirs record the manners and customs of the court in vivid detail. The following extract gives his impressions of the King's character. From Duke de Saint-Simon, Memoirs of Louis XIV and the Regency, *Bayle St. John, trans. (Washington: M. Walter Dunne, 1901), Vol. III, p. 359 (language simplified and modernized by John M. Good).*

At twenty-three years of age, Louis became King in fact as well as in name, under the most favorable conditions. His ministers were the most skillful in all Europe; his generals the best; his court was filled with illustrious and clever men.

Louis XIV was made for a brilliant court. His figure, his courage, his grace, his beauty, his grand bearing, even the tone of his voice and his majestic and natural charm set him apart from other men as the king bee. Even if he had been born a simple private gentleman, he still would have excelled in all social festivities. However, intrigues against the King during his childhood made Louis suspicious of intelligent, educated, noble, and highly principled men, and as he advanced in years, he began to hate them. He wished to reign by himself, and his jealousy on this point soon became a weakness. He concerned himself with little things; he never could reach great things. The superior ability of his early ministers and generals soon wearied him. He liked no one to be in any way superior to him. He chose his ministers, therefore, not for their knowledge, but for their ignorance; not for their capacity, but for their want of it. He liked to teach them even the most trifling things. . . . He was naturally fond of trifles. He unceasingly concerned himself with the smallest details of his troops, his minor household officials, and the way his mansions were built and maintained. He would even instruct his cooks, even though he taught them things they had known for years.

His vanity, his unreasonable desire to be admired, ruined him. His ministers, his generals, his mistresses, his courtiers soon understood this fatal weakness. They praised him and spoiled him, for it was the one way they could approach him. This is why his ministers, drawn from the non-noble class, had so much authority. They had better opportunity to flatter him and tell him that all good works came from his actions and that they owed everything to him.

3. A Day in the Life of the King
DUC DE SAINT-SIMON

Saint-Simon's Memoirs *contain very detailed descriptions of the life at Louis' court at Versailles. The following excerpt explains the daily routine of the King. Saint-Simon,* op. cit., *pp. 30–37.*

At eight o'clock the chief *valet de chambre* on duty, who alone had slept in the royal chamber . . . awoke the King. The chief physician, the chief surgeon, and the nurse (as long as she lived), entered at the same time. The last-mentioned kissed the King; the others rubbed [him] and often changed his shirt, because he was in the habit of sweating a great deal. At the quarter, the grand chamberlain was called (or, in his absence, the first gentleman of the chamber), and those who had what was called the *grandes entrées.* The chamberlain (or chief gentleman) drew back the curtains which had been closed again and presented the holy water from the vase at the head of the bed. These gentlemen stayed but a moment, and that was the time to speak to the King, if anyone had anything to ask of him; in which case the rest stood aside. . . . The same officer gave him his dressing gown; immediately after, other privileged courtiers entered, and then everybody, in time to find the King putting on his shoes and stockings. . . .

As soon as he was dressed, he prayed to God, at the side of his bed, where all the clergy present knelt, the cardinals without cushions, all the laity remaining standing; and the captain of the guards came to the balustrade during the prayer, after which the King passed into his cabinet.

He found there . . . a very numerous company, for it included everybody in any office. He gave orders to each for the day; thus within a half a quarter of an hour, it was known what he meant to do; and then all this crowd left directly. . . . It was then a good opportunity for talking with the King; for example, about plans of gardens and buildings; and conversation lasted more or less according to the person engaged in it.

All the Court meantime waited for the King in the gallery, the captain of the guard being alone in the chamber seated at the door of the cabinet. . . . During this pause the King gave audiences when he wished to accord any, spoke with whomever he might wish to speak secretly to, and gave secret interviews to foreign ministers. . . .

The King went to mass, where his musicians always sang an anthem. . . . While he was going to and returning from mass, everybody spoke to him who wished. . . . During the mass the ministers assembled in the King's chamber where distinguished people could go and speak or chat with them. The King amused himself a little upon returning from mass and asked almost immediately for the council. . . .

On Sunday, and often on Monday, there was a council of state; on Tuesday a finance council; on Wednesday council of state; on Saturday finance council. Rarely were two held in one day or any on Thursday or Friday. Once or twice a month there was a council of dispatches on Monday morning. . . .

Thursday morning was almost always blank. It was the day for audiences that the King wished to give. . . . On Friday after the mass, the King was with his confessor, and the length of their audiences was limited by nothing. . . . At Fontainebleau [one of the King's palaces] on the mornings when there was no council, the King usually passed from mass to Madame de Maintenon's and so at Trianon and Marly [two more of the King's palaces]. It was the time of their tête-à-tête without interruption. . . .

Upon leaving the table (after the noon meal), the King immediately entered his cabinet. That was the time for distinguished people to speak to him. He stopped at the door a moment to listen, then entered; very rarely did anyone follow him, never without asking him for permission to do so; and for this few had the courage. . . .

Upon returning home from walks or drives, anybody might speak to the King from the moment he left his coach till he reached the foot of his staircase. He changed his dress and rested in his cabinet an hour or more, then went to Madame de Maintenon's, and on the way anyone who wished might speak to him.

At ten o'clock his supper was served. . . . A quarter of an hour after the King came to supper, and from the antechamber of Madame de Maintenon to the table again, anyone spoke to him who wished. This supper was always on a grand scale, the royal household at table, and a large number of courtiers and ladies present, sitting or standing. . . .

After supper the King stood some moments, his back to the balustrade of the foot of his bed, encircled by all his court; then, with bows to the ladies, passed into his cabinet, where on arriving, he gave his orders. He passed a little less than an hour there, seated in an armchair [with the royal family].

The King, wishing to retire, went and fed his dogs; then said good night, passed into his chamber . . . , where he said his prayers, as in the morning, then undressed. He said good night with an inclination of the head, and while everybody was leaving the room, stood at the corner of the mantlepiece, where he gave the order to the colonel of the guards alone. Then commenced what was called the *petit coucher,* at which only the specially privileged remained. That was short. They did not leave until he got into bed. It was a moment to speak to him. . . .

SUGGESTED READINGS

ALEXANDER, JOHN W. and MORROE BERGER, "Is the Town Meeting Finished," *Capitol, Courthouse and City Hall,* pp. 233–36.
   Question: What appears to be the role of the town meeting in Winston, Richfield, and Barrington? How do you explain the difference between the popular notion of a town meeting and what the authors found when they conducted a study of town meetings in these three areas?
ARMSTRONG, JOHN A., "The Police State and Its Limitations," *Ideology, Politics, and Government in the Soviet Union,* pp. 84–89.
   Question: What are the limitations of a police state?
BEAN, LOUIS H., "The Head, the Heart, or the Pocketbook?", *Profile of American Politics,* pp. 98–102.
   Question: Under what conditions do voters appear to respond to "head and heart" issues, rather than "pocketbook" issues?
CATER, DOUGLAS, "The Fourth Branch of Government," *Profile of American Politics,* pp. 141–45.
   Question: How does the press influence government decisions?
COMMAGER, HENRY STEELE, "Who Is Loyal to America?", *Political Institutions,* pp. 282–86.
   Question: According to Henry Steele Commager, what constitutes loyalty to the American political system?
FARLEY, JAMES and LEONARD HALL, "How Politicians Get Your Vote," *Profile of American Politics,* pp. 102–06.
   Question: According to Mr. Hall and Mr. Farley, what is most likely to influence voters? Have their observations been proved accurate by recent studies of voter behavior?
FRANKEL, MAX and TOBIA, "New Soviet Plan—Feminine Females," *Communism in Theory and Practice,* pp. 111–17.
   Question: What impact does the desire of women to be feminine have on Soviet political decision-makers?

FRIEDRICH, CARL J., "The Unique Character of Totalitarian Society," *Political Institutions*, pp. 51–53.

Question: What are the characteristic features of a totalitarian society?

HARRIS, LOUIS, "Some Characteristics of the American Voter," *Capitol, Courthouse and City Hall*, pp. 292–94.

Question: What is the profile of the American voter as drawn by Louis Harris?

HUTCHINS, ROBERT, "The Responsibility of a Free Press," *Profile of American Politics*, pp. 150–54.

Question: Do you agree with Mr. Hutchins that a commission could force newspapers to do a better job of educating the public?

JACOBS, PAUL, "The Boys on Gorki Street," *Communism in Theory and Practice*, pp. 121–29.

Question: What do you consider the significance of the black market operations of the "boys on Gorki Street"?

LASCH, ROBERT, "Pride and Prejudice: The Fourth Estate," *Profile of American Politics*, pp. 147–50.

Question: What is the danger of supporting newspapers that editorialize in their news columns?

LIFE MAGAZINE, "To Reach the People: What Really Happened Before the TV Debate?", *Democracy in Action*, pp. 96–100.

Question: How have campaign techniques changed over the years? Have these changes affected the role of the citizen in the American political system?

POLYAKOV, VLADIMIR, "The Story of a Story," *The USSR and Communism*, pp. 221–25.

Question: Does the encouragement of creativity conflict with the goals of of an authoritarian government?

RENFIELD, RICHARD, "Soviet Education," *The USSR and Communism*, pp. 227–30.

Question: How does a society's educational system serve as an arm of its political system?

SCAMMON, R. M., "Uncontested Elections," *Communism in Theory and Practice*, pp. 79–81.

Question: According to this account, why are elections held in the USSR? Do you agree with the author?

STEVENSON, ADLAI E., "The One-Party Press," *Profile of American Politics*, pp. 145–47.

Question: Do you think Mr. Stevenson's evaluation of the political influence of the press is accurate? Why?

SMITH, T. V., "Our Issue with Russia," *Political Institutions*, pp. 43–45.

Question: What does Professor Smith see as the basic difference between the American political system and that of the Soviet Union?

WHITNEY, THOMAS P., "The Pasternak Incident," *Political Institutions*, pp. 68–69.

Question: Why is it difficult for authoritarianism and freedom to go hand in hand?

"Why Participate in Party Politics?", and "The Reformer," *Capitol, Courthouse and City Hall*, pp. 356–57.

Question: Which do you consider the most vital of the two roles defined for individuals wishing to participate in the political system?

Unit Six
Rights and Liberties in a Democracy

IN UNIT FIVE you compared the role of the individual citizen in the United States with the role of the individual citizen in the Soviet Union. You studied the way in which the citizen influenced decisions made by his government. In the process you compared elections in the societies, studied the degree to which citizens had access to accurate political information, and investigated the activities of men who were alienated from the systems. Studying the roles played by citizens in the two societies helps to make the differences between them more clear.

Unit Six does not compare two political systems. Instead, it examines some of the liberties and rights guaranteed to Americans. Thomas Jefferson put the matter of individual rights in classic form in the Declaration of Independence, which says: "We hold these truths to be self-evident: that all men are created equal, that they are endowed by their Creator with certain unalienable rights, that among these are life, liberty, and the pursuit of happiness. That, to secure these rights, governments are instituted among men, deriving their just powers from the consent of the governed. . ." This famous document clearly states that individual rights came first and that government was begun to protect them.

Unit Six discusses conflicts which have arisen in the United States over the interpretation of rights, liberties, and obligations established by the Constitution. The conflict recounted in the first reading arose when the government tried to guarantee rights which are granted by the Constitution but which may be ignored in practice The next two readings discuss cases of individuals who felt that the government invaded their liberties. All of the readings raise issues which are vital to a full and meaningful life in a democracy.

Chapter 15

The Protection of the Individual

STATING THE ISSUE Any government imposes restraints on the freedom of the individual. Without restraints, society cannot function. If the government did not require people to pay taxes, it could not build highways. If it did not prevent drivers from speeding through the city at ninety miles an hour, no one would be safe on the streets. Without restraints, men like Frederick John Kasper could overthrow the government and replace the rule of law with the rule of force. Clearly, some degree of government restraint is needed. The question is, "How much?"

The American political system has traditionally placed as few restraints upon the individual as possible. Many states ratified the Constitution only after they had been promised that a Bill of Rights would be added to protect the individual's rights from abuse by the government. The privileges guaranteed to citizens by the Constitution, such as freedom of the press and freedom of speech, are referred to as civil liberties.

The Fourteenth Amendment states that "No state shall make or enforce any law which shall abridge the privileges or immunities of citizens of the United States; nor shall any state deprive any person of life, liberty, or property, without due process of law; nor deny to any person within its jurisdiction the equal protection of the laws." For over half a century the courts ruled that "equal but separate facilities" for Negroes met the requirements of this amendment. In 1954, however, the Supreme Court ruled that "Separate educational facilities are inherently unequal; segregation itself is a denial of equal protection." This Supreme Court decision was one of a series of decisions designed to bring into being constitutional rights long denied by custom. Equal protection of the laws is one example of an American's civil rights.

Chapter 15 analyzes the nature of both civil rights and civil liberties. It may raise more questions than it will answer. When should the government step in to protect a minority group from the will of the majority? What comes first, a boy's duty to his conscience or his duty to his government? Where do you draw the line between an individual's right to do as he pleases and his responsibility to respect the wishes of the larger community?

57 The Protection of Civil Rights

Negro Americans have yet to achieve full equality as citizens. While the Constitution grants them equality, local laws and practices often deny it. In many areas Negroes are not allowed to enroll in certain public schools or to eat in restaurants. Many jobs and residential areas are closed to Negroes. The 1954 ruling of the Supreme Court was one of a series of judicial decisions which brought the power of the federal government to bear on the problem of securing for the Negro community the rights granted by the Thirteenth, Fourteenth, and Fifteenth Amendments to the Constitution. Many of these decisions came in response to an organized civil rights movement.

When the modern civil rights movement emerged as a political force on the American scene, some Americans saw the Negro's claim to equality as a violation of other people's civil liberties. In Little Rock, Arkansas, the Mothers' League of Central High School resisted the ruling of the Supreme Court. In the opinion of members of that league, admitting Negroes to Central High would deny their own freedom to send their children to schools which enrolled only white students. They saw the practice of exclusion as a right they wished to preserve. The two parties to the case—the Negroes and the white people—saw two conflicting sets of rights involved, not just one.

Reading 57 involves another instance when rights as interpreted by two parties came in conflict. In 1951, before the Supreme Court decision, a twenty-nine-year-old Negro war veteran and his family moved into an apartment in Cicero, Illinois, an area by custom closed to Negroes. Reading 57 describes the reaction of the community when this move took place. As you read, consider the following questions:

1. How did this conflict begin? Why did it get out of hand? How might it have been avoided?
2. Whose rights were involved in this case? Did each side think its rights had been violated?
3. What is the fair way to settle a controversy like this one?

Violent Harvest
ARNOLD FORSTER AND BENJAMIN R. EPSTEIN

The events described in this account took place in Cicero, Illinois, a suburb of Chicago, on the evenings of July 10, 11, and 12, 1951. From The Troublemakers *by Arnold Forster and Benjamin R. Epstein. Copyright 1952 by The Anti-Defamation League of B'nai B'rith. Reprinted by permission of Doubleday & Company, Inc. The Anti-Defamation League of B'nai B'rith is an organization which was formed in 1913 to combat prejudice against Jewish citizens and to promote better inter-group relations.*

Cicero has a population of about seventy thousand; most of its wage earners work for the Western Electric Company or the Hurley Manufacturing Company. They represent more than twenty-two nationality groups, with a predominance of persons of Slovak, Polish, Lithuanian, Italian, and German origin, in that order.

But there were no Negroes living in Cicero. Harvey E. Clark, Jr., a twenty-nine-year-old Negro war veteran and graduate of Fisk University, was not aware of this fact. He and his wife, Johnetta, and their two children, aged eight and six, lived in one half of a small two-room apartment on Chicago's South Side. It was obviously unsuitable: the place was vermin-infested; and it was twenty-four miles from the terminal where Clark started and ended his daily run as a bus driver. The rent was $56 a month.

When, in March 1951, Clark found the five-room apartment at 6132-42 West 19 Street, in Cicero, he was delighted. The rent was $60 a month, the apartment was in a building which had been bought by a group of Negroes some time before, and the place was clean and modern.

On March 8, the Clarks loaded their furniture into a moving van and drew up before the building on West 19 Street. They were met by Charles S. Edwards, a rental agent, who was there to help them—and some members of the Cicero police force.

The police would not let the furniture be moved into the building without a permit—although subsequent investigation did not disclose the need for such a permit in any other case.

Mr. Edwards described the events that followed in an affidavit:

About 6 P.M. the chief of police of Cicero rushed out of the alley nearby followed by about twenty men and rushed up and grabbed my arm. The police in cars out front got out of their cars and rushed up toward us. The chief said to me, "You should know better—get going—get out of here fast. There will be no moving into this building. I'm not going to endanger the lives of nineteen families for the likes of you."

During these statements, the chief held my left arm with his strong left arm, and he kept hitting me in the back with his right fist, especially at my right shoulder and on my right side below the shoulder. He hit me about eight times while he was pushing me ahead of him toward my car which was parked across the street. I was trying to walk, but he was trying to make me move faster.

When we reached my car, I opened the door, and the chief shoved me inside and said, "Get out of Cicero and don't come back in town, or you'll get a bullet through you." There were three—four officers with the chief . . . I have not been back to Cicero since, and my clients, the Clarks, have not been allowed to move into the apartment which is theirs.

Edwards and Clark brought the matter to the attention of local civic agencies. They in turn decided to bring criminal prosecution against Cicero's civil authorities under the United States code which prohibits a conspiracy to deprive citizens by force and violence of their right of freedom of movement. They also filed a $200,000 damage suit against Cicero.

U.S. District Judge John P. Barnes issued a temporary injunction restraining the town and its officials from "shooting, beating, or otherwise harassing Mr. Clark and his family." He warned Cicero officials: "If you don't obey the order, you're going to be in serious trouble . . . You're going to exercise the same diligence in seeing that these people move in as you did in trying to keep them out."

The Illinois Interracial Commission, the Chicago Council Against Discrimination, and other groups tried to help prepare the community for the Clarks' arrival as tenants of the building. The Church Federation of Greater Chicago requested all Protestant ministers in Cicero and nearby Berwyn to make a statement from their pulpits, asking their people to maintain peace and order.

Then came the troublemakers.

The Clarks moved their furniture into the apartment building on Tuesday, July 10. A crowd gathered that night and broke the windows of the Clark apartment with stones.

Rumors swept the town the following morning. The other nineteen tenants moved out most of their furniture during the day to save it from destruction. By 7:30 P.M. of the night of July 11, some eight hundred people had gathered outside the building. By the time darkness had set in, the eight hundred had swelled to more than four thousand. It was a wild, noisy crowd, composed of people of all ages, including women and children. An American Civil Liberties Union observer reported:

> The most active were teen-agers, some in gangs. Police did nothing to break up the gangs . . . Police watched women pass stones from a rock pile back to the throwers in the crowd and made no effort to stop them. The police, for the most part, were in a jovial mood, cracked jokes with the crowd, and some made Jim Crow remarks . . . Firecrackers were thrown, and one man, said to be a plainclothesman, went up to the group of kids, and was heard to say, "Cut out the firecrackers. In case you're searched, don't have any on you. We don't care how many stones you throw, but get rid of the firecrackers."

The frames of the windows of the Clark apartment were knocked out. A gang went upstairs, vandalized the apartment, and turned on gas and water. Furniture was thrown out the window and set afire by the people below.

At 11:30 P.M. the gang was in the basement, tearing up the plumbing. One member ran out of the building to report that his group was losing to the police downstairs. A larger gang rushed to help. For ten minutes the police effectively held back the mob with tear gas — then the gang took control.

Cook County Sheriff Babb tried to disperse the crowd. A police loudspeaker blared that the Clarks had agreed not to return to the apartment—a false report, incidentally. The Clarks were miles away from the scene at the time but too aghast by the events to make any decision at the moment.

Past midnight, youngsters pulled down a half dozen poplar trees in front of the apartment house. The mob cheered and applauded as each twenty-five-foot tree snapped and fell.

The following morning, Thursday, July 12, Sheriff Babb was informed that nightfall would again bring out the mob. In the absence of the mayor of Cicero—on vacation in Antioch, Illinois—the Sheriff called Governor Adlai Stevenson, requesting that National Guard units be sent to Cicero to restore peace.

The guardsmen arrived at Cicero Town Hall at 7:30 P.M. Before they were summoned into action, the sheriff's deputies and as many other police as could be gathered from neighboring Cook County towns were assigned to keep the fast-gathering crowd in order. The police formed a cordon at all intersections within two blocks of the building. By 9:30 the mob had grown to about five thousand persons and had broken through the police lines.

The guardsmen were called into action. They stood shoulder to shoulder, bayonets poised, to keep the mob from surging closer to the building. For an hour they all stood their ground—the police, the young soldiers, and the mob, which continued to throw stones and flares and firecrackers. Then the guardsmen slowly pushed the crowd back as it heaped abuse upon them. . . Stones dented the soldiers' helmets, policemen were hit, police cars were overturned, members of the mob were cut by bayonets. In the end, the mob retreated.

Nineteen people were injured. The police arrested about seventy persons. By 3:00 A.M., the sound of fury had subsided, the stone-throwers were gone. The guardsmen stayed on duty during the next few days to forestall any further rioting.

58 The Protection of Civil Liberties

In the very act of forming a government, Americans restricted the freedom of the individual. In keeping with the Constitution, citizens have to choose leaders with particular qualifications such as age; men and women who do not have these qualifications cannot be elected. Citizens have to obey laws passed by Congress. To protect the individual from an over-zealous government, the Constitution specifies the extent to which government can restrict individual freedom. The limits on governmental power are stated both in the Articles of the Constitution itself and in the Amendments. They include the following provisions:

1. No person can be held in jail or prison without being told the charges against him (writ of habeas corpus).
2. No laws shall restrict a person's right to worship as he pleases.
3. No laws shall restrict freedom of speech, freedom of the press, or freedom of people to assemble.
4. Individuals shall be allowed to bear arms to protect themselves.
5. Homes cannot be searched, and items found cannot be seized unless a warrant has been issued permitting the search. Warrants shall not be issued without good reason to believe evidence will be found of illegal activities.
6. In a criminal case, no person will be compelled to be a witness against himself. (A criminal case is one in which the person is accused by the government of breaking a law.)
7. In all criminal prosecutions the accused shall
   a. have a speedy and public trial
   b. have an impartial jury
   c. be informed of the nature of his crime
   d. be confronted by the witnesses against him
   e. have the right to compel witnesses in his behalf to testify
   f. have a counsel to assist him in his defense.
8. No person shall be tried for the same offense twice.
9. No person shall be deprived of life, liberty, or property without fair treatment under the law (due process of law).
10. Excessive bail shall not be required, nor excessive fines imposed, nor cruel and unusual punishments inflicted.
11. In civil cases, when the value in controversy exceeds twenty dollars, the defendant, if he wishes, shall be tried by a jury. (A civil case is brought by one individual against another for protection of private rights.)
12. Private property shall not be taken for public use without just compensation.
13. Laws cannot be passed to convict persons of crimes committed before the law was passed (ex post facto laws).
14. Legislatures cannot pass laws designed to try, convict, and punish a person without a jury trial.
15. Work required of prisoners is the only form of forced labor permitted in the United States.
16. The right of citizens to vote shall not be denied or abridged on account of race, color, or previous condition of servitude.
17. No religious oath or test shall be required as qualification for public office.

These provisions of the Constitution protect the individual citizen. But in specific cases, it is often not clear that a right has been violated. When such a case occurs, a court can often decide the issue. If one of the parties to a case feels that the decision is incorrect, he can appeal to a higher court.

Reading 59 gives details about five court cases. It presents each case as it was handled in court the first time. In all cases, the judgments by lower courts were later appealed to higher courts on the basis of violations of individuals' civil liberties. As you read each case, consider the following questions:

1. What were the facts of this case? What civil liberty was involved?
2. What do you think the correct decision should be? Why?
3. How do the courts protect the rights and liberties of citizens?

Liberty Under Law:
True Stories of Our Constitutional
Rights and Responsibilities

From Liberty Under Law: True Stories of Our Constitutional Rights and Responsibilities, *Columbus, Ohio: American Education Publications, 1963. Reprinted by permission.*

I

Clarence Earl Gideon was charged with breaking and entering a poolroom [a criminal offense], in Panama City, Florida, on August 4, 1961. He said he could not afford a lawyer and asked the Florida state court where he was tried to appoint counsel for him. The following exchange then took place:

COURT: "Mr. Gideon, I am sorry, but I cannot appoint counsel to represent you in this case. Under the laws of the State of Florida, the only time the court can appoint counsel to represent a defendant is when that person is charged with a capital offense. . . ."

MR. GIDEON: "The United States Supreme Court says I am entitled to be represented by counsel!"

Without a lawyer, Mr. Gideon defended himself as well as he could. He made an opening statement to the jury, cross-examined the state's witnesses, presented his own witnesses, and refused to testify himself. He also made a short argument that he was innocent of the charge against him.

Nevertheless, he was found guilty. The court sentenced him to five years in the state prison.

II

Walt Smith was charged with assault with intent to kill. Police said it happened this way:

Mr. Smith and Guy Fulsom had had a dispute over money. When Mr. Smith hit Mr. Fulsom and knocked him down, Mr. Fulsom gave him all the money he had—$6.75. Mr. Fulsom then got up and went home.

Later Mr. Smith showed up at the Fulsom house with a gun and said he was going to kill Mr. Fulsom. After he fired three shots into the house, Mr. Smith was arrested.

At his trial, Mr. Smith pleaded not guilty by reason of insanity. But the prosecution introduced in evidence psychiatric reports of a state hospital which said he was not insane. The doctors who made the examinations and wrote the reports did not testify at the trial.

Mr. Smith was convicted and sentenced to one year in prison. . . .

III

Wilbert Rideau brought the Supreme Court the issue of "trial by television."

He faced the death penalty. The charges against him—a murder which followed a bank robbery and kidnaping—were grave. Yet, he said, television had spoiled the usual calm temper of justice in his case.

Rideau was accused of looting a bank in Lake Charles, Louisiana, of $14,000 on February 16, 1961. He had held the bank manager and two women tellers at gunpoint while they stuffed money into a bag. Then he forced the three to go with him in a car owned by Mrs. Julia Ferguson, one of the tellers.

After escaping the scene, it was charged, he shot all three. Mrs. Ferguson died of her wounds.

A few hours later Rideau was captured. On the next morning, newsmen from the Lake Charles television station came to the jail. Their cameras and sound equipment recorded a talk between the sheriff and Rideau. The movie included Rideau's admission that he had committed the robbery, kidnaping, and murder.

Television audiences saw the film later in the day and again on the next two days. By the end of that time, station officials estimated, the confession had been seen and heard by 106,000 of the 150,000 people in the area.

When the case came to court two weeks later, Rideau's lawyers charged that the televised confession made it impossible for their client to get a fair trial. They asked for a *change of venue*—arrangements to hold the trial in a different part of the state where feeling about the crime did not run so high.

Their request was denied. The trial went on. Rideau was convicted, on evidence which included a written confession he had signed. The television film was not shown in court.

IV

Down with segregation—I am proud to be a Negro—Signs like these swayed over the heads of the marchers on the grounds of South Carolina's State House.

The 187 Negro demonstrators, most of them high school and college students, had gathered on the morning of March 2, 1961, at a downtown church in Columbia, South Carolina. About noon, they had broken into clusters of about fifteen and gone through the streets to regroup at the capitol grounds.

Their march began in a parklike area, about two city blocks in size, which was open to the general public.

Police authorities, alerted to the demonstration as soon as it began, sent thirty officers to the scene. Onlookers began to gather as the sign-carrying demonstrators marched silently. By the time the march had gone on for thirty minutes, more than two hundred persons were in the watching crowd. Though they were also quiet, the Columbia city manager thought he recognized some "possible troublemakers" among them.

Police officials discussed the situation with the city manager. Then they informed the demonstrators that they would be arrested if they did not disperse in fifteen minutes.

The demonstrators instead began to sing "The Star-Spangled Banner." They listened to a speech by one of their leaders. They stamped their feet and clapped their hands to the rhythm of a hymn, "I Shall Not Be Moved."

At the end of the fifteen minutes they were all arrested on charges of breach of the peace. All 187 were fined, in amounts ranging from $5 to $100, and given jail sentences of from five to thirty days. South Carolina courts upheld the view that they were "disturbing the public tranquility by inciting to violence."

V

The place was a street corner in Syracuse, New York. The date was March 8, 1949. The time was about six o'clock in the evening.

Irving Feiner, a university student, stood on a large wooden box speaking to a group of people. He urged them to attend a meeting that night at the Syracuse Hotel.

But Mr. Feiner also was giving his views on a number of other topics. He called the President of the United States a "bum" and the mayor of Syracuse a "champagne-sipping bum."

The listening crowd included Negroes and whites. Mr. Feiner made some remarks that the police later thought were stirring up one race against the other.

At 6:30 police received a complaint about the meeting, and two officers were sent to investigate. They saw a crowd of seventy-five or eighty people blocking the sidewalk and standing in the street. Mr. Feiner was addressing them in a "loud, high-pitched voice" through a loud-speaker.

The officers first tried to move the crowd onto the sidewalk, then mingled with the listeners. People were milling about restlessly. One man told the officers that if they did not take Mr. Feiner off the box, he would.

Finally, an officer asked Mr. Feiner to step down. He refused. Then Mr. Feiner was "told" and at last "commanded" to get down because he was under arrest. He announced over the microphone that "the law has arrived, and I suppose they will take over now."

The speaker was first charged with "unlawful assembly." This was changed to "disorderly conduct." Found guilty on the second charge, he was sentenced to thirty days in the county penitentiary.

The conviction was supported by two other New York courts. Mr. Feiner at last made an appeal to the Supreme Court of the United States.

He claimed that his constitutional right of free speech had been violated. The First Amendment says "Congress shall make no law . . . abridging the freedom of speech." The Fourteenth Amendment says, in part, ". . . nor shall any state deprive any person of life, liberty, or property without due process of law."

Mr. Feiner appealed under the Fourteenth Amendment, which is considered to include and apply the First Amendment specifically to state governments.

59 Civil Disobedience

During the 1960's, the American government became involved in a major military conflict in Vietnam. The political background of the conflict was extremely complex, and there was substantial difference of opinion about the wisdom of American involvement. Some saw the activities of the Vietcong as part of a campaign to destroy democratic government all over the world. Others saw the fighting as a local skirmish between two factions competing for the right to govern a small country.

In the midst of this controversy, young men between the ages of eighteen and twenty-six were being drafted into the armed services. The great majority of men who were drafted decided to serve. Some young men, however, questioned the government's right to send them to fight a war in which they felt the United States should not be involved. Other young men opposed any war as a means of resolving conflicts. They registered as conscientious objectors. These men, if drafted, were either assigned to noncombat duty in the army, usually as medical attendants, or to civilian jobs with recognized service organizations.

The problem of the conscientious objector was widely debated. Should the status be reserved for those belonging to religious groups known to preach pacifism? Is it necessary to believe in God to be a conscientious objector? What is a man's duty to his country? Does a man owe first allegiance to his conscience or to his nation? All of these questions were raised, and many different answers were given.

Tom Rodd was a young man who asked himself these questions. Finally, he concluded that the draft law itself violated his principles. Five days after his eighteenth birthday, the time limit set by law for registering for the draft, he went to the federal attorney's office and asked to be arrested. He felt that as a conscientious objector, he could not support war even to the extent of registering for the draft. As you read about Tom Rodd, keep the following questions in mind:

1. Why did Tom refuse to register for the draft? What would happen if everyone, or even a majority, refused to serve in the armed forces?
2. Why did Judge Rosenberg sentence Tom to four years in a federal reformatory?
3. What is civil disobedience? Is it a form of dissent or alienation? Is it ever justifiable?

Four Ways To Go: Tommy Rodd Went to Jail
BERNARD WEINRAUB

This account appeared in Esquire *Magazine, September 1966. Reprinted by permission of* Esquire *Magazine.* © *1966 by Esquire, Inc.*

Dear Friend:

I love you. Stripped to the bare essentials, that is my message: I care for you; I rejoice in your existence. If, like me, you are often casting about for certainties to hold onto, let my love for you become one of them. And if you accept this love, I am presumptuous enough to ask you to read and hear the rest of this message.

My name is Tom Rodd. I am nineteen years old and was raised in Pittsburgh, Pennsylvania . . .

Thomas Whitney Rodd, 31522, began his "I love you" message shortly before entering the federal reformatory in Petersburg, Virginia, for four years. He is a pacifist who refused to register for the draft and violated his parole by demonstrating against the Vietnamese war. . . .

. . . It could have been so easy for Tommy Rodd. . . . Tommy had advantages, the best of upper-middle-class advantages: a quiet street, a fourteen-room house built by the mayor of Pittsburgh in 1902, his own room . . .

To his friends and neighbors, Tommy was simply a good-looking aristocrat who never appeared to suffer . . .

And yet on the gray morning of March 26, 1964, five days after Tommy Rodd turned eighteen, he showed up in Room 633 of the federal building in downtown Pittsburgh and told Federal Attorney Gustave Diamond that he would not register for the draft. . . .

Tommy, who had already notified Diamond that he wouldn't register, was accompanied by three friends.

"Mr. Diamond?"

"Yes, sir, what can I do for you?"

"I've come to turn myself in for violation of the U.M.T.S.A. [Universal Military Training Service Act]."

"Yes, I've read your literature. I've decided I will not arrest you at this time."

"In the letter I sent you, I stated my intention to remain here until I was arrested."

"Right. Like any other citizen you are entitled to the use of the office and building, as long as you conduct yourself in a gentlemanly manner."

The two shook hands, and Tommy walked into an outer office and then sat down, placing his sleeping bag and briefcase on the bench and opening up his Rilke paperback. . .

Tommy was not arrested. He waited—one day, two days, three days—sleeping on the bench, sitting in the chilly lobby, sipping coffee, reading Rilke . . . Then he went home.

In April Tommy was indicted by a federal grand jury for his failure to register for the draft. One month later, at Tommy's arraignment, Federal Judge Joseph P. Willson refused to accept his guilty plea because he had insisted on representing himself . . .

On June 9 a sentence hearing was held before Judge Louis Rosenberg in federal court.

. . . Tom [testified]: "Yes . . . obviously I am trying to raise the question of the draft; that is one of my motives. But even if I didn't, and even if the penalty were possibly twenty-five years, and I couldn't get it into the papers and I couldn't get people talking about it, and there was no one in the courtroom, then I would still do it, because it is something my conscience and my God have led me to.

". . . I am a civil disobedient. That was the term that was coined by Henry David Thoreau. It means that a person so respects the institution of law, and the laws of our country, that he openly, willingly, submits himself to prosecution while that law exists.

". . . I suppose I could have gone to Canada and not registered at all. But it was because of this duty to our laws and because of this duty to society that has set up these laws that I have turned myself in. That is why I stand here today. And my conscience is very clear. And life has been very good to me. Thank you."

. . . Judge Rosenberg questioned Tom. "Do you think the Russians would respect the nonviolence that you are preaching? Do you think they would stay on their own side and let us alone?"

"I think as human beings and as children of God, they have souls too; they can be appealed to."

"All right."

269

Tommy was sent to the Ashland, Kentucky, Federal Correctional Institution for "observation and study.". . .

One morning Judge Rosenberg received a three-page letter from Tommy Rodd, who was still in Ashland. Tommy knew that the judge had three choices once the Ashland period was over: to parole him if he could get into college; to place him on probation and work out a two-year sentence with a court-approved service agency; or to sentence him to five years in a federal jail. Tommy would have preferred college, possibly the University of Chicago or Pittsburgh.

In the letter, Tommy recalled an incident in Binghamton, New York: he was standing on the downtown courthouse steps lashing out at the draft when a youth walked up and smashed him in the jaw.

"I fell down, then got up. Several of his friends were restraining him; I asked them to let him go and told him I wouldn't fight back, that I bore him no hatred, and would he like to talk. He walked away, but came back. We talked, had coffee—his father had been killed at Iwo Jima. I spent that night at his house; in the morning he gave me a St. Christopher's medal which I have today. What would have happened if I had hit him? This sort of thing has happened too often to let me avoid the conclusion that true communication cannot be based upon violence.

"Sometimes, your honor, civil disobedience is a mandatory act. No United States law can be ruled unconstitutional until a person breaks it—so decided Justice Marshall. What of the Boston Tea Party? Those who courageously defied the Fugitive Slave Law? What was Eichmann's crime, essentially? [Adolph Eichmann was convicted and executed for his part in the killing of Jews during World War II.] It was that he obeyed the law, even when it contradicted a higher morality. This is the essence of the Nuremberg decision: that when conscience and the state conflict, conscience must be obeyed."

Tommy returned to the Allegheny County jail for five weeks. . .

On August 18 he was called before Judge Rosenberg. The judge, armed with the report from Ashland, said that "This young man has perhaps been guided and taught wrongly from early childhood, because, when he was eight years old, he had already told his teacher how things should be run.

"He knew better than the teacher, and later in his life he did the same thing. He was one of those who demonstrated . . . not because it was for the sake of canceling out war, but because it put him into a position where he could exhibit his own ego."

"I can't send you to college," said the judge a few moments later. "You have put yourself in the position that you did. I didn't put you there. You are there, and you will have to face it.

"And if you think that your martyrdom will carry you through, that is your function in a constitutionally free America. In governments such as we have, even you are permitted to violate the law, even serious law, in chaotic fashion, but we must deal with you for the purpose of preservation of society. And that is what I propose to do."

Tommy was ordered to join an approved service group, such as the Peace Corps or the International Voluntary Services, Inc., or go to prison for five years. Later, when the plan for probation was worked out, the probation included a provision that Tommy could not participate in any demonstrations. . . .

For one year Tommy worked at the American Friends warehouse, processing and shipping clothes to Algerian refugees. He grew a little beard and wore baggy Army fatigue pants and a T-shirt and thirty-nine-cent rubber thongs and would walk down Union Street in West Philadelphia carrying his banjo and shouting, "Whatcha doin'?" to the little Negro kids, who all knew him.

In the second year, Tommy moved to 3945 Fairmount Avenue in Mantua, in the heart of the ghetto, where he was a weekend work-camp leader for the Friends Social Order Committee. He shared the fire-scarred building, a former warehouse, with two V.I.S.T.A. workers and a large, gentle Negro conscientious objector. By day, the four worked in the neighborhood, painting houses, nailing, fixing broken windows. At night they worked on their own house.

Tommy adored it. He adored sitting on a curb and teaching a kid the banjo and eating what appeared to be an inexhaustible supply of government-issue peanut butter on bread and tinkering with the broken television set and playing on the warped ping-pong table and listening to Copland's *Billy the Kid*, and going to the Royal Theatre nearby to scream with all the kids who were watching *Help!* . . .

There was also tutoring of the neighborhood kids and speeches to Quaker groups and, on weekends, freshmen from Haverford or Temple would show up and work in the neighborhood during the day and sleep on the blankets and in the sleeping bags in Tommy's third-floor bedroom. They would have parties, and Tommy would take over, of course, singing *Arkansas Traveler* in that funky twang, and break up everybody with the corn pone. ("How much is thirty-eight and thirty-eight?" "Seventy-six." "That's the spirit!")

"So here is Tom Rodd. I have tried, Lord knows, to obey this probation. I wanted to go to Selma and walk to Montgomery — but I didn't. I wanted to go to Washington and confront the President — but I didn't. I wanted to picket Girard College in Philadelphia — but I didn't. I wanted to help picket a nonunion store on Lanchester Avenue in West Philadelphia — but I didn't.

"But this war is too immediate, too pressing, too terrible for me to have to say later: 'but I didn't.'"

The Vietnam war was escalating, and Tommy's friends were demonstrating in Washington, Pittsburgh, Philadelphia, and New

York. How could he stand by? How could he watch? What was this commitment, this labor, this devotion for? *"This war is a sin."*

In November 1965 Norman Morrison burned himself to death outside the Pentagon to protest the war. Tommy was stunned. "I had to do something. I could have waited a few months until my probation period ended, but it was a question of living with myself. I decided to break my probation."

On a cold and gray morning, December 30, 1965, about 160 pickets demonstrated at the Boeing Corporation's Vertol Division in Morton, Pennsylvania, to protest Vertol's production of helicopters for the war. They carried the usual signs, "Withdraw U.S. Troops from Vietnam," and the 250 American Legionnaires across the street carried *their* usual signs, "Free Matches and Gas for You Peace Creeps," and there were the usual arrests (twenty-six of them), and one of the demonstrators arrested was nineteen-year-old Tom Rodd.

Weeks before, he had sent a letter to everyone — to Judge Rosenberg, Bill and Betts [his parents], neighbors in Pittsburgh and Philadelphia, "brave friends already in prison, girls I have kissed, guitar-picking comrades, Presidents, congressmen, peace actionists, men and women of good will all over the world.

"I now take action and will continue to take action that will invite you, force you to abandon this war or do violence to me. One is never sure of the truth, but if I am right, and if I and all others like myself are firm and loving in our noncooperation and our sacrifice, I believe that we will prevail, someday."

On January 7, 1966, Tommy again confronted Judge Rosenberg. The courtroom was packed. Outside, four young men and women staged a silent vigil and carried a sign: "He Did It for Love."

Tommy looked gaunt and frightened. The $8 suit that he had bought in Mantua sagged. He asked and was given permission to read a statement.

"I am forced by my conscience to stand as a representative of the suffering millions of Vietnam. I am forced to stand for the girl child burned to death in Bien Hoa, for the refugee cold and hungry in a camp on the outskirts of Saigon, for the weary guerrilla fighter, for the Buddhist monk who is now a handful of ashes, for the thousands with no legs, thousands more with no eyes, yes, and even for the U.S. Marine now slowly dying in a Philadelphia hospital.

"These people are my constituency. I stand for them. And my word from them to this government, to this country is this: 'Stop this war! Your dominoes, your escalation, your computer theories, your phony negotiations are at best inhuman madness and at worst insidious, deliberate lies. Your war, all wars, are immoral and insane. Stop it. Withdraw U.S. troops now. End the war in Vietnam.'"

He spoke for eight minutes. Judge Rosenberg then summoned him to the bar and in thirty seconds ordered him placed in federal prison for four years.

Tommy blinked. The audience was stunned. . . .

60 A Summary Exercise

You have now completed your study of comparative political systems. You have identified five characteristics shared by all political systems, and examined two systems in terms of these characteristics. Throughout the course there has been an emphasis on the analysis of political systems. Therefore, more time and space have been given to "what is" rather than to "what ought to be." But you cannot conclude your course without giving attention to "what ought to be."

Who is to say what is "better"? You know from your comparative analyses that one system can be made to look superior to another if the criteria by which they are compared are carefully chosen. Does this fact imply that all systems are equally "good"? As Americans, we obviously do not think so. We bring our own values to our study of comparative political systems. We bring our belief in the importance of questioning; thus, we naturally favor a system that permits us to ask questions. We bring our commitment to the value of an individual's opinion; thus, we are attracted to a system that encourages us to express ourselves freely. We bring ourselves, what we are and what we believe in, to our task; therefore, we must constantly question our own conclusions to make sure that our answers to questions about what ought to be are not mere reflections of the society in which we live.

For tomorrow you are to write a short essay. Give it careful thought, for it is, in a sense, an evaluation of everything you have learned throughout this course. In preparation, review your notes, particularly those in which you analyzed and compared characteristics of the Soviet and American political systems. Then answer the following questions:

What do you think are the three most important tasks of modern government?

How would you rate the United States government in the performance of these tasks?

How would you rate the government of the Soviet Union in the performance of these tasks?

SUGGESTED READINGS

HUTCHINS, ROBERT M., "Is Democracy Possible?", *Political Institutions,* pp. 350–54.

Question: What does Dr. Hutchins think is needed to make democracy operate most effectively? Do you agree?

MENCKEN, H. L., "Democracy: Rule of the Mob," *Political Institutions,* pp. 31–34.

Question: How could Mr. Mencken's charges be refuted?

MERYMAN, RICHARD S., JR., "South Dakota's Christian Martyrs," *Politics, U.S.A.,* pp. 155–61.

Question: Do the Hutterites constitute a threat to democracy?

MILL, JOHN STUART, "The Superiority of Democratic Government," *Political Institutions,* pp. 34–36.

Question: What did John Stuart Mill mean by the term *democracy?*

MILLIS, WALTER, "Outlook for Our Civil Liberties," *Profile of American Politics,* pp. 68–72.

Question: Why is it easier to talk about civil liberties than it is to enforce them?

LIPPMANN, WALTER, "The People Are Often Wrong," *Profile of American Politics,* pp. 12–15.

Question: What is the dilemma posed by Mr. Lippmann? How would you respond to Mr. Lippmann?

REDFIELD, ROBERT, "Talk with a Stranger," *Political Institutions,* pp. 354–59.

Question: How do you think "the stranger" would define the role of a democratic government?

RODELL, FRED, "The Law," *Political Institutions,* pp. 263–66.

Question: According to the author, what is "the law"?

ROSSITER, CLINTON, "The Democratic Process," *Politics, U.S.A.,* pp. 2–20.

Question: What are the strengths of the democratic process? What are the responsibilities?

SLAPPEY, STERLING, "I Saw It Happen in Oxford," *Politics, U.S.A.,* pp. 117–22.

Question: What role did the federal government play in the incident described by Sterling Slappey?

U.S. NEWS AND WORLD REPORT, "The Mississippi Tragedy," *Politics, U.S.A.,* pp. 111–17.

Question: What principles of government were tested at Oxford?

Appendix

The Constitution of the United States

(The portions of the Constitution printed in brackets are either out of date or changed by amendment. The descriptive headings have been added for your convenience.)

PREAMBLE

We, the people of the United States, in order to form a more perfect Union, establish justice, insure domestic tranquillity, provide for the common defense, promote the general welfare, and secure the blessings of liberty to ourselves and our posterity, do ordain and establish this CONSTITUTION for the United States of America.

Article 1. LEGISLATIVE DEPARTMENT

SECTION 1. CONGRESS

All legislative powers herein granted shall be vested in a Congress of the United States, which shall consist of a Senate and House of Representatives.

SECTION 2. HOUSE OF REPRESENTATIVES

1. *Election and term of office.* The House of Representatives shall be composed of members chosen every second year by the people of the several states, and the electors in each state shall have the qualifications requisite for electors of the most numerous branch of the state legislature.

2. *Qualifications for representatives.* No person shall be a representative who shall not have attained to the age of twenty-five years, and been seven years a citizen of the United States, and who shall not, when elected, be an inhabitant of that state in which he shall be chosen.

3. *Apportionment of representatives and direct taxes.* Representatives [and direct taxes] shall be apportioned among the several states which may be included within this Union, according to their respective numbers, [which shall be determined by adding to the whole number of free persons, including those bound to service for a term of years, and excluding Indians not taxed, three-fifths of all other persons.] The actual enumeration shall be made within three years after the first meeting of the Congress of the United States, and within every subsequent term of ten years, in such manner as they shall by law direct. The number of representatives shall not exceed 1 for every 30,000, but each state shall have at least 1 representative; [and until such enumeration shall be made, the state of New Hampshire shall be entitled to choose 3; Massachusetts, 8; Rhode Island and Providence Plantations, 1; Connecticut, 5; New York, 6; New Jersey, 4; Pennsylvania, 8; Delaware, 1; Maryland, 6; Virginia, 10; North Carolina, 5; South Carolina 5; and Georgia 3.]

4. *Filling vacancies.* When vacancies happen in the representation from any state, the executive authority thereof shall issue writs of election to fill such vacancies.

5. *Election of officers; impeachment.* The House of Representatives shall choose their Speaker and other officers; and shall have the sole power of impeachment.

SECTION 3. SENATE

1. *Number of senators and term of office.* The Senate of the United States shall be composed of two senators from each state, [chosen by the legislature thereof,] for six years, and each senator shall have one vote.

2. *Classification; filling vacancies.* [Immediately after they shall be assembled in consequence of the first election, they shall be divided as equally as may be into three classes. The seats of the senators of the first class shall be vacated at the expiration of the second year, of the second class at the expiration of the fourth year, and of the third class at the expiration of the sixth year, so that one-third may be chosen every second year; and if vacancies happen by resignation, or otherwise, during the recess of the legislature of any state, the executive thereof may make temporary appointments until the next meeting of the legislature, which shall then fill such vacancies.]

3. *Qualifications for senators.* No person shall be a senator who shall not have attained to the age of thirty years, and been nine years a citizen of the United States, and who shall not, when elected, be an inhabitant of that state for which he shall be chosen.

4. *President of the Senate.* The Vice-President of the United States shall be president of the Senate, but shall have no vote, unless they be equally divided.

5. *Other officers.* The Senate shall choose their other officers, and also a President *pro tempore,* in the absence of the Vice-President, or when he shall exercise the office of President of the United States.

6. *Trials of impeachment.* The Senate shall have the sole power to try all impeachments. When sitting for that purpose, they shall be on oath or affirmation. When the President of the United States is tried, the Chief Justice shall preside; and no person shall be convicted without the concurrence of two thirds of the members present.

7. *Punishment for conviction.* Judgment in cases of impeachment shall not extend further than to removal from office, and disqualification to hold and enjoy any office of honor, trust, or profit under the United States; but the party convicted shall nevertheless be liable and subject to indictment, trial, judgment, and punishment, according to law.

SECTION 4. ELECTIONS AND MEETINGS OF CONGRESS

1. *Regulation of elections.* The times, places, and manner of holding elections for senators and representatives shall be prescribed in each state by the legislature thereof; but the Congress may at any time by law make or alter such regulations, except as to the places of choosing senators.

2. *Meetings.* The Congress shall assemble at least once in every year, [and such meeting shall be on the first Monday in December,] unless they shall by law appoint a different day.

SECTION 5. RULES OF PROCEDURE

1. *Membership and sittings.* Each house shall be the judge of the elections, returns, and qualifications of its own members, and a majority of each shall constitute a quorum to do business; but a smaller number may adjourn from day to day, and may be authorized to compel the attendance of absent members, in such manner, and under such penalties, as each house may provide.

2. *Proceedings.* Each house may determine the rules of its proceedings, punish its members for disorderly behavior, and with the concurrence of two thirds, expel a member.

3. *Journal.* Each house shall keep a journal of its proceedings, and from time to time publish the same, excepting such parts as may in their judgment require secrecy; and the yeas and nays of the members of either house on any question shall, at the desire of one fifth of those present, be entered on the journal.

4. *Adjournment.* Neither house, during the session of Congress, shall, without the consent of the other, adjourn for more than three days, nor to any other place than that in which the two houses shall be sitting.

SECTION 6. PRIVILEGES AND RESTRICTIONS

1. *Salary and privileges.* The senators and representatives shall receive a compensation for their services, to be ascertained by law and paid out of the Treasury of the United States. They shall in all cases, except treason, felony, and breach of the peace, be privileged from arrest during their attendance at the session of their respective houses, and in going to and returning from the same; and for any speech or debate in either house, they shall not be questioned in any other place.

2. *Restrictions.* No senator or representative shall, during the time for which he was elected, be appointed to any civil office under the authority of the United States, which shall have been created, or the emoluments whereof shall have been increased, during such time; and no person holding any office under the United States shall be a member of either house during his continuance in office.

SECTION 7. METHOD OF PASSING LAWS

1. *Revenue bills.* All bills for raising revenue shall originate in the House of Representatives; but the Senate may propose or concur with amendments as on other bills.

2. *How a bill becomes a law.* Every bill which shall have passed the House of Representatives and the Senate shall, before it becomes a law, be presented to the President of the United States; if he approve, he shall sign it, but if not, he shall return it, with his objections, to that house in which it shall have originated, who shall enter the objections at large on their journal, and proceed to reconsider it. If after such reconsideration two thirds of that house shall agree to pass the bill, it shall be sent, together with the objections, to the other house, by which it shall likewise be reconsidered, and, if approved by two thirds of that house, it shall become a law. But in all such cases the votes of both houses shall be determined by yeas and nays, and the names of the persons voting for and against the bill shall be entered on the journal of each house respectively. If any bill shall not be returned by the President within ten days (Sundays excepted) after it shall have been presented to him, the same shall be a law, in like manner as if he had signed it, unless the Congress by their adjournment prevent its return, in which case it shall not be a law.

3. *Presidential approval or veto.* Every order, resolution, or vote to which the concurrence of the Senate and House of Representatives may be necessary (except on a question of adjournment) shall be presented to the President of the United States; and before the same shall take effect, shall be approved by him, or being disapproved by him, shall be repassed by two thirds of the Senate and House of Representatives, according to the rules and limitations prescribed in the case of a bill.

SECTION 8. POWERS DELEGATED TO CONGRESS

The Congress shall have power

1. To lay and collect taxes, duties, imposts, and excises, to pay the debts and provide for the common defense and general welfare of the United States; but all duties, imposts, and excises shall be uniform throughout the United States;

2. To borrow money on the credit of the United States;

3. To regulate commerce with foreign nations, and among the several states, and with the Indian tribes;

4. To establish a uniform rule of naturalization, and uniform laws on the subject of bankruptcies throughout the United States;

5. To coin money, regulate the value thereof, and of foreign coin, and fix the standard of weights and measures;

6. To provide for the punishment of counterfeiting the securities and current coin of the United States;

7. To establish post offices and post roads;

8. To promote the progress of science and useful arts by securing for limited times to authors and inventors the exclusive right to their respective writings and discoveries;

9. To constitute tribunals inferior to the Supreme Court;

10. To define and punish piracies and felonies committed on the high seas and offenses against the law of nations;

11. To declare war, [grant letters of marque and reprisal,] and make rules concerning captures on land and water;

12. To raise and support armies, but no appropriation of money to that use shall be for a longer term than two years;

13. To provide and maintain a navy;

14. To make rules for the government and regulation of the land and naval forces;

15. To provide for calling forth the militia to execute the laws of the Union, suppress insurrections, and repel invasions;

16. To provide for organizing, arming, and disciplining the militia, and for governing such part of them as may be employed in the service of the United States, reserving to the states, respectively, the appointment of the officers, and the authority of training the militia according to the discipline prescribed by Congress;

17. To exercise exclusive legislation in all cases whatsoever, over such district (not exceeding ten miles square) as may, by cession of particular states, and the acceptance of Congress, become the seat of government of the United States, and to exercise like authority over all places purchased by the consent of the legislature of the state in which the same shall be, for the erection of forts, magazines, arsenals, dockyards, and other needful buildings;—and

18. To make all laws which shall be necessary and proper for carrying into execution the foregoing powers, and all other powers vested by this Constitution in the government of the United States, or in any department or officer thereof.

SECTION 9. POWERS DENIED TO THE FEDERAL GOVERNMENT

1. [The migration or importation of such persons as any of the states now existing shall think proper to admit shall not be prohibited by the Congress prior to the year 1808; but a tax or duty may be imposed on such importation, not exceeding $10 for each person.]

2. The privilege of the writ of *habeas corpus* shall not be suspended, unless when in cases of rebellion or invasion the public safety may require it.

3. No bill of attainder or *ex post facto* law shall be passed.

4. No capitation or other direct tax shall be laid, unless in proportion to the census or enumeration herein before directed to be taken.

5. No tax or duty shall be laid on articles exported from any state.

6. No preference shall be given by any regulation of commerce or revenue to the ports of one state over those of another; nor shall vessels bound to, or from, one state, be obliged to enter, clear, or pay duties in another.

7. No money shall be drawn from the Treasury, but in consequence of appropriations made by law; and a regular statement and account of the receipts and expenditures of all public money shall be published from time to time.

8. No title of nobility shall be granted by the United States; and no person holding any office of profit or trust under them, shall, without the consent of the Congress, accept of any present, emolument, office, or title, of any kind whatever, from any king, prince, or foreign state.

SECTION 10. POWERS DENIED TO THE STATES

1. No state shall enter into any treaty, alliance, or confederation; grant letters of marque and reprisal; coin money; emit bills of credit; make anything but gold and silver coin a tender in payment of debts; pass any bill of attainder, *ex post facto* law, or law impairing the obligation of contracts, or grant any title of nobility.

2. No state shall, without the consent of the Congress, lay any imposts or duties on imports or exports, except what may be absolutely necessary for executing its inspection laws; and the net produce of all duties and imposts, laid by any state on imports or exports, shall be for the use of the Treasury of the United States; and all such laws shall be subject to the revision and control of the Congress.

3. No state shall, without the consent of Congress, lay any duty of tonnage, keep troops, or ships of war in time of peace, enter into any agreement or compact with another state, or with a foreign power, or engage in war, unless actually invaded, or in such imminent danger as will not admit of delay.

Article 2. EXECUTIVE DEPARTMENT

SECTION 1. PRESIDENT AND VICE-PRESIDENT

1. *Term of office.* The executive power shall be vested in a President of the United States of America. He shall hold his office during the term of four years, and together with the Vice-President, chosen for the same term, be elected as follows:

2. *Electoral system.* Each state shall appoint, in such manner as the legislature thereof may direct, a number of electors, equal to the whole number of senators and representatives to which the state may be entitled in the Congress; but no senator or representative, or person holding an office of trust or profit under the United States, shall be appointed an elector.

3. *Election of President and Vice-President.* [The electors shall meet in their respective states, and vote by ballot for two persons, of whom one at least shall not be an inhabitant of the same state with themselves. And they shall make a list of all the persons voted for, and of the number of votes for each; which list they shall sign and certify, and transmit sealed to the seat of the government of the United States, directed to the president of the Senate. The president of the Senate shall, in the presence of the Senate and House of Representatives, open all the certificates, and the votes shall then be counted. The person having the greatest number of votes shall be the President, if such number be a majority of the whole number of electors appointed; and if there be more than one who have such majority, and have an equal number of votes, then the House of Representatives shall immediately choose by ballot one of them for President; and if no person have a majority, then from the five highest on the list the said House shall in like manner choose the President. But in choosing the President the votes shall be taken by states, the representation from each state having one vote. A quorum for this purpose shall consist of a member or members from two-thirds of the states, and a majority of all the states shall be necessary to a choice. In every case, after the choice of the President, the person having the greatest number of votes of the electors shall be the Vice-President. But if there should remain two or more who have equal votes, the Senate shall choose from them by ballot the Vice-President.]

4. *Time of elections.* The Congress may determine the time of choosing the electors,

and the day on which they shall give their votes; which day shall be the same throughout the United States.

5. *Qualifications for President.* No person except a natural-born citizen, [or a citizen of the United States, at the time of the adoption of this Constitution,] shall be eligible to the office of President; neither shall any person be eligible to that office who shall not have attained to the age of thirty-five years, and been fourteen years a resident within the United States.

6. *Filling vacancies.* In case of the removal of the President from office, or of his death, resignation, or inability to discharge the powers and duties of the said office, the same shall devolve on the Vice-President, and the Congress may by law provide for the case of removal, death, resignation, or inability, both of the President and Vice-President, declaring what officer shall then act as President, and such officer shall act accordingly, until the disability be removed, or a President shall be elected.

7. *Salary.* The President shall, at stated times, receive for his services, a compensation, which shall neither be increased nor diminished during the period for which he shall have been elected, and he shall not receive within that period any other emolument from the United States, or any of them.

8. *Oath of office.* Before he enter on the execution of his office, he shall take the following oath or affirmation:—"I do solemnly swear (or affirm) that I will faithfully execute the office of President of the United States, and will to the best of my ability, preserve, protect, and defend the Constitution of the United States."

SECTION 2. POWERS OF THE PRESIDENT

1. *Powers over the military and executive departments; reprieves and pardons.* The President shall be Commander in Chief of the Army and Navy of the United States, and of the militia of the several states, when called into the actual service of the United States; he may require the opinion, in writing, of the principal officer in each of the executive departments, upon any subject relating to the duties of their respective offices, and he shall have power to grant reprieves and pardons for offenses against the United States, except in cases of impeachment.

2. *Treaties and appointments.* He shall have power, by and with the advice and consent of the Senate, to make treaties, provided two thirds of the senators present concur; and he shall nominate, and by and with the advice and consent of the Senate, shall appoint ambassadors, other public ministers and consuls, judges of the Supreme Court, and all other officers of the United States, whose appointments are not herein otherwise provided for, and which shall be established by law; but the Congress may by law vest the appointment of such inferior officers, as they think proper, in the President alone, in the courts of law, or in the heads of departments.

3. *Filling vacancies.* The President shall have power to fill up all vacancies that may happen during the recess of the Senate, by granting commissions which shall expire at the end of their next session.

SECTION 3. DUTIES OF THE PRESIDENT

He shall from time to time give to the Congress information of the state of the Union, and recommend to their consideration such measures as he shall judge necessary and expedient; he may, on extraordinary occasions, convene both houses, or either of them, and in case of disagreement between them, with respect to the time of adjournment, he may adjourn them to such time as he shall think proper; he shall receive ambassadors and other public ministers; he shall take care that the laws be faithfully executed, and shall commission all the officers of the United States.

SECTION 4. IMPEACHMENT

The President, Vice-President, and all civil officers of the United States, shall be removed from office on impeachment for, and conviction of, treason, bribery, or other high crimes and misdemeanors.

Article 3. JUDICIAL DEPARTMENT

SECTION 1. FEDERAL COURTS

The judicial power of the United States shall be vested in one Supreme Court, and in such inferior courts as the Congress may from time to time ordain and establish. The judges, both of the Supreme and inferior courts, shall hold their offices during good behavior, and shall, at stated times, receive for their services a compensation, which shall not be diminished during their continuance in office.

SECTION 2. JURISDICTION OF FEDERAL COURTS

1. *General jurisdiction.* The judicial power shall extend to all cases, in law and equity, arising under this Constitution, the laws of the United States, and treaties made or which shall be made, under their authority; to all cases affecting ambassadors, other public ministers and consuls; to all cases of admiralty and maritime jurisdiction; to controversies to which the United States shall be a party; to controversies between two or more states; [between a state and citizens of another state;] between citizens of different states; between citizens of the same state claiming lands under grants of different states, and between a state, or the citizens thereof, and foreign states, citizens, or subjects.

2. *Supreme Court.* In all cases affecting ambassadors, other public ministers and consuls, and those in which a state shall be a party, the Supreme Court shall have original jurisdiction. In all the other cases before mentioned, the Supreme Court shall have appellate jurisdiction, both as to law and fact, with such exceptions, and under such regulations as the Congress shall make.

3. *Conduct of trials.* The trial of all crimes, except in cases of impeachment, shall be by jury; and such trial shall be held in the state where the said crimes shall have been committed; but when not committed within any state, the trial shall be at such place or places as the Congress may by law have directed.

SECTION 3. TREASON

1. *Definition.* Treason against the United States shall consist only in levying war against them, or in adhering to their enemies, giving them aid and comfort. No person shall be convicted of treason unless on the testimony of two witnesses to the same overt act, or on confession in open court.

2. *Punishment.* The Congress shall have power to declare the punishment of treason, but no attainder of treason shall work corruption of blood or forfeiture except during the life of the person attainted.

Article 4. RELATIONS AMONG THE STATES

SECTION 1. OFFICIAL ACTS

Full faith and credit shall be given in each state to the public acts, records, and judicial proceedings of every other state. And the Congress may by general laws prescribe the manner in which such acts, records, and proceedings shall be proved, and the effect thereof.

SECTION 2. PRIVILEGES OF CITIZENS

1. *Privileges.* The citizens of each state shall be entitled to all privileges and immunities of citizens in the several states.

2. *Extradition.* A person charged in any state with treason, felony, or other crime, who shall flee from justice, and be found in another state, shall on demand of the

executive authority of the state from which he fled, be delivered up, to be removed to the state having jurisdiction of the crime.

3. *Fugitive slaves.* [No person held in service or labor in one state, under the laws thereof, escaping into another, shall in consequence of any law or regulation therein, be discharged from such service or labor, but shall be delivered up on claim of the party to whom such service or labor may be due.]

SECTION 3. NEW STATES AND TERRITORIES

1. *Admission of new states.* New states may be admitted by the Congress into this Union; but no new state shall be formed or erected within the jurisdiction of any other state; nor any state be formed by the junction of two or more states, or parts of states, without the consent of the legislatures of the states concerned as well as of the Congress.

2. *Power of Congress over territories and other property.* The Congress shall have power to dispose of and make all needful rules and regulations respecting the territory or other property belonging to the United States; and nothing in this Constitution shall be so construed as to prejudice any claims of the United States, or of any particular state.

SECTION 4. GUARANTEES TO THE STATES

The United States shall guarantee to every state in this Union a republican form of government, and shall protect each of them against invasion; and on application of the legislature, or of the executive (when the legislature cannot be convened) against domestic violence.

Article 5. METHODS OF AMENDMENT

The Congress, whenever two thirds of both houses shall deem it necessary, shall propose amendments to this Constitution, or, on the application of the legislatures of two thirds of the several states, shall call a convention for proposing amendments, which, in either case, shall be valid to all intents and purposes, as part of this Constitution, when ratified by the legislatures of three fourths of the several states, or by conventions in three fourths thereof, as the one or the other mode of ratification may be proposed by the Congress; provided that [no amendments which may be made prior to the year 1808 shall in any manner affect the first and fourth clauses in the Ninth Section of the First Article; and that] no state, without its consent, shall be deprived of its equal suffrage in the Senate.

Article 6. GENERAL PROVISIONS

1. *Public debts.* All debts contracted and engagements entered into, before the adoption of this Constitution, shall be as valid against the United States under this Constitution, as under the Confederation.

2. *The supreme law of the land.* This Constitution, and the laws of the United States which shall be made in pursuance thereof, and all treaties made, or which shall be made, under the authority of the United States, shall be the supreme law of the land; and the judges in every state shall be bound thereby, anything in the constitution or laws of any state to the contrary notwithstanding.

3. *Oaths of office; no religious test.* The senators and representatives before mentioned, and the members of the several state legislatures, and all executive and judicial officers, both of the United States and of the several states, shall be bound by oath or affirmation, to support this Constitution; but no religious test shall ever be required as a qualification to any office or public trust under the United States.

Article 7. RATIFICATION

The ratification of the convention of nine states shall be sufficient for the establishment of this Constitution between the states so ratifying the same.

DONE in Convention by the unanimous consent of the States present the seventeenth day of September in the year of our Lord one thousand seven hundred and eighty-seven and of the independence of the United States of America the twelfth. In witness whereof we have hereunto subscribed our names.

Amendment 1. FREEDOM OF RELIGION, SPEECH, PRESS, ASSEMBLY, AND PETITION (1791)

Congress shall make no law respecting an establishment of religion, or prohibiting the free exercise thereof; or abridging the freedom of speech, or of the press; or the right of the people peaceably to assemble, and to petition the government for a redress of grievances.

Amendment 2. RIGHT TO KEEP ARMS (1791)

A well-regulated militia, being necessary to the security of a free state, the right of the people to keep and bear arms shall not be infringed.

Amendment 3. QUARTERING OF TROOPS (1791)

No soldier shall, in time of peace, be quartered in any house, without the consent of the owner; nor in time of war, but in a manner to be prescribed by law.

Amendment 4. SEARCHES AND SEIZURES; WARRANTS (1791)

The right of the people to be secure in their persons, houses, papers, and effects, against unreasonable searches and seizures, shall not be violated; and no warrants shall issue but upon probable cause, supported by oath or affirmation, and particularly describing the place to be searched, and the person or things to be seized.

Amendment 5. RIGHTS OF ACCUSED PERSONS (1791)

No person shall be held to answer for a capital, or otherwise infamous, crime, unless on a presentment or indictment of a grand jury, except in cases arising in the land or naval forces, or in the militia, when in actual service in time of war or public danger; nor shall any person be subject for the same offense to be twice put in jeopardy of life or limb; nor shall be compelled, in any criminal case, to be a witness against himself; nor be deprived of life, liberty, or property, without due process of law; nor shall private property be taken for public use, without just compensation.

Amendment 6. RIGHT TO SPEEDY AND PUBLIC TRIAL (1791)

In all criminal prosecutions, the accused shall enjoy the right to a speedy and public trial, by an impartial jury of the state and district wherein the crime shall have been committed, which district shall have been previously ascertained by law, and to be informed of the nature and cause of the accusation; to be confronted with the witnesses against him; to have compulsory process for obtaining witnesses in his favor, and to have the assistance of counsel for his defense.

Amendment 7. JURY TRIAL IN CIVIL CASES (1791)

In suits at common law, where the value in controversy shall exceed twenty dollars, the right of trial by jury shall be preserved, and no fact tried by a jury shall be otherwise reexamined in any court of the United States than according to the rules of the common law.

Amendment 8. BAIL, FINES, PUNISHMENTS (1791)

Excessive bail shall not be required, nor excessive fines imposed, nor cruel and unusual punishments inflicted.

Amendment 9. POWERS RESERVED TO THE PEOPLE (1791)

The enumeration in the Constitution, of certain rights, shall not be construed to deny or disparage others retained by the people.

Amendment 10. POWERS RESERVED TO THE STATES (1791)

The powers not delegated to the United States by the Constitution, nor prohibited by it to the states, are reserved to the states respectively, or to the people.

Amendment 11. SUITS AGAINST STATES (1798)

The judicial power of the United States shall not be construed to extend to any suit in law or equity, commenced or prosecuted against one of the United States, by citizens of another state, or by citizens or subjects of any foreign state.

Amendment 12. ELECTION OF PRESIDENT AND VICE-PRESIDENT (1804)

The electors shall meet in their respective states, and vote by ballot for President and Vice-President, one of whom, at least, shall not be an inhabitant of the same state with themselves; they shall name in their ballots the person voted for as President, and in distinct ballots the person voted for as Vice-President, and they shall make distinct lists of all persons voted for as President, and of all persons voted for as Vice-President, and of the number of votes for each, which lists they shall sign and certify, and transmit, sealed, to the seat of government of the United States, directed to the President of the Senate; the President of the Senate shall, in the presence of the Senate and House of Representatives, open all the certificates and the votes shall then be counted; the person having the greatest number of votes for President shall be the President, if such number be a majority of the whole number of electors appointed; and if no person have such majority, then from the persons having the highest numbers not exceeding three on the list of those voted for as President, the House of Representatives shall choose imme-diately, by ballot, the President. But in choosing the President, the votes shall be taken by states, the representation from each state having one vote; a quorum for this purpose shall consist of a member or members from two thirds of the states, and a majority of all the states shall be necessary to a choice. [And if the House of Representatives shall not choose a President whenever the right of choice shall devolve upon them, before the fourth day of March next following, then the Vice-President shall act as President, as in the case of the death or other constitutional disability of the President.] The person having the greatest number of votes as Vice-President, shall be the Vice-President, if such number be a majority of the whole number of electors appointed, and if no person have a majority, then, from the two highest numbers on the list, the Senate shall choose the Vice-President; a quorum for the purpose shall consist of two thirds of the whole number of senators, and a majority of the whole number shall be necessary to a choice. But no person constitutionally ineligible to the office of President shall be eligible to that of Vice-President of the United States.

Amendment 13. SLAVERY ABOLISHED (1865)

SECTION 1. Neither slavery nor involuntary servitude, except as a punishment for crime whereof the party shall have been duly convicted, shall exist within the United

States, or any place subject to their jurisdiction.

SECTION 2. Congress shall have power to enforce this article by appropriate legislation.

Amendment 14. RIGHTS OF CITIZENS (1868)

SECTION 1. *Citizenship defined.* All persons born or naturalized in the United States and subject to the jurisdiction thereof, are citizens of the United States and of the state wherein they reside. No state shall make or enforce any law which shall abridge the privileges or immunities of citizens of the United States; nor shall any state deprive any person of life, liberty, or property, without due process of law; nor deny to any person within its jurisdiction the equal protection of the laws.

SECTION 2. *Apportionment of representatives.* Representatives shall be apportioned among the several states according to their respective numbers, counting the whole number of persons in each state, excluding Indians not taxed. But when the right to vote at any election for the choice of electors for President and Vice-President of the United States, representatives in Congress, the executive and judicial officers of a state, or the members of the legislature thereof, is denied to any of the male inhabitants of such state, being twenty-one years of age and citizens of the United States, or in any way abridged, except for participation in rebellion, or other crime, the basis of representation therein shall be reduced in the proportion which the number of such male citizens shall bear to the whole number of male citizens twenty-one years of age in such state.

SECTION 3. *Disability for engaging in insurrection.* No person shall be a senator or representative in Congress, or elector of President and Vice-President, or hold any office, civil or military, under the United States, or under any state, who, having previously taken an oath, as a member of Congress, or as an officer of the United States, or as a member of any state legislature, or as an executive or judicial officer of any state, to support the Constitution of the United States, shall have engaged in insurrection or rebellion against the same, or given aid or comfort to the enemies thereof. But Congress may, by vote of two thirds of each house, remove such disability.

SECTION 4. *Public debt.* The validity of the public debt of the United States, authorized by law, including debts incurred for payment of pensions and bounties for services in suppressing insurrection or rebellion, shall not be questioned. But neither the United States nor any state shall assume or pay any debt or obligation incurred in aid of insurrection or rebellion against the United States, [or any claim for the loss or emancipation of any slave;] but all such debts, obligations, and claims shall be held illegal and void.

SECTION 5. *Enforcement.* The Congress shall have power to enforce, by appropriate legislation, the provisions of this article.

Amendment 15. RIGHT OF SUFFRAGE (1870)

SECTION 1. The right of citizens of the United States to vote shall not be denied or abridged by the United States or any state on account of race, color, or previous condition of servitude.

SECTION 2. The Congress shall have power to enforce this article by appropriate legislation.

Amendment 16. INCOME TAX (1913)

The Congress shall have power to lay and collect taxes on incomes, from whatever source derived, without apportionment among the several states, and without regard to any census or enumeration.

Amendment 17. ELECTION OF SENATORS (1913)

SECTION 1. *Method of election.* The Senate of the United States shall be composed of two senators from each state, elected by the people thereof, for six years; and each senator shall have one vote. The electors in each state shall have the qualifications requisite for electors of the most numerous branch of the state legislatures.

SECTION 2. *Filling vacancies.* When vacancies happen in the representation of any state in the Senate, the executive authority of such state shall issue writs of election to fill such vacancies: *Provided* that the legislature of any state may empower the executive thereof to make temporary appointments until the people fill the vacancies by election as the legislature may direct.

[SECTION 3. *Not retroactive.* This amendment shall not be so construed as to affect the election or term of any senator chosen before it becomes valid as part of the Constitution.]

Amendment 18. NATIONAL PROHIBITION (1919)

[SECTION 1. After one year from the ratification of this article the manufacture, sale, or transportation of intoxicating liquors within, the importation thereof into, or the exportation thereof from, the United States and all territory subject to the jurisdiction thereof for beverage purposes is hereby prohibited.

SECTION 2. The Congress and the several states shall have concurrent power to enforce this article by appropriate legislation.

SECTION 3. This article shall be inoperative unless it shall have been ratified as an amendment to the Constitution by the legislatures of the several states, as provided in the Constitution, within seven years from the date of the submission hereof to the states by the Congress.]

Amendment 19. WOMAN SUFFRAGE (1920)

SECTION 1. The right of citizens of the United States to vote shall not be denied or abridged by the United States or by any state on account of sex.

SECTION 2. Congress shall have power to enforce this article by appropriate legislation.

Amendment 20. "LAME DUCK" AMENDMENT (1933)

SECTION 1. *Beginning of terms.* The terms of the President and Vice-President shall end at noon on the 20th day of January, and the terms of senators and representatives at noon on the 3d day of January, of the years in which such terms would have ended if this article had not been ratified; and the terms of their successors shall then begin.

SECTION 2. *Beginning of congressional sessions.* The Congress shall assemble at least once in every year, and such meeting shall begin at noon on the 3d day of January, unless they shall by law appoint a different day.

SECTION 3. *Presidential succession.* If at the time fixed for the beginning of the term of the President, the President-elect shall have died, the Vice-President-elect shall become President. If a President shall not have been chosen before the time fixed for the beginning of his term, or if the President-elect shall have failed to qualify, then the Vice-President-elect shall act as President until a President shall have qualified; and the Congress may by law provide for the case wherein neither a President-elect nor a Vice-President-elect shall have qualified, declaring who shall then act as President, or the manner in which one who is to act shall be selected, and such person shall act accordingly until a President or Vice-President shall have qualified.

SECTION 4. *Filling Presidential vacancy.* The Congress may by law provide for the case of the death of any of the persons from whom the House of Representatives may choose a President whenever the right of choice shall have devolved upon them, and for the case of the death of any of the persons from whom the Senate may choose a Vice-President whenever the right of choice shall have devolved upon them.

[SECTION 5. *Effective date.* Sections 1 and 2 shall take effect on the 15th day of October following the ratification of this article.

SECTION 6. *Time limit for ratification.* This article shall be inoperative unless it shall have been ratified as an amendment to the Constitution by the legislatures of three fourths of the several states within seven years from the date of its submission.]

Amendment 21. REPEAL OF PROHIBITION (1933)

SECTION 1. The eighteenth article of amendment to the Constitution of the United States is hereby repealed.

SECTION 2. The transportation or importation into any state, territory, or possession of the United States for delivery or use therein of intoxicating liquors, in violation of the laws thereof, is hereby prohibited.

[SECTION 3. This article shall be inoperative unless it shall have been ratified as an amendment to the Constitution by conventions in the several states, as provided in the Constitution, within seven years from the date of the submission hereof to the states by the Congress.]

Amendment 22. TWO-TERM LIMIT FOR PRESIDENTS (1951)

SECTION 1. No person shall be elected to the office of the President more than twice, and no person who has held the office of President, or acted as President, for more than two years of a term to which some other person was elected President shall be elected to the office of the President more than once. [But this Article shall not apply to any person holding the office of President when this Article was proposed by the Congress, and shall not prevent any person who may be holding the office of President, or acting as President, during the term within which this Article becomes operative from holding the office of President or acting as President during the remainder of such term.]

[SECTION 2. This article shall be inoperative unless it shall have been ratified as an amendment to the Constitution by the legislatures of three fourths of the several states within seven years from the date of its submission to the states by the Congress.]

Amendment 23. PRESIDENTIAL ELECTORS FOR DISTRICT OF COLUMBIA (1961)

SECTION 1. The District constituting the seat of Government of the United States shall appoint in such manner as the Congress may direct:

A number of electors of President and Vice-President equal to the whole number of senators and representatives in Congress to which the District would be entitled if it were a State, but in no event more than the least populous State; they shall be in addition to those appointed by the States, but they shall be considered, for the purposes of the election of President and Vice-President, to be electors appointed by a State; and they shall meet in the District and perform such duties as provided by the twelfth article of amendment.

SECTION 2. The Congress shall have power to enforce this article by appropriate legislation.

Amendment 24. POLL TAX BANNED IN NATIONAL ELECTIONS (1964)

SECTION 1. The right of citizens of the United States to vote in any primary or other election for President or Vice-President, for electors for President or Vice-President, or for senator or representative in Congress, shall not be denied or abridged by the United States or any state by reason of failure to pay any poll tax or other tax.

SECTION 2. The Congress shall have the power to enforce this article by appropriate legislation.

Amendment 25. PRESIDENTIAL DISABILITY AND SUCCESSION (1967)

1. In case of the removal of the President from office or his death or resignation, the Vice-President shall become President.

2. Whenever there is a vacancy in the office of the Vice-President, the President shall nominate a Vice-President who shall take the office upon confirmation of a majority vote of both houses of Congress.

3. Whenever the President transmits to the President *pro tempore* of the Senate and the Speaker of the House of Representatives his written declaration that he is unable to discharge the powers and duties of his office and until he transmits to them a written declaration to the contrary, such powers and duties shall be discharged by the Vice-President as Acting President.

4. Whenever the Vice-President and a majority of either the principal officers of the executive departments or of such other body as Congress may by law provide, transmit to the President *pro tempore* of the Senate and the Speaker of the House of Representatives their written declaration that the President is unable to discharge the powers and duties of his office, the Vice-President shall immediately assume the powers and duties of the office as Acting President.

Thereafter, when the President transmits to the President *pro tempore* of the Senate and the Speaker of the House of Representatives his written declaration that no inability exists, he shall resume the powers and duties of his office unless the Vice-President and a majority of either the principal officers of the executive department or of such other body as Congress may by law provide, transmit within four days to the President *pro tempore* of the Senate and the Speaker of the House of Representatives their written declaration that the President is unable to discharge the powers and duties of his office. Thereupon Congress shall decide the issue, assembling within forty-eight hours for that purpose if not in session. If the Congress, within twenty-one days after receipt of the latter written declaration, or, if Congress is not in session, within twenty-one days after Congress is required to assemble, determines by two-thirds vote of both houses that the President is unable to discharge the powers and duties of his office, the Vice-President shall continue to discharge the same as Acting President; otherwise, the President shall resume the powers and duties of his office.

The Constitution (Fundamental Law)
of the Union of Soviet Socialist Republics

(Chapters 1 to 6 and Chapter 8, as amended to January 1, 1964)

Chapter I THE SOCIAL STRUCTURE

ARTICLE 1. The Union of Soviet Socialist Republics is a socialist state of workers and peasants.

ARTICLE 2. The political foundation of the U.S.S.R. is the Soviets of Working People's Deputies, which grew and became strong as a result of the overthrow of the power of the landlords and capitalists and the conquest of the dictatorship of the proletariat.

ARTICLE 3. All power in the U.S.S.R. belongs to the working people of town and country as represented by the Soviets of Working People's Deputies.

ARTICLE 4. The economic foundation of the U.S.S.R. is the socialist system of economy and the socialist ownership of the instruments and means of production, firmly established as a result of the liquidation of the capitalist system of economy, the abolition of private ownership of the instruments and means of production, and the elimination of the exploitation of man by man.

ARTICLE 5. Socialist property in the U.S.S.R. exists either in the form of state property [belonging to the whole people] or in the form of cooperative and collective-farm property [property of collective farms, property of cooperative societies].

ARTICLE 6. The land, its mineral wealth, waters, forests, mills, factories, mines, rail, water and air transport, banks, communications, large state-organized agricultural enterprises [state farms, machine and tractor stations, and the like], as well as municipal enterprises and the bulk of the dwelling-houses in the cities and industrial localities, are state property, that is, belong to the whole people.

ARTICLE 7. The common enterprises of collective farms and cooperative organizations, with their live stock and implements, the products of the collective farms and cooperative organizations, as well as their common buildings, constitute the common, socialist property of the collective farms and cooperative organizations.

Every household in a collective farm, in addition to its basic income from the common, collective-farm enterprise, has for its personal use a small plot of household land and, as its personal property, a subsidiary husbandry on the plot, a dwelling-house, live-stock, poultry and minor agricultural implements—in accordance with the rules of the agricultural artel [collective association of laborers].

ARTICLE 8. The land occupied by collective farms is secured to them for their use free of charge and for an unlimited time, that is, in perpetuity.

ARTICLE 9. Alongside the socialist system of economy, which is the predominant form of economy in the U.S.S.R., the law permits the small private economy of individual peasants and handicraftsmen based on their own labor and precluding the exploitation of the labor of others.

ARTICLE 10. The personal property right of citizens in their incomes and savings from work, in their dwelling houses and subsidiary home enterprises, in articles of domestic economy and use and articles of personal use and convenience, as well as the right of citizens to inherit personal property, is protected by law.

ARTICLE 11. The economic life of the U.S.S.R. is determined and directed by the state national-economic plan, with the aim of increasing the public wealth, of steadily raising the material and cultural standards of the working people, of consolidating the independence of the U.S.S.R. and strengthening its defensive capacity.

ARTICLE 12. Work in the U.S.S.R. is a duty and a matter of honour for every able-bodied citizen, in accordance with the principle: "He who does not work, neither shall he eat."

The principle applied in the U.S.S.R. is that of socialism: "From each according to his ability, to each according to his work."

Chapter II THE STATE STRUCTURE

ARTICLE 13. The Union of Soviet Socialist Republics is a federal state, formed on the basis of a voluntary union of equal Soviet Socialist Republics, namely:

The Russian Soviet Federative Socialist Republic
The Ukrainian Soviet Socialist Republic
The Byelorussian Soviet Socialist Republic
The Uzbek Soviet Socialist Republic
The Kazakh Soviet Socialist Republic
The Georgian Soviet Socialist Republic
The Azerbaijan Soviet Socialist Republic
The Lithuanian Soviet Socialist Republic
The Moldavian Soviet Socialist Republic
The Latvian Soviet Socialist Republic
The Kirghiz Soviet Socialist Republic
The Tajik Soviet Socialist Republic
The Armenian Soviet Socialist Republic
The Turkmen Soviet Socialist Republic
The Estonian Soviet Socialist Republic

ARTICLE 14. The jurisdiction of the Union of Soviet Socialist Republics, as represented by its higher organs of state power and organs of state administration embraces:

a) Representation of the U.S.S.R. in international relations; conclusion, ratification and denunciation of treaties of the U.S.S.R. with other states; establishment of general procedure governing the relations of Union Republics with foreign states;

b) Questions of war and peace;

c) Admission of new republics into the U.S.S.R.;

d) Control over the observance of the constitution of the U.S.S.R.; and ensuring conformity of the constitutions of the Union Republics with the constitution of the U.S.S.R.;

e) Confirmation of alterations of boundaries between Union Republics;

f) Confirmation of the formation of new Autonomous Republics and Autonomous Regions within Union Republics;

g) Organization of the defense of the U.S.S.R.; direction of all the Armed Forces of the U.S.S.R.; determination of directing principles governing the organization of the military formations of the Union Republics;

h) Foreign trade on the basis of state monopoly;

i) Safeguarding the security of the state;

j) Determination of the national-economic plans of the U.S.S.R.;

k) Approval of the consolidated state budget of the U.S.S.R. and of the report on its fulfillment; determination of the taxes and revenues which go to the Union, the Republican, and the local budgets;

l) Administration of the banks, industrial and agricultural institutions and enterprises, and also trading enterprises of all-Union subordination; general guidance of industry and construction of Union-Republic importance;

m) Administration of transport and communications of all-Union importance;

n) Direction of the monetary and credit system;

o) Organization of state insurance;

p) Contracting and granting of loans;

q) Determination of the basic principles of land tenure and of the use of mineral wealth, forests, and waters;

r) Determination of the basic principles in the spheres of education and public health;

s) Organization of a uniform system of national-economic statistics;

t) Determination of the fundamental principles of labor legislation;

u) Determination of the fundamental principles of legislation concerning the judicial system and judicial procedure; and of the fundamental principles of criminal and civil legislation;

v) Legislation concerning Union citizenship; legislation concerning rights of foreigners;

w) Determination of the fundamental principles of legislation concerning marriage and the family;

x) Issuing of all-Union acts of amnesty.

ARTICLE 15. The sovereignty of the Union Republics is limited only in the spheres defined in Article 14 of the constitution of the U.S.S.R. Outside of these spheres each Union Republic exercises state authority independently. The U.S.S.R. protects the sovereign rights of the Union Republics.

ARTICLE 16. Each Union Republic has its own constitution, which takes account of the specific features of the Republic and is drawn up in full conformity with the constitution of the U.S.S.R.

ARTICLE 17. The right freely to secede from the U.S.S.R. is reserved to every Union Republic.

ARTICLE 18. The territory of a Union Republic may not be altered without its consent.

ARTICLE 18-a. Each Union Republic has the right to enter into direct relations with foreign states and to conclude agreements and exchange diplomatic and consular representatives with them.

ARTICLE 18-b. Each Union Republic has its own Republican military formations.

ARTICLE 19. The laws of the U.S.S.R. have the same force within the territory of every Union Republic.

ARTICLE 20. In the event of divergence between a law of a Union Republic and a law of the Union, the Union law prevails.

ARTICLE 21. Uniform Union citizenship is established for citizens of the U.S.S.R. Every citizen of a Union Republic is a citizen of the U.S.S.R.

[Articles 22–29–b deal with the geographic structure of the Union Republics.]

Chapter III THE HIGHER ORGANS OF STATE POWER IN THE UNION OF SOVIET SOCIALIST REPUBLICS

ARTICLE 30. The highest organ of state power in the U.S.S.R. is the Supreme Soviet of the U.S.S.R.

ARTICLE 31. The Supreme Soviet of the U.S.S.R. exercises all rights vested in the Union of Soviet Socialist Republics in accordance with Article 14 of the constitution, in so far as they do not, by virtue of the constitution, come within the jurisdiction of organs of the U.S.S.R. that are accountable to the Supreme Soviet of the U.S.S.R., that is, the Presidium of the Supreme Soviet of the U.S.S.R., the Council of Ministers of the U.S.S.R., and the Ministries of the U.S.S.R.

ARTICLE 32. The legislative power of the U.S.S.R. is exercised exclusively by the Supreme Soviet of the U.S.S.R.

ARTICLE 33. The Supreme Soviet of the U.S.S.R. consists of two chambers: the Soviet of the Union and the Soviet of Nationalities.

ARTICLE 34. The Soviet of the Union is elected by the citizens of the U.S.S.R. voting by election districts on the basis of one deputy for every 300,000 of the population.

ARTICLE 35. The Soviet of Nationalities is elected by the citizens of the U.S.S.R. voting by Union Republics, Autonomous Republics, Autonomous Provinces and National Districts on the basis of twenty-five deputies from each Union Republic, eleven deputies from each Autonomous Republic, five deputies from each Autonomous Province and one deputy from each National District.

ARTICLE 36. The Supreme Soviet of the U.S.S.R. is elected for a term of four years.

ARTICLE 37. The two chambers of the Supreme Soviet of the U.S.S.R.—the Soviet of the Union and the Soviet of the Nationalities—have equal rights.

ARTICLE 38. The Soviet of the Union and the Soviet of Nationalities have equal powers to initiate legislation.

ARTICLE 39. A law is considered adopted if passed by both chambers of the Supreme Soviet of the U.S.S.R. by a simple majority vote in each.

ARTICLE 40. Laws passed by the Supreme Soviet of the U.S.S.R. are published in the languages of the Union Republics over the signatures of the President and Secretary of the Presidium of the Supreme Soviet of the U.S.S.R.

ARTICLE 41. Sessions of the Soviet of the Union and of the Soviet of Nationalities begin and terminate simultaneously.

ARTICLE 42. The Soviet of the Union elects a Chairman of the Soviet of the Union and four Vice-Chairmen.

ARTICLE 43. The Soviet of Nationalities elects a Chairman of the Soviet of Nationalities and four Vice-Chairmen.

ARTICLE 44. The Chairmen of the Soviet of the Union and the Soviet of Nationalities preside at the sittings of the respective chambers and have charge of the conduct of their business and proceedings.

ARTICLE 45. Joint sittings of the two chambers of the Supreme Soviet of the U.S.S.R. are presided over alternately by the Chairman of the Soviet of the Union and the Chairman of the Soviet of Nationalities.

ARTICLE 46. Sessions of the Supreme Soviet of the U.S.S.R. are convened by the Presidium of the Supreme Soviet of the U.S.S.R. twice a year.

Extraordinary sessions are convened by the Presidium of the Supreme Soviet of the U.S.S.R. at its discretion or on the demand of one of the Union Republics.

ARTICLE 47. In the event of disagreement between the Soviet of the Union and the Soviet of Nationalities, the question is referred for settlement to a conciliation commission formed by the chambers on a party basis. If the conciliation commission fails to arrive at an agreement, or if its decision fails to satisfy one of the chambers, the question is considered for a second time by the chambers. Failing agreement between the two chambers, the Presidium of the Supreme Soviet of the U.S.S.R. dissolves the Supreme Soviet of the U.S.S.R. and orders new elections.

ARTICLE 48. The Supreme Soviet of the U.S.S.R. at a joint sitting of the two chambers elects the Presidium of the Supreme Soviet of the U.S.S.R., consisting of a President of the Presidium of the Supreme Soviet of the U.S.S.R., fifteen Vice-Presidents—one for each of the Union Republics—a Secretary of the Presidium and sixteen members of the Presidium of the Supreme Soviet of the U.S.S.R.

The Presidium of the Supreme Soviet of the U.S.S.R. is accountable to the Supreme Soviet of the U.S.S.R. for all its activities.

ARTICLE 49. The Presidium of the Supreme Soviet of the U.S.S.R.:
   a) Convenes the sessions of the Supreme Soviet of the U.S.S.R.;
   b) Issues decrees;
   c) Gives interpretations of the laws of the U.S.S.R. in operation;
   d) Dissolves the Supreme Soviet of the U.S.S.R. in conformity with Article 47 of the constitution of the U.S.S.R. and orders new elections;
   e) Conducts nation-wide polls [referendums] on its own initiative or on the demand of one of the Union Republics;

f) Annuls decisions and orders of the Council of Ministers of the U.S.S.R. and of the Councils of Ministers of the Union Republics if they do not conform to law;

g) In the intervals between sessions of the Supreme Soviet of the U.S.S.R., releases and appoints Ministers of the U.S.S.R. on the recommendation of the Chairman of the Council of Ministers of the U.S.S.R., subject to subsequent confirmation by the Supreme Soviet of the U.S.S.R.;

h) Institutes decorations [orders and medals] and titles of honor of the U.S.S.R.;

i) Awards orders and medals and confers titles of honor of the U.S.S.R.;

j) Exercises the right of pardon;

k) Institutes military titles, diplomatic ranks, and other special titles;

l) Appoints and removes the high command of the armed forces of the U.S.S.R.;

m) In the intervals between sessions of the Supreme Soviet of the U.S.S.R., proclaims a state of war in the event of military attack on the U.S.S.R., or when necessary to fulfill international treaty obligations concerning mutual defense against aggression;

n) Orders general or partial mobilization;

o) Ratifies and denounces international treaties of the U.S.S.R.;

p) Appoints and recalls plenipotentiary representatives of the U.S.S.R. to foreign states;

q) Receives the letters of credence and recall of diplomatic representatives accredited to it by foreign states;

r) Proclaims martial law in separate localities or throughout the U.S.S.R. in the interests of the defense of the U.S.S.R. or of the maintenance of public order and the security of the state.

ARTICLE 50. The Soviet of the Union and the Soviet of Nationalities elect Credentials Committees to verify the credentials of the members of the respective chambers.

On the report of the Credentials Committees, the chambers decide whether to recognize the credentials of deputies or to annul their election.

ARTICLE 51. The Supreme Soviet of the U.S.S.R., when it deems necessary, appoints commissions of investigation and audit on any matter.

It is the duty of all institutions and officials to comply with the demands of such commissions and to submit to them all necessary materials and documents.

ARTICLE 52. A member of the Supreme Soviet of the U.S.S.R. may not be prosecuted or arrested without the consent of the Supreme Soviet of the U.S.S.R., or, when the Supreme Soviet of the U.S.S.R. is not in session, without the consent of the Presidium of the Supreme Soviet of the U.S.S.R.

ARTICLE 53. On the expiration of the term of office of the Supreme Soviet of the U.S.S.R., or on its dissolution prior to the expiration of its term of office, the Presidium of the Supreme Soviet of the U.S.S.R. retains its powers until the newly-elected Supreme Soviet of the U.S.S.R. shall have formed a new Presidium of the Supreme Soviet of the U.S.S.R.

ARTICLE 54. On the expiration of the term of office of the Supreme Soviet of the U.S.S.R., or in the event of its dissolution prior to the expiration of its term of office, the Presidium of the Supreme Soviet of the U.S.S.R. orders new elections to be held within a period not exceeding two months from the date of expiration of the term of office or dissolution of the Supreme Soviet of the U.S.S.R.

ARTICLE 55. The newly-elected Supreme Soviet of the U.S.S.R. is convened by the outgoing Presidium of the Supreme Soviet of the U.S.S.R. not later than three months after the elections.

ARTICLE 56. The Supreme Soviet of the U.S.S.R., at a joint sitting of the two chambers, appoints the Government of the U.S.S.R., namely, the Council of Ministers of the U.S.S.R.

Chapter IV THE HIGHER ORGANS OF STATE POWER IN THE UNION REPUBLICS

ARTICLE 57. The highest organ of state power in a Union Republic is the Supreme Soviet of the Union Republic.

ARTICLE 58. The Supreme Soviet of a Union Republic is elected by the citizens of the Republic for a term of four years.

The basis of representation is established by the constitution of the Union Republic.

ARTICLE 59. The Supreme Soviet of a Union Republic is the sole legislative organ of the Republic.

ARTICLE 60. The Supreme Soviet of a Union Republic:

a) Adopts the constitution of the Republic and amends it in conformity with Article 16 of the constitution of the U.S.S.R.;

b) Confirms the constitutions of the Autonomous Republics forming part of it and defines the boundaries of their territories;

c) Approves the economic plan and the budget of the Republic; forms economic administrative regions of the Republic;

d) Exercises the right of amnesty and pardon of citizens sentenced by the judicial organs of the Union Republic;

e) Decides questions of representation of the Union Republic in its international relations;

f) Determines the manner of organizing the Republic's military formations.

ARTICLE 61. The Supreme Soviet of a Union Republic elects the Presidium of the Supreme Soviet of the Union Republic, consisting of a President of the Presidium of the Supreme Soviet of the Union Republic, Vice-Presidents, a Secretary of the Presidium and members of the Presidium of the Supreme Soviet of the Union Republic.

The powers of the Presidium of the Supreme Soviet of a Union Republic are defined by the constitution of the Union Republic.

ARTICLE 62. The Supreme Soviet of a Union Republic elects a Chairman and Vice-Chairmen to conduct its sittings.

ARTICLE 63. The Supreme Soviet of a Union Republic appoints the government of the Union Republic, namely, the Council of Ministers of the Union Republic.

Chapter V THE ORGANS OF STATE ADMINISTRATION OF THE UNION OF SOVIET SOCIALIST REPUBLICS

ARTICLE 64. The highest executive and administrative organ of the state power of the Union of Soviet Socialist Republics is the Council of Ministers of the U.S.S.R.

Article 65. The Council of Ministers of the U.S.S.R. is responsible and accountable to the Supreme Soviet of the U.S.S.R., or, in the intervals between sessions of the Supreme Soviet, to the Presidium of the Supreme Soviet of the U.S.S.R.

Article 66. The Council of Ministers of the U.S.S.R. issues decisions and orders on the basis and in pursuance of the laws in operation, and verifies their execution.

Article 67. Decisions and orders of the Council of Ministers of the U.S.S.R. are binding throughout the territory of the U.S.S.R.

Article 68. The Council of Ministers of the U.S.S.R.:

a) Coordinates and directs the work of the Supreme Council of National Economy U.S.S.R. of the Council of Ministers of the U.S.S.R., and of the all-Union and Union-Republican Ministries of the U.S.S.R., and of the State Committees of the Council of Ministers of the U.S.S.R., and of other institutions under its jurisdiction;

b) Adopts measures to carry out the national-economic plan and the state budget, and to strengthen the credit and monetary system;

c) Adopts measures for the maintenance of public order, for the protection of the interests of the state, and for the safeguarding of the rights of citizens;

d) Exercises general guidance in the sphere of relations with foreign states;

e) Fixes the annual contingent of citizens to be called up for military service and directs the general organization of the armed forces of the country;

f) Sets up State Committees of the U.S.S.R. and also, whenever necessary, special Committees and Central Administrations under the Council of Ministers of the U.S.S.R. for economic and cultural affairs and defense.

Article 69. The Council of Ministers of the U.S.S.R. has the right, in respect of those branches of administration and economy which come within the jurisdiction of the U.S.S.R., to suspend decisions and orders of the Councils of Ministers of the Union Republics, to annul orders and instructions of Ministers of the U.S.S.R. and also administrative acts of other institutions subject to their jurisdiction.

Article 70. The Council of Ministers of the U.S.S.R. is appointed by the Supreme Soviet of the U.S.S.R. and consists of:
The Chairman of the Council of Ministers of the U.S.S.R.;
The First Vice-Chairmen of the Council of Ministers of the U.S.S.R.;
The Vice-Chairmen of the Council of Ministers of the U.S.S.R.;
The Ministers of the U.S.S.R.;
The Chairman of the Council of National Economy U.S.S.R.;
The Chairman of the State Council for Construction U.S.S.R.;
The Chairman of the State Planning Committee U.S.S.R.;
The Chairman of the Committee of Party-State Control of the Central Committee of the C.P.S.U. and of the Council of Ministers of the U.S.S.R.;
The Chairman of the State Committee on Labor and Wages;
The Chairman of the State Committee for the Coordination of Scientific Research Work U.S.S.R.;
The Chairman of the U.S.S.R. Council of Ministers' State Committee for Radio Broadcasting and Television;
The Chairman of the U.S.S.R. Council of Ministers' State Committee for the Moving Picture Industry;
The Chairman of the U.S.S.R. Council of Ministers' State Committee for the Press;

The Chairman of the U.S.S.R. Council of Ministers' State Committee for Trade;

The Chairman of the U.S.S.R. Council of Ministers' State Committee for Grain Procurement;

The Chairman of the U.S.S.R. Council of Ministers' State Committee for Foreign Economic Relations;

The Chairman of the U.S.S.R. Council of Ministers' State Committee for Cultural Relations with Foreign Countries;

The Chairman of the U.S.S.R. Council of Ministers' State Committee for State Security;

The Chairman of the Board of the U.S.S.R. State Bank;

The Director of the U.S.S.R. Council of Ministers' Central Statistical Administration;

The Chairmen of the Union Republic Councils of Ministers are members ex officio of the Council of Ministers of the U.S.S.R.

ARTICLE 71. The government of the U.S.S.R. or a Minister of the U.S.S.R. to whom a question of a member of the Supreme Soviet of the U.S.S.R. is addressed must give a verbal or written reply in the respective chamber within a period not exceeding three days.

ARTICLE 72. The Ministers of the U.S.S.R. direct the branches of state administration which come within the jurisdiction of the U.S.S.R.

ARTICLE 73. The Ministers of the U.S.S.R., within the limits of the jurisdiction of their respective Ministries, issue orders and instructions on the basis and in pursuance of the laws in operation, and also of decisions and orders of the Council of Ministers of the U.S.S.R., and verify their execution.

ARTICLE 74. The Ministries of the U.S.S.R. are either all-Union or Union-Republican Ministries.

ARTICLE 75. Each all-Union Ministry directs the branch of state administration entrusted to it throughout the territory of the U.S.S.R. either directly or through bodies appointed by it.

ARTICLE 76. The Union-Republican Ministries, as a rule, direct the branches of state administration entrusted to them through corresponding Ministries of the Union Republics; they administer directly only a definite and limited number of enterprises according to a list confirmed by the Presidium of the Supreme Soviet of the U.S.S.R.

ARTICLE 77. The following Ministries are all-Union Ministries: Foreign Trade; Merchant Marine; Transportation.

ARTICLE 78. The following Ministries are Union-Republican Ministries: Higher and Specialized Secondary Education; Public Health; Foreign Affairs; Culture; Defense; Communications; Agriculture; Finance.

Chapter VI THE ORGANS OF STATE ADMINISTRATION OF THE UNION REPUBLICS

ARTICLE 79. The highest executive and administrative organ of the state power of a Union Republic is the Council of Ministers of the Union Republic.

ARTICLE 80. The Council of Ministers of a Union Republic is responsible and accountable to the Supreme Soviet of the Union Republic, or, in the intervals between sessions of the Supreme Soviet of the Union Republic, to the Presidium of the Supreme Soviet of the Union Republic.

ARTICLE 81. The Council of Ministers of a Union Republic issues decisions and orders on the basis and in pursuance of the laws in operation of the U.S.S.R. and of the Union Republic, and of the decisions and orders of the Council of Ministers of the U.S.S.R., and verifies their execution.

ARTICLE 82. The Council of Ministers of a Union Republic has the right to suspend decisions and orders of the Councils of Ministers of its Autonomous Republics, annul decisions and orders of the Executive Committees of the Soviets of Working People's Deputies of its Territories, Provinces and Autonomous Provinces, and also decisions and orders of the Republic Council of National Economy and of the Councils of National Economy of the economic administrative regions of the Republic.

ARTICLE 83. The Council of Ministers of a Union Republic is appointed by the Supreme Soviet of the Union Republic and consists of:

The Chairman of the Council of Ministers of the Union Republic;
The Vice-Chairmen of the Council of Ministers;
The Ministers;
The Chairmen of the State Committees, Commissions, and Directors of the other departments of the Council of Ministers, organized by the Supreme Soviet of the Union Republic in accordance with the constitution of the Union Republic.

ARTICLE 84. The Ministers of a Union Republic direct the branches of state administration which come within the jurisdiction of the Union Republic.

ARTICLE 85. The Ministers of a Union Republic, within the limits of the jurisdiction of their respective Ministries, issue orders and instructions on the basis and in pursuance of the laws of the U.S.S.R. and of the Union Republic, of the decisions and orders of the Council of Ministers of the U.S.S.R. and the Council of Ministers of the Union Republic, and of the orders and instructions of the Union-Republican Ministries of the U.S.S.R.

ARTICLE 86. The Ministries of a Union Republic are either Union-Republican or Republican Ministries.

ARTICLE 87. Each Union-Republican Ministry directs the branch of state administration entrusted to it, and is subordinate both to the Council of Ministers of the Union Republic and to the corresponding Union-Republican Ministry of the U.S.S.R.

ARTICLE 88. Each Republican Ministry directs the branch of state administration entrusted to it and is directly subordinate to the Council of Ministers of the Union Republic.

Chapter VIII THE LOCAL ORGANS OF STATE POWER

ARTICLE 94. The organs of state power in Territories, Provinces, Autonomous Provinces, Areas, Counties, Cities, and rural localities [Stanitsas, Villages, Hamlets, Kishlaks, Auls] are the Soviets of Working People's Deputies.

ARTICLE 95. The Soviets of Working People's Deputies of Territories, Provinces, Autonomous Provinces, Areas, Counties, Cities, and rural localities . . . are elected by the working people of the respective Territories, Provinces, Autonomous Provinces, Areas, Counties, Cities, or rural localities for a term of two years.

ARTICLE 96. The basis of representation for Soviets of Working People's Deputies is determined by the constitutions of the Union Republics.

ARTICLE 97. The Soviets of Working People's Deputies direct the work of the organs of administration subordinate to them, ensure the maintenance of public order, the observance of the laws and the protection of the rights of citizens, direct local economic and cultural affairs, and draw up the local budgets.

ARTICLE 98. The Soviets of Working People's Deputies adopt decisions and issue orders within the limits of the powers vested in them by the laws of the U.S.S.R. and of the Union Republic.

ARTICLE 99. The executive and administrative organ of the Soviet of Working People's Deputies of a Territory, Province, Autonomous Province, Area, County, City, or rural locality is the Executive Committee elected by it, consisting of a Chairman, Vice-Chairman, a Secretary, and members.

ARTICLE 100. The executive and administrative organ of the Soviet of Working People's Deputies in a small locality, in accordance with the Constitution of the Union Republic, is the Chairman, the Vice-Chairman, and the Secretary elected by the Soviet of Working People's Deputies.

ARTICLE 101. The executive organs of the Soviets of Working People's Deputies are directly accountable both to the Soviets of Working People's Deputies which elected them and to the executive organ of the superior Soviet of Working People's Deputies.

Index

Italicized page numbers preceded by *c* refer to a chart.
Boldface page numbers refer to definitions of political science terms.

Malenkov, G. M., 102, 115, 210-12
Mansfield, Mike, 72
Marshall, Thurgood, 159, 164
Marx, Karl, 53, 246; *The Manifesto of the Communist Party*, 46, 48, 49-50
Massachusetts Bay Company, 30
Matthews, Donald R., study of senators by, 71-72
Mayflower Compact, 30
McArthur, Donna, 83
McClellan, John, 74
McCone, John, 98
McNamara, Robert, 98
Meany, George, 99
Meeker, Leonard, 139
Meredith, James, 164-65
Meretskov, Vasily A., 125-26
Metcalf, Lee, 73
Meyer, Alfred G., 191
Mikoyan, Anastas, 111, 115, 182, 211; named Soviet President, 188-90
Molotov, Vyacheslav, 115, 125, 210, 211
Morgenthau, Hans, 229

Nineteenth Amendment, 82, 286
Nixon, Richard M., 69
Norris, George, 73

O'Brien, Larry, 97
Okudzava, Bulat, 242-45
Oppenheimer, J. Robert, 224
Oregon, state legislature of, 167-70

Pacifism, 267-72
Pake, George E., 231
Paton, B. Ye., 181
Peive, J. V., 180
Peltier-Zamoyska, Helene, 199
Penn, William, 30
People's assessors, 196-97
Peters, Burton C., 175
Plessy vs. Ferguson, 157-58
Pocket veto, 39
Podgorny, N. V., 182
Political information, individual access to, in Soviet Union, 238-41; in United States, 221-26
Political parties, 86-87
Polyansky, Dmitri S., 125
Powell, Adam Clayton, 149
Pravda, 111, 113
Premier of the U.S.S.R., 51
President, of Soviet Union, 187-90
President, of United States, choosing candi-

date for, 87-90; decision-making by, 137-45; powers of, 40; transfer of power of, 95-99
President pro tempore, 38
Proletariat, 48, 49

Radio, FCC regulation of, 162-63
Ratify, 41
Reams, Frazier, 224
Red Robe (Indian), 22-24
Reeves, Earl, 231
Referendum, 7; bond-issue, 92-95
Republican form of government, 36
Republican Party, 65, 80, 87
Residual powers, 33
Revenue, 39
Revolutionary War, 32
Richardson, William, on Russian serfs, 47
Rideau, Wilbert, 265
Rights and freedoms, under U. S. Constitution, 41-43, 257-67
Rodd, Tom, 268-72
Roosevelt, Franklin D., 222
Roper, Elmo, 219
Rosenberg, Louis, 269-70, 272
Ross, Edmund G., 75-80
Ruoff, Richard, 84
Rusk, Dean, 97, 144, 145, 231
Russell, Richard, 74
Russia, background for revolution in, 46-48

School integration, 155-60, 232-36
Schultz, Herman, 174
Schweitzer, Mitchell D., 44
Senate, characteristics of successful members, 70-74; decision-making by, 145-53; establishment of, 34, 38; impeachment proceedings in, 38, 75-80; powers of, 38, 39; terms of members, 70
Separation of powers, 37-40
Serfs, Russian, 47
Shelepin, A. N., 181
Sinyavsky, A. D., 193, 197-203
Smirnov, L. N., 197, 198
Smith, Howard M., 150, 151
Smith, Reverend Robert L. T., 165
Smith, Walt, 264-65
Snow, Roger, 92-93
Sokolov, P. V., 197, 198
Sorensen, Theodore, 140, 142
Soviet government, structure of, *c* 51
Sprague, William, 77
Stalin, Joseph, and Communist Party membership, 54, 56; death of, 102, 210, 211;

as First Secretary, 194, 209; and purges, 118-19; replaces Lenin, 50
Stanton, Edwin M., 76, 77
Stevens, Thaddeus, 76, 78
Stevenson, Adlai, 65, 89-90, 99, 144-45
Sticks Everything Under His Belt (Indian), 18-20
Stoerpenberg Camp, political system of, 2-11
Summers, Joseph, 231
Sumner, Charles, 77
Sun Dance, 18-20
Supreme Court, of Russian Republic, 197; of Soviet Union, 196
Supreme Court of the United States, 37, 154-60, c 154, 259, 264-67
Supreme Soviet, 178-82
Suslov, Mikhail, 115, 125
Symington, Stuart, 89-90

Taft, Robert A., 65, 73
Taylor, Robert L., 233
Teach-in, 227-31
Television, FCC regulation of, 163-66
Thirteenth Amendment, 259, 284-85
Toledo Blade, 222-25
Topeka, Kansas, 155-57
Truman, Harry S, 99, 222
Tumanov, P., "Guarantees of Democratism," 121-24
Two Twists (Indian), 23-24

Udall, Stewart L., 148

Uhlman, Laila, 84
Uhlman, Wes, 82-86
Usharenko, Irina B., 126

Vandenberg, Arthur, 73
Van Laue, Theodore H., 230-31
Veto, 30, 39; pocket, 39
Voroshilov, Kliment Y., 189
Voting, in Soviet Union, 125, 237
Voting, in United States, 124-25; in colonial America, 31; and Fifteenth Amendment, 82; and Nineteenth Amendment, 82; voter behavior, 219-21; voting machines, 124. *See also* Elections.

Wanamaker, Jim, 83
Washington, George, 32
Webster, Daniel, 73
Wells, H. V., Jr., 236
Wilkins, Roy, 147
Williams, John, 74
Willson, Joseph P., 269
Wilson, Harold, 119
WLBT (television station), 164-66
Woodward, Julian, 219

Yasnov, M. A., 180
Yevtushenko, Yevgeny, meeting with Khrushchev, 128-30
Young, Whitney, Jr., 147-48

Zaitsov (worker), 246-50
Zenger, Peter, 32
Zhukov, Georgi K., 115, 118, 210-12